The Book of Psalms

From Suffering to Glory

Volume 1: Psalms 1–72

The Servant-King

Philip Eveson

Evangelical Press, an imprint of 10Publishing
Unit C, Tomlinson Road, Leyland, PR25 2DY, England
epbooks@10ofthose.com
www.epbooks.org

British Library Cataloguing in Publication Data available

ISBN 978-1-78397-020-9

Unless otherwise indicated, Scripture quotations are the author's own
translation.

To Jen

Preface

The Psalms have been very much a part of my life from early childhood, especially through hearing the Metrical Version of some of them each Lord's Day. Others were memorised from the Authorised Version of the Bible. They have been a wonderful source of comfort and encouragement over the years through the ups and downs of life. The academic study of the Psalms has in no way dampened my enthusiasm for this biblical treasure. It has been a delight to lecture and preach from this book and preparing this commentary has been a labour of love and of great spiritual benefit.

It must be well over ten years ago that David Clark of Evangelical Press set me the task of producing this commentary for the Welwyn series. More recently, Graham Hind, the managing director of Evangelical Press, has given me every encouragement and has even allowed me the unique privilege of extending the commentary over two volumes! It has been the task of Trudy Kinloch to edit the manuscript and I am grateful for all her input and advice. I pray that the commentary will contribute a little more to an understanding of the text and that the message of the Psalms will challenge and convict as well as bring comfort and hope. Above all, I trust it will lead to a deeper appreciation of our Lord's inner life as the suffering Messiah as well as of the glory that followed.

A special word of thanks must go to my dear wife Jennifer, who has been my best friend and support for forty-five years. She has read

5

through various drafts of this commentary, checked all my references and often suggested better ways of expressing my thoughts.

Philip H. Eveson
Wrexham
August 2014

Contents

Introduction to Psalms

The Psalms continue to have an enormous influence on people's lives all round the world and down the centuries they have brought comfort and encouragement to countless millions of people. Dag Hammarskjöld, the second Secretary-General of the United Nations, died in a plane crash in 1961. His briefcase was recovered from the crash site and among the items it contained were a copy of the New Testament and the Book of Psalms.[1]

In the New Testament the most quoted book of the Old Testament is the Psalms.[2] Jesus clearly committed them to memory and found them speaking to him and for him concerning his ministry in life and death. The Apostles turned to the Psalms in their preaching as well as when praying for boldness in the face of strong persecution. Following the example set by our Lord, the writers of the New Testament saw them as pointers to the person and work of Christ (Acts 2:25-35; 4:11; 24-31; 13:33-36).

Psalms were sung by the early Christians and prayers and songs were offered to God in accord with the pattern set by the Psalms and the teaching of Jesus (Matthew 6:9-13; Mark 14:26; Acts 16:25; 1 Corinthians 14:26; Ephesians 5:19-20; Colossians 3:16; James 5:13). In the early second century Christian teachers like Clement, bishop of Rome around AD 96, were using the Psalms to point to Christ, while Ignatius in Syrian Antioch around AD 100 introduced the singing of the Psalms antiphonally. Expositions and commentaries on the Psalms dating from the third century onwards have been preserved and early

13

testimonies indicate the place of the Psalms in Christian devotion in the home and individual people's lives in their workplace as well as in communal worship. Among the famous commentators on the Psalms in the early period stand Augustine, bishop of Hippo in North Africa (354–430) and Cassiodorus, a Roman writer and statesman, who in his retirement founded a monastery (c. 485–580).

Some of the statements made about the Psalms show how important they have been to Christians throughout history. Athanasius of Alexandria (c. 295–373) called the Psalms 'an epitome of the whole Scripture and is reported to have said that 'Most of Scripture speaks to us, the Psalms speak for us.' Basil, bishop of Caesarea in Cappadocia (c. 329–379) regarded the Psalms as 'the compendium of all theology'. Martin Luther (1483–1546), who began lecturing on the Psalms in 1513, spoke of the book as 'a little Bible, and the summary of the Old Testament'. For John Calvin (1509–1564), who first preached on the Psalms and then wrote a commentary on the Hebrew text which is still of immense value, the book is 'An Anatomy of all the Parts of the Soul' and he explained that 'the Holy Spirit has brought to life all the grief, sorrows, fears, doubts, hopes, cares, perplexities, in short, all the distracting emotions with which our minds are agitated'.

The Name

There are two English names given to the book and both are derived via the Latin Bible from the Greek version. The most popular name is 'Book of Psalms', as in our English Bibles, which is the heading to the psalm collection in the 4th century AD Vaticanus manuscript of the ancient Greek version of the Old Testament called the Septuagint (see also Luke 20:42; Acts 1:20). To the Greeks the term 'Psalm' meant music produced by a stringed instrument and was used to translate the equivalent Hebrew term found in many of the headings to individual psalms (see Psalm 3). It referred originally to a song accompanied by musical instruments. By New Testament times it seems to be just another name for a 'song' that Christians used (1 Corinthians 14:26). The other English name for the book is 'Psalter', which is the heading in the 5th century AD Alexandrinus manuscript of the Septuagint and was perhaps a term that emphasised the instrument used such as a harp. In the Hebrew Bible from earliest times the Rabbis called the psalm collection, 'Praises' (see Psalm 145 where the singular is found in the psalm's heading). No title does justice to the wide range of compositions in the collection that include prayers of lament and thanksgiving, teaching and wisdom psalms, in addition to hymns of praise.

The Psalm Headings

Many of the psalms have introductory headings that mention the author or a particular collection. Sometimes the heading will give an idea of when it was written (Psalms 3 and 51); it will indicate whether it is a song or a word of instruction and it may suggest the instruments to be used and perhaps even an appropriate tune (Psalms 4-9). Similar notifications are also found outside the Psalter, as in the introduction to David's thanksgiving psalm (2 Samuel 22:1) and in the heading and postscript to Habakkuk's psalm (Habakkuk 3:1,19). Some of these headings, as well as the word 'Selah' that appears at the end of some verses (see Psalm 3), may not be original to the psalm but they are certainly very early and were present when the final edition was made. In the Hebrew Bible these headings are seen as part of the text and regarded as the first verse. Our English versions do not follow this custom and it results in the English text being one verse behind the Hebrew original in many of the psalms. For example, Psalm 3 verse 1 in our English Bibles is verse 2 in the original text. What the Hebrew text indicates is that the headings are to be treated as part of God's Word and not ignored or dismissed out of hand. These headings must be clearly distinguished from the attempts in some Bible versions to provide titles to indicate a psalm's content.

The Psalm Collection

There are individual psalms that span almost a thousand years from Moses (Psalm 90) to the time when the Jews experienced exile in Babylon (Psalm 137) and perhaps even afterwards. At least half the psalms are associated with David, the 'sweet psalmist of Israel' (2 Samuel 23:1; see Psalms 3-32; 34-41; 51-65; 68-70; 86; 101; 103; 108-110; 138-145) and there are numerous psalms belonging to Korah and Asaph (Psalms 42-50; 73-83; 84-85; 87-88).

A distinction must be made between the individual compositions and the final editing process that occurred in the post-exilic period perhaps during the time of Ezra and Nehemiah or when Chronicles was written. The person or persons used by God to bring the whole collection together found various psalms already bundled together under personal names like David and Asaph or the Sons of Korah. At the end of Psalm 72 we are informed that the 'prayers of David the son of Jesse are ended' and yet further psalms associated with David appear later as noted above.

The collection of 150 psalms in our Bibles is divided into five parts (called 'books'), each terminating with a doxology—Psalms 1–41; 42–72; 73–89; 90–106; 107–150. This division was probably influenced by the Law of Moses which also consists of five books. Psalms 1 and 2 provide a fitting opening to the whole collection with the final Hallelujah psalms (Psalm 146–150) forming a grand conclusion.

The way the psalms have been collected into this final fivefold form suggests the compiler had an important aim in mind for his people living as they were under foreign domination and still awaiting the fulfilment of promises God had made to Abraham and David. It encouraged God's people to look with confidence to their covenant God as the universal ruler who would bring to completion everything that he had purposed and prophesied.

Book One focuses on David, the highs and lows of his life and how God delivered such a one who belongs to the poor, oppressed righteous community. It also draws our attention to God's law and the importance of trusting God and coming into his presence. In Book Two the promises God made to David provide the background and are coupled to the importance of Zion and worship at the central sanctuary. God's deliverances are again prominent and it ends with a view of the universal reign of David's greater son. Book Three introduces a sobering note and suggests that the exile is in mind. Israel's covenant failures are prominent and the promises to David are in jeopardy. The curses of God on account of Israel's rebellion are brought to our attention and yet positive things are still said of Zion which give grounds for hope. In Book Four with the exile still in the compiler's thoughts, God's kingship is highlighted with summaries of his powerful activities throughout history and it ends with prayer for a return from Israel's exile. Book Five reflects the post-exilic era with an emphasis on restoration and renewal. God's steadfast love is often mentioned and a series of psalms attributed to David are also included. We are given a glimpse of the future Davidic ruler who will have priestly functions, and worship in Zion is prominent. The oppressed righteous do eventually receive justice and the enemies of God and his people are punished so that at the close of the collection, as in the book of Revelation, the 'hallelujah chorus' can resound to the glory of God (Psalm 150; see Revelation 19:1-6).

A clear distinction exists between the first three books (Psalms 1-89) and the final two (Psalms 90-150). In the first three almost all the psalms have headings and many give fulsome information concerning authorship, historical background, the type of psalm it is—whether a song or for instruction—and with details concerning instruments for accompaniment and with reference to the chief musician. On the other hand, the last two books in comparison have few headings and those that do have titles, give little information. Again, in the first three books laments predominate whereas the final two are characterised by thanksgiving and praise.

Holy Scripture

The Psalms head up the third part of the Jewish Scriptures, which is perhaps the reason Jesus specifically speaks of the Law, the Prophets and Psalms as he shows his disciples from the whole of the Old Testament the things relating to himself (Luke 24:27,44-46). This unique collection of psalms is therefore God-breathed Scripture. More noticeable than in other parts of the Bible, the human authorship is very pronounced so that we are made aware of the various moods and concerns of so many of the individual authors. Nevertheless, the whole collection is part of the written Word of God and its purpose, like the rest of Holy Scripture, is to make people wise about salvation through faith in Jesus the Messiah and profitable for God's people in the development of their spiritual lives (2 Timothy 3:15-17).

Psalms Types

It is helpful to be aware of the main types and to show their distinctive characteristics but it must be remembered that some psalms defy the pigeon-hole treatment and many do not fit neatly into their 'box' but display features belonging to other types as well.

Praise psalms—The typical praise psalm can be clearly identified. It begins with a call to worship and gives reasons why praise should be offered. Grounds for praise are often introduced by the word translated 'for' or 'because'. It can also have a concluding call to praise. Examples of this type are Psalms 33, 96, 100, 117, 147. Included within the praise group are the kingship, royal and Zion psalms. The kingship psalms such as Psalms 29, 47, 93, 97-99 proclaim God's rule and a number of them begin with the declaration 'The LORD reigns'. Royal psalms or psalms relating to the Lord's anointed include Psalms 2, 45, 72, 89, 110 and 132 but psalms belonging to other types can be included such as Psalms 18, 20–21, 101 and 144. Zion songs draw attention to the significance of God's city (see Psalms 46, 48, 76, 84, 87, 122).

Prayer psalms—These have often been segregated into individual 'I' petitions and communal 'we' prayers but this is too simplistic as the psalmist may well be speaking as the leader of the community. There are some psalms that oscillate between the singular and the plural. They can be divided into prayers of lament where the psalmist expresses penitence or often protests his innocence in the face of false accusations and severe persecution, and prayers of trust and confidence in God. In the laments there is an appeal to God to listen and this is supported with reasons. Pleas for help can sometimes begin the psalm or occur after the complaint has been made. The prayer may often conclude with a profession of trust and a promise to praise God. Psalm 22 begins as a cry for help but closes with a remarkable act of praise. Examples of the lament include Psalms 3, 5–7, 17, 26, 35, 38, 41, 56–57, 59, 88, 109. The communal element is strong in Psalms 44, 74, 79, 83, 85, 89, 137. Psalms of trust and confidence include 11, 16, 23, 27, 62, 91, 121, 125.

Thanksgiving psalms—There are fewer psalms specifically dedicated to giving thanks than those of the prayer type. Many references to thanksgiving or testimony are hidden when the verb 'give thanks' is translated 'praise' as sometimes happens in English versions. These psalms are characterised by expressions of thanks and gratitude, a description of the trouble from which the psalmist has been delivered, a testimony to others concerning God's deliverance and an exhortation to join in acknowledging God's goodness. Psalms of this nature include 18, 30, 34, 92, 116, 118.

Preaching psalms—These can be sub-divided into wisdom, Torah (Law), historical, teaching and exhortation psalms. The wisdom psalms are similar to passages that we find in Proverbs, especially when a contrast is drawn between the righteous and the wicked and the two ways (see Psalms 1, 37, 73, 128). Torah psalms focus on God's specially revealed Word (see Psalms 1, 19, 119). The historical psalms use the account of Israel's history to teach and urge the people to change their ways as well as to praise (see Psalms 78, 105–106). Teaching psalms are concerned about the character of true worshippers (Psalms 15, 24,

32). There are teaching elements in many other psalms like 18, 25, 33, 111–112, 147–148. As for the exhortation psalms, these are similar to the kind of preaching we find in prophets like Isaiah and Jeremiah (see Psalms 50, 81, 95).

Poetry

Poetry is more musical than prose and both music and poetry can have a much more powerful effect upon the human psyche than a straight piece of narrative. They speak to the heart as well as the mind. Poetry is much easier to sing to than prose and judging by the musical references many of the psalms were meant to be sung.

Hebrew poetry is well-adapted to being translated into other languages. Instead of sound, as is often the case in English poetry with its rhyme endings, Hebrew rhythm is conveyed more by sense. Two or sometimes three lines form a unit and present similar or contrasting ideas or a developing theme. This enables the reader or singer to think more about what is being stated instead of moving quickly on as prose narrative tends to encourage.

These units are classified into three main types. Synonymous (or 'affirming') parallelism is when the second line uses similar wording to express the sense of the first line. A perfect example of this type is Psalm 6:9, 'The LORD has heard my supplication;/The LORD will receive my prayer' (see also Psalm 2). The second line often modifies the thought of the first line in some way. Antithetical (or 'opposing') parallelism is when the second line presents a contrast to the first as in Psalm 90:6, 'In the morning it flourishes and grows up;/In the evening it is cut down and withers' (see also 37:21). A third type is synthetic (or 'advancing') parallelism in which the second line advances or completes the thought of the first line as in Psalm 2:6, 'Yet I have set my king/ On my holy hill of Zion'. A subset of this third type is climactic (or ascending) parallelism where the first line is held in suspense with the second line providing the completing thought. This 'step-like' parallelism is very prominent in the Songs of Ascents (Psalms 120–134) but it is seen in earlier psalms like 29:1, 'Give unto the LORD, O you mighty ones,/Give unto the LORD glory and strength'.

Music

As seems clear from the headings, not all the psalms were intended to be sung so it is somewhat misleading to call the whole collection 'the hymnbook of the second temple', that is to say the psalms sung from the time when the Jews built the temple after their return from Babylonian exile (see Ezra 3–5) to the fall of Jerusalem in AD 70. For the Jews when Jesus lived on earth, the Book of Psalms was first and foremost viewed as part of Holy Scripture as we have already emphasised. Some of the psalms, like the Songs of Ascents (Psalms 120–134), had special significance at festival times and were sung by the people in their own homes as well as when they made their way to Jerusalem on pilgrimage (see Mark 11:9; 14:26).

The musical accompaniment used in the temple included the lyre, harp, the ten-stringed instrument, trumpets and cymbals (1 Chronicles 16:5,42; 25:6; 2 Chronicles 5:12–13; see Psalm 150 for details). There is no mention of the tambourine (or 'timbrel') or dance forming a part of temple worship. Only on special outdoor occasions do we read of these two expressions of praise being used (Exodus 15:20; Judges 11:34; 1 Samuel 10:5; 2 Samuel 6:5; 1 Chronicles 13:8; Psalms 68:25; 149:3; 150:4).

With the final destruction of the temple by the Romans the choirs and instrumentalists belonging to the Levite families also came to a sudden end. The musical instruments mentioned in Psalms and Chronicles all disappear with only the ram's horn surviving to be used to signal important times in the Jewish calendar. Although much reduced and even banned by some rabbis (understandably in the light of the temple's destruction in AD 70; see Psalm 137:1–4), singing survived and there is some evidence that psalms were sung in the Jewish synagogues to tunes learnt in the temple. Musical instruments, however, were permanently banned from religious worship.

After the New Testament period, there is no record of musical accompaniment when Christians sang their hymns and songs and when references are made to musical instruments, it is only to condemn their use. Two arguments were used. First, the temple instruments were seen as appropriate to the 'childish' era and regarded as part of the Jewish types. Second, musical instruments were associated with sensual pagan practices.

Unaccompanied vocal singing continued to be the norm in communal worship for many centuries and only gradually did an early form of the organ appear in the Western Church from around the 8th century. In the Eastern Orthodox churches it never caught on although some ancient percussion instruments were introduced at an early point in the Coptic and Ethiopian churches.

The Protestant Reformation re-introduced congregational singing into the communal acts of worship after centuries where the people had become mere spectators rather than participants. Luther encouraged the singing of hymns as well as the biblical psalms and although he objected to the organ probably because of its associations with the Roman Catholic system, he was not totally against the use of musical instruments. Calvin, on the other hand, allowed only unaccompanied singing of the psalms or other scriptural passages in church services. He has an interesting remark on musical instruments in his comment on Psalm 71:22. On the basis of Paul's words in 1 Corinthians 14:13 he argues that while the private use of musical instruments is not forbidden they are now banished from the churches by the plain command of the Holy Spirit 'that we must praise God, and pray to him only in a known tongue'!

When it comes to the communal worship of God, Calvin is right to emphasise that all that is superfluous to worship in spirit and truth should be set aside. His grounds for banning all musical accompaniment however are weak. Musical accompaniment is not even mentioned in the Mosaic law as part of the ceremonial law that has been fulfilled in Christ. If the heavenly singing employed the harp in John's visions (Revelation 5:8; 14:2; 15:2) then such instruments cannot be viewed as 'shadows of a departed dispensation'. The danger is always there, however, for secondary issues like music to become central and to cause needless divisions.

Depending on one's taste all kinds of musical forms can be enjoyed and appreciated. Some tunes, music and instruments can have negative associations but this will vary from person to person and country to country. Hard and fast rules cannot be set down and freedom must be given within the bonds of Christian love (see Romans 14).

Using the Psalms

Many of the individual psalms have been composed out of the psalmist's own personal experiences or as expressions of how the whole company of God's people felt and reacted when they passed through difficult times. It is not always possible to pinpoint the particular situations that led to the compositions but that is no hindrance to appreciating their value. The fact that the final editor(s) of the Psalter applied these individual psalms to the situations in which the people of God found themselves after the return from the Babylonian exile encourages Christians today to use them in expressing their own concerns and desires. Nevertheless, we must not lose sight of the overall purpose of the Psalms which is to lead us to Jesus the Messiah, the Saviour of the world and to view his presence among the people of Zion in the new creation with every enemy defeated and where the sovereign Lord is praised by all.

Personal devotion

The psalms provide the Christian with a devotional handbook of hymns, prayers and exhortations. In all the trials and sorrows of the psalmists we can identify with them and their words can so often speak for us. Such psalms remind us of the personal relationship that God's people can have with the living God and ample examples are given of what Psalm 55:22 encourages us to do, 'Cast your burden on the LORD, and he shall sustain you' (see 1 Peter 5:7). There is boldness in prayer where the psalmist pours out his grief and is not afraid to express his feelings. The flesh and blood enemies that the psalms constantly mention will vary from age to age but they all witness to the fact that we have a spiritual enemy. Ultimately, 'we do not wrestle against flesh and blood, but against principalities and powers, against the rulers of the darkness of this age, against spiritual hosts of wickedness in the heavenly places' (Ephesians 6:12). Paul urges us not to be anxious but in everything by prayer and supplication to make our requests known to God but he adds 'with thanksgiving' (Philippians 4:6) and the prayer psalms often include thanksgiving and praise in addition to psalms specifically dedicated to thanksgiving and praise.

Christians are encouraged to sing hymns and spiritual songs when they are feeling cheerful and also when suffering persecution (Acts 16:25; James 5:13).

Communal worship

Chronicles was written in the post-exilic period and the compiler of that material was eager to encourage his people to trust the God of Israel, to pray earnestly and expectantly, and to sing his praises. It is the Chronicler who records how Hezekiah restored the Temple worship according to the standards set by King David. As the congregation of Israel assembled for worship, Hezekiah commanded the Levites to sing praise 'with the words of David and of Asaph the seer' (2 Chronicles 29:25-30). As one commentator points out, 'It is a good illustration of the use of Scripture in worship'.[3]

The New Testament does not advocate exclusive psalmody when singing spiritual songs in church services, but as our prayers should follow the pattern set in God's Word so should our songs. If the singing in heaven includes direct references to the Lamb who was slain for us (Revelation 5:8-14; 15:3), it would be strange if the church on earth was confined to the language of the Old Testament and prevented from singing clearly and directly of Jesus and his atoning death and glorious resurrection as expressed in the language of the New Testament. We live after all in the era of the new covenant and of the giving of the Holy Spirit (John 7:39; 16:24; Acts 2:16-21; 1 Corinthians 14:15; Romans 15:9).

Book One

Besides being an introduction to the whole psalm collection, Psalms 1 and 2 are particularly appropriate as a prelude to the psalms in Book One.

There are twenty-five beatitudes in the Psalter ('Blessed/Happy ...') of which eight are in Book One. What is surprising is the way the beatitudes are placed in this first book. Not only do we find a group in the centre (Psalms 32:1,2; 33:12; 34:8) but they also act like bookends, with two at the beginning (Psalms 1:1; 2:12) and two at the end (Psalms 40:4; 41:1). The overall impression that this arrangement conveys is that the highly favoured state does not follow the general worldly view that sees a person's happy situation in terms of material success and physical wellbeing. The righteous do not prosper in that sense. It is the wicked, the ones who persecute the humble poor, who seem to do well and have the best of life.

Coupled with the beatitudes is a strong emphasis on the poor finding refuge in God. The word for 'to take refuge' or 'trust' appears fourteen times in the psalms of Book One and they reveal that God is committed to these poor righteous members of the covenant community (see for example Psalms 5:11; 7:1; 11:1; 18:2,30; 34:22). The first seven beatitudes clearly indicate that despite outward circumstances to the contrary, the happy state involves trusting God and being found in a right relationship to him (see Psalm 34:8), while the final beatitude (Psalm 41:1) reveals that this favoured condition also means that such people begin to act like God in their commitment

to those who, like themselves, are poor and needy. David is a prime
example of this relationship with God that results in concern for the
poor.[4] These are similar to the poor, meek, persecuted people whom
Jesus pronounces as blessed at the beginning of the Sermon on the
Mount (Matthew 5:3–10; see Luke 6:20–26).[5]

The message of Book One is that God is true to his word and despite
evidences to the contrary he does come to the support of his king
who is associated with the poor righteous members of God's covenant
community (see Psalms 1–2). While the psalms can be applied to the
individual believer, we are encouraged to see in the ups and downs
of David's life, a picture of the true King, Jesus Christ, who endured
persecution and the curse of God yet was vindicated and delivered
because of his godly fear.

Psalm 1

The LORD's True Worshippers

When we think of the Psalms perhaps our first thought is of singing and praising God, giving thanks to him, or praying fervently to him with confession of sin and heartfelt desires to see God honoured. But the psalm that heads up the whole collection is not what we might expect.

The Psalms begin by preaching to us. Would-be worshippers are reminded that true worship of the living God centres on teaching revealed by God that is meant to have a positive effect on our daily lives.

This is something we all need to keep in mind. We can get so caught up with the kind of communal worship we think is attractive and acceptable that we can lose sight of or ignore what really counts. Our attention is drawn not to music and song but to a message that pulls us up short and makes us consider where we stand before God.

It is not the only psalm of this nature. There are other preaching psalms scattered throughout the Psalm collection but the emphasis from the beginning is to encourage right worship. How different Israel's worship was to be from the pagan worship with which they were familiar! Far from making their lives wholesome, pagan worship more often than not added to the depravity of people's lives. And when Israel's worship was contaminated by pagan elements the same results ensued. Because of our sinful natures there is always a tendency for true religion to degenerate and become no better than paganism as witnessed in so many medieval church practices and is still evident where Roman Catholicism is in a dominant position as well as in numerous modern Protestant practices.

God's word has been given that we might humble ourselves and mend our ways. We are called to reform our worship and our lives in accord with the teaching of God's revealed Word. This is why the Bible is to be central in our worship. It must never be thought of as something secondary or separate from communal worship. We are grateful to the Protestant Reformers for reminding us that the Word of God must be at the heart of worship.

Psalm 1 not only functions as an introduction to the entire collection but also to the third section of the Hebrew Bible called 'The Writings'[6] and reminds us that first and foremost the Book of Psalms is divine revelation, part of Holy Scripture, making us wise about salvation and profitable for the building up of God's people (2 Timothy 3:15-17).

As in Proverbs and other parts of the Bible a contrast is drawn between the 'righteous' and the 'wicked'. The first three verses highlight the righteous while the following two verses consider the wicked with the final verse depicting a parting of the ways.

The psalm is a very carefully constructed poem of contrasting pictures. From start to finish two lifestyles are in view. No sooner does it mention the happy person than it refers to the ungodly or wicked with whom the godly do not associate (verse 1) but rather find delight in God and his word (verse 2). When the wicked are the subject they are contrasted with the happy (compare verse 4 with verse 3) and find themselves excluded from the company of the righteous (verse 5 and in contrast to verse 1). Contrasting with the first word 'blessed' (verse 1), the last word of the psalm is 'perish' which is the destiny of the wicked (verse 6; similarly Psalm 112:1,10).[7]

The Godly (verses 1–3)

Jesus was not the first to proclaim beatitudes at the beginning of a sermon (see Matthew 5:1-11) for this wisdom or preaching psalm opens with one. 'Blessed' (verse 1) is not the more common religious word often translated 'blessed' in the sense of bestowing a blessing on someone ('the Lord bless you', Numbers 6:24) or that is used in reference to worshipping God ('Bless the Lord', Psalm 103:1). The term found here belongs to the same word family as Asher, the name of one of Jacob's sons (Genesis 30:13) and Asherah, the Canaanite goddess of fortune and happiness. Like its Greek equivalent it is an exclamation, 'O the happiness of!' or 'How fortunate!' This is the person's pleasing position or situation. It is never used of God but it is one of the characteristic ways of encouraging God's people to live lives pleasing to him, especially in Proverbs (see Proverbs 3:13; 8:32,34; etc. and Psalm 41:1).

Charles Spurgeon once reminded his Victorian London congregation that many people think of religion as a sad and miserable affair and the preacher added, 'and perhaps their religion is just that'! But true religion, the religion of the Bible is quite different. 'Religion never was designed to make our pleasures less', wrote the hymn writer, Isaac Watts.

There is a general longing for happiness and the world offers so many ways of achieving it but too often they lead to more unhappiness and eventually to final misery. From God's perspective the sort of person who is truly happy is the one described here. It is another way of describing the wise person who like Job steered clear of evil and feared God (Job 1:1; Proverbs 3:7; Romans 12:9).

Shunning the evil (verse 1)

Interestingly, three negative statements are presented first which may not be a 'user friendly' approach but it is often the biblical way because as Lloyd-Jones reminds us, the Bible is a realistic book and starts with the world as it is, and because it emphasises our need to repent of the evil of sin and follow God's unique way.[8] The worldly lifestyle is to be avoided at all costs. Do not envy the ungodly or think of them as fortunate. All they have at best are the fleeting pleasures of sin. It is the one who is in a right relationship with God who is the happy person, one who keeps away from all that is morally dirty, vile and unwholesome.

The verbs 'walks', 'stands' and 'sits' (see Deuteronomy 6:7) may have been used deliberately to suggest the downward spiral of evil but the main point is to express the whole life attitude of the wicked. To walk 'in the counsel of the ungodly' is to model one's life on the schemes and plans of those who are opposed to God's revealed word. The phrase 'stands in the path (or 'way') of sinners' does not mean getting in other people's way but adopting their conduct and participating in their way of life. To sit 'in the seat of the scornful' denotes enjoying the company of those who scoff at people who are not like them. Paul describes the position of those outside Christ as ones who walk 'according to the course of this world' (Ephesians 2:2) and urges Christians not to be conformed to this world (Romans 12: 2).

Of the three terms for the unrighteous, 'the ungodly' or better 'the wicked' are those who would be judged guilty in a court of law and 'sinners' describes those who have missed the mark and whose lives are dominated by their evil desires. Both terms are used interchangeably throughout the psalm collection. As for 'the scornful' or 'mockers', this is a much more specific term for hardened apostates who arrogantly disdain the words of the wise (see Proverbs 1:22; 15:12).

Clinging to the good (verse 2)

After the negatives of verse 1 the alternative lifestyle is introduced with a 'But', which could be translated as 'But rather' to bring out the force of the original. Surprisingly, instead of a contrasting three-fold positive description of this most happy and fortunate person, only one thing is said but it is crucial and sufficient. Over-against the thinking, values and conduct of the wicked stands the Lord's instruction, what God thinks and plans. This is the truly happy worshipper: one whose 'delight' (see Psalm 112:1) is in 'the law of the LORD', who 'meditates' on it continually (see Psalm 119:47–48). It is not an irksome legalistic duty but a pleasurable activity that is as enjoyable as eating a good meal (see Deuteronomy 8:3; Psalm 19:10). Jesus said, 'blessed are those who hear the word of God and keep it' (Luke 11:28).

While 'law' often refers to God's law through Moses and later to the five books of Moses it can also be used more generally for 'instruction' and for the 'teaching' that we find, for instance, in wisdom books like Proverbs. It must certainly not be confined to what we think of as the Ten Commandments. The Law of Moses contains narrative, advice and warnings as well as legal directives. By the time this psalm came to head up the whole collection 'law' was probably applied to the whole of God's written word.[9] Paul uses the word 'law' for the whole of the Old Testament (see Romans 3:10–19; 1 Corinthians 14:21). It is divine instruction and therefore profitable to the people of God. Other psalms that focus on the 'law of the LORD' are Psalms 19 (near the middle of Book One) and 119 (near the centre of Book Five).

The verb 'meditate' (see also Psalm 2:1) suggests muttering God's word in a low voice as it was read or remembered. It was no mere intellectual exercise neither was it a ritualistic activity to gain merit as some holy books are memorised and repeated ad nauseam without understanding. This was done with a view to taking to heart God's revealed instruction and living by it. Meditating day and night in God's law echoes the words of God to Joshua on the death of Moses (Joshua 1:8). It is therefore no surprise to read that a copy of the law-book was to be given to the king so that it might be with him to read 'all the days of his life' that he might learn to fear God and observe his statutes (Deuteronomy 17:18–20).

The resulting picture (verse 3)

The highly favoured wise person who shunned intimate associations with the wicked and clung instead to the good word of God is likened to a tree (see Jeremiah 17:5–8). We are again reminded of wisdom and the wise who are depicted as 'a tree of life' (Proverbs 3:18; 11:30; 15:4). Unlike trees in the wild whose leaves wither and their fruit drops before it is ripe through lack of water, the godly are like trees specially planted or more literally 'transplanted' beside irrigation channels ('streams of water'; see Proverbs 21:1), which grow strong and healthy, yielding mature fruit at the right time. The godly are nourished by the life-giving word of God so that they 'prosper' in all that they do. In other words, like the flourishing tree, they fulfil the purpose of their existence. They 'flourish like the palm tree ... they still bear fruit in old age (Psalm 92:12–15). They live to honour God and benefit others, and find their satisfaction in doing so. The Christian produces the righteous fruit of the Spirit and seeks to help others to become Christians (John 15:8,16; Romans 1:13; Galatians 5:22–23; Ephesians 5:9; Hebrews 12:11).

The kind of prosperity we read of here is not material reward for surrendering to God as the prosperity gospellers claim but a natural outcome of drawing on 'the fountain of life' himself through his word (see Psalm 36:9). It is true that the wicked can 'prosper' in their evil ways and can increase their material wealth (Psalms 37:7; 73:12), but what about 'their end'? It is said of the Lord's Servant that through all his sorrows and suffering the will of the Lord would 'prosper' in his hand (Isaiah 53:10).

The Godless (verses 4–5)

'Not so the wicked' is the terse way it is put in the original followed
by another strong 'but rather' to introduce the contrasting picture.
It takes four or five lines to depict the godly but just one line is
enough to picture the wicked. There is very little to say about 'chaff'
(verse 4), those husks of corn and seed and bits of straw. What could
be more different to a well-established, thriving tree than chaff! It
is the difference between life and death. Chaff (see Psalm 35:5) is
insubstantial, lifeless, rootless, easily blown away. This is the stark
truth concerning the ungodly. Such people are what Proverbs and
some of the psalms will refer to as the 'fool' (see Psalm 14:1; Proverbs
12:15).

The conclusion is introduced by 'Therefore' (verse 5). With words
and ideas from the opening verse, the end of the 'ungodly' ('wicked')
'sinners' is brought to our attention. Those who have stood where
sinners tread will not be able to stand up 'in the judgment'. They are
not among those who can stand upright before God in the present
and if they remain in that rebellious state on the final day of judgment
they will not be able to endure his anger but will want to hide in
terror from the presence of the great judge of all the earth (Isaiah
2:10-11,19; Nahum 1:6; Revelation 6:15-17). Those who have followed
wicked counsel do not belong to the 'assembly' or 'congregation of the
righteous'. They do not belong to what other psalms will describe as
God's holy city of Zion, the company of God's redeemed people (Psalms
24:3-6; 87:1-7; see Revelation 22:14-15).

The Two Ways (verse 6)

The final verse introduced with the word 'For' or 'because' brings the
two contrasting lifestyles to a concluding climax and particularly
considers their situation on judgment day. It summarises the whole
psalm with the image of two ways, picking up the reference to 'path'
in verse 1 (here translated 'way'). As in Proverbs the contrast is drawn
between the paths of the wise and the foolish, the righteous and the
wicked. The two phrases, 'the way of the righteous, but the way of
the ungodly' refer to the character and conduct of the two types of
people. The 'righteous' people have been introduced in the previous
verse. They are the ones who stand in a right legal relationship to God
and are therefore not terrified on the final day of wrath but belong to
that company whose names are written in heaven. All the 'righteous'

can be identified with the person congratulated at the beginning of the psalm. And they can be even more encouraged, because the LORD, their covenant-keeping God, 'knows' their way. There is the ongoing 'knowing' that expresses personal care and concern (see Genesis 18:19; Exodus 2:25; Amos 3:2; Psalm 144:3; 2 Timothy 2:19). It is not only that God knows all the facts about their lives, which of course he does as the all-knowing one, but that he is intimately concerned about every step the righteous take (see Psalm 37:18). This is the personal care that God has for his people. He walks with them through the dark valley and brings them safely to life and fulness of joy (Psalms 16:11; 23:1-6)

The 'ungodly' are the same wicked people mentioned throughout the psalm who are not accounted righteous in God's sight and have no place among God's people as the previous verse has made clear. In other words, their whole rebellious way of life, if left unchanged, 'shall perish'; it ends in ruin (see Psalms 37:20; 73:27; Proverbs 14:12). That is the solemn note on which the psalm ends in complete contrast to the happy opening word.

Throughout Scripture the two ways are set before us. Moses preached to Israel: ' ... I have set before you life and death, blessing and cursing; therefore choose life, that both you and your descendants may live' (Deuteronomy 30:19). So did Joshua (Joshua 24:14-25), prophets like Samuel and Elijah (1 Samuel 7:3; 1 Kings 18:21), the wisdom of Proverbs 4:10-19 and supremely Jesus at the end of his Sermon on the Mount (Matthew 7:13-27).

Our psalmist-preacher has provided us with an important introduction and message for appreciating the entire collection of psalms. At the same time, we come to see that this picture of the blessed man who loves and meditates on God's Law is the kind of king described in Deuteronomy 17:18-19 of whom Joshua is a type (Joshua 1:7-8) and who is introduced to us in Psalm 2. With Luther we can say that the first psalm 'speaks literally concerning Christ'[10] and it is in and through King Jesus that we are blessed and are found among the righteous.

Psalm 2

The LORD's King

Like Psalm 1, this second psalm is not a hymn of praise or a prayer but a sermon. Psalms 1 and 2 have been specially chosen by the final editor, perhaps someone like Ezra the scribe after the return from exile in Babylon, to serve as an introduction to the entire collection of psalms. Unless we appreciate what these two psalms are saying we shall miss the overall message of the whole book of Psalms. The Psalms are about God's rule in the face of human and devilish opposition. Dominion over the created world as God's representatives was the role given from the first to human beings (Genesis 1:26–28; see Psalm 8). God's aim in setting apart one nation as his kingdom on earth including his special promises to David, was in order to fulfil his purposes for the entire world. What God did in Israel during the David-Solomon era is a small sketch of the future universal kingdom. The human representative from David's family line will fulfil this divine plan, through much suffering, to the eternal praise of God. With that overarching theme in mind, individuals are encouraged to seek God, to trust him despite enemy opposition and to look in sure and certain hope for all that God has in store for them as members of the heavenly city.

The link between Psalms 1 and 2 is close and some early Christian leaders in the Church treated them as one.[11] Beatitudes frame the two psalms: 'Blessed is the man ...' (Psalm 1:1) and 'Blessed are all ...' (Psalm 2:12). Psalm 1 describes God's man in contrast to the wicked; Psalm 2 describes God's king in contrast to the rebellious kings of the earth. Unless the rebellious kings of Psalm 2 submit to the Lord and his anointed they will 'perish' like the ungodly of Psalm 1. Whereas the people of Psalm 2 foolishly 'plot' ('murmur') against God, the man to be congratulated in Psalm 1 'meditates' ('murmur') on God's law. This righteous one depicts the kind of king that God desires who will read the law all the days of his life and will be careful to observe it (Deuteronomy 17:18-19). In turn, the king's observance of God's law will be an example to the people.

Psalm 2 like the opening psalm has no heading but Peter attributes the authorship to David (Acts 4:25). It is quoted and alluded to many times in the New Testament, the most obvious references being Acts 4:25-26 in the church's urgent prayer to God on account of the threats by the Jerusalem authorities and Acts 13:33 where Paul uses it to support Jesus' resurrection and actually refers to it as 'the second psalm'. Hebrews also quotes from the psalm (Hebrews 1:5; 5:5) as does the apostle John (Revelation 2:27).

It is a well-constructed poem. Each of the four sections introduces us to a different voice with each one picking up and amplifying an important item from the preceding section. The two outer sections refer to the kings who firstly voice their opposition to God and his anointed (verses 1-3) but who, in the final section, are urged to submit and serve God and his son (verses 10-12). In the two inner sections God first speaks concerning his king (verses 4-6) and then the son announces the divine promise about his universal rule (verses 7-9). The psalm is a good example of one of the distinctive features of Hebrew poetry, namely, synonymous parallelism, where the second line reinforces the first (see especially verses 1,3,4,5,9,10 and 11). For example, 'And the ends of the earth for your possession' parallels 'The nations for your inheritance' (verse 8).

Rulers revolt (verses 1-3)
As with so many of the psalms, particularly in the first half of the collection, this one arises out of the experiences of the David-Solomon era. God so planned it that the nation of Israel under the Davidic monarchy was to picture, albeit in faint and imperfect outline, the deeper truth concerning worldly reaction to God's authority and that

of his Son, Jesus the Messiah. That old kingdom of God on earth in Israel was constantly under threat from foreign enemies, either from closely related neighbours like Moab, Ammon and Edom or from peoples and nations like the Philistines, Phoenicians, Syria and Egypt. 2 Samuel 8 and 10 give us examples of David's foreign foes. Attacking Israel and its divinely appointed king implied an attack on God himself by these nations. David and his descendants represented God's rule. They ruled on God's throne over God's kingdom—'he has chosen my son Solomon to sit on the throne of the kingdom of the Lord over Israel' (1 Chronicles 28:5; see 1 Chronicles 29:23; 2 Chronicles 13:8).

The psalm opens with a rhetorical question 'Why?' (verse 1). It is not expecting an answer but expressing astonishment. The question is not a cry of desperation or frustration but a statement of confidence. It expresses the folly of the non-Israelite 'nations' and the 'people' groups within those national boundaries that they could be so insane as to engage in such a senseless exercise. They 'rage'; they are like a noisy restless gathering of pilgrims (see Psalm 55:14) only they are assembling not to worship but to rebel. The verb 'plot' is the same as that translated 'meditate' in Psalm 1:2. While the godly 'mutter' God's law, the ungodly world 'mutter' useless thoughts. Nothing can be more futile ('vain') than plotting to rebel against God.

From the local scene of ungodly people within Israel with their worldly opinions, life-style and attitudes (Psalm 1:1), the spotlight has turned in Psalm 2 to view what this looks like on an international level with 'kings' and 'rulers' conspiring 'together' against the 'Lord' (Yahweh/Jehovah) and his 'Anointed' (verse 2). Our English word 'Messiah' comes from this Hebrew term 'Anointed' applied first to the high priest (Leviticus 4:3) and then to the kings of Israel anointed by God's command (1 Samuel 12:3; 16:13; 24:6) and especially to David's family line of kings and the future Messiah (1 Samuel 2:10,35; Psalms 18:50; 132:10; Daniel 9:25–26; Zechariah 4:14) of whom Cyrus the Persian was a type (Isaiah 45:1). Those who fail to honour and obey the Anointed deny the authority of God (John 5:22).

The 'bonds' and the 'cords' (verse 3) are symbols of subjection (see Jeremiah 2:20: 30:8) and the picture we are given is of these foreign leaders seeking to break free from God's rule exercised through God's king (see Jeremiah 2:20; 30:8). 'Freedom' has been the watchword of Satan's party from the beginning. The first couple believed the snake's lie that the restrictions God had placed upon them were not for their good but hindered them from achieving their true potential (Genesis 3:1–5) and that has been the belief of fallen humanity ever since. 'I did it my way' sums up the lifestyle of the ungodly. The rebellion reached a notable peak when Jew and Gentile clamoured together to put Jesus, God's Messiah, on the cross (Acts 4:27–28). Their attitude was that of the citizens in one of Jesus' parables, 'We will not have this man to reign over us' (Luke 19:14). The world of fallen humanity hates God and his Anointed and, as Jesus informed his disciples, it hates God's people too (John 15:18–19) and persecutes them (Acts 4:23–31).

Divine response (verses 4–6)

God's response is graphically portrayed. The LORD (Jehovah/Yahweh) who is enthroned as king forever 'shall laugh' and 'hold them in derision' (verse 4; see Psalms 37:13; 59:8). This is anthropomorphic language where human actions and emotions are applied to God. The dramatic imagery is meant to convey the utter stupidity of human scheming against God. This is why such plotting is useless. We might be impressed or intimidated by the hostile intentions and forceful efforts of those opposed to God and his people, but from God's vantage point it is ludicrous. How absurd, how irrational, how futile the attempts made by puny humans to rebel against God! They are like a race of pygmies where the ruling giant is in a position to put an end to them all with one stamp of his foot.

The God who derides their plots then speaks in his wrath and troubles them in his fury. He does not negotiate with rebels but proclaims his purposes. Our attention is drawn not as we might have expected to an announcement of punishment on the nations united in revolt but to a divine declaration concerning the Lord's appointed ruler against whom they are conspiring. The national rulers say 'Let us ...' but God says, 'Yet I ...' (verse 6). God's plans are already worked out and the centrepiece concerns his 'King', the one called 'his Anointed' in verse 2.

It is important at this point to make clear some truths relating to God's rule:

First, God is the supreme ruler. He is sovereign over everything. God 'sits' enthroned in the heavens. As creator of all he is the ruler of all. Nothing is outside his dominion or control (see Psalms 29:10; 9:1–2; 99:1). However, rebellion against God's authority has taken place on earth. His sovereignty has been challenged and his revealed will is not being done on earth as it is in heaven.

Second, humans were created to rule. They were made in God's image and likeness to exercise dominion over the other creatures (Genesis 1:28; Psalm 8:6–8). The first human couple were appointed as God's viceroys to govern the earth. But they rebelled and submitted to the snake. Instead of serving God they served God's enemy, who is revealed as Satan or the Devil (Revelation 12:9). This usurper then became the ruler of this world with the earthly kingdoms under his control and influence.

The big storyline of the Bible is how God acts so that the kingdoms of this world come to acknowledge his rule once more. It is the story of how humans are finally rescued from the snake's control to reign over the created order on God's behalf. God is not thwarted in his original plans for it is through a human that God overcomes the evil one and establishes his rule over the whole earth where humans fulfil their destiny. The formation of Israel into a nation and the appointment of David and his family line as kings over God's people were part of the preparations toward the final goal and provided a small and imperfect preview of God's kingdom on earth.

The announcement that God's king who will rule the world has been installed on God's 'holy hill of Zion' (verse 6) seems something of an anticlimax because Zion referred originally to the hill fortress that David conquered from the Jebusites. It was a tiny area that lay on the south-eastern slopes of Jerusalem and yet it was there that David made his home and the capital of his kingdom (2 Samuel 5:5,7). The name also came to be used for the mount where the temple was built (Psalm 132:13; Isaiah 8:18) and as another term for Jerusalem (Isaiah 10:24) and for the whole company of God's people (Psalms 48:11; 149:2).

From those early beginnings on Zion's hill the kingdom grew into an empire that stretched from the Euphrates to the borders of Egypt with the kings of the earth coming to Jerusalem to hear Solomon's wisdom (1 Kings 4:20–34). That era was in fact a picture, an imperfect copy, of the future real eternal city-state made up of God's people from all time and nations that will fill the whole earth, when God will be as much at home on earth as in heaven. The David-Solomon period was pointing forward to the real king of David's line who came preaching God's kingdom and pointing to himself as the king. Through weakness and insignificance God's rule on earth was established by Jesus, the God-

Man. Like David, he becomes the humble, poor, oppressed righteous one. By his life of obedience to God and his atoning death he has gained the victory over Satan and has been raised to that supreme position at the Father's right hand where he reigns till all his enemies are under his feet. John sees Jesus, the Lamb who was slain, standing on Mount Zion together with the redeemed elect (Revelation 14:1-5). Jesus the Messiah is God's response to all the rebellion. The remaining verses expand on this unexpected statement. How can the anointed King among his people bring such terror to the rebels?

Divine decree (verses 7-9)

The king himself now speaks, the one referred to in verse 2 as the Lord's anointed. He emphasises that it was the 'Lord' (Jehovah/Yahweh) who spoke the decree. This formal declaration concerned the Davidic king and the re-establishment of God's kingdom on earth.

First, it speaks of his legal position: 'You are my Son' (verse 7). The background to understanding this relationship between God and his king is to be found in the covenant that God made with David. Among the promises made, God states, 'I will be his Father and he shall be my son' (2 Samuel 7:14; Psalm 89:26-27). The phrase 'today I have begotten you' is another way of saying 'I have now become your Father'. It is not speaking about the king's birth but of his coronation. It is the language of adoption and comes into effect on the occasion of the king's installation (see verse 6).

Jesus is not only God's unique Son, the second Person of the Holy Trinity but in becoming truly human he is appointed to fulfil the promises made to David as well as the ones made to Adam and Eve and Abraham. At Jesus' baptism there are echoes of this verse where God acknowledges him as 'my beloved Son' and interestingly, Luke follows this up immediately by introducing Christ's genealogy emphasising his association with Adam 'the son of God' (Luke 3:22-38). Jesus is appointed God's viceroy like Adam to have dominion and as the second Man all those united to him will reign with him (see Psalm 8). He is also appointed, as the angel informed Mary, to bring to realisation the promises made to David that God would give to him 'the throne of his father David' (Luke 1:32-33). At Jesus' resurrection the installation is complete (Acts 13:30-34). By the resurrection it was publicly and powerfully revealed that Jesus is the Son of God. He was vindicated and exalted to God's throne (Romans 1:3; Hebrews 1:5; 5:5). All authority has been given to him as the Anointed one and he shall reign till all his enemies are under his feet. And when death, the last enemy, has been destroyed, then the Son, having delivered the kingdom to God the Father, 'will also be subject to the one who put all things under him, that God may be all in all' (1 Corinthians 15:24–28). We must be careful not to confuse Jesus' sonship as the Messiah which is the main point of this psalm and his eternal Sonship as the second Person of the triune God (Matthew 28:19; Luke 1:35; John 1:14,18), nevertheless they are intimately connected in that as the Messiah he is God the Son (Hebrews 1).

Second, there is the promise of worldwide rule: '... the nations for your inheritance ... the ends of the earth for your possession' (verse 8). It is God's gift to his anointed who is in willing submission to God. 'Ask of me, and I will give'—Jesus was tempted to achieve universal sway by worshipping God's enemy Satan but unlike Adam and Israel he did not succumb but remained faithful and received the inheritance by his obedience even to the death of the cross. As Jesus predicted his death he declared, 'Now is the judgment of this world; now the ruler of this world will be cast out. And I, if I am lifted up from the earth, will draw all *peoples* to myself' (John 12:31–32). Psalm 72 looks forward to this universal reign of Messiah in a renewed earth (see also Zechariah 9:10). The David-Solomon empire gave a little taster of this future under great David's greater son.

Third, there is a description of his powerful rule: it will be 'with a rod of iron ...' (verse 9). The 'rod' can denote a shepherd's crook (Psalm 23:4) or a king's sceptre (Genesis 49:10). This rod, the sign of kingly authority, is an iron one suggesting firm, no-nonsense rule that is prepared to use force when necessary. We have expressions like 'iron lady' applied to Britain's first woman Prime Minister. Not all will submit voluntarily to the king's rule and a contrast is drawn between the strength of iron and the fragile nature of a 'potter's vessel'. Though the opposition may appear invincible as it clubs together to present a united show of strength (see verses 1–3) its power is broken, smashed to smithereens by this king set up by God. The apostle John uses the same imagery to indicate that ultimate victory belongs to Jesus the Messiah when he comes to exercise vengeance on all his enemies. His faithful followers, who have shared Messiah's sufferings, will also be involved in judging the nations and in the glory of that final victory (Revelation 2:26–27; 12:5; 19:15; 2 Thessalonians 1:7–10).

Wisdom warns (verses 10–12)

In the light of that awesome day of the Lamb's wrath, the question is, 'who is able to stand?' (Revelation 6:15–17; Malachi 3:2). The answer provided in Revelation 7 is the same as the one we find in these remaining lines of Psalm 2. It is a gospel message, a word of hope. Those kings and governors mentioned earlier who had taken counsel together are themselves counselled. They are urged to be wise and receive instruction so that they might be effective rulers. The wisdom of this age and of the rulers of this age is of no help. If the rulers of this age had known gospel wisdom they would not have crucified the Lord of glory (1 Corinthians 2:6–8).

Here is God's gracious invitation. All in rebellion against God and his Messiah are called to submit respectfully to the LORD (Jehovah/ Yahweh). In other words they must turn from their idols and their hatred of God and turn to worshipping and honouring the true and living God (see Jeremiah 10:16; 1 Thessalonians 1:9). Unlike Queen Elizabeth II who in her eighties rededicated herself on the occasion of her diamond jubilee to serve her people, ancient monarchs did not see their rule in quite that way! Yet such rulers are commanded to 'serve' with fear. But to be in the Lord's service is not painful or servile. It is truly satisfying, for God made us to bring him honour and in that service we find true enjoyment (see Psalm 100:2). In God's presence is fulness of joy (Psalm 16:11) but that rejoicing must not turn into irreverent presumption. We 'rejoice with trembling' (verse 11).

To honour and serve God means submitting to the Son.[12] The 'kiss' was one of the ways of paying homage to a king (see 1 Samuel 10:1). Encouragements to submit come with the call.

On the negative side there is a threat to avoid—'lest he be angry and you perish in the way' (verse 12) which suggests being suddenly struck dead when they think they are only midway through their course of life. Human death is not a part of the natural evolutionary process but is God's judgment on sin. Physical death reveals God's wrath (see Psalm 90:7–12) but it will be fully displayed on the final day of judgment in the second death which is described as the torment of the lake of fire (Revelation 20:9,13–15).

On the positive side there is a privileged position to enjoy—'Blessed are all those who put their trust in him' or more literally, 'O how fortunate are all who seek refuge in him!' The theme of finding refuge in God is a dominant one in the psalms particularly in the first half of the collection (see for example Psalms 5:11; 7:1; 34:22; 71:1). The inclusion in this closing verse of the two words 'perish' and 'blessed' that were found at the beginning and end of the first psalm, is yet another indication that these two initial Psalms belong together and form the introduction to the whole collection. They focus on the righteous King, the Lord's Anointed and encourage us to trust him and live that life that his pleasing to the Lord.

Psalm 3

Deliverance belongs to the LORD

After the two introductory psalms we might have expected to have songs in praise of the Lord. Instead, the following psalms contain pleas for help and expressions of trust in crisis situations.

As the headings suggest the psalms in Book One (Psalms 1–41), with the possible exception of 10 and 33, are associated with David. The word 'Psalm' is a technical term occurring fifty-seven times in the Psalter. It originally meant a song to be sung to a musical instrument. When the psalms were collected into their present order and divided into five books after the Jews returned from Babylonian exile, the various headings became part of the Hebrew text of Scripture that the scribes then methodically copied. They are important and to be distinguished from the titles often added by well-meaning editors of the English versions to indicate something of the content of the individual psalms.

Lament (verses 1–2)
The title tells us that this psalm was composed when David 'fled from Absalom his son', who had secretly conspired against his father's rule (see 2 Samuel 15–19). It is one of the royal psalms calling on God for protection but it opens with a lament.

David speaks of the increasing numbers of his enemies and of the 'many' rising up against him. In the prophetic history we read of how Absalom gradually 'stole the hearts of the men of Israel' as he made friendly gestures to those who came to him for justice. As a result of his treasonable actions, 'the conspiracy grew stronger, for the people with Absalom continually increased in number' (2 Samuel 15:4–6,12b).

His enemies were saying that God was not on David's side (verse 2). When Zadok the priest and the Levites brought the ark of the covenant to David outside the city, he insisted that it should be returned to Jerusalem and this, no doubt, added more fuel to the idea that God was not with David and therefore would not help him (2 Samuel 15:25–26). It was no surprise, then, to find a man like Shimei, a member of Saul's family, cursing the king (2 Samuel 16:8).

This was certainly a low point in David's kingship. The greatness of the problem is emphasised by the repeated references to the 'many' who are against him. It is a reminder of the enemies set against the Lord and his anointed in Psalm 2.

The 'Selah' might be a musical direction, indicating an instrumental interlude or pause. In many cases there seems no logical reason for its presence. As with some of the notices in the headings we are at a loss to know precisely what its significance is and why it appears where it does.

Confidence (verses 3–6)
Despite all his grievous sin, David was a man 'after God's own heart'. He knew the Lord in a personal way and acknowledged him as his deliverer. In reply to those who were saying that he would receive no help from God, David confidently asserts that the covenant God of Israel is his 'shield', which is a way of emphasising that God is his protector. It reminds us of God's reassuring word to Abram after his triumph over the kings of the East (Genesis 15:1). But David goes further and speaks of the Lord as his 'glory'. At that time David was inglorious. It seemed that God had left him. His head was low and covered in dust as a sign of mourning (2 Samuel 15:30). But he believes that the Lord will come to him and restore his honour and be the means of lifting his head up high again.

Furthermore, though he had left the ark, the symbol of God's presence, in Jerusalem, known as God's 'holy hill' of Zion, David is confident that the Lord will hear him. When Daniel was in Babylon he prayed toward Jerusalem and God heard his pleas. Christians do not need to turn east in order to pray and confess faith or have arrows pointing in a particular direction. By faith we direct our prayers, under the new covenant, through God's Son, Jesus Christ (John 16:23-24; Hebrews 10:19-22).

David can go to sleep without worrying and awake refreshed, confident of the Lord's protection—'for the LORD sustained me' (verse 5). The danger of night attack was very real. Ahithophel counselled Absalom that with twelve thousand men they could pursue David at night while he was weary and weak (2 Samuel 17:1-2). David was well and truly outnumbered yet with the Lord as his shield (verse 3) he 'will not be afraid of ten thousands of people' against him all around (verse 6).

Calling on God (verses 7-8)

The opening plea for God to act in this desperate situation takes up what is said in the opening lines of the psalm. With the many rising up against him he calls out 'Arise, O LORD'. The petition recalls the battle cry of the Israelites when they moved camp in the wilderness with the ark of the covenant at the head of the procession: 'Rise up, O LORD! Let your enemies be scattered, and let those who hate you flee before you' (Numbers 10:35-36). Though the symbol of God's presence was in Jerusalem, David looks to this living and true God, whom he knows personally, to rescue him—'Save me, O my God!' His attitude was so different to Israel's when Eli and his sons governed the people. They had a superstitious view of the ark, believing that only if the ark was with them in battle would they obtain victory.

From Psalm 2 we learn that the enemies of God's anointed are God's enemies too (Psalm 2:2). David therefore calls for the enemies' strength to be broken, that they would be shamed and made ineffective. The enemies, who are also described as the wicked or 'ungodly' (see Psalm 1:4-6) are like demonic beasts with ravenous jaws and fangs. The psalm then ends on a confident note. Victory is secure for it does not depend on David and his resources but on the Lord. This is what we find in 2 Samuel: David was victorious, Absalom and those with him were defeated and it was all the Lord's doing.

David could say what Jonah said later: 'Salvation belongs to the LORD' (verse 8: Jonah 2:9). The psalm ends with David calling down a blessing on God's people who have been deceived by God's enemies.

Saving David, the Lord's anointed, in turn leads to God's people being
blessed (verse 8).

David's experiences prefigure those of Jesus, the Lord's Messiah.
Psalm 2 has prepared us for this as the New Testament indicates.
The history of David during this low period in his reign, as 2 Samuel
suggests and this psalm underlines, is a shadowy preview of our
Lord's humiliation and sufferings. Many rose up against him and the
opposition increased throughout his public ministry culminating in
the cries to be rid of him and crucify him. As he was mistreated and
hung on a Roman cross people jeered, confident that such an impostor
would get no help from God. Like David, Jesus made his way out of
Jerusalem and was cursed but throughout his sufferings, the Father
kept his Anointed. At no time was Jesus ruffled by the enemy. He could
sleep any time, anywhere, even in a boat with a storm raging. After the
enemies had done their worst, Jesus committed his spirit to his Father
and awoke on the resurrection morning. In the days of his flesh, the
Son of God 'offered up prayers and supplications with vehement cries
and tears to him who was able to save him from death and was heard
because of his godly fear' (Hebrews 5:7). Blessing comes to God's people
through the curse that the Anointed one endured (Galatians 3:13–14).

But David's prayer is appropriate for all God's people. In every
affliction as believers we are encouraged to lay our concerns before
our God and cry to him to deliver us in times of trouble, knowing that
deliverance comes from him.

Psalm 4

Living Securely

There are indications that this 'Psalm of David' comes from the same period as the previous one. David was forced to leave the security of his palace and sleep rough during the period when Absalom his son usurped the throne. The troublers who cause 'distress' (verse 1; see Psalm 3:1), and the 'many who say' (verse 6; see 3:2) were still around and David calls to the Lord for a hearing (verse 1; see 3:4). In both psalms, David speaks of 'my glory' (verse 2; see 3:3) and introduces the themes of prayerful trust and sleeping peacefully (verse 8; see 3:5). Like Psalm 3 it is one of the royal psalms of protection. But an even more confident note is struck in the way David addresses his opponents (see verses 2–5).

This is the first of the psalms with musical directions in the title. It is possible that originally not many of the psalms were composed to be sung. 'To the Chief Musician' may mean that the psalm is one belonging to the musical director's collection. It is used fifty-five times in the Psalter and is also found in Habakkuk 3:19. We find the word 'chief musician' or 'director of music' used a number of times in Chronicles for those overseeing the Temple worship, particularly the music. 'With stringed instruments' is found six times in the Psalter and once in the singular (see Psalm 61). For this psalm quiet accompaniment is needed such as lyre and harp, not the louder wind instruments and percussion (see Psalm 150 for more details on musical instruments). The Selah again might stand for an instrumental interlude, thus allowing for a pause in the psalm.

Urgent prayer (verse 1)

The psalm begins abruptly with this call for God to 'hear' him (literally 'answer') in his distress. 'O God of my righteousness' probably means 'God who vindicates my right standing' as in Jesus' parable of the unjust judge. God vindicates his own who cry to him (Luke 18:7). The God who puts us legally right with himself through his Son is the one who will publicly vindicate his people on the day of resurrection and judgment. David is looking to be vindicated by God despite what his enemies are saying and doing.

There is good reason to read 'You have relieved me', not as a statement of what God has done for David but his actual prayer. It should be translated as a cry to God in his distress: 'Give me relief 'or more literally 'Give me room'. In a situation where the enemy is pressing in upon him and confining him he asks God to give him space. His appeal is to God's unmerited favour ('have mercy' or better, 'be gracious') so that he would listen to his plea.

Here then is an urgent call for help that rests on God's righteousness and grace. We are again reminded of the enemies set against the Lord's anointed in Psalm 2.

Address to the enemy (verses 2–5)

David, the Lord's anointed, makes an authoritative appeal to his enemies whom he describes as 'sons of men' (verse 2) which is an idiom for 'influential people', those prominent men of power who have removed David from office. As in Psalm 2, the enemy is boldly addressed with a series of commands: know, tremble, don't sin, commune with yourself, be still, offer sacrifice, trust in the Lord (verses 3–5).

It is difficult to decide whether 'my glory' refers to the Lord's honour and reputation (see Psalm 106:20) or David's. The kingly office in Israel was, in any case, closely associated with the Lord so that God's glory or honour was at stake when David's honour was brought into disrepute. David rebukes these high and mighty ones, who have rebelled against his rule and so bring God's honour to shame, love what is worthless and seek after lies.

The enemy needs to know that the LORD (Jehovah/Yahweh) has set apart for himself the 'godly' (verse 3; often translated 'saints' as in Psalm 30:3), those who love the Lord and are loyal to his covenant. That is why David is confident that the Lord will 'hear when I call' (verse 3), echoing the 'hear' and 'when I call' of verse 1. The king is committed to God and his cause.

Instead of 'Be angry' (verse 4) a better translation is 'tremble' or 'stand in awe' and along with 'do not sin' suggests a call to repentance. In Psalm 99:1 and Isaiah 64:2 peoples and nations must 'tremble' at the presence of the Lord who reigns supreme. They should quieten their rebellious thoughts and 'meditate' within themselves (literally, 'say in your hearts') while lying on their beds and 'be still'. The same call appears later: 'Be still and know that I am God (Psalm 46:10). Instead of offering 'the sacrifice of fools' (Ecclesiastes 5:1), they are urged to offer righteous sacrifices and trust in the Lord (verse 5). Their actions show a rebellious attitude toward the Lord and his anointed and so all their worship is a sham. This was so with Absalom and those associated with him. They belonged to the nation that God had set apart for himself, yet they were behaving like enemies of God and his people by rebelling against the Lord's anointed. All their worship of God at the Jerusalem sanctuary was futile as long as they showed contempt for the king. Likewise, those who profess to be Christian yet live as if Christ is not their Lord and Saviour, need to repent and return to their first love.

Quiet confidence (verses 6–8)

We are not sure who the 'many' are (verse 6). They may be disheartened and disgruntled members of David's loyal followers. Although they trust God they are beginning to feel the pressure and are starting to crumble under the strain and to question whether any good can come out of this evil. In distressing times it is an added danger to have such people around. Paul's answer to such a question is that 'all things', even the very worst of situations, 'work together for good to those who love God ...' (Romans 8:28).

On the other hand, the 'many' could be the people addressed in verses 2–5 and belong to the 'many' of Psalm 3, in which case they are David's enemies. They are spreading lies (verse 2) and suggesting that David's rule has not produced the good they expected. Absalom had been active in administering justice and clearly making out he would serve the people better than his father (see 2 Samuel 15:2–6).

To overcome the temptation to doubt God's goodness or to counteract the denigration of God's anointed, David remembers the ancient priestly blessing: 'Lord, lift the light of your face upon us' (Numbers 6:24–26). He is praying that the Lord would do them good, both materially and spiritually, but it is the inner spiritual satisfaction that is uppermost in David's mind in the closing sentences.

Experiencing the presence and blessing of the Lord gives more joy than all the merrymaking that takes place during the festival of Tabernacles when all the harvest has been gathered in (verse 7; see Leviticus 23:39–40). Peace is a gift from God of which the ungodly know nothing (Isaiah 48:18,22; 52:7; 53:5; 57:19–21). As in the priestly blessing (Numbers 6:26) peace is another result of knowing that God is for and not against us. There is no indication that the troubles are over, yet David can know joy and peace as he places his trust in the Lord. It also means that David can sleep soundly, for God is his ultimate protector. To 'dwell in safety' (verse 8b) includes security from enemy assault and, more positively, resting in the provisions that God gives (Leviticus 25:18–19; 1 Kings 4:24–25).

Like the previous psalm, this one prefigures the experience of Jesus the Lord's Anointed. When he suffered at the hands of God's enemies, he committed himself to the God who judges justly. He looked to God to vindicate him. During his earthly ministry he was the most fulfilled person who has ever lived. He spoke to his disciples of a fulness of joy that he knew and a peace that belonged to him and he desired them to possess both (John 14:27; 15:11). Jesus could sleep through a raging storm and after his atoning work on the cross lie down to sleep in death having committed his spirit into the safe hands of his Father (Luke 23:46).

Like David, we too are to have a similar faith in God. We are encouraged to pray and have confidence in a good God, to challenge those who oppose him and to know the joy and peace of the Lord. Those justified through faith in Jesus Christ 'have peace with God' and 'rejoice in hope of the glory of God' (Romans 5:1–2). Later Paul writes: 'Therefore do not let your good be spoken of as evil; for the kingdom of God is not food and drink, but righteousness and peace and joy in the Holy Spirit' (Romans 14:17). After urging Christians to rejoice in the Lord always, Paul encourages them to be anxious for nothing but to express their needs to God with thanksgiving 'and the peace of God, which passes all understanding, will guard your hearts and minds through Christ Jesus' (Philippians 4:4-7). The believers to whom Peter writes, though they were passing through severe trials, were rejoicing greatly 'with joy inexpressible and full of glory' (1 Peter 1:6-8). A conscience cleansed by the blood of Jesus enables the person to sleep contentedly and when the sleep of death comes we can be assured that anyone 'who dies believing dies safely' through Christ's love.[13]

Psalm 5

Joy in the LORD

Deception in various forms, from clever advertisements and fraudulent activity to the flattering speeches of those who seek power, pervades the worldly society and enslaves and endangers the lives of many. When however it invades the church's life and ministry it is particularly damaging to its individual members as well as to the good of the whole and the honour of God. This is the kind of context in which this psalm was born.

It is another of David's compositions and like the previous one belongs to the musical director's collection. But unlike the previous psalm the accompaniment to which it was later to be sung is not from the string but the wind section of the orchestra. Pipes or 'flutes' are used in this prayer that includes both lament and confidence (see Matthew 9:23; 11:17).

It is the king who speaks on behalf of himself and his followers who are again troubled by enemies ('my enemies', verse 8), similar to those in the previous psalms. As in Psalm 2 the anointed one's enemies are God's enemies (verse 10c). All that David says about them in verses 4–6 concerning falsehood and deceit becomes pointed and direct in verse 9. The background may still be the period of Absalom's rebellion when deception and flattery were the order of the day. Whereas the previous psalm pleaded with the rebels to repent (Psalm 4:4), this psalm prays against them suggesting a much later time when all hope had gone of a change of heart (verse 10).

David's praying is not only an example to the Christian but also prefigures his greater son, Jesus the Messiah, who often withdrew alone to pray early in the morning and sometimes spent whole nights in prayer (Mark 1:35; Luke 5:16; 6:12). In praying for his people as well as himself, David also pictures Christ and his concern for all whom the Father had given him (John 17).

The same two groups that we observed in Psalm 1 are present here, the righteous and the wicked, with blessing for the righteous and punishment for the wicked.

An urgent appeal (verses 1-3)

Here is someone who knows where to turn in times of trouble. The introductory words of David's prayer so characteristic of the psalms of lament (Psalms 17:1; 55:1-2), express the urgency of his appeal. He calls for God's attention—'Give ear ... consider ... Give heed (listen)' that he would listen to 'my words ... my meditation ... the voice of my cry' (verses 1-2). The noun 'meditation' belongs to the same word family as the verb used in the first two psalms (1:2; 2:1) and suggests inaudible muttering (see Psalm 39:3). He addresses the covenant-keeping 'LORD' as 'my King and my God' (verse 2; see Psalms 68:24; 84:3). Israel's God who revealed himself so wonderfully at the time of the deliverance from Egypt is the ruler over all creation (see Psalm 2:4) and yet he is approachable and can be personally known (see Hosea 2:23). God can speak of the Davidic ruler as 'my King' (Psalm 2:6) while the Davidic ruler in turn can call God 'my King'. God's kingship runs right through the psalms and the Davidic king rules as God's representative under his authority.

The double reference to 'in the morning' (verse 3) suggests an earnest desire to call out to God before engaging in anything else. Morning was one of the set times for prayer and praise (Psalms 55:17; 59:16; 88:13) but this was no ritualistic act for David. He was up early to pray because of his deep concerns. He is determined to 'direct' or more literally, 'arrange' or 'set in order' his prayers as carefully as the wood and sacrifice were set out on the altar (Leviticus 1:7-8) or as Job desired to present his legal case before God (Job 23:4). Prayer is sometimes likened to presenting a legal case to God (see Psalm 17) as well as in terms of offering a sacrifice (Psalm 141:2). It is an encouragement to us to be more orderly in our praying, especially in public. We have the example given by Jesus in the pattern prayer he taught his disciples (Matthew 6:9–13). David prayed in faith, looking out in eager expectation for an answer like a watchman in his tower (see Habakkuk 2:1; Micah 7:4).

Faith in God's justice (verses 4–6)

The 'For' at the beginning of verse 4 introduces the basis for David's confidence that God will hear his cries. He calls to mind God's character and in so doing identifies his cause with God's. Unlike the gods of the nations, the true God is not one who delights in 'wickedness'. In addition, to the question that will later be put concerning 'who may abide' or 'sojourn' in God's tabernacle (Psalm 15:1) David states that no 'evil' can 'dwell' with God in the sense that it cannot take up temporary residence or 'sojourn' with him. God is good and such goodness is incompatible with evil (see Habakkuk 1:13).

The 'evil' is spelled out in the following two verses in terms of sinners who engage in evil practices—the 'boastful', the 'workers of iniquity', 'who speak falsehood', the 'bloodthirsty and deceitful man'. Such people cannot 'stand' in God's sight (see Psalm 24:3–4). He cannot bear the presence of these arrogant people. J. A. Alexander comments, 'Sin is not only opposed to God's will, but repugnant to his nature. By ceasing to hate it, he would cease to be holy, cease to be perfect, cease to be God.' It has become fashionable to speak of God hating the sin and loving the sinner and while there is a sense in which that distinction is valid in that he loved a world of sinners like us (John 3:16), there is no getting away from the fact that God hates the sinner who engages in those rebellious activities. It is the sinner who deserves to perish (Psalms 1:6; 2:12; also John 3:16).

What God hates and finds abhorrent he must 'destroy'. The examples of the sinners David mentions in verse 6 are those who are a particular problem to him in his present crisis. They are people who are after his life ('bloodthirsty'; see Psalm 139:19), who speak lies and are deceitful (see Psalm 4:2). His strong belief in God's just punishment of the wicked means that David can pray for the overthrow of his enemies and the deliverance of his people. In addressing such words to God, David is concerned for God's honour and reputation. Such prayers would have also forced David to consider whether his own thoughts and actions were abhorrent to God (see Psalm 139:19,23–24).

Prayer for protection (verses 7–10)

The introductory 'But as for me' expresses the sharp contrast between the Lord's rejection of the wicked and his acceptance of David. While the wicked are barred from God's presence (verse 4), David has access not on account of his own superior morality but by the abundant, overflowing, steadfast love of God. God's 'mercy' (verse 7) is his 'unfailing love' toward his people and this is the first of many occurrences of the term in the Psalms. But he does not come to God in a presumptuous and careless way. In Dale Ralph Davis's language, 'David is both lured by grace yet sobered by fear—just the right packaging for worship!'[14] As subjects respectfully bow down in the presence of their ruler, so David, God's servant, will bow ('worship') reverently ('in fear') before the King (see verse 2) in God's holy palace. Though the temple was not built during David's life, the tabernacle had been called God's 'house' and 'temple' ('palace') from the time when the ark was at Shiloh (see 1 Samuel 1:9,24; 2:22; 3:3; 4:3–4). The people of God under the old covenant prayed 'toward' the place associated with God's earthly presence where the sacrifices were offered (1 Kings 8:35,38,42; Daniel 6:10). Christians under the new covenant do not pray toward an earthly sanctuary but come into the true Holy Place through Jesus Christ who has offered the perfect once for all sacrifice and is seated at God's right hand (Hebrews 10:12,19–22).

Only in verse 8 does David actually begin his petition and refer to those who are causing him great trouble. It is on account of 'my enemies', those whom he literally calls 'my watchers' (see Psalms 27:11; 59:10), that he makes his plea. He describes more precisely in verse 9 these people who are lying in wait for him. They are deceivers, smooth talkers with murderous hearts and mouths ('their inward part destruction, their throat an open tomb'). The tongue can be used to deadly effect (James 3:8). Therefore he prays that his covenant-keeping 'LORD' would 'lead' him like a shepherd does his sheep in paths of righteousness (see Psalm 23:3). God is righteous and true to his character in all his actions and he can be depended on to lead his servant in a way that is right and secure from those bent on destroying him. Like soldiers clearing a path through a minefield, so David asks that God would clear away all the dangerous obstacles that he might tread safely.

'Pronounce them guilty, O God!' (verse 10), David urges God, as if he were the prosecuting counsel in a court of law and he calls for an appropriate sentence on the enemy. He prays that they will fall prey to their own deadly plots ('counsels', verse 10) and be banished from God's presence. David's enemies are God's in that their treatment of David, who is the Lord's anointed, is an indication of their rebellion against God (see Psalm 2:1–2). It is not personal revenge that David is calling for, but for God to be true to his righteous nature as confessed in verses 4 to 6. While David comes near to God 'in the multitude' of God's mercy (verse 7), the rebellious must be cast out 'in the multitude of their transgressions' (verse 10). What happened to Absalom, to Ahithophel and Judas should be a warning to others not to follow their rebellious example.

The second half of verse 9 is used by Paul in his list of Old Testament quotations to underline his contention that the whole of humanity, Jew and Gentile alike, is under the rule of sin (Romans 3:13).

Experiencing God's protection (verses 11–12)

David prays and speaks for the people under his charge as well as for the God he represents. The king's protection and deliverance by God from the enemy is to his people's advantage. These verses pick up on items already mentioned in previous psalms particularly the two introductory ones (Psalms 1:1–2,6; 2:12; 3:5–6,8; 4:7–8). While the wicked are driven away from God's presence and have no place among God's people, 'all who put their trust in' or better 'all who take refuge in' God (see 2:12) will experience his protection. He will 'cover' ('defend') them like a hen protects her young under her wings (see Psalm 91:4). Everyone who is right with God ('the righteous', verse 12) he will 'bless', guarding each individually with his 'favour' like a body-sized 'shield' (see Psalm 91:4). The word for 'surround' is only used elsewhere to describe how Saul and his men were 'circling in', in the sense of 'closing in', on David (1 Samuel 23:26). What a blessing to know God's gracious protective care! Such people who 'love his name', those, in other words, who love all that God has revealed of himself, have every reason to 'rejoice', 'shout for joy' and to 'be joyful' (verse 11).

Psalm 6

Greatly Troubled

This is one of seven psalms known since the early church period as the 'penitential psalms' (Psalms 6, 32, 38, 51, 102, 130, 143). However, there is no confession of sin or prayer for forgiveness. It is a lament arising from David's personal experience but it was later given 'To the Chief Musician' for use by the temple choirs. As in Psalm 4 the quieter string accompaniment is appropriate for this moving prayer. The phrase 'On an eight-stringed harp' translates a Hebrew term associated with the word for 'eight'. Other scholars suggest that it refers to the psalm's tune or less likely to the musical pitch—an octave higher or lower (see Psalm 12; 1 Chronicles 15:20-21). Like the previous two psalms the background may be the same as that described in the heading of Psalm 3 where David was fleeing from his son Absalom. David sees his predicament as evidence of God's disciplining rod and prays that God will have mercy on him and that in the end his enemies will know the terror he has experienced.

Appeal (verses 1-5)
David is expressing his spiritual state under the image of sickness and death. There is no need to think that he is actually suffering from some bodily disease or ill health. He is distressed by the severe circumstances he is in, which has been made worse by the sense of God's displeasure

and by the attitude of his enemies. There are three parts to the appeal: do not rebuke ... nor chasten me (verse 1); 'Have mercy ... heal me' (verses 2–3) and 'Return ... deliver ... save me' (verses 4–5).

In each of the first four verses David appeals to God using the special covenantal name 'LORD' (Jehovah/Yahweh). He is conscious of being under the divine wrath. God is likened to a father whom David acknowledges has the right to 'rebuke' and 'chasten' wayward sons just as God declared in the covenant he made with him (2 Samuel 7:14). But he prays that this will not be done in 'anger' and 'hot displeasure' (verse 1) as described in Psalm 2:12. While David is willing to receive God's disciplining rod, it would seem he does not understand why it is so severe or why it seems more like punishment than discipline with no end in sight. Jeremiah prayed similarly, 'O Lord, correct me, but with justice; not in your anger lest you bring me to nothing' (Jeremiah 10:24).

David therefore appeals to God to be gracious ('Have mercy', verse 2; see Psalm 4:1) and 'heal' him by restoring him to his former situation. As he makes this plea he describes exactly how he feels using the kind of vivid language associated with lack of water and physical pain and distress. The word 'weak' is used of vegetation languishing in the fields (Isaiah 16:8; 24:7) and of a city fainting for lack of water (Jeremiah 14:2) and it speaks of David's low condition as a result of his circumstances. His 'bones' (verse 2) and his 'soul' (verse 3) in this context refer to his whole inner being (see Psalm 35:9-10), which he describes as in a terror-stricken state. The word 'troubled' (verses 2–3) does not bring out the strength of feeling. He was 'terrified out of his wits' as Jacob's sons were when Joseph their brother revealed to them who he was (Genesis 45:3).

This part of his plea closes with an agonising cry that does not form a proper sentence. To bring out the intensity of the emotion, it could be translated 'But you! LORD! How long?' The phrase 'how long?' (verse 3) is one often heard in the psalms (see Psalm 13:1-2) and is not to be thought of as a request for information but a cry of desperation for an immediate end to his distressing state.

David's final appeal is bold as he calls on God to 'Return' (verse 4). He has no awareness that God is with him and he pleads that God would give some indication of his presence with him. It may mean that David is asking God to 'turn' from seeming inactivity on David's behalf.

He also calls on God to 'deliver' and 'save' (verse 4) him from his life-threatening plight.

At this point David brings forward in verses 4–7 a number of arguments to back up his urgent appeal. We find this many times in David's prayers and Christians can be encouraged to follow his example.

1. The first argument is the strongest and most important: 'for your mercy's sake' (verse 4; see Psalm 5:7). His appeal rests upon the truth concerning who God is. God's 'mercy' or 'faithful love' had been promised to David and his descendants (2 Samuel 7:15; 22:51) and David holds God to his word.

2. David's second argument is that if the enemy assassinated him he would not be able to call to mind or commemorate ('remembrance') God's gracious activity and lead his people in thanksgiving to God. The body lies silent in the 'grave' (verse 5; Psalm 30:9). The word for 'grave' is 'Sheol', the realm of the dead. This verse is echoed later by Hezekiah after his miraculous recovery from a terminal illness (Isaiah 38:18).

Anguish (verses 6–7)

David, as part of his lament, gives yet more indications of his current difficult situation and at the same time these provide further reasons why God should act to rescue his anointed.

3. He speaks first of his 'groaning', his 'tears' and his 'grief'. His groaning has made him weary like someone exhausted from hard work. The build-up of exaggerated language, typical of poetry, expresses his deep distress, with his bed swimming at night and his couch dripping ('drench') with his tears. Can God allow the one who rules legitimately over God's people as his viceroy to be in such a condition? This is a powerful plea for God to show him grace and act according to his unfailing love.

4. The last argument that David brings forward introduces us to his enemies and this confirms that the sufferings he is enduring are not health problems but the result of enemy opposition, although opposition from foes can have its effects on our mental and physical well-being. His 'eye wastes away because of grief' (verse 7; see Psalm 31:9) and 'grows old' before its time on account of his sorrow. The word 'grief' has an element of anger attached to it for the word occurs when God or people are provoked to anger (Deuteronomy 32:19; 1 Samuel 1:6; 1 Kings 21:22). The king's enemies are God's enemies and so this

is another powerful argument for God to act to rescue his deeply distressed servant.

Assurance (verses 8–10)

There is a sudden change of mood and it would appear that this has happened while he has been in prayer. In his weakness David has appealed to the only one who could change his situation. Even though, like Job, David thought that God was dealing with him in anger, he still brought his complaint to God. He appeals to the God who seems to have abandoned him. But through the course of this prayer he has come to believe that he will be delivered from his foes. Prayer changes things because God uses prayer to bring us into a closer relationship with himself and to a complete dependence on him. Often this leads to an assurance that all will be well.

He addresses his enemies from the position of one who has been 'heard' (see Isaiah 38:5) and accepted ('receive') by Israel's covenant keeping 'LORD'. Three times God's personal name is mentioned (verses 8b–9). Reading between the lines, it would seem that the enemies had been accusing David of sin and that God would not hear and deliver him. But he is vindicated and as king over God's people he pronounces judgment on them. His words, 'Depart from me, all you workers of iniquity' (verse 8), are very familiar to us for they are used by Jesus in his warning to those who assumed they were supporters but who were in effect workers of lawlessness (Matthew 7:23).

The end result is that David's enemies will be proved wrong and the tables will be turned. They will be made to 'turn back' (verses 10; the same verb is translated 'return' in verse 4) from their evil activities against the Lord's anointed and will find themselves experiencing what David expresses in his lament. We read in verse 10 that as he was 'greatly troubled' or 'terrified' (see verse 3) they will be terrified and experience shame. David's desperate cry, 'how long' (verse 3), will be answered by the suddenness of the shame that will overcome his foes.

The Psalm expresses the spiritual distress of God's people in every generation who are conscious of sin and the disciplining rod of God. Enemies, demonic and human, can add to our distress. We are encouraged to express our anguish to God and directly appeal to him for deliverance on the basis of his loving commitment to his people.

David's experience also prefigures that of Messiah, our Lord Jesus. The Son of God in his human nature became the man of sorrows fulfilling the prophecies concerning the Suffering Servant and recapitulating to new depths the experiences of David. He who knew no sin prepared himself for suffering God's hot displeasure as our representative head and substitute. Jesus appropriated the words of verse 3 as he contemplated the cross (see John 12:27). We also find him, like David, offering up 'prayers and supplications, with vehement cries and tears to him who was able to save him from death, and was heard because of his godly fear (Hebrews 5:7).

Psalm 7

An Appeal for Justice

This is probably another psalm from the period when Absalom rebelled against his father. The tribe of Benjamin, from which Saul the first king of Israel came, 'held some bitter enemies of David' (Kidner). One was Shimei, a relative of Saul, who continually cursed as David and his followers were forced to leave Jerusalem (2 Samuel 16:5–8). Then there was Sheba who, in a later rebellion against David, drew away the northern half of Israel (2 Samuel 20:1–2). We are therefore not surprised that there were others from that tribe not mentioned in the prophetic history, like this 'Cush, a Benjamite', who sought to undermine David's authority.

The psalm is clearly a lament which may be the meaning of the word translated 'Meditation', a term that only occurs in this heading. A similar word appears in Habakkuk 3:1.[15] This 'lamentation' was one that David 'sang to the LORD', indicating that even some of his cries for help were originally composed to be sung rather than spoken.

An urgent appeal (verses 1–2)

The covenant God of Israel is David's God—'LORD my God' in whom he has put his trust or taken refuge and in whom he continues to find shelter (see Psalms 2:12; 5:11). This is a strong position from which to cry out to God for help in his present perilous circumstances. He wastes no time in calling for God to 'save' (see Psalm 3:2) and 'deliver' ('snatch out'; see Psalm 6:4) him from his persecutors or pursuers (see 1 Samuel 24:14).

Lions were quite common in Israel during biblical times and David knew from experience as a young shepherd lad how one of these hungry animals could tear its victim to pieces (1 Samuel 17:34-37; see Psalm 17:12). He uses this vivid imagery to describe his helpless state in the face of such vicious enemies who are ready to attack him. God's people will always find themselves subject to enemy attack in one form or another in this world. Cain was the first persecutor and our Lord warned his disciples to expect persecution (Matthew 5:11; John 15:20).

An oath of innocence (verses 3-5)

Like Job, David protests his innocence. He is not claiming moral perfection but asserting his innocence of the charges levelled against him. Again his appeal is introduced by calling on God as 'O LORD my God' (see verse 1). He is appealing to his covenant keeping God who is also the judge of all the earth who has perfect knowledge of every situation (verses 8-9). His claim of innocence is made in the form of a self-curse as we find Job doing in Job 31:5-40. The implication is that 'if' he has done the things he is accused of then he is saying 'let me be cursed'. It was a most emphatic way of asserting his innocence. If the slanders are really true then 'Let the enemy pursue me and overtake me ...' (verse 5). If there was some truth in the smear campaign then he would deserve to die: to be trampled underfoot (see 2 Kings 7:20; 9:33) and to be disgraced as king by having his 'honour' (literally 'glory'; see Psalms 4:2) brought down to the dust. But in fact he has not wronged his enemy by repaying with evil someone with whom he is at peace, nor has he robbed his adversary for no reason. The testimony of a good conscience before God is a great blessing even though it will not necessarily exempt anyone from being unfairly slandered (2 Corinthians 1:12).

Call for the righteous judge (verses 6-13)

The 'Selah' at the end of verse 5 (see Psalm 3:2) is appropriate at the point where the declaration of innocence ends and the appeal for God to act begins. David, the innocent sufferer, calls out boldly to Jehovah/ Yahweh ('O LORD') to 'Arise' (see Psalm 3:7) and to 'lift yourself up'. As the enemy is raging so he summons God to act in anger against them, the thought being that if God is provoked then justice will be done. Of course this is picturesque language to convey the urgency of the appeal. God neither slumbers nor sleeps but his call for God to 'awake' for his benefit is a forceful way of urging God to take action. God has 'commanded' or ordained 'judgment' (verse 6). There is a final day of judgment but that is not what David calls for here. Rather, in anticipation and as a kind of preview of that awesome day, David looks to his God to vindicate him in his present crisis situation. He pictures this justice being administered before a great international assembly ('the congregation of the peoples', verse 7) and calls for God to 'return' in the sense of to resume his place on the heavenly judgment throne. God's implied inaction, sleep and absence from the judgment seat are in the words of J. A. Alexander, 'bold metaphors' for God's seeming failure to save his servant.

There is a general judgment when God 'shall judge the peoples' (verse 8), righting all wrongs and punishing all who oppose him. Paul made this clear to the Athenians that God 'has appointed a day on which he will judge the world in righteousness' (Acts 17:31). Here David calls for that justice to be anticipated in his present situation—'Judge me, O LORD', in other words, 'show me to be in the right in this law suit'. His plea of personal 'righteousness' and inner 'integrity' must be seen in the context of his oath in the previous section. David is not claiming absolute perfection but, as in a court of law, he is appealing to the judge who has all the evidence in this legal case, to decide in his favour.

As David prays he thinks more generally of the need for God to set the world to rights by bringing 'to an end' the evil of all 'the wicked' and so 'establish the just' or righteous person (verse 9). The king represents God's righteous people and he is concerned that justice will be done for them too. As the 'righteous God' (verse 9) he tests the innermost beings (literally 'hearts and kidneys') of all. Jeremiah speaks similarly as he describes the human heart as 'deceitful above all things' (Jeremiah 17:9–10).

David looks to God to protect him for he is one who rescues 'the upright in heart', those who are straightforward and of proven integrity and by saying this he is again asserting his innocence. The word translated 'defence' (verse 10) is literally 'shield' as in Psalms 3:3 and 5:12. In the following verses David supports his plea by calling attention to God's universal sovereignty and justice. God is a 'just (righteous) judge' (verse 11) and, unlike humans whose zeal fluctuates,

there is a constancy and consistency to his indignation—'God is angry
... every day' (verse 11). The object of God's indignation is not actually
expressed but it is clearly toward the 'wicked' described in verse 9. If
such ungodly rebels will not repent ('turn back' verse 12) then God is
likened to a soldier preparing his weapons for battle.[16] The military
imagery portrays God as an archer poised ready to fire deadly flaming
arrows at the enemy (verses 12–13).

The enemy's punishment (verses 14–16)

The psalm moves to depicting the enemy as a pregnant woman who
has conceived 'mischief' or 'trouble' and is in labour 'with iniquity'
and gives birth to lies or 'falsehood' (verse 14), which could either refer
to the false accusations that are now being levelled against David or
more likely in view of the following verses, that the trouble they had
intended failed to materialise and so it issued in disappointment and
disillusionment. Using ancient hunting imagery David graphically
portrays the fate of the wicked as falling into their own 'pit' that they
have dug out for others. The 'mischief' or 'trouble' they had planned
for others has boomeranged so that the 'violence' they intended has
rebounded and landed on their own heads and hairy scalps (see Psalm
68:21). In the story of Esther, Haman was hanged 'on the gallows he
had prepared for Mordecai' (Esther 7:10).

We must not think that all God's judgments are a matter of
impersonal cause and effect. Yes, what we sow we shall reap and
the punishment fits the crime but we must not think in terms of
natural law like getting our hand burned if we put it too near the
fire. God's wrath is personal to him as is true of his love. The God we
have offended we must face and receive from him the judgment we
deserve and it is 'a fearful thing to fall into the hands of the living God'
(Hebrews 10:31; Revelation 6:16).

Grateful thanks (verse 17)

In view of God's righteous rule ('according to his righteousness') in
which he shields the righteous and punishes the wicked, David closes
on a note of thanksgiving ('I will praise' is more precisely 'I will give
thanks' or 'testify') to his covenant keeping God, the 'LORD' (Jehovah/
Yahweh).

The psalm has not shown much evidence of being one that David
could have sung (see the heading) but it ends by making music ('sing

praise') to the God who had revealed himself as the 'LORD Most High'. The God who had shown his being and character to Moses and the people of Israel as the 'LORD' (Jehovah/Yahweh; Exodus 3:13–15; 6:3; 34:5–7) is the same as the one who had made himself known to Abraham and Melchizedek as God 'Most High' (Genesis 14:18–20,22). This latter title, used twenty-nine times in the Old Testament as a divine name, is most appropriate in the context of God as the universal ruler and judge (see Daniel 4:34: 5:21; 7:27).

David, the anointed king, had his enemies and what is presented here becomes prophetic and symbolic of the Messiah's enemies depicted in Psalm 2. Christians too can expect the same kind of malicious gossip and false accusations as were levelled against David and his greater son, Jesus our Saviour. Our formidable enemy is the devil, 'the accuser' of God's people (Revelation 12:10) but we praise God that he has been judged and vanquished as a result of Christ's atoning death. 'Who shall bring a charge against God's elect? It is God who justifies. Who is he who condemns? It is Christ who died, and furthermore is also risen, who is even at the right hand of God, who also makes intercession for us' (Romans 8:33–34).

Psalm 8

Why Humans?

Among the goodwill messages etched on a small silicon disk and left by the first humans to set foot on the surface of the moon is the full text of this psalm.[17]

Unlike Psalms 3 to 7 that reflect the king's experiences in the face of enemies we now have David's meditation on the majesty of God (verses 1-2,9) and the place of humans in God's creation (verses 3-8). Psalm 7 ended with a firm commitment on David's part to make music to the LORD and this psalm is a wonderful example of a song of praise. It opens as it closes by contemplating the greatness of God. Although it is one of the praise psalms it does not contain the usual calls to praise and reasons for doing so that we find in other hymns (see Psalms 100,111,149). The whole psalm is addressed to God with David speaking for his people using the royal plural 'our' (verses 1,9) but with the singular 'I' (verse 3) found at the opening of the central section.

To the now common heading indicating that David is the author and associating the psalm with the musical director, there is added 'On the instrument of Gath' or more literally 'according to Gittith'. The phrase occurs later with Psalms 81 and 84. 'Gittith' may stand for a particular type of melody associated with the city of Gath or a musical instrument such as 'the Gittite lyre' (similar to the way we speak of a Spanish guitar). The word itself means 'winepress' and may suggest that the hymn was used at the autumn festival of Tabernacles (Booths), also known as Ingathering, when all the fruit, including the grapes, had been harvested.

God's glory (verses 1–2)

The people's representative addresses God as 'Lord our Lord'. 'Lord' (Yahweh or Jehovah) is God's covenant name associated with the deliverance of his people from Egyptian slavery and the special agreement that he made with them at Sinai. 'Lord' (without all the capital letters) is the address of respect toward those in authority. Depending on the context, it could be translated 'sir', 'lord' or 'master'. Here it applies to the living God, the creator and universal ruler.

God's name is 'excellent' or magnificent in all the earth. It is more excellent than the mountains (Psalm 76:4). It is superior to all other names. The word 'name' not only represents all that God is in himself but especially what he has revealed of himself. At the time of the exodus God indicated the greatness of his name, in the defeat of Pharaoh and the Egyptian gods and in the rescuing of his people from bondage. When Moses asked God about himself and his name he was told to tell the Israelites, 'I AM has sent me to you' (Exodus 3:14). The Lord later proclaimed the divine characteristics associated with his name when Moses was allowed to see the afterglow of God's majestic splendour (see Exodus 33:18–34:8). The majesty of God displayed in creation (see Psalm 19:1) is revealed even more in the redemption of his people. Through the plagues on Egypt and the calling out of Israel to be God's people they were taught that 'the earth is the Lord's (Exodus 9:29; 19:5). When the shadows gave way to the real spiritual redemption through Jesus Christ it was again in this world that the drama of salvation was played out and, as a result, we look forward to the earth being full of the knowledge of the glory of God.

But the display of God's majestic being is not confined to the earth. The heavenly world is even more aware of it (Psalms 96:6; 145:5). We should perhaps read: 'Above the heavens your majesty is recounted'.[18]

The greatness and power of God are even seen in the way he puts to silence those who are out of tune with him, like the rebels of Psalm 2. 'Out of the mouths of babes and infants' God has appointed 'strength' (or a 'bulwark') because of his enemies. Over against the strength of his enemies, God establishes his strength through symbols of weakness and simplicity. When 'babies' and 'sucklings' are mentioned in the Old

Testament they are usually the victims of war, oppression and death (see Psalm 137:9; Lamentations 1:5; 2:11,19,20; 4:4) and this is also the case when Herod slaughtered all the baby boys two years old and under (Matthew 2:16-18). Their cry was normally out of pain and injustice and they became symbolic of the despised people of God. Jesus quoted these words to the chief priests and scribes who demanded that he silence the children who were still singing their hosannas to 'the son of David' on the day after his triumphal entry into Jerusalem (Matthew 21:15-16). It is the leaders of Judaism that turn out to be God's enemies while the little ones of Jerusalem represent those who embrace God's Messiah and praise the name of Jesus.[19] Praise expressed so spontaneously was God's way of silencing his enemies. Earlier, Jesus had given thanks to his Father for the childlike humility of believers in contrast to the wise and knowledgeable of this world (Matthew 11:25-26).

David may have remembered how, as the despised shepherd boy he was victorious over the Philistine giant, Goliath (1 Samuel 17:14,26-28,42-47). God takes the weak and insignificant in the eyes of the world to shame and confound the mighty (1 Corinthians 1:27). This was even more gloriously obvious in the great victory that David's greater Son and Saviour accomplished on the cross of Calvary over the devil.

Human glory (verses 3-8)

In comparison with God's stunning greatness revealed in creation, human beings seem so insignificant and unimportant. Again, David's experience as a young shepherd on the hills near Bethlehem, contemplating a night sky unpolluted by modern artificial light, could well have prompted the concerns he reveals here. God's greatness and mysteriousness was impressed upon him when he looked up into the vast heavens with the moon and stars shining out so brightly, all of it the work of God. It raised a natural question: 'What is man that you are mindful of him and the son of man that you visit him?' The phrase 'son of man' in this context is merely a synonym for human being.[20]

If this was the reaction of David how much more should it be ours who live in the era of space exploration! 'Who are we?' 'Why should God remember frail, puny human beings and care for them?' It is staggering to think that the God who is responsible for the Milky Way and the innumerable galaxies millions of light years away should take an interest in us. But it is true! The Lord, whose fingers formed the mass of heavenly lights, condescends to attend to the needs of such specks of dust. He has literally visited us in the person of his Son, Jesus Christ.

We often take it for granted that we humans are the centre of the universe, despite all the evidence to the contrary. What is more, an assumption has arisen that imagines we have gained a supremacy over the world and the solar system through our own abilities. This psalm reminds us that what greatness we do possess is due to our creator God alone: 'For you have made him ... you have crowned him ... You have made him ... you have put all *things* under his feet' (verses 5–8).

Three important truths about humans are presented in these verses.

First, the psalmist reminds us that we have been made in the divine image to be rulers. The expressions 'crowned', 'dominion' and 'under his feet' all denote rule and authority. What is associated with God and his rule is applied to humans: 'glory and honour' (see Psalm 96:6–7). The word 'dominion' calls to mind how God's image bearers are to have authority over the living creatures of the earth, both domestic and wild animals (Genesis 1:26–28), a fact that is obvious wherever humans live. Charles Darwin said, 'man has become, even in his rudest state, the most dominant animal that has ever appeared on this earth'. We humans are now realising afresh that we should care for the creatures under our control, be concerned for the environment and take responsible actions to preserve and prevent pollution. All this expresses the truth taught here and in Genesis that we are not on the same level as the rest of creation.

Second, we have been made 'a little lower than the angels'. The Hebrew word for 'angels' here is the common word for 'God' (*Elohim*) in the Old Testament. But it can also be used for supernatural spirits or heavenly beings and their earthly counterparts whether human rulers or pagan gods (1 Samuel 28:13; Psalm 82:1,6; Exodus 20:3; see also 'sons of *elohim*' Job 1:6; 38:7). Humans have been made just slightly inferior to angels.

Third, while 'a little lower' suggests that angels are ranked higher than humans, 'little' can sometimes mean, in Hebrew as well as Greek, 'for a little while lower' and that is what is implied by the writer to the Hebrews (Hebrews 2:7,9).[21] The implication then is, that although humans are at present in a position that is lower than angels, their future and final status is to be higher than angels. Paul can speak of humans judging angels (1 Corinthians 6:3) and Hebrews teaches that they are to be our future servants (Hebrews 1:14).

Hebrews sees the purposes of God for human beings in this world realised in God's Son, Jesus the Messiah. We humans are associated with the first man, Adam, and his sin, so that we are flawed image bearers and even though we may tame the creatures of this world we find it impossible to tame ourselves and our tongues (James 3:7-9). What is more, humans by nature are God's 'enemies' who do not see and acknowledge his majestic splendour (verse 2). Such rebellion has caused a rift between us and the Almighty resulting in such questions as, 'What is man that you are mindful of him?' (see Psalm 144:3-4 and Job 7:16-18 on the fleeting, frustrating nature of human life). God's curse as a result of the Fall has affected human life in this world.

Jesus is the second man, the last Adam. He is the representative head of a new humanity that brings to realisation what was denied the old humanity in sin. In him we see our true humanity. Jesus is the Son of Man *par excellence*, who became not only our representative head but our substitute. He underwent the penalty that our sin deserves. The human Jesus, God incarnate, died our death and is now risen and ascended, 'crowned with glory and honour'. Jesus shall reign till all his enemies are under his feet (1 Corinthians 15:25). The last enemy is death. United to him we who believe are already risen with him and made to sit with him in the heavenly realms (Ephesians 2:5-6). That is our present position in Christ. But we await the consummation when Christ returns when we all shall be changed and have glorified bodies like Christ's and live and reign with him in the new creation. Paul quotes a well-known early Christian saying that is true: 'For if we died with him, we shall also live with him. If we endure, we shall also reign with him' (2 Timothy 2:11-12).

For the writer to Hebrews to see Jesus in this psalm is not imposing something alien to the text for this Davidic psalm reminds us of Psalm 2 where there is a specific reference to God's anointed ruler and it prepares us for Psalm 72 where his universal righteous reign is depicted.

God's glory (verse 9)

The opening line is repeated at the end to envelop the whole psalm with the thought that it is God who is the most glorious being in the whole creation. However wonderful his creatures they cannot take the glory to themselves and woe betide humans who abuse the authority given them or maltreat those under their care. We look forward to the day when 'the earth will be filled with the knowledge of the glory of the LORD, as the waters cover the sea' (Habakkuk 2:14). This will come through this second man, the last Adam. 'Even so, come, Lord Jesus!' (Revelation 22:20).

Psalm 9

Praise and Petition
to the World's Judge

We see Christians persecuted in many parts of the world and we wonder why God allows such atrocities to continue. Here is a psalm that reminds us that similar concerns were felt hundreds of years before God's Son appeared on earth. It expresses our own anguish of heart and encourages us to trust the judge of all the earth.

It is almost certain that Psalms 9 and 10 were originally one psalm. But in the final arrangement of the Psalter as we have it they are treated as two separate works. The reason the final editor treated them as separate compositions is probably due to the difference in mood and type, for Psalm 9 is mainly a hymn of praise and Psalm 10 a lament.[22]

In this hymn of praise that was to be sung to the tune the 'Death of the Son',[23] David recounts the wonders of God's saving power (verses 1-12) and on this basis prays that God would be further praised when he finally arises to bring about the complete destruction of the wicked (verses 13-20). This is the first of the acrostic psalms in which verses begin in turn with each successive letter of the Hebrew alphabet. It would be like starting verse 1 with 'Applause to the Lord', verse 3 with 'Back my enemies turn' and verse 5 with 'Castigate the nations',

73

etc. In addition to Psalms 9 and 10, there are seven other psalms that display this poetic feature (Psalms 25, 34, 37, 111, 112, 119, 145). Outside the book of Psalms we find the same device in Proverbs 31:10-31 and Lamentations 1-4. In this Psalm the first eleven letters of the Hebrew alphabet are employed with the exception of the fourth letter. The second half of the alphabet is used in a similar way in Psalm 10.

Praise (verses 1–2)

The opening lines beginning with the first Hebrew letter (Aleph), echo the closing verse of Psalm 7. It is the believer's joy to give thanks to the Lord ('I will give thanks' rather than 'I will praise'; see Psalm 7:17). Paul encourages us to 'Rejoice in the Lord always; again I say, Rejoice' and to make our requests known to God 'with thanksgiving' (Philippians 4:4-6). In speech and song we are called to give testimony to what God has done. The Psalms love to recount God's wonderful deeds or 'marvellous works' (verse 1). We find reference to God's wonders some twenty-seven times in the Psalter and they refer especially to his acts of creation, judgment and salvation (see Psalms 26:7; 75:1; 96:3; 105:5; etc.). God's 'name' (verse 2) stands for the revelation of himself through his words and acts. It was at the time when God redeemed his people from Egyptian slavery that he especially revealed his stunning greatness (see Exodus 3:13-14; 9:16; 15:1-3; 34:5-7), but in the person and work of our redeemer, Jesus Christ, we have the supreme revelation of God and witness even more of God's wonders in judgment and grace.

Reasons for praise (verses 3–10)

These verses take us through from the second Hebrew letter to the sixth and introduce us to David's enemies. Because the Lord is on the king's side (verse 4) his enemies will retreat, stumble and perish before God ('at your presence', verse 3). The psalm recollects God's past activity in bringing nations to ruin (verses 5-6). In mind especially would be the account of Egypt's defeat at the Red Sea (Exodus 14:13; 15:6-10), the destruction of the cities of Canaan under Joshua and 'blotting out' Amalek's memory (Exodus 17:14; Numbers 24:20). In contrast to the defeated foes eliminated 'for ever' (verses 5-6), the Lord remains secure 'for ever' on his judgment throne (verse 7; 'endure' is literally 'sit'). The words of verse 4 expressing justice for the king are used in verses 7 and 8 to emphasise God's universal rule in administering justice to all peoples. God is scrupulously fair. When God's people become faithless he judges them too. That God judges 'the world in righteousness' (verse 8) is not only a present reality it is a sure and certain hope. Similar words are used to describe the Lord's end-time judgment (see Psalms 96:13; 98:9).

In the meantime, God's upright administration means that 'the oppressed' (also called the 'needy' or 'humble poor', see verse 12) can find refuge in the Lord (verse 9). While the names of the enemies of God's people are blotted out (verse 5) those who acknowledge God's name (see verse 2) have a sure place of trust (verse 10; see Psalm 91:14). As Israel was called under the old covenant to have a knowledge of God that included confidence in him and concern for God's people, so it is the privilege of each individual member of the new covenant to 'know the Lord from the least of them to the greatest of them' (Jeremiah 31:34), to show brotherly love and to be confident that he will never disappoint those who depend on him in time of need (see Hebrews 13:1,5-6).

Praise (verses 11-12)

The seventh letter of the Hebrew alphabet is used to summon songs of praise to the LORD, an appropriate response after recounting who God is and what he has done. The one who sits enthroned on high (verses 4b,7) is at the same time enthroned in Zion, among his worshipping people (see Psalm 2:6). The Jerusalem sanctuary, with the ark of the covenant symbolising God's presence, was the earthly counterpart of the heavenly temple. This praise expressing God's deeds is meant for public consumption (verse 11b). The deeds in question involve, in particular, God's intervention on behalf of those who cry out to him. As Abel's blood cried out from the ground for vengeance (Genesis 4:10) so God is the avenger (literally 'seeker') of bloodshed (verse 12) on behalf of those who seek him (see verse 10b). He does not forsake them but remembers his 'humble', afflicted, oppressed people by acting on their behalf. However, the gospel speaks better things than the blood of Abel (Hebrews 12:24). God's greatest work involved the shedding of the blood of Jesus in order that God's enemies and ours might be defeated. The atoning death of Christ has resulted in a moral victory over sin, Satan, death and hell. On the day of Pentecost, those filled with the Spirit in that Jerusalem upper room, began speaking in such a way that the representatives of the nations who had gathered for the festival, heard them telling out, in their own languages, 'the wonderful works of God' (Acts 2:1–11).

Petition (verses 13–14)

The Hebrew word for grace or 'mercy' begins with the eighth letter of the alphabet and introduces the plea for deliverance. In view of the Lord's past actions on behalf of his suffering people, the king, as their representative, calls on God to look in pity on him in his present weak, poor state engineered by those who hate him. He feel near to death's door but is confident that the Lord can lift him out before he goes down into that city below. Burial suggested descent into the city of the dead. The dead cannot praise God for their bodies lie silent in the grave (see Psalm 6:5). David prays for deliverance from 'the gates of death' so that he can tell out God's praises within 'the gates of' Zion (see Psalm 87:2) and rejoice in his salvation. In contrast to death, Zion, the city of God, the home of God's people, is pictured as a young girl, 'daughter Zion' (only here in the Psalms but frequently in Isaiah and Jeremiah, but see Psalm 45:13), a place of life and vitality (see Psalm 87:7). Peter encourages the people of the new covenant to 'proclaim the praises of him who called you out of darkness into his marvellous light' (1 Peter 2:9).

Reasons for praise (verses 15–18)

With the ninth Hebrew letter used to open this section, the psalm moves on by recalling once again the Lord's actions on behalf of his people. The enemy nations (see verses 3 and 5) find that the pit and the net for catching the weak become the trap that brings about their own downfall (see Psalm 7:15). Commenting on the judgment that God executes (verse 16), Calvin remarks that when the wicked nations find their evil plans redounding on themselves, this did not happen by chance, 'but was the work of God and a notable proof of God's judgment'.

This expression of God's just dealings calls for a pause (Selah) and a moment of reflection (verse 16b) suggested by the Hebrew word that could mean 'Meditation' (see Psalms 1:2; 19:14).[24]

The tenth and eleventh letters of the Hebrew alphabet are used respectively in verses 17 and 18 to draw out the contrast between the fate of the wicked nations who forget God and God's weak and needy people who seem forgotten by God. To forget God is associated with forsaking him (see Isaiah 65:11) and death ('hell' or 'sheol') is the punishment, where 'there is no remembrance' of God (Psalm 6:5). While there is to be an end to the wicked, the needy, who often feel their pleas are being ignored by God, find that their hope does not finally perish. It is the enemies of God and his people who fall and perish (verse 3). In the final analysis, as Israel's own history showed at the time of the exodus (Exodus 2:23-25; 3:7-9), God does not forget the cry of the humble poor (verse 12).

Petition (verses 19-20)

As in Psalm 7:6 the appeal recalls the words of Moses when they moved camp with the ark of the covenant leading them. (Numbers 10:35). The God who raised a barricade ('something strong') against attackers (8:2) cannot allow mere mortals to prevail ('to be strong'). Though God is acknowledged to be in control (see verses 4 and 7) David calls for action now. The plea is that the Lord would exercise judgment in the present and humble the arrogant nations so that they realise that they are not God but frail human beings. This is what happened to Egypt at the time of the exodus when God appointed plagues that 'put them in fear', forcing Pharaoh to acknowledge: 'The LORD is righteous and my people and I are wicked' (Exodus 9:27).

The psalm thanks God for his past actions in saving his people from enemy action and has a strong belief in the final day of judgment when God will judge the world in righteousness. But the cry of the heart is that he would execute justice immediately, that he would act in the present to bring relief to his beleaguered people and deliver them from evil. The emphasis on praise puts into practice the thought of Psalm 8 where the praises of the defenceless provide a stronghold against the enemies of the Lord and his people.

Psalm 10

When God Seems Absent

Having grown up in a country where God has often blessed with periods of spiritual awakening it is hard to believe that God would so remove his felt presence that he would allow people to believe that he is no different to the gods of this world and leave sceptics to convince themselves that the one true God does not exist. Psalms like this one indicate that it is not a new situation. It shows how the arrogant react in open rebellion to God's apparent absence while the humble poor are moved earnestly to cry to God and confidently expect him to act on their behalf.

The psalm begins by using the twelfth of the twenty-two letter Hebrew alphabet, picking up where it left off in the previous psalm (9:18; see the introduction to Psalm 9). But then the alphabetic order breaks off for a time and continues with the final four letters in verses 12,14,15 and 17 respectively.

Pleading with the Lord (verses 1–2)

Appearances often conflict with faith. The previous psalm confidently asserted that the Lord will be a refuge for the oppressed 'in times of trouble' (Psalm 9:9) but this lament begins by questioning God over his inactivity and absence 'in times of trouble'. Taking up the imagery of Psalm 9:15–16 the call is that those who chase after the humble poor would be caught by their own schemes (verse 2) as happened to Haman who was hanged on the gallows he prepared for Mordecai (Esther 5:14; 7:9-10).

Reasons for the complaint (verses 3-11)

A description of the arrogant oppressors is now presented to support the plea for God to intervene. It is so depressingly true of what we see around us today. Instead of boasting in God and praising him, the godless boast of their plans for gain, worship the greedy and treat the Lord with contempt (verses 3-4). For all practical purposes God is left out of the account (see Psalm 14:1). They suppress the truth they have of God, accept lies, and worship and serve the creature rather than the creator (Romans 1:18-25).

God's 'judgments', the standards that he enforces, are viewed as ineffective. They do not appear to have any bearing on everyday life. Any who felt strong enough to counter attack the wicked are treated with disdain—'he sneers at them' (verse 5), and he rests secure in his positive thinking—'I shall not be moved ...' (verse 6). His speech gives expression to his whole attitude (verse 7). It is 'from within, out of the heart of men', Jesus taught, that such evils as wickedness, deceit and blasphemy proceed (Mark 7:20-23). Paul makes use of his Greek version of verse 7 to prove that the whole human race is morally guilty before God (Romans 3:14).

The description of the ruthless oppression of the helpless, humble poor continues under the vivid imagery of a murderous robber lurking in the village waiting his moment (verse 8), a ravenous lion ready to pounce (verses 9-10) and a skilful hunter making use of his net (verse 9b). The prophets give evidence that what is portrayed here was widespread in later Israelite society (Jeremiah 7:9; Hosea 6:9; Amos 5:11-12). Wisdom instructs the inexperienced to avoid the company of those who for personal gain lie in wait to ambush the innocent (Proverbs 1:10-19).

The psalmist returns to the thinking behind the evil actions (verse 11; see verses 4-6). The unrighteous activity emanates from an ungodly attitude that imagines that God is not interested and therefore no action will be taken. Paul may only have quoted one verse from this section of the psalm but he clearly has the whole in mind as he indicates that the wrath of God is against all human ungodliness and unrighteousness (Romans 1:18).

Pleading with the Lord (verses 12–15)

Having poured out his heart, the psalmist reverts to petition and with it the use of the Hebrew alphabetic arrangement. The battle cry goes up again—'Arise, O Lord' (verse 12; see 7:6; 9:19). Lifting up the hand, in this context, suggests taking firm action against the oppressor (see 2 Samuel 20:21). The call is that God would not ignore the humble poor as the oppressor said the Lord did, the implication being that the Lord would act to bring deliverance. The 'why' of verse 1 returns but with the confidence that God will not allow the wicked to win as the verses that follow indicate. He reminds the Lord of what the oppressor has said 'in his heart' (verse 13; see verses 6,11) concerning his proud boast that he will not be accountable to God for his actions. Despite present appearances (see verse 11) God does observe all that goes on and will act to punish the perpetrators of evil. The 'fatherless' or 'orphans' are examples of the 'helpless' and humble poor in society who throw themselves on God for rescue (verse 14). He has seen and acted in the past and this is the basis for the present plea.

In order for the needy to be rescued the might of the oppressor must be broken. A person's 'arm' was often a symbol of strength (Psalm 89:13; Isaiah 59:16; Luke 1:51). We have the phrase 'strong arm tactics'. The prayer for God to break the enemy's power is with the aim of bringing to an end all his rebellious activity. The verb 'seek' has been used in the sense of 'avenge', 'require an account' (see 9:12; 10:13) and that might be the thought here also.

At Calvary the enemy's power was broken when Christ ransomed his people from all nations but we must wait till the end-time judgment day for the eradication of all evil. For the persecuted believer we have the example of Jesus 'who when he was reviled, did not revile in return; when he suffered, he did not threaten, but committed himself to him who judges righteously' (1 Peter 2:23; 4:19).

Confidence in the Lord (verses 16–18)

The psalm ends on a triumphant note. Just as the cry, 'Arise O Lord' recalled Israel's strong confidence in the Lord's ability to lead them forward against every obstacle in their pilgrimage to the promised land (verse 12; see Numbers 10:35) so the declaration, 'The Lord is King forever and ever' also looked back to the Lord's victory over the Egyptians (Exodus 15:18). God's kingship also picks up the thought of the previous psalm that speaks of the Lord's judgment throne and the end of the nations (9:4–7,15–17). In addition, as the Lord heard the cries of his needy people at the time of the exodus (Exodus 3:7), in a similar way he bends his ear to the present appeals for justice and strengthens the hearts of the humble poor. While the terrorists are removed, who are, after all, mere mortals of the earth (see 9:20), God judges in favour of the socially unprotected and oppressed people.

Christians in many countries are being tortured and killed because of their Christian profession. Why does God not act to stop such cruelty to his defenceless people? This psalm encourages us to trust the Lord and to remember there is a day of reckoning. The Lord is not indifferent. His apparent slowness to act is on account of his patience and mercy, 'not willing that any should perish but that all should come to repentance' (2 Peter 3:9).

Psalm 11

Trust in Testing Times

Here is a confession of confidence in the Lord that contains no direct appeals to God for help. It was probably composed around the same time as the previous psalms of David (Psalms 4–7) when Absalom plotted to usurp his father's position as king. At a moment of great uncertainty for the nation, David encouraged himself and his people with this strong statement of faith in the Lord's righteous rule. The same heading appears as in Psalms 4 and 5 but without the references to musical instruments.

Counsel of despair (verses 1–3)

David had received well-meaning advice to flee for safety by abandoning his kingdom and going into hiding. Just as a bird flies out of harm's way by soaring up to its favourite mountain ledge (see 1 Samuel 26:20) so David is urged to find refuge in a safe haven. The wilderness or exile in another country would be the most likely hiding places.

This counsel of despair is backed up with a description of the enemy that is reminiscent of the previous psalm. The 'wicked' are like hunters ready to shoot (see Psalm 37:14). They are operating in the shadows, away from the public eye. In other words, they are acting deceitfully, which is typical of the terrorist. Their sights are on people like David

who are 'the upright in heart' (verse 2) and who are described in the
next verse as 'the righteous' (verse 3). If the foundations of the national
kingdom are being broken up on account of these attackers what can
the Lord's people do but make a quick getaway? It is a natural and
understandable response when the rule of law has been replaced by the
rule of lawlessness.

But David retorts, 'How can you say such things!'—'In the LORD I put
my trust' (verse 1). For him to abandon his responsibilities as king of
God's earthly kingdom in moments of crisis would have meant a denial
of his trust in God. Nehemiah experienced a similar temptation to quit,
only his came from the enemies of Israel. His reply was, 'Should such
a man as I flee?' (Nehemiah 6:11). Flight may be the best policy in some
instances. English reformers fled to the continent during Queen Mary's
reign. But when devilish temptations come to abandon the work to
which God has called us, whether from friend or foe, we take the shield
of faith to ward off all the fiery darts of the evil one (Ephesians 6:16).

Confidence in God (verses 4–7)

David's confidence in God is not the result of so-called 'blind faith'.
Good reasons are now presented for his belief. Basically his trust is in
Israel's covenant God. All the emphasis falls on the 'LORD' (Jehovah/
Yahweh) in verses 4 and 5. It is the LORD who reigns supreme in his
heavenly temple palace;[25] his eyes observe and scrutinize humans; the
Lord tests the righteous and the wicked; his very being abhors 'the one
who loves violence'.

It is possible that 'his holy temple' refers to the Lord's presence in
the Jerusalem sanctuary (see 5:7), in which case David encourages
us to remember that God who is with his people is at the same time
the transcendent ruler whose 'throne is in heaven'. Solomon later
confessed when the newly constructed temple was dedicated that the
heaven of heavens could not contain God let alone the temple he had
built (1 Kings 8:27). The LORD is in full control and it is from his exalted
position that he views all that goes on in the world of human beings.
His gaze is intense, his 'eyelids' are always open to examine carefully
people's attitudes and activities. Like a refiner of metal, the Lord
tests or assays his people to discover the truth (see Psalms 7:9; 17:3).
To suggest from this that God does not 'automatically know' what is
going on but chooses to look and needs to take a look is to apply vivid
imagery in a literal way.[26] God does not have human eyes in the first

place. He is pure spirit and is an all-knowing (omniscient) God. But the illustration impresses upon us how completely and discriminately he knows us.

The testing of the wicked terrorist results not in a fire that purifies but punishes. It will be a repeat of what happened to Sodom and Gomorrah when God rained on them burning sulphur (Genesis 19:24). The awesome power of fire and sulphur, such as is seen in a volcanic eruption, became symbolic of God's final curse on Israel (Deuteronomy 29:23) and a warning of the sudden and ultimate judgment of God on the world (Luke 17:28–32; 2 Peter 2:6–9). The scorching east wind, the sirocco, further presses home the punishment that the wicked will receive (see Jeremiah 4:11).

The 'portion of their cup', in this context, means the cup of God's wrath which the wicked will receive (see Lamentations 4:21). In Psalm 16:5 we have the opposite thought where those who trust the Lord have him as their portion and cup. The word 'portion' is used of the priest's share of the people's offerings to God (Leviticus 6:17). It is what has been allocated to them and the 'cup' contains the allotted share.

The final verse is a reminder of the Lord's righteous character. The psalm highlights the concerns of 'the righteous' and demonstrates that the Lord carefully tests 'the righteous'. They need have no fears and that is why David has such assurance (verse 1). The foundations will not be destroyed because the righteous Lord 'loves righteousness'. Not only does he himself do righteous deeds but he delights in the righteous lifestyle of his people. The last line should probably read 'the upright behold his face'. In verse 4 the Lord's eyes 'behold' or gaze while here the upright 'behold'. Exactly the same form of the verb is used in both cases. In verse 2 the 'upright' are called 'the upright in heart'. This is the expectation of David, the man 'after God's own heart': 'As for me, I will see your face in righteousness' (Psalm 17:15). It is the pure in heart who will see God (Matthew 5:8). The hope of every contrite, believing heart is that they 'shall see his face' (Revelation 22:4).

> Why should I fear the darkest hour,
> Or tremble at the tempter's power?
> Jesus vouchsafes to be my tower.
> Though hot the fight, why quit the field?
> Why must I either fly or yield,
> Since Jesus is my mighty shield?   (John Newton)

Psalm 12

Human Words of Flattery and God's Pure Words

We can well understand David's lament if this psalm comes from the time when he found that his enemies included his son Absalom and trusted advisers like Ahithophel (see 2 Samuel 15:1-12, 31). It seemed as if no one could be trusted. They were saying one thing to the king and doing another. As in Psalm 6 this Davidic psalm for the musical director is to be sung either to a particular tune ('according to Sheminith') or to the accompaniment of ('on') 'an eight-stringed' instrument (see 1 Chronicles 15:21). A clear contrast is drawn between the smart talk of the wicked and the sure speech of the Lord.

Appeal for help against flattering lips (verses 1-4)

Like a drowning man, David cries out 'Help!' The Hebrew word is usually translated 'Save!' His desperate cry is directed to the Lord. Only he can rescue in this situation. The reason for the urgent appeal is that the 'godly' (Psalm 4:3; sometimes translated 'saints' as in Psalms 30:4; 31:23), those loyal to God and his covenant, have ceased; 'the faithful', those true to the commitments they make, have vanished from the earthly scene. These terms describe the humble, righteous people like

David the king. It is a situation that later prophets describe. Elijah felt this loneliness with his lament, 'I alone am left' (1 Kings 19:10; see Isaiah 57:1; Micah 7:2).

The only people left in his world were those who spoke lies to one another, which was quite contrary to the behaviour expected of those within the covenant community. Their smooth talk ('flattering lips') meant that they said one thing but their intentions were different. They operated with two minds (literally 'heart and heart'), not in the sense that they were unstable and uncertain like the double-minded person of James 1:8. These people were hypocrites. John accuses Judas of being like this (John 12:4–6).

David calls on the Lord to terminate these smooth talkers with their boastful speech (verses 3–4). They talk big, claiming they can smooth-talk their way to success. They trust in the power of their words to bring them victory. No one can match them. James may have had these verses in mind when he called attention to the power of the tongue (James 3:5–12).

Answer from the Lord (verse 5)

In Psalm 6 we have David's lament (verses 1–7) followed abruptly by the conviction that the Lord has heard (verses 8–10). Some scholars assume that a prophetic word came from the Lord to bring about the change of mood or that David himself received a direct word of assurance but there is nothing in that psalm to prove it. Here, however, for the first time in the Psalter, we have an example of a divine oracle that turns the lament into a confession of trust in God's promises (see Psalms 60:6–8; 85:8; 95:8–11; 108:7–9).

Instead of picking up on the lying words of the wicked, the Lord mentions another aspect, namely, that the humble poor are being oppressed. As in the case of the sighs or groans of God's people at the time of the exodus (Exodus 2:24) God acts to bring his needy ones to the safety for which they pant.[27] The idea of God arising either in judgment or salvation is not an uncommon picture. In earlier psalms, David called upon God to arise (7:6; 9:19). Again, we are not to take this vivid allusion literally. It serves to emphasise God acting to change situations for the better.

Appreciative response (verses 6–8)

The Lord's words of promise are 'pure' unlike the implied dross of the oppressors. Their purity is likened to the purity of refined silver that has been completely tested ('seven times' tested). They come through the strictest quality control. It means that when God says he will do something he is not like the smooth talkers, he actually does what he promises. The Lord keeps the promises of blessing associated with his covenant with Israel as well as the curses. He always preserves his people from the evil age in which they live ('this generation', verse 7; see Matthew 17:17).

It does not mean that in this life all the opposition will evaporate. The wicked are still confidently walking around with heads held high because the society in which they strut about ('the sons of men', verse 8; see verse 1) still regards their worthless words with respect ('vileness is exalted').

Christians can expect to experience what David knew from a society that is godless, but too often this worldly situation enters church life. Paul urges Christians to put away lying and to 'speak truth with his neighbour, for we are members of one another' (Ephesians 4:25; see Colossians 3:9).

Psalm 13

When Trouble Seems Endless

Christians in Britain have been protected for many years from the severe persecutions that have afflicted Christ's followers in so many parts of the world. It was hard for believers in Russia before 1917 when they were persecuted by the State Church and then afterwards under the Communist State. It seemed as if there would be no end to the differing forms of unjust treatment they endured. This lament expresses the distress that so many have felt after years of harassment. Yet, it does not display distrust or disillusionment. In fact, it does the very opposite, for it drives David to prayer and to a deeper confidence in God.

The complaint (verses 1–2)

Four times the cry goes out: 'How long ... ?' It is not a request for information as in 'tell me how many more weeks I shall have to endure this?' but a rhetorical question implying that David finds his situation intolerable and wishes it would end immediately. The first occurrence, 'How long, O LORD?' is an introduction to what follows. The rest of the section expresses in more detail what has prompted David's troubled state. His complaint concerns the Lord, his inner self and his outward circumstances.

The fundamental grievance relates to the Lord's apparent

indifference. David wonders whether the Lord is going to ignore him forever and withhold the help he needs. To 'forget' means that no help is forthcoming. On the other hand, when God remembers people it is an indication that he is going to act on their behalf. The Lord heard the groan of the Israelites in Egypt and he remembered his covenant with their forefathers and moved to change their desperate situation (Exodus 2:24).

David also considers that God is displeased with him. For God to 'hide' his face usually meant he was inflicting punishment. It was the very opposite of the peace and tranquillity expressed in the priestly blessing of Numbers 6:24-26. God's people often feel that the sufferings they endure are a consequence of God punishing them for past or present sins.

David then moves from thinking of his position before the Lord to the conflicts in his inner, psychological life (verse 2). In his mind and innermost being there is turmoil of thought. How often this is so in the experience of Christians as they try to come to terms with what is happening to them. They toss plans over in their minds and consider options relating to the troubles. Introspection can often make the sorrows worse.

Finally, David refers to the enemy who has gained the ascendancy over him, 'exalted over me' (see Psalm 12:8). The enemy could be an individual member of the covenant community, a political rival such as Saul and Absalom, or a national enemy like the Philistines. Paul reminds us that the last enemy is death (1 Corinthians 15:26) and that might also be a factor in David's thinking (see verse 3). It is unlikely that his fear of the nearness of death is the result of some severe illness.

The call (verses 3-4)

Though he considers that God has turned from him David still directs prayer to him. In this he follows men like Job who pleaded with God against God. In fact, he views the covenant Lord as his God—'Lord my God'. Reminding God of the relationship makes the prayer more powerful and urgent as he calls on the Lord to ignore him no longer but 'consider' him (literally 'look') and 'hear' (literally 'answer me'). Instead of 'hiding his face' David calls for God to 'enlighten' his eyes. The priestly prayer was that the Lord would 'make his face shine' (see Numbers 6:25) and that is how David prays later (Psalm 31:16). Here however, using the same form of the verb ('make shine'), David prays that his own eyes might shine. Instead of his eyes wasting away with grief (see Psalm 6:7; Job 17:7) he wants them to sparkle with life again. Similarly, after praying earnestly to God in the tabernacle and conversing with Eli, the previously sorrowful Hannah went away with a changed face (1 Samuel 1:18).

Only as a result of the Lord's activity, with David's face alight with life and health, would the enemy be deprived of the satisfaction of seeing him dead. Sleep is often used in the Bible to describe death (see Job 3:13; 1 Corinthians 15:51). David's concern is for God's honour. If the enemy were to see him dead and overthrown ('moved'; literally, 'shaken', 'totter') they would be triumphant. It would mean victory for God's enemies as well as David's.

The commitment (verses 5–6)

The psalm ends with an expression of confidence in the Lord. The complaint does not come from the lips of one who has become disillusioned with life and has lost faith in God. Far from it! David's trust is in God's enduring love ('mercy'). There is emphasis on the 'I'—'But I have trusted'. Even when God seems to ignore him and be uninterested in his situation, he holds on to what he knows of God. While humans fail God remains true to the promises he has made to his people. David then makes his own commitment. The 'heart' that is presently sorrowful (see verse 2) 'shall rejoice' (verse 5) in the deliverance he expects from God; he 'will sing' to the 'LORD' (Jehovah/Yahweh) because he has 'dealt bountifully' with him, meaning that God has taken complete care of him. The Prayer Book Version follows the ancient Greek Septuagint version by closing with the additional line: 'I will praise the Name of the Lord most High'.

What David experienced was true of his greater son. His great enemy was the devil (Matthew 13:39; Luke 10:18–19). Throughout Jesus' public life the devil continually attacked him. How the devil's agents were 'glad' when Judas agreed to betray him to them (Luke 22:5). The enemy seemed to have triumphed when he was hung on the cross as a common criminal until he died and his body was placed in a tomb. But our Lord committed himself to his Father and rejoiced that through his death and resurrection the devil would be defeated (John 12:31–32).

The Church of Jesus Christ passes through times when it appears that the enemy has the upper hand and God seems deaf to the earnest cries of his people—'How long, O LORD?' We are encouraged to hold on and not despair, confident that the Lord will bring deliverance and rejoicing that he deals with us so fully and lovingly. In more private situations, too, when trouble overwhelms us with no light in sight, and we call out in desperation for an end to the agony, we go on trusting, making our requests known to God and expressing our commitment to him.

One of Jesus' disciples who knew all about the enemy's subtle attacks wrote, 'casting all your care upon him, for he cares for you. Be sober, be vigilant; because your adversary the devil walks about like a roaring lion, seeking whom he may devour. Resist him, steadfast in the faith knowing that the same sufferings are experienced by your brotherhood in the world' (1 Peter 5:7-9).

Psalm 14

Fool's Paradise and Zion's LORD

At the beginning of the 21st century Richard Dawkins has become quite a celebrity in Britain for his atheistic fundamentalism. He rubbishes the God of the Bible and denounces Christianity in a most vicious and belligerent way. Though few would be so bold as to accept all his anti-God and anti-Christian pronouncements the bulk of society live as if God did not exist. Theoretical atheists are a rare breed but the world is full of practical atheists and this psalm draws attention to them.

Psalm 53 presents another version of what we have here and it is there that the differences will be noted. The psalm has some similarities to wisdom books like Proverbs with its reference to the fool but it also reads like a prophetic denunciation of the evils of society (see Isaiah 59:3-4; Jeremiah 5:1). As in previous psalms, the humble poor are the ones who feel the effects of a godless society but David's trust is in the Lord's ability to change things for the better.

The general state of humanity (verses 1-3)

The fool is one who scoffs at God, is irreligious and immoral, lacking all decency (see Psalm 74:22; Isaiah 32:5-6). By declaring in the heart, by thinking that 'There is no God' the fool is suppressing the truth about God as revealed in creation, through the conscience and special revelation, and positively and deeply dismissing God from everyday life and treating him as an irrelevance (see Psalms 10:4; 53:1).

The fool is no isolated individual but typical of society as a whole, hence the first verse continues in the plural: 'They are corrupt ...' Where ungodliness exists there unrighteousness will flourish (Romans 1:18-32). This was the situation prior to the Flood (Genesis 6:12) and while God promises never to destroy the human race in that way again he recognises that 'the imagination of man's heart is evil from his youth' (Genesis 8:21). It is also the natural condition of humanity to do 'abominable works'. Such loathsome activity covers all that is typical of paganism including idolatry, sexual sins, pride, lying, murder and dishonesty (Leviticus 18:26-30; Deuteronomy 7:25-26; Proverbs 6:16-19; 11:1). 'There is none who does good' is David's conclusion and his son Solomon acknowledged that 'there is no one who does not sin' (1 Kings 8:46). The Preacher does not mince his words when he tells us, 'For there is not a righteous man on earth who does good and does not sin' (Ecclesiastes 7:20). Who can claim to be innocent?

This is the state of the human race generally and of each individual person born into the world. The Lord is pictured as looking out of his window in heaven (see Genesis 11:5) to see whether there is anyone who is not a fool. This description of God is what we call anthropomorphism, presenting God in human terms. It graphically suggests the divine concern that the whole human race (literally 'the sons of man') does not 'understand' or 'seek God'. They may be experts in science and politics but they have no spiritual insight and they have no desire to have a personal relationship with God and to enjoy God. Unlike David who will in a later psalm express his longings after God (Psalm 63:1) everybody by nature is more interested in self-seeking than desiring the true and living God.

All have 'turned aside' (verse 3), which means they are unfaithful to God and his law. Israel quickly 'turned aside' from the way God had commanded them when they worshipped the golden calf at the foot of Mount Sinai (Deuteronomy 9:12). Israel repeated the rebellion of Adam and Eve. They turned from God's way and went their own way and this is the tragedy of the human race. It has turned its back on God and the true path and is travelling through life on the road that leads to ruin. 'All we like sheep have gone astray; we have turned, every one, to his own way' (Isaiah 53:6).

The verb translated 'become corrupt' (verse 3) is different from the 'corrupt' of verse one. Here it means 'tainted' in the sense of morally polluted. Eliphaz uses the same word to describe humanity as 'filthy' (Job 15:16). All over the world, west as well as east, we see more and more disgusting expressions of people's inner moral filth.

For the sake of emphasis and to convict the self-righteous, the last lines of verse one are repeated with the addition 'no, not one'. There are many who would want to be thought of as 'good' because they might have a concern to help others or believe they have never harmed anyone. But from God's vantage point no one is good. No one comes up to God's standard. The 'good' which sinful humans engage in is not done for the glory of God. All our so-called good activity is polluted at source. All our righteous deeds are like filthy rags in God's sight (Isaiah 64:6). This is the unpleasant reality preached by David and underlined by Paul (see Romans 3:9-19, 23). It was also the teaching of Jesus who said, in one of his encounters with the most morally respectable group in Jewish society, 'You are those who justify yourselves before men, but God knows your hearts. For what is highly esteemed among men is an abomination in the sight of God' (Luke 16:15). The natural goodness to which the media draws our attention and praises is hated by God because he sees right into the human psyche and finds that it is tainted and flawed.

The local situation (verses 4-6)

Up to this point the situation seems desperate with no one who does good and folly reigning supreme in the world. Yet, now we read of 'my people' (verse 4), 'the generation of the righteous' (verse 5) and 'the poor' (verse 6) who take refuge in the Lord. Other psalms have made a distinction between the righteous and the wicked (Psalms 1; 11:5). It is important to remember that the psalms, like the Bible as a whole, present human beings as belonging to either one of two states—the righteous and the wicked, the godly and the ungodly, the wise and the foolish. In New Testament terms these states can be described as 'under grace' and 'under sin' or belonging to the kingdom of God and the kingdom of this age.

There are people who can be called righteous because of God's grace. Contrary to the common trend, such people have an understanding of spiritual realities, have had a change of heart, seek God with all their hearts, have been brought on to God's path and can rejoice in God's salvation. These are God's people who are poor in spirit, who recognise their need of God and take refuge in the Lord.

Because of the general attitude of humanity toward God it is not surprising to find God's people being treated with disdain. The situation that David describes in this section of the psalm is one with which he himself can identify as we have found from previous psalms. The godless fools in the local situation are 'the workers of iniquity' (verse 4). Their sinful state results in sinful actions. They are people within the old covenant community who are acting against fellow members in a most unbrotherly way. They are providing for their own comforts and well-being by oppressing the true people of God—they 'eat up my people'. They do not have that knowledge of God that results in caring for fellow members of their community (see Jeremiah 22:16). They do not 'call on the Lord' for the food that God provides and they have no regard for their neighbours. There is no true love for God and therefore they do not love their neighbour. The same truth is taught by James and John. Jesus will say to the hypocrites who claim to serve him, 'Depart from me you who practise lawlessness' (Matthew 7:23).

This lament in verse 4 gives way to an unexpected reaction in these oppressors. They have not calculated on the possibility of God being among his covenant people—'the generation (or 'society, company') of the righteous' (verse 5). When God is active among his people, the ungodly begin to panic. The fools who convince themselves that God is not involved in the world and seek to shame the plans and thoughts of the humble poor believers find that the Lord is the refuge of his people. The 'refuge' or 'shelter' (verse 6) was a place where humans and animals could take cover from attack or from inclement weather (see Psalms 61:3; 104:18). It is a word that is often used in the psalms to convey the idea of God's protection of his people (see Psalms 46:1; 62:7-8). Such a shelter we find in our Lord Jesus Christ. We have seen in recent decades how anti-God and anti-Christian forces have sought to eradicate all traces of God and Christianity. There is panic among segments of the Chinese hierarchy at the advance of Christianity in that land. They have seen God at work among his people.

David's prayer wish (verse 7)

On behalf of the righteous David longs for God to deliver and restore the oppressed people of God. Zion is used as an expression for the whole company of God's people with the presence of the Lord at the centre of their life and worship (See Psalms 2:6; 3:4). The living God, whose home is in heaven (verse 2) ordained to live among his people in the tabernacle, later in the Jerusalem temple, and this presence was represented by the ark of the covenant in the holy of holies. Deliverance for God's people comes from the God who lives among them. The reference to 'captivity' need not mean that the psalm comes from the time when the Jews were exiled in Babylon. Most commentators recognise that 'brings back the captivity' can be taken in a much more general sense for 'restores the fortunes' (literally it could read; 'turn the turning'). Each experience in Israel's past of God's saving activity is, of course, a pointer to the ultimate deliverance from the slavery of sin, Satan and death, which was achieved through God's Son, Jesus Christ. It results in God's covenant people ('Jacob'/'Israel') responding in joyful worship. Those justified through faith in Christ rejoice in hope of the glory of God (Romans 5:1–2).

'The fool is not a rare subspecies within the human race; all human beings are fools apart from the wisdom (and grace) of God' writes Peter Craigie.[28] This is why Paul uses the text to emphasise the universal sinfulness of the human race, both Jew and Gentile, those with Bibles and those without. God's gospel proclaims a righteousness from God in Jesus Christ that enables foolish sinners to be right with God (Romans 3:9–26). From the human perspective, God's wisdom appears foolish and yet it is through the 'folly' of the cross and the preaching of the cross that God saves people the world over from the consequences of their folly in dismissing God and living in rebellion against him. It was from Zion, both historically and spiritually that the word of salvation was proclaimed to all nations (Acts 2). The Lord Jesus has promised to be with his people down the Christian centuries to the end of the age as they seek to propagate the good news of God's saving grace.

Psalm 15

God's Guests

There are a number of features about this psalm that may concern Christians who rightly believe that we are accepted before God not because of what we are or have done but entirely on the basis of who Christ is and what he has done on our behalf. This psalm seems to be a legalistic approach that denies the gospel of God's free grace. As we shall see, however, that is not what the psalm preaches. Another concern that some Christians have about a psalm like this is that it assumes that worship has to do with coming together to some place to meet God instead of the New Testament emphasis on worship as a lifelong activity that we engage in through Jesus who offers direct access into God's holy presence to all who trust him.

It is true that in and through Jesus the one and only mediator between God and humanity we have boldness to enter the presence of the holy God at any time and anywhere. It enables us to offer up prayer in all kinds of situations and we can, like Nehemiah, make those sudden, quick cries of the heart (Nehemiah 2:4). This, however, does not rule out the setting apart of times for more solemn secret communion with God where prayer involves humbling ourselves before him and acknowledging our own unworthiness, as Nehemiah again shows (Nehemiah 1:4-11). Likewise, when we are urged to come together as God's people it is not merely to encourage and build one another up but to seek God as an assembly by humbling ourselves before him, remembering who he is and the access he has provided into his presence through Jesus. The last book of the Bible encourages the communal worship of God in the sense of bowing our hearts before him, praising him, thanking him and making our supplications to him. Receiving the preached Word with a believing heart that adores God for his amazing grace and that seeks to put into practice what is heard is also part of true worship.

This psalm with its brief heading, 'Psalm of David', follows on quite naturally from the previous one. Psalm 14 describes the character of the godless while here we are shown the character of the godly. In addition, reference was made in the previous psalm to 'Zion' and the people of God and they are again in mind here but in a more indirect way. In Psalm 14 God is with his people while in Psalm 15 God's people are with him. Both psalms remind us of the first two introductory psalms in their emphasis on the wicked and the godly, and God's 'holy hill'.

A vital question (verse 1)

David raises this most important question as to who may reside in God's presence and he does so in the form of a prayer. It is a question not about making annual visits as a pilgrim to worship but of living with God and it is addressed not to a priest or temple gate-keeper but to the covenant-keeping God of Israel, 'LORD' (Jehovah/Yahweh). While the way the psalm is set out, may resemble ancient Near Eastern practices where worshippers were made aware of the necessary qualifications for admittance to the place of worship, there is no real evidence that such a formal entrance liturgy took place in Israel. The same form is used in Psalm 24:3–4 and Isaiah 33:14–16.

God's 'tabernacle' reflects the period before Solomon's temple was built, especially the time when David brought the ark of the covenant to Jerusalem and set it in the tent that he had erected for it (2 Samuel 6:17; 7:2). The tabernacle is associated with the 'holy hill' of Zion (see Psalm 2:6) and they both signified God's earthly residence among his people, as the song of Moses indicated (Exodus 15:17). But these were pictures and pale reflections of the real tabernacle and Zion to which all God's people belong (Hebrews 12:22–24). They point ultimately to the scene presented by John when in the new creation, the tabernacle of God is with men and he will dwell with them on the earth and when the new Jerusalem descends from heaven without any need for a temple, because God and the Lamb are there (Revelation 21:2-3,10-11,22-23; 22:3). Isaiah uses these earthly types as he looks to the glorious future when God in Christ will reign in the midst of his people and will be seen in his beauty in the new creation (Isaiah 32:1-8,16-20; 33:17).

The question is about what kind of person may 'sojourn' ('abide') in God's presence. The word implies residing as a guest. It is God's home and humans have no automatic rights there, yet David is assured of being God's guest forever (Psalm 61:4). The second verb translated 'dwell' has the idea of to 'settle down' or 'encamp'. John uses the Greek equivalent when speaking of the Word made flesh who 'dwelt' or 'tabernacled' among us (John 1:14).

To live with the holy God is to be in the presence of one who is a consuming fire (Deuteronomy 4:24; Hebrews 12:29). And sinners and hypocrites may well ask, 'Who among us shall dwell (sojourn) with the devouring fire? Who among us shall dwell (sojourn) with everlasting burnings?' By God's grace there is forgiveness for repentant sinners and the true people like Isaiah who have humbled themselves to receive God's cleansing work (Isaiah 6:1-7) begin to display the characteristics of a changed life (Isaiah 33:14-24).

Many scholars see this psalm as an 'entrance liturgy' with the would-be worshipper asking the conditions of entry into the sanctuary forecourt and a priest giving the reply. The law did exclude certain people from the worshipping company of God's people (Deuteronomy 23: 1-6) and we learn that from the time of David some of the Levites acted as gate-keepers so that no unclean person according to the ceremonial law of Leviticus could enter God's house (2 Chronicles 23:18-19). But these examples are no proof that a special ceremony existed for worshippers entering the temple. This psalm like Psalm 24 is not a list of qualifications that a priest or Levite would tick off at the temple gate before entrance was granted. They belong with those great passages in the law, the prophets and the wisdom books that prick the consciences of the people and emphasise the importance of a heart devoted to God, that expresses that devotion in love toward others. That same concern is found in the New Testament letters (see for instance, Romans 13:8-14; James 1:21-27; 1 John 4:12-21).

A definitive reply (verses 2–5a)

Like the Ten Commandments of Exodus 20 the answer presents a catalogue of ten characteristics that God expects to find in his people. It is not an exhaustive list as we see from other similar passages (Psalm 24:3-5; Isaiah 33:14-16; Micah 6:6-8). The ethical emphasis must not be taken out of context as if the basis for entry into God's presence is our good deeds. This is not salvation by works in which good behaviour puts us right with God and atones for past wrongs. The reply to the opening question is not really a list of requirements for entrance but a portrait of those who are already guests of the Lord. As Michael Wilcock helpfully puts it, "The 'ten commandments' of Psalm 15 are not conditions for people who want to belong, but descriptions of people who do belong."[29] They are like the eight characteristics of a true disciple of Christ set out in the opening to the Sermon on the Mount (Matthew 5:3-10).

This is the portrait of everyone who has taken refuge in God (Psalms 2:12; 7:1), who loves God (Psalm 5:11), who belongs to the humble poor (Psalm 9:9,12,18) and is among the congregation of the righteous (Psalms 1:5-6; 14:5). In other words such individuals belong to the true covenant community that the Lord brought together to be his special treasure, a kingdom of priests and a chosen nation (Exodus 19:5-6; 1 Peter 2:9-10).

The ten representative characteristic features of a righteous person are divided into three positive (verse 2) and three negative (verse 3) items with an additional two positive (verse 4) and two negative (verse 5a) ones to close. What is particularly noticeable is that they all have to do with character and ethical behaviour and not with ritual matters such as correct sacrifices and attendance at festivals. In this the emphasis is the same as that found in the preaching of Moses and prophets such as Isaiah, Amos and Micah. Unlike so much that went on in pagan religion, the true religion of the Bible is a heart religion where inner attitudes and desires rather than outward show and pretence are all important.

Three positive statements (verse 2)

1. Heading the list is a way of life that shows no obvious defects—'walks uprightly' ('blamelessly'). Noah was 'blameless' in his day and Abraham was called to 'walk before God and be blameless' (Genesis 6:9; 17:1). In the case of Job, God indicated to Satan that he was 'blameless'

(Job 1:1,8; 2:3). The word is sometimes translated 'perfect' or 'complete' and is used of sacrificial animals that are free of blemish. Clearly it does not mean in the case of Noah and Abraham sinless perfection but it does suggest wholeness of character with no discernible flaws. This is the calling of every Christian. Jesus said, 'Be perfect, even as your Father in heaven is perfect' (Matthew 5:48). The final destiny of all who belong to God through Jesus is to be like God in moral perfection.

2. The person who 'works righteousness' is the exact opposite of the 'workers of iniquity' in the previous psalm (Psalms 5:5; 14:4). This is one who is true to the covenant demands, doing what is right and fair in the sight of God and fellow humans especially those within the covenant community. Those who are justified by faith alone, in Christ alone are also the ones who seek to do what is righteous, just as Christ is righteous (see 1 John 3:7). To 'work righteousness' is not simply a matter of performing actions that are right, for 'everyone who practises righteousness is born of God' (1 John 2:29).

3. To speak 'truth in his heart' is not merely to say correct things but to speak sincerely. The hypocrite can say what he thinks you wish to hear but in his inner being he has other ideas like the flattering lips of Psalm 12:2. A godly person's speech expresses what he really believes. Such a one is unlike those whom God denounces, people who 'draw near to me with their mouths and honour me with their lips but have removed their hearts far from me' (Isaiah 29:13).

Three negative statements (verse 3)

Whereas in Psalm 1 negative descriptions of the godly person came before the positive, here the negatives follow the positive.

4. 'He does not backbite with his tongue' ('slander on his tongue') and is one who goes about maliciously spreading false tales about people (see Leviticus 19:16). Mephibosheth's servant, Zeba, 'slandered' his master to King David (2 Samuel 19:27). James has much to say about the tongue and the evil it can spread (James 3:3-8).

5. In relation to his 'neighbour', one with whom he is in frequent contact, he does him no hurt ('evil'). He is seeking, in other words, to love his neighbour as himself (Leviticus 19:18).

6. The person belonging to God's people does not seek to discredit ('take up a reproach against') his friend. Within the covenant community there is to exist a brotherly love that encourages and helps people rather than injures them emotionally or socially.

Final two positive statements (verse 4)

7. Despising the 'reprobate' or 'rejected' ('vile person') and honouring 'those who fear the LORD', as in Psalm 1, shows where the loyalty of the godly person lies. Such a one, like God, takes no pleasure in wickedness (see Psalm 5:4) but respects all those who reverence the LORD.

8. The one whom God approves is prepared to keep his promises even if it results in personal hurt or loss (see Psalm 24:4; Matthew 5:33–37). Promises made on oath are serious commitments (see Leviticus 27). The Bible never forces people into making vows but if God's people do make such promises then they should be kept (Deuteronomy 23:21–22; Ecclesiastes 5:4–5). Christians are to view vows as part of their total commitment to the Lord. To cheat on God or fellow humans is not taken lightly as we see in the case of Ananias and Sapphira (Acts 5:1–11).

Final two negative statements (verse 5a)

9. The person found in God's home is not motivated by financial gain. Those with money are not to take advantage of poorer members by charging interest on loans ('usury'). Like God, such people are considerate toward the poor and needy within the covenant community (Psalm 12:5). While there was no general ban on Israel exacting interest on business loans (see Leviticus 25:35–37; Deuteronomy 23:20) Israel was forbidden to gain at the expense of a brother's misfortune (Exodus 22:25). This concern for the poor is emphasised under the new covenant especially toward those of the household of faith (Galatians 6:10; Ephesians 4:28; 1 Timothy 6:18; 1 John 3:17–18).

10. As God judges in righteousness (Psalm 9:4) so those of God's people who are in positions of power must not engage in corrupt dealings. Again, it was often the poor who were taken advantage of in legal proceedings by unscrupulous people who bribed either the witness or the judge to condemn the innocent and justify the guilty. The practice was rife in ancient as in modern societies and the law and the prophets speak out against it (Exodus 23:7–8; Deuteronomy 16:19; Isaiah 1:23; Micah 3:11; Proverbs 17:23). James has strong words for those who claim to be Christians yet show partiality toward the rich at the expense of the poor (James 2:1–9).

A concluding promise (verse 5b)

Unlike the hypocrite and arrogant oppressors who presume they will not be moved (Psalm 10:6), it is the person whose life exhibits these ten characteristics who will never totter or 'be moved' (see Psalm 55:22). Who are the ones who may reside in God's tabernacle? (verse 1). They are the righteous ones (verses 2–5a) and whatever may happen they are God's permanent guests in that holy place that is immoveable (see Psalm 46:5; Isaiah 33:20). Though constantly disturbed by enemies who would take great delight in seeing them 'moved' (Psalm 13:4), the Lord's people are assured of this fundamental stability. They belong to that city and kingdom that is firmly established which will not be shaken when everything else is shaken and consumed (Hebrews 11:10,16; 12:26–29).

Psalm 16

Present Confidence, Future Joy

The close relationship between the psalmist and the Lord, so typical of King David's fellowship with God, provides the setting for its application as a prophecy concerning Jesus. Both Peter and Paul use the psalm in their preaching to Jews to demonstrate that Jesus' resurrection was in the plan of God all along and that he is the long awaited Messiah.

The psalm is described as a 'Michtam of David'. It appears in five other psalm headings (Psalms 56-60). Many suggestions as to the meaning of 'michtam' have been put forward but on present knowledge there can be no certainty over any of them. One view that is widely supported today is that it is related to the Hebrew verb 'to inscribe'. Perhaps David considered the content so important that he wished it to be inscribed in such a way that it would stand as a permanent record. Before expressing those famous lines concerning his own death and resurrection when he will see his redeemer God, Job calls for his words to be inscribed forever in a book or engraved on a rock with an iron pen and lead (see Job 19:23-27). Like Psalms 4 and 11 this psalm describes the king's confidence in the Lord his God.

Present Confidence (verses 1-8)

This part of the psalm begins with prayer and ends with praise.

Prayer of faith (v. 1)—As God's protection has been known in the past so the king pleads that God would keep or 'preserve' him in the present and through all that is to come. The plea comes with the argument that he has made God his refuge. It is the same wording as in Psalms 7:1 and 11:1 where in all three cases 'I put my trust' is more literally 'I have taken refuge'.

Profession of faith (v. 2)—The Hebrew of verses 2 to 4 is difficult and various interpretations are possible. In the phrase 'you have said' the 'you' is feminine in the original and could be a reference to David's 'soul' which in Hebrew is a feminine noun. This is why some translations add 'O my soul' to the text. The psalmist often addresses himself in this way (see Psalm 103:1). On the other hand, the Hebrew could be read as 'I have said' and this is how the ancient versions took it.

David's profession of faith 'to the LORD' is 'You are my Lord'. He is confessing Israel's God, the LORD, (Yahweh/Jehovah) as his sovereign or master in contrast to the ungodly who confidently call out 'who is master over us?' (see Psalm 12:4).

David also confesses that whatever good he enjoys, all is due to God who redeemed Israel from Egypt and entered into a special relationship with them. This involves reading the original as 'I have no good apart from you'. The nature of the 'good' will be spelled out in verses 5-11 but here David acknowledges with James that 'Every good and perfect gift is from above' (James 1:17). Further, only in relation to God can the things we enjoy be considered good. 'Nothing is ultimately good if it is abstracted from God.'[30]

Partnership in faith (v. 3)—after speaking to the Lord, it may be that David turns to address the 'saints'. The word used here for 'saints' can often be applied to heavenly beings or foreign gods (see Psalm 89:5, 7) which is the reason why some commentators take verses 3 and 4 together and apply it all to false worshippers who delight in their gods. On the other hand, 'saints' can refer to God's people on earth (see Psalm 34:9). This is the probable sense here. The Hebrew suggests two groups—'they' (the saints) and the 'excellent ones' or 'nobles' of the people, a reference either to the leadership in general or the priests in particular. David takes delight in all God's people. If we love and delight in God we should have similar feelings for fellow worshippers. 'And this commandment we have from him: that he who loves God must love his brother also' (1 John 4:21).

Protestations of faith (v. 4)—Those who 'hasten *after* another', that is, after a false god, will experience an increase in their sorrows. The multiplying of sorrows reminds us of the curse that fell on Eve as a result of the original rebellion against God (Genesis 3:16). Not only do worshippers of false gods waste time and money on what is futile (see Jeremiah 2:13) but as Calvin observes they 'overwhelm themselves with new troubles by provoking God's wrath against themselves'. This is in contrast to the 'good' that David enjoys.

In view of his prayer and confession of faith David insists that he will have nothing to do with blood libations to false gods or, as the text implies, use their names in prayer or for oaths. Syncretism, the merging of religious beliefs and practices, has always been a temptation for God's people as we find when Israel set up the golden calf at the foot of Mount Sinai. David will have nothing of it.

Provisions of faith (verses 5–6)—In contrast to the sorrows of the idolaters, David enjoys the blessing of knowing God. To understand the thought of these verses we need to bear in mind how the land of Canaan was divided up among the tribes of Israel. The country was measured out and each tribe and each family was given a share as their inheritance. Lots were cast, probably using the Urim and Thumim (see Joshua 13:14ff., 18:2ff.). The tribe of Levi, however, which included the priests, was given no land (see Joshua 13:14; 14:4) for we are told that the Lord himself was to be their portion and inheritance which meant that they lived off the sacrifices presented to the Lord by the rest of the people (see Numbers 18:20; Deuteronomy 10:9). This made them totally dependent on the Lord. As a kingdom of priests, it was also true that Israel as a whole as well as each individual was to consider the Lord to be their 'portion' (see Jeremiah 10:16a; Lamentations 3:24; Psalm 119:57).

David uses this thought as he expresses his contentment. The LORD (Jehovah/Yahweh) is his allotted share and his inheritance. And instead of a cup of burning wrath (see Psalm 11:6) he partakes of God's cup of salvation and blessing, the word 'cup' being used as another term for 'lot'. All the present 'good' of verse 2 is his because of his relationship to the living and true God, the source of all good. Like so many of the blessings of God's covenant at Sinai, the blessing of knowing God is associated with the land, as David expresses it to Saul (see 1 Samuel 26:19). It is also the Lord who maintains David's lot ('you hold my lot') so that no one could snatch it from him.

The idea of apportioning out land is continued in the following verse where 'the lines' (verse 6) refer to the measuring ropes that marked out the allotted plot of land (see Psalm 78:55; Micah 2:5). But of course it is the actual allocation itself that is meant and David is very pleased with it as he confesses, 'I have a good inheritance'.

Praise (v. 7)—It is because the Lord has guided him ('given me counsel') that he enjoys such blessing. The way that divine guidance came to David was through 'inward enlightening' (Calvin). The 'heart' is literally 'the kidneys', which the Hebrews used for the seat of the emotions. During the 'night seasons' he has been instructed (see Psalm 17:3). He therefore desires to 'bless' God, which implies an attitude of reverence and the payment of homage (see Psalm 34:1).

Perseverance (v. 8)—David has great confidence for the future because his eyes are continually on God who is his 'right hand' helper (Psalms 109:31; 121:5). Unlike the ungodly (Psalm 10:6) and self confident (Psalm 30:6), David can be assured through his dependence on God, that he will 'not be moved' (see Psalm 15:5). Christ was able to sustain himself through all his trials and persevere to the end in the sure knowledge that God was there to help and sustain him and at the right moment to vindicate him. Calvin uses this passage against those who would call into question the final perseverance of the saints.

Future joy (verses 9–11)

Assured of God's help and protection he can rejoice with all his being. Here the Hebrew word translated 'heart' often means the mind or the centre of human personality. His 'glory' (see Psalm 7:5 and Genesis 49:6) is used here as another term for a person's self. We remember that humans were created in God's image for fellowship with God (see Psalm 8:5). The ancient Greek translation, the Septuagint, reads 'my tongue'. All three words, 'heart', 'glory' and 'flesh' sum up the whole human person. Not only can he be full of gladness but he can 'rest' safely. The word translated 'rest' is most often translated 'dwell' or more literally 'encamp' (see Psalm 15:1), while the word 'hope' has the idea of being safe and secure.

Because of David's trust and confidence in the Lord he is assured that he will not be delivered over to Saul. He is assured that he will not die but live. This assurance is on account of God's promises to him that he will reign in place of Saul. God will therefore not abandon his 'soul' to 'Sheol' (verse 10). 'Soul' is another term to describe the whole person.

Neither will God permit his 'holy one' to see the pit. The word which is translated 'holy one' is used to describe people who are committed in love to the Lord and his people (see 'godly' in Psalm 4:3) and often translated by the term 'saint' (see Psalms 37:28; 50:5) but not the same word that is translated 'saints' in verse 3. 'Sheol' is the word for where the dead go and 'pit' (in our version 'corruption') is a poetic synonym. This latter word comes from the idea that bodies were sometimes buried in the ground rather than being placed in a tomb hewn out of rock. A similar sounding word means 'corruption' which is how the ancient Greek, the Septuagint, translates it.

After the negative assertions of verse 10 we have the corresponding positive statements of the final verse. The deliverance from death that is assured is not merely survival but it leads to life in all its fulness ('the path of life', verse 11). Experiencing God's 'presence' (literally 'face') brings fulness of joy and lasting pleasures (see Psalm 4:7), while God's 'right hand' is symbolic of blessing (see Genesis 48:13-20). The thought is similar to the priestly blessing that speaks of God causing his face to shine (Numbers 6:25). It is an expression of God's pleasure with his people and the consequent blessings they receive from him.

As we have found with previous psalms there are three levels of interpretation, all of which are true and biblical. We have seen how it applies to David's own situation and the possible circumstances in which he found himself during the time when he was on the run from Saul. It can also be applied by extension to every believer in the Lord. All Christians can make this psalm their own. In the light of the New Testament and our Lord's coming we can take to heart the promise emphasised by Jesus that death itself cannot interrupt the fellowship we have with God. The Old Testament saints saw the fulness of life in very shadowy ways through the physical blessings of life in the land but people like Enoch and Elijah did point the way to an even fuller life with God that death could not touch.

However, the real subject of this psalm is Jesus. David is not only a type of the true anointed one, but out of his own experiences he can speak prophetically of the coming messiah. After quoting the Greek translation of verses 8-11 of this Psalm, Peter actually states that David could not have been referring to himself since he did eventually die and was buried. He then continued: 'Therefore being a prophet, and knowing that God had sworn with an oath to him that of the fruit of his body, according to the flesh, he would raise up the Christ to sit on his throne, he, foreseeing this, spoke concerning the resurrection of the Christ, that his soul was not left in Hades, nor did his flesh see corruption. This Jesus God has raised up, of which we are all witnesses.' (Acts 2:30-32). To balance this we must remember what Peter also said later that the prophets did not fully appreciate what they wrote when by the Spirit of Christ they predicted his sufferings and glory (1 Peter 1:10-12). By God's Spirit David was able to write words that would only finally be realised in his great descendant, Jesus the Messiah.

Luke also records that Paul quoted this psalm in Pisidian Antioch as he reasoned with the Jews concerning Jesus' resurrection and justification through Christ alone (Acts 13:35-39). This Jesus who was crucified on account of our sins and raised for our justification (Romans 4:25) is the only one who can give those solid joys and lasting pleasures of the new creation of which Christians have foretastes here and now.

Psalm 17

Prayer for Vindication

What are you to do when you are falsely accused and your position undermined by innuendo and gossip? This psalm encourages us to pray to the Lord in the way that Jesus taught in the parable of the unjust judge (Luke 18:1-8).

Like Psalm 7, David's plea to God may well have arisen at the time when his son Absalom rebelled against him. Unlike that psalm, however, there is a strong assertion of innocence. David's use of many of the words from the previous psalm suggests that Psalms 16 and 17 come from the same time and situation—'night' (verse 3, Psalm 16:7); 'path' (verse 4, Psalm 16:11); 'keep' or 'preserve' (verses 4 and 8, Psalm 16:1); 'uphold' or 'maintain' (verse 5, Psalm 16:5); 'not slip' or 'not be moved' (verse 5; Psalm 16:8); 'God' (El) (verse 6, Psalm 16:1); 'trust' (verse 7, Psalm 16:1); 'portion' (verse 14, Psalm 16:5); 'fulness' or 'satisfied' (verse 15, Psalm 16:11); 'presence' or 'face' (verse 2 and 15, Psalm 16:11). This psalm indicates that the attacks are more personal and the pressures more severe than in Psalm 16.

This is the first of five psalms to be described as a 'Prayer'. The others are Psalms 86, 90, 102, 142 (see also Habakkuk 3:1). Though not designated as such, there are many other psalms that can be described as prayers of David as the note at the end of Psalm 72 makes clear.

Appeal to God (verses 1–2)

This royal lament opens with a petition based on David's sincerity. It is a 'just' or 'righteous' plea that he makes. It is not two-faced for his prayer is not from 'deceitful' or lying lips (see Psalm 31:18). He therefore looks to the 'LORD' (Yahweh/Jehovah), the God of the covenant, for his case to be settled. Psalm 11:4 has already informed us that the Lord looks from his holy heavenly temple and tests a person's integrity, so we are not surprised to find David acknowledging that God looks on what is straight or 'upright'. He calls on the Lord to bring about his 'vindication' (literally, 'my judgment'). Similarly, Job, when he was accused by his 'comforters' of having committed grave sins for him to be in such a miserable and destitute state, looks for a heavenly vindicator (Job 19, etc.). David, like Job, is not being self-righteous and claiming moral perfection but looking to the Lord to vindicate him and declare him innocent of the false charges levelled against him.

Some scholars think that David is looking for the Lord's vindication as he appears at the tabernacle before the Lord's representative, the priest, who will use the Urim method of obtaining an answer (see Deuteronomy 17:8–11). But following on from the previous psalm which speaks of fulness of joy in God's presence (Psalm 16:11) and seeing God's face in the final verse of this psalm, 'from your presence' suggests that, like Job, David has in mind a divine vindication that is more personal and direct.

Declaration of loyalty (verses 3–5)

It is David's integrity that is under attack and it is only God who can examine a person's true motives. He is able to examine the 'heart', the very centre of one's being. Using language for refining metal, David speaks of being 'tested' and 'tried' by the Lord like gold refined in the fire with no dross being found. In other words, David is not guilty of the rumours spread by his enemies. This testing (see Job 7:18) has taken place 'in the night', the time when many lie alone on their beds with their innermost thoughts (see Psalms 4:4; 36:4; 77:6). God discerns whether we are sincere and true. There are scholars who now suggest that God does not 'automatically' know everything and that the psalmist pictures the Lord choosing to investigate in order to ascertain what people are really like on the inside.[31] But as often found in the Bible, human ways of expression are used to emphasise that in fact nothing is hidden from God (see Psalm 139).

The Hebrew text from the latter part of verse 3 to the end of verse 5 is difficult to interpret and translate. What is clear is that David affirms that in neither speech nor action will he follow the example of his enemies. On the contrary, he desires to remain true to the Lord's word ('the word of your lips') and to move forward in the paths of the Lord which, as we know from Psalm 119, means living according to what God has revealed in his word. The phrase 'the works of men' refer to human wrongdoing and 'the paths of the destroyer' to the violence they display. Both describe David's ruthless enemies.

Appeal for God to act (verses 6–9)

As at the start of his prayer, David again calls for a hearing but also confidently requests action. In words reminiscent of Moses' song at the Red Sea (Exodus 15:11-13) David asks that God would do for him what he did at the time of the exodus. As God revealed his 'wonders', his 'mercy' or 'faithful love' and the 'right hand' of his power in Egypt so he prays that God would show the wonders ('marvellous'; see Psalm 9:1) of his 'faithful love' ('loving-kindness' or 'mercy') by his powerful 'right hand' by delivering those who flee ('those who trust') from enemy hands.[32]

The exodus theme continues with echoes of another song of Moses from Deuteronomy 32:10-11. As God kept Israel as 'the apple of his eye' so David pleads that God would keep him. The tender Hebrew idiom (literally, 'as the little one, daughter of an eye') probably refers to the tiny image of the little one in the pupil of the mother's eye as she looks down on the baby at her breast. Further, as God protected Israel like an eagle with its wings outspread so David asks that he would find a hiding place 'under the shadow of your wings' from the wicked enemies who surround him and are after his life.

The lament (verses 10–12)

To back up his plea, David now gives further information concerning the enemy. Using the various parts of the body he emphasises the cruelty of his opponents. In the phrase 'they have closed up their fat' we have another Hebrew idiom and a further allusion to Moses' song (Deuteronomy 32:15). To grow fat and thick is to be arrogant. Making the heart fat is to make it stubbornly rebellious and proud (Isaiah 6:10). In addition, the enemy is surrounding the one whose steps or paths have been following the Lord (verse 11; see verses 4-5). The thought of the enemy encircling the king is further developed in Psalm 22:12–18. It culminates at Calvary's cross where we see sinful humanity's rebellion in all its ugly horror. In place of the Lord's eyes looking on the things that are upright (verse 2), the eyes of the enemy are set to extend over the earth. The verb translated 'crouching down' or 'cast' would be better rendered 'extend' or 'stretch' as when God is said to stretch out the heavens like a curtain. David's enemies have greedy eyes and they seek to gain whatever they can from the royal domain. The metaphor then changes and the enemies are now like hungry lions ready to pounce on their prey. As David is a type of Christ so David's enemies are a type of the Devil and his evil spirits.

Appeal for God to act (verses 13–14)

David no longer needs to seek God's attention. Having described the desperate situation, he calls for action. This appeal is made using four verbs: 'Arise', 'Confront', 'cast him down' and 'Deliver'. Against the enemies that have arisen (verse 7) the plea is that the Lord himself would rise up. David uses military language ('with your sword', verse 13; see Psalms 3:7; 7:6; 10:12) to express the deliverance that God will give him.

The Hebrew text of verse 14 is difficult to translate. Spurgeon writes: 'Almost every word of this verse has furnished matter for discussion to scholars, for it is very obscure.' Traditionally, the whole verse is taken as a reference to David's enemies. These wicked people who seem so high and mighty are described here as 'men ... men of the world' (verse 14).[33] The word for 'men' in both cases means 'mere mortals' and the unusual term for 'world' emphasises that these humans live in a transient world, a passing age (see Psalm 49:1). Their outlook is limited and their life so fragile. They have their fleeting satisfactions in this world and like Passion in John Bunyan's *Pilgrim's Progress*, 'they have their best things first, and revel during their little hour'. They know nothing of the Lord as their portion (see Psalm 16:5). As part of his judgments in this world, God sometimes gives people, from 'his hidden treasure' what they crave. To have numerous children to whom they can pass on the plenty they have accrued in this life is what pleases and satisfies them. God gives people over to their passions and folly. Jesus speaks of people belonging to this world who hate him and his disciples (Luke 16:8; John 15:18–19), and Paul describes the enemies of the cross of

Christ as those 'whose god is their belly, and whose glory is in their shame—who set their mind on earthly things' (Philippians 3:19).

Assurance (verse 15)

In contrast to the earthly, material pleasures of verse 14, there is the solid satisfaction of meeting with God. David began by offering a 'just' or 'righteous' plea and now is confident that because of his righteous standing before God he will view God's face and awake to be satisfied with God's 'likeness' or 'form'. This goes beyond asking that the Lord would cause his face to shine upon him. Israel was not allowed to see God's form nevertheless God did reveal himself in a visible way to Moses, Aaron and other select individuals (Exodus 24:10-11; Numbers 12:8; Deuteronomy 4:12,15; 34:10). Later, Isaiah 'saw the LORD' (Isaiah 6:1). It is a familiar desire for David to seek God's face and this is often associated with the tabernacle sanctuary (see Psalms 11:7; 24:6; 42:1-4; 63:1-2; 84:7). Calvin suggests that David compares his troubles to slumber so that his assurance lies in the certainty that he will awake from the enemy's harassment and be able to meet with God in the earthly sanctuary where he has ordained to live. He also comments that 'none enjoy substantial happiness, save those that are satisfied with God alone'.

There are indications that David may be saying more than this. The testimony concerning Enoch points to life beyond this present world order (Genesis 5:22-24). As in Isaiah 26:19 and Daniel 12:2 the 'awake' refers ultimately to the resurrection and the time when all opposition to God and his people will be at an end, when death itself will be no more and believers will 'see his face' (Revelation 22:4). 'Blessed are the pure in heart for they shall see God (Matthew 5:8). In contrast to Christ's enemies, are the citizens of heaven who eagerly await the Saviour, the Lord Jesus Christ, who will see him as he is and be like him (Philippians 3:19-20; 1 John 3:2).

How helpful this psalm is when Christians, who are certain they have acted honourably and in a transparently righteous way, find themselves being accused and hunted down by those who oppose them. We are to look to our God and Saviour. He will vindicate his own who cry to him day and night. Not only can we be certain of final vindication but we can pray for more immediate action in terms of the downfall of the opposition and the assurance of God's felt presence.

The psalm finds its ultimate significance in the life and ministry of

Jesus Christ. Of him alone could the Father say, 'This is my beloved Son in whom I am well pleased'. Only he could say to his enemies, 'Which of you convicts me of sin?' Yet his opponents accused him falsely of being in league with the devil and stirring up rebellion. But he did not take revenge. As the Suffering Servant, 'despised and rejected by men', he 'was led as a lamb to the slaughter and as a sheep before its shearers is silent, so he opened not his mouth' (Isaiah 53:3,7; Mark 15:1–5). Jesus looked to God to vindicate him. He 'committed himself to him who judges righteously' (1Peter 2:23). And God did vindicate him. By the resurrection he was justified or vindicated (1 Timothy 3:16; Romans 1:4). And because of his death and resurrection all who put their trust in him are also justified and look forward to their final public vindication when they rise from the dead to be for ever with the Lord in the new creation. With Job we can confess 'in my flesh I shall see God, whom I shall see for myself, and my eyes shall behold, and not another. How my heart yearns within me!' (Job 19:26–27).

Psalm 18

David's Final Testimony

What have we got to shout about? When we come to retire from the work that has occupied us most of our lives will we have cause to offer a hymn that extols the true and living God?

A version of this thanksgiving psalm appears toward the close of 2 Samuel. Chapters 21 to 24 emphasise some key issues from David's reign and the psalm in 2 Samuel 22 provides a theological commentary on his life balancing the prayer of Hannah at the beginning of the prophetic history (1 Samuel 2:1–10).

The introduction to David's testimony is almost identical to that given in 2 Samuel 22:1 and is a reminder that the headings in the Psalter must not be dismissed as later additions that are not part of God's word. In the Hebrew Bible they form the first verse of the text and are therefore authoritative. These introductions, however, must not be confused with the editorial titles that sometimes appear in Bible versions, which give an idea of the contents but are no part of the original text.

Psalm 18 gives extra introductory information. It not only has the more typical psalm heading mentioning the musical director as in previous psalms like Psalm 14 but David is referred to as 'the servant of the Lord' (see Psalms 36; 78:70; 89:3). Moses, Joshua and the prophets

116

are described as God's servants (Joshua 1:1,13; 24:29; 2 Kings 17:13) and
the Lord speaks of Job in this way too (Job 1:8; 2:3). The phrase is also
used to denote Israel as the people of God and the one whom Isaiah
prophesies will be the representative of God's people (Isaiah 41:8-9;
42:1; 52:13). It speaks of a person's exusive allegiance to God and of
the protection that the person can expect from God. To be a servant
of Yahweh/Jehovah is both a privileged and responsible position (see
Psalm 105:6). It is not a coincidence that it should be used here in the
introduction for at the close of the psalm a matching phrase is found,
'his (the Lord's) anointed'. That David should be described here in
the introduction in these terms and then at the close of the psalm as
the LORD's 'anointed' (18:50) is significant. By this means the psalm is
already pointing us forward to great David's greater Son.

In this the third longest psalm after 78 and 119, David first praises
God and gives an account of his trouble (verses 1-6); a description
of God's deliverance is presented in very graphic terms (verses 7-19)
followed by an affirmation of his faith in God's justice (verses 20-30);
a description of God's deliverance is again emphasised (verses 31-45)
and the psalm concludes as it began with praise to the God who
has delivered David from his troubles (verses 46-50). Besides the
superb poetry, this is a carefully constructed psalm where praise and
descriptions of salvation surround the central section (verses 20-30).

Praise (verses 1-3)

The opening words, 'I will love you', are not found in 2 Samuel 22:2
but they are a fitting opening as David surveys the ups and downs of
his life. They express a resolute declaration of intense love toward God
that rises from within him as he contemplates all that God has been to
him. It is quite startling to find the almighty God being addressed in
this way. While the form of the verb used here is unique, another form
from the same verb is often employed to describe God's compassionate
love for his people (see Psalm 116:5). In Psalm 116:1 David uses the more
common word for love but here his emotions are more deeply affected
as he considers the special relationship he has known with God over
the years. He is moved to speak of the LORD (Yahweh/Jehovah) in a
most intimate way as 'my rock' (or 'crag'), 'my fortress', 'my deliverer',
'my God', 'my strength' (or 'rock'), 'my shield', 'the horn of my salvation'
(that is, 'my saving strength'), 'my stronghold'. The whole emphasis is
on the LORD as his place of safety and security. This build-up of terms

taken from his experiences of hiding in caves and rocks express his trust and complete dependence on the Lord. Others before him had expressed themselves in similar ways. Moses had sung about God as his rock (Deuteronomy 32:4,15,18,31) and there are early personal names that contain the same imagery, such as Elizur, 'My God is a Rock' (Numbers 1:5).

An animal's horn, such as the wild ox, was a symbol of strength and David draws on this example to show that God was not a passive protector but an active one. The Lord is strong to save his people from the enemy.

Out of this explosion of praise comes the confident cry for help. David calls to the one who is to be praised knowing God will deliver him.

Distress (verses 4-6)

These verses express the desperate state in which David found himself at times. Using vivid language he speaks of 'death' and 'Sheol' trapping him with ropes and snares (both 'pangs' and 'sorrows' translate the original term 'cords' in verses 4-5). The phrase 'floods of ungodliness' is literally 'streams of Belial' (see Psalm 41:8) and is a further description of his death-like situation, where overwhelming torrents terrify him. David was not exaggerating for he makes this comment to Jonathan in more prosaic language: 'there is but a step between me and death' (1 Samuel 20:3).

In his distress David testifies that he called out to the LORD his God ('my God', verse 6; see also verse 21) who heard him from his heavenly temple (see Psalm 11:4). Unlike the gods of the nations, the LORD is the living God who does hear and respond. God informed Moses that 'the cry of the children of Israel has come to me' (Exodus 3:9). To the rich oppressors James, in the spirit of an Amos, states that 'the cries of the reapers have reached the ears of the Lord of Sabaoth' (James 5:4). God's distressed people are encouraged to believe that their cries do not go unheard.

Deliverance (verses 7-19)

Terrible though David's troubles were, they were nothing compared with the terror of God's presence scattering David's enemies and bringing him to a place of safety and freedom. The Lord's activity in bringing about David's deliverance is expressed graphically using language reminiscent of the exodus account. It includes the shaking of the earth, smoke, fire, darkness, thick clouds, thunder, lightning and hailstones (verses 7-15). In fact, God's amazing supernatural acts of judgment and salvation are frequently depicted in terms of natural occurrences like thunderstorms, volcanic eruptions and earthquakes (see Psalm 97:2-6). Cherubs are also mentioned for they are often associated with the revelation of the Lord's stunning splendour and holy wrath. What literally happened in the past is used by David to express in a figurative and vivid way God's intervention in scattering his enemies.

Verses 16 to 19 describe the resulting deliverance of David in words that are reminiscent of Israel's experience in Egypt and at the Red Sea through to their entrance into the openness and freedom of the land of Canaan. David acknowledges that it was God alone who 'sent' from on high, who 'took' him, 'drew' him from the deep, who 'rescued' him, who was his 'support' and 'brought' him into 'a broad place' and 'delivered' him. Instead of being in 'distress' (see verse 6 and Psalm 4:1, where 'distress' has the idea of being hemmed in as if in prison), he is now free. This freedom from the enemy is like the experience of a kidnapped person held in a small, stuffy room and then released into the spacious, airy countryside.

Again, the reason for David's deliverance is reminiscent of God's reason for redeeming Israel and bringing them into Canaan. It was because the Lord 'delighted' in him (verse 19; see Deuteronomy 7:8; 10:15; 23:5). As Christians we can sing of the great deliverance from bondage to sin and Satan because of God's grace and love toward us.

Affirmation (verses 20-30)

Some make heavy weather of this section suggesting that David could not have said these words of himself or that if he did he was displaying a boastful, self-righteous spirit or possessed a weak sense of sin. Another view is that David could only have written such words before his outrageous treatment of Uriah and Bathsheba which led to the humble repentant spirit of Psalm 51. But David utters similar sentiments in Psalm 17:1-5 where it is clear that he is not claiming sinless perfection or being hypocritical. Neither is David contradicting Paul with a salvation based on human works instead of one based on divine grace.

In this whole section David is extolling the Lord's unfailing love. He does this, firstly, by drawing on his own experience (verses 20-24), then by reflecting generally on God's dealings with his people (verses 25-27) and finally, by presenting personal examples of divine help (verses 28-30).

The almost identical lines that envelop the first subsection (verses 20 and 24) emphasise God's faithfulness toward David ('The Lord rewarded me ... the Lord has recompensed me ...'). It is in response to David's own loyalty ('according to my righteousness ... according to my righteousness'). Divine aid has come to him not because of his own meritorious works but because of God's grace. The intervening verses 21-23 help explain the 'righteousness' and 'cleanness' of which David writes. Unlike so many of the kings who came after him, David remained true to the covenant demands by following God's commands—'the ways of the LORD' (see Deuteronomy 8:6). Though David 'had sometimes *weakly* departed from his duty', as Matthew Henry helpfully puts it, 'he had never *wickedly* departed from his God'. He remained 'a man after God's own heart'.

God's 'judgments' (judicial rulings) and 'statutes'—familiar words that summarise God's law in Deuteronomy—determined the way he governed his kingdom.

When David claims to be 'blameless' (verse 23), he is declaring his undivided commitment toward God. He is a man of integrity. He is right to plead his innocence when his enemies have wrongly accused him. On the other hand, he confesses his weaknesses and his need to keep himself from falling into those sins to which he is susceptible—'I kept myself from my iniquity' (verse 23). David is not claiming moral perfection but professing to be a loyal servant of the Lord, one who has not rejected the Lord and his commandments 'with a high hand'. There is all the difference in the world between those who deliberately and blatantly treat God and his laws with disdain and those who through fleshly passions and weaknesses fall into sin and deeply regret it later and desire with all their hearts to honour and serve God. Later kings of Judah are often judged on the basis of whether they were true to the Lord as David was (see 2 Kings 18:3; 22:2).

Though God's ways are inscrutable they are not irrational and irresponsible. He acts according to his own righteous standards and does not disappoint those who are committed to him—'with the merciful (or better 'with the committed' or 'loyal') you will show yourself merciful' (or 'show yourself committed'). David has already used the words 'blameless' ('integrity') and 'pure' ('moral cleanness') in relation to himself (verses 20, 23, 24). Now he repeats them to indicate that God is true to himself and to his covenant relationship with his people. On the other hand, those who despise the relationship and reject God's rule cannot expect God's blessing, but rather only the covenant curses (see Leviticus 26; Deuteronomy 27-28). The final couplet emphasises this, except that the pattern is broken of matching the second half of the sentence with first—'with the devious' God shows himself 'shrewd'.[34] This change is probably done to indicate that the corresponding action of God does not arise from any moral failure on the part of God. God is not sinfully devious and twisted, nevertheless, he will act in a matching way to make life difficult for such a person. He will punish the ungodly in a way that fits their crime. A similar idea to this is found in Leviticus 26:21-24: 'if you walk contrary to me ... I will walk contrary to you' (see also 2 Timothy 2:11-13).

As we have seen in previous psalms, God is gracious to the 'humble poor' but brings low those with haughty looks (verse 27). David belongs to the former group while his son Absalom and King Saul belong to the latter. The 'humble poor' are the ones Jesus congratulated as he began his great Sermon on the Mount.

David can thus announce that it is the LORD (Yahweh/Jehovah) who gives light in deathly dark situations. The light might seem inadequate—a wick in a bowl of oil—yet it is sufficient, for it is lit by God. With God's help no obstacle is too great. David can attack an enemy ('a troop') and scale city walls. This is David's testimony. It is also Christ's firm conviction that the gates of Hades will not prevail against his Church as Christ's people fight against their spiritual enemies.

Deliverance (verses 31-45)
Rather than addressing the Lord, David first presents statements about God (verses 30-34) using language already expressed in the first section (verses 1-3).

He acknowledges that God's way of working in David's life has been 'perfect' or without blemish and that the divine words of response to his requests have been reliable (tested like metal is tried and shown to be without any dross; see Psalms 12:6; 119:140). He is probably thinking of those times when in tricky situations he had asked for an oracle from God. We often hear it said, 'David inquired of the Lord ... And the Lord said to David' (see 1 Samuel 23:2,4,9–12). Returning to the thought of verse 2, David also confesses that God shields those who trust him (see Proverbs 30:5).

Reminiscent of Exodus 15:11, David emphasises that the LORD is the only true and living God, his protector (verse 31; see verse 2). It is from the safety of this Rock that he can fight the enemy with the Lord's help (verses 31–34). The Christian has the whole armour of God in order to withstand the devil's devices (Ephesians 6:10–18).

David returns to addressing God where he admits his entire dependence on God who has provided the shield of salvation and all his support and who has kept his feet from slipping (verses 35–36). God's 'humbleness', in the sense of his condescension, rather than his 'gentleness'[35] had made David great. It was that same condescension that was seen in the God-Man, Jesus Christ, who stooped to raise his people up to glory.

The language of victory and conquest pervades the following verses 37–45. All who would set themselves against the Lord's anointed are roundly defeated. The Lord does not answer the cry of those stubbornly in rebellion against him. Just as Joshua's men put their feet on the necks of five of the kings of Canaan before they were executed (Joshua 10:22–27), so David speaks in a similar way of the total subjugation of his enemies (verses 37–42). His words remind us of Psalm 2:9. With this second psalm in mind we can appreciate that David not only subdued those within Israel who opposed him but foreign lands too came under his dominion. By the end of his life David had defeated not only the Philistines and the Jebusites of Jerusalem, but had brought the Moabites, the Arameans of Damascus and the Edomites under his authority (2 Samuel 8:1–14).

Confession (verses 46–48)

While other psalms speak of the 'LORD' (Yahweh) as the living God (Psalms 42:2; 84:2), only here do we have the declaration that Israel's covenant God is alive ('The LORD lives!'). It is because the Lord really is the true and living God that deliverance and victory have been possible for David. God has vindicated him and subdued his enemies and these are grounds for humble worship picking up wording he has used in verse 2 ('my Rock', 'my salvation' (verse 46).

Praise (verses 49–50)

In the light of God's activity through his earthly king, David gives thanks to the Lord and enhances God's reputation among the Gentile nations with songs of praise. There is a cosmic aspect to David's victories. It is a sign of God's loving commitment toward David, 'his anointed', that God has given great deliverance to him and 'to his seed for ever'. We are encouraged to look forward to the events surrounding the coming of Jesus Christ, the Saviour, the Lord's Anointed one or Messiah. Paul uses verse 49 to indicate that Gentile participation in God's gospel of salvation in Christ was prefigured in the kingdom set up by God on earth in Israel with David as his representative ruler (Romans 15:9).

While we can encourage ourselves as believers through the experiences of David as we fight the good fight of faith, the psalm ultimately points to Jesus Christ, his victory over the powers of darkness when the ropes of death encompassed him. With strong cries and tears he called out to God and was heard, and God brought him up from the snares of death and Sheol, vindicated him and granted him victory over all his enemies.

Psalm 19

Revelation: Natural and Supernatural

The heavens declare thy glory Lord;
In every star thy wisdom shines;
But when our eyes behold thy word,
We read thy name in fairer lines.

(Isaac Watts)

God has revealed himself through the things he has created. This is what theologians describe as natural revelation. He has also given us special or supernatural revelation in the Bible. In David's time it was the first part of the Bible that Israel, God's people, possessed. The Law or the Torah, as the Jews call it, consists of the first five books of our Bible. This was God's Word through Moses which the priests and Levites were to look after and from which the people were to be instructed.

Psalm 1 stressed the importance of God's special revelation and it will be unforgettably emphasised in Psalm 119. We have also been introduced to the revelation of God in creation in Psalm 8 and we shall find this theme reappearing in Psalms 104 and 148. Psalm 19, however, brings the two themes together abruptly without any comment on their relationship. In the first six verses we are told of how God speaks through the created order but from verse seven we are introduced to God's written word. The final three or four verses present David's response. C. S. Lewis, writing as a specialist in literary works was of the opinion that this was 'the greatest poem in the Psalter and one of the greatest lyrics in the world'.

The voice of the skies (verses 1–6)

David draws our attention to the heavens, by which he means the sky or expanse, as the parallelism suggests (verse 1). It takes us back to Genesis 1 and how God made the expanse or firmament, which not only includes our atmosphere with its clouds but also the planets and stars. From our earthly vantage point the sky looks like a gigantic canopy. Whether by day or by night the expanse is preaching to us. In the daytime there are the cloud formations and on a clear night whole new worlds come into being. The message presented is continuous—it daily 'utters' or better 'pours out' speech (verse 2). There is a constant flow like a fountain.

What is the communication conveyed by the heavens? It is calling out to us that this is all the work of the one true God. What an amazing creator! It reveals 'the glory of God' (verse 1). It demonstrates, in other words, his stunning greatness and importance. The very creation 'reveals knowledge' (verse 2) in that it makes us all aware of the existence of the creator God.

We have a saying that actions speak louder than words so we can appreciate what David is saying: that though there is no literal audible proclamation with words yet the message of the heavens is conveyed to every part of the earth (verses 3–4). It may be inarticulate but it is real and it is universal.

Verse 3 is not saying that there is no language group in the world where the knowledge taught by the heavens does not reach (as the Authorised, New International and New King James Versions suggest by adding 'where' to the text). That truth is eloquently expressed in the next verse. It is the paradox and power of inarticulate speech that is conveyed here. Rather than our ears hearing what is proclaimed, it is our eyes that are receiving the message. The sky's 'measuring line' stretches across the world so that every part of the earth receives the signal. The whole of humanity is without excuse, for as Paul puts it, God's 'invisible attributes, namely, his eternal power and divine nature, have been clearly perceived, ever since the creation of the world, in the things that have been made' (Romans 1:20).

From the last part of verse 4 David considers the greatest wonder of the heavens—the sun. It so impressed many in the ancient world that they began to worship it. From the start the psalmist counteracts such thoughts. It is God who is responsible for the sun. He has provided it with a place to stay overnight in the sky—'he has set a tent for the sun' (verse 4). The real God is outside of creation and rules over the whole of it including the sun. Genesis 1 also teaches that the heavenly lights have no independent existence but are created by God but unlike the plain narrative style of Genesis we have the sun's journey across the sky described in very poetic language. First, the sun is depicted as emerging from its tent on the eastern horizon like an eastern bridegroom coming out of the nuptial chamber for a celebratory procession. In the other illustration the sun is like a champion who can joyfully run the track event. During the course of the day the sun circuits the whole earth and there is nothing that can hide from its heat. The point is again made, this time more graphically, that the message of the sky gets to every part of the world.

Paul's use of this text in Romans 10:18 in which he likens his commission to the sky's universal proclamation gives no warrant for the allegorical interpretation of these verses in which the sky becomes a type of the church and the sun a type of the gospel. As often in Paul, he uses the text with the whole context in mind including the verses that follow. He is illustrating how the gospel word has spread throughout the Roman world. How much more so is that true today!

The voice of Scripture (verses 7–11)

This sudden change draws our attention to the greater wonder of God's written words. Like Genesis 1–3 we move from the creation of the sky and the sun to the important place of God's Word in human life. In Genesis 1 the general name for God is used (Elohim) whereas in Genesis 2 we find God's personal name 'Lord' used alongside 'God'. Interestingly, David also introduces in verse 7 God's covenant name 'Lord' (Yahweh/Jehovah). This is the name that became special to Israel at the time when the almighty Creator redeemed Israel from captivity and entered into an arrangement with them at Sinai, called a covenant, giving them his written Law through Moses. In contrast to the single use of 'God' in the first section, the name 'Lord' is repeated six times in the following three verses.

Like Psalm 119 this reflection on the Lord's Word introduces us to a variety of terms for the Mosaic instruction. The word 'law' or 'Torah' can, of course, be applied to all Scripture as is suggested by Paul when he quotes from the prophets and psalms (see Romans 3:10–19). All Scripture is the inspired Word of God (2 Timothy 3:16).

Six terms are used with six matching descriptions and effects (in Psalm 119 eight different terms are used for God's revelatory words). This build up of synonyms presses home the greater clarity and significance of God's special revelation.

1. Verse 7—'The law of the LORD' is the LORD's instruction. It is 'perfect'. There is a completeness and consistency about it (see Psalm 18:30). It has not only a life-giving or 'converting' effect but also a life-renewing result like hungry people satisfied with food (Lamentations 1:11).

2. The parallel line follows the same pattern stating that the LORD's 'testimony' or his solemn declaration is 'sure' or reliable. The word 'testimony' is used of the Ten Commandments that were put in 'the ark of the Testimony' (Exodus 25:16,21–22). As in the wisdom literature the 'simple' are the inexperienced or untaught who could easily be swayed and dragged down into foolish ways (Proverbs 1:4; 9:16). The LORD's written word makes a person 'wise'. Timothy had been taught the Scriptures from childhood making him wise about salvation through faith in Jesus Christ (2 Timothy 3:15).

3. Verse 8—'The statutes of the LORD' are his precepts or ordinances that 'are right'. They are straight or upright; there is nothing crooked about them (see Proverbs 8:8–9). Far from being burdensome, they gladden the heart. What a blessing to have God's word and to know what is right and pleasing to him!

4. The parallel line introduces us to 'The commandment of the LORD' that is 'pure', or 'clear'. It is so clear and bright that it lights the eyes either in the sense of 'enlightening', 'giving understanding' or better, in view of the parallel, 'giving joy', 'lighting up the eyes with gladness'.

5. Verse 9—'The fear of the LORD' may here be a synonym of the 'law'. If the 'testimony of the Lord' makes the simple wise, the fear of the Lord, as Proverbs reminds us is the beginning of wisdom (see Psalm 111:10; Proverbs 1:7; 9:10). On the other hand, it is probably better to understand the expression as the godly life taught by the LORD. Reverence for the LORD is what the law teaches (see Deuteronomy 4:10) and it is 'clean', which is unlike so much of the paganism of ancient and modern times. God's law that instructs in the godly way is an 'enduring' word, it stands for ever.

6. 'The judgments of the LORD' are his regulations or judicial rulings and they are reliable and entirely righteous (Psalm 119:142, 160). Jesus stated in his prayer: 'Your word is truth' (John 17:17).

Only two items come to mind when comparing the worth of God's written revelation. When it comes to riches it is for the finest gold that people crave and as for those with a sweet tooth it is not the common date honey that is coveted but the honey that resides in a honeycomb. Unlike Adam and Eve who found the forbidden fruit of the garden more appealing than God's regulations, for David the Lord's Word was far more valuable than the wealth of this world and far more desirable than its sweetest foods (verse 10). How highly do we treasure the Holy Scriptures?

God's Word is given for our good (verse 11). While Adam and Eve refused the warnings of God's word, David, as God's 'servant' (see the introductory words to Psalm 18), takes it to heart and finds much blessing in keeping it. Paul reminds us that 'the law is holy, and the commandment holy and just and good' (Romans 7:12). To Timothy he writes that God's Word is profitable for doctrine, for reproof, for correction, for instruction in righteousness, that the man of God may be complete, thoroughly equipped for every good work' (2 Timothy 3:16–17).

The voice of the godly (verses 12–14)

No doubt with Genesis 3 in mind and in the light of his meditation on God's law, David senses his own unworthiness and proneness to sin. Even when he knows what is best for him he still goes astray. He therefore asks the Lord to cleanse him from hidden faults and to preserve him from wilful acts of rebellion against God. The godly person is no longer in the realm of sin but he must pray and desire not to be ruled by any particular sin (see Romans 6:12–14). The 'great transgression' (verse 13) is the sin of apostasy. What happened in the Garden of Eden was repeated at Sinai when Israel made and worshipped the golden calf. It is described as 'a great sin' (Exodus 32:21, 30–31).

The psalm closes with a plea that his own voice and inner meditations would be acceptable to God (verse 14). From what he has just said he is aware of how easily he could be deceiving himself. His prayer like the previous psalm is made to the 'LORD' (Yahweh/ Jehovah) his 'strength' (or more literally 'rock'; see Psalm 18:2) and his 'redeemer'. This final description of the LORD is the first use of this familiar biblical word. The 'redeemer' in Israelite society was the next of kin who came to the aid of a family member. It was applied to God when he redeemed Israel from slavery. They belonged to him through his covenant with Abraham and he came to rescue them when they were in grave trouble. This is the same God who in the Son Jesus Christ came to his people's aid when they were in deep distress on account of their slavery to sin and Satan and redeemed them at the cost of his own precious blood.

Psalm 20

'God save the King!'

This psalm and the following one form a pair. Both are concerned with the king, his enemies, deliverance and the prayers of God's people. Here the people pronounce blessings on their king before he sets out for battle, whereas Psalm 21 is praise and joy at the king's victory over the enemy. They both have the same heading like Psalm 19 (see Psalm 11).

The psalm divides into two parts.

Prayer-wish for the king (verses 1–5)

Before going out to meet the enemy, sacrifice was offered and the whole enterprise was committed to the Lord. In 2 Chronicles 20 we read of Jehoshaphat proclaiming a fast and offering prayer to the LORD in which he asked for help when enemy forces united to invade Judah.

This prayer-wish is not a straightforward intercessory prayer. It is not addressed to God but to the king. The 'you' and 'your' are singular in all these verses and the person addressed is identified in the second half of the psalm as the 'anointed' (verse 6) and the 'King' (verse 9). It is similar to the priestly blessing of Numbers 6:24–26 in that the benefits invoked are directed towards the king. The anointed king is the recipient of those blessings. This corporate invocation of blessing was perhaps expressed by the priest on behalf of the people (see Psalm

72:15). In 1 Kings 1:47 we read of the king's servants going 'to bless our lord, king David' and later all the people who attended the dedication of the temple when they departed 'blessed' king Solomon (1 Kings 8:66).

The 'LORD' (Jehovah/Yahweh) is invoked. The use of the word 'name' in the parallel expression (verse 1) is another way of referring to the Lord, particularly all that he has revealed under that name—his character and activity. The expression, 'the name of the God of Jacob' (see Psalm 84:8), associates God Almighty (El Shaddai), the name by which God revealed himself to Abraham, Isaac and Jacob, with the name that became so precious to God's people at the time of the exodus. By his name the 'LORD' (Jehovah/Yahweh) God revealed his redemptive activity and so much more of his character. God graciously associates himself with his people and it is a reminder of the covenant he made originally with Abraham that was later confirmed with Isaac and then Jacob (Exodus 3:13-15; 6:2-8; 34:5-7). To us God is now known as the God and Father of our Lord Jesus Christ (Romans 15:6; 2 Corinthians 1:3; Ephesians 1:3; 1 Peter 1:3).

Jacob was one of the sons of Isaac and his name came to be used for the whole nation of Israel (Psalm 78:5, 71). The 'day of trouble' or 'distress' (verse 1; see Psalm 50:15) is a time of crisis like that recalled by Jacob when he originally prayed to God at Bethel (Genesis 35:3). This may be the reason why reference is made to Jacob's God rather than Abraham's. The verb 'defend you' is literally 'set you on high'. The blessing requested is that the king will be out of the enemy's reach.

Asking that help and support might be sent from the 'sanctuary' or 'holy place' is appropriate, for David brought God's ark, the symbol of his presence, into the tabernacle on Zion's hill before the temple was built (2 Samuel 6:15-17). 'Zion' came to be another name for Jerusalem but at first it denoted the hill that David took and fortified and where the worshipping people met (see 2 Samuel 5:6-9; Psalms 65:1; 128:5; 132:13). The sanctuary in Jerusalem is the earthly representation of God's heavenly home. There is no contradiction between God's special presence on Mount Zion and God's special presence in 'his holy heaven' (see verse 6).

It is here at Zion that the congregation of God's people and the king are gathered and it is here that the king would have offered sacrifices (2 Samuel 6:17-18). There is no thought of God actually forgetting when the psalmist prays that God would 'remember' (verse

3). Neither is there any thought that the sacrifices are offered as a way of manipulating God as in pagan offerings (see Psalm 50). It is a humble desire that God would accept the king's worship and act accordingly.

Though the word for 'offerings' is the general term for a 'gift' or any kind of sacrifice (see Genesis 4:3–4; 32:13; 43:11), it is used specifically for the grain offering especially when it is coupled with the burnt offering. Part of the grain offering was also burnt on the altar of burnt offering (see Leviticus 2; 1 Samuel 1:24). The verb 'accept' (verse 3) is literally 'find fat' or 'regard as fat', the thought being that the Lord would regard all the offerings as fat and therefore his by right because 'all the fat is the LORD's' (Leviticus 3:16). Fat was considered a delicacy in ancient Israel and such offerings would be an indication of whole-hearted commitment to God. The prayer is that God would regard with favour the offerings the king presented.

The blessing continues in verse 4 and as with the previous verses the second line as it parallels the first, helps to make the point of the first line clear. It is assumed that the king is formulating plans that are in harmony with God's will. The prayer is that God would grant what he has set his heart on doing (literally 'according to your heart'). The defeat of the enemy is the great object and that is also God's concern for his anointed and his people.

As the form of the verb in verse 5 is the same as those in the previous verses, where they are translated 'may he (the Lord)', it is better to continue as 'May we' than 'We will'. In other words, rather than a declaration of what they will do at the assured outcome, the people continue in prayer, this time invoking a blessing for themselves. The desire of the king's subjects is that they might rejoice and unfurl their banners in God's name when the king finds divine deliverance. The king's 'salvation' or deliverance from the enemy is their deliverance. Positively, it means victory over the enemy. The displaying of 'banners' has a military connotation in the Bible. Under the tribal banners or standards Israel camped in the desert like a mighty army (Numbers 1:52; 2:2, 34; see also Song of Solomon 6:4, 10).

The final line, 'May the LORD fulfil all your petitions' (verse 5c), not only repeats the thought of verse 4 it summarises all the requests made in the previous verses.

Confidence in God (verses 6–9)

It is not necessary to assume that a prophet or priest is responding at this point. In the light of the words of blessing addressed to the king it is better to see the words of verse 6 as the king's own reaction.

The king's assurance (verse 6)—The king is the 'anointed one' (see Psalms 2:2; 18:50). 'Now I know', like Jethro's reply to the words of Moses (Exodus 18:11), is a confession of faith. It is David's response to the people's blessing in verses 1-5. In his testimony he echoes with similar words to theirs: 'the LORD saves'; 'saving strength (or power)' (see verse 5); 'he will answer' (verse 1); 'from his holy heaven' (see verse 2). The sanctuary at Mount Zion was expressive both of God's presence with his people and symbolic of his heavenly home. In Psalm 18:6 a reference is made to requests coming to God in his temple and then of God acting with all the powers of nature at his command (Psalm 18:7-15). This is what David can expect. God's powerful 'right hand' (see Psalm 89:25) brings mighty acts of deliverance as seen at the time of the exodus.

The people's assurance (verses 7-8)—These verses revert to the words of the people, possibly again through a prophet or priest as their representative. Again, these verses pick up phrases in the previous blessing: 'remember' (see verse 3); 'the name' along with 'LORD' (Jehovah/Yahweh) our God' (verses 1 and 5). The references to 'chariots' and 'horses' (verse 7) suggest that the psalm is set in the context of a war situation. Pharaoh put his trust in his horses and chariots but they proved inadequate when God gave Israel victory at the Red Sea (Exodus 14). The same was true when the Lord routed Sisera and all his chariots (Judges 4:12-16). In the laws concerning warfare, Israel was taught that when they went to war against their enemies and 'see horses and chariots' and an army larger than their own 'you shall not be afraid of them, for the Lord your God is with you, who brought you up out of the land of Egypt' (Deuteronomy 20:1-2). Joshua urged the people to trust the Lord 'since it is the Lord your God who fights for you just as he promised you' (Joshua 23:10). The latest military equipment is formidable but the people of David's time remember that God possesses 'superior power and guardian grace'. That lesson was lost in Isaiah's day for the prophet pronounced judgment on Judah's leaders for relying on horses and chariots (Isaiah 31:1).

If their trust is in the Lord then the outcome is assured. Like Sisera the enemy would sink and fall (Judges 5:27) while God's people would be victorious.

The people's prayer (verse 9)—There are difficulties in knowing how best to translate the verse. If we take the traditional reading, 'Save, Lᴏʀᴅ! May the King answer us', the psalm now calls directly on God to deliver his 'anointed' king (see verse 6). The 'King' of verse 9 is then understood to be a reference to God (Deuteronomy 33:5; 48:2; Matthew 5:35). In praying for the king's safety as leader of his people, this will lead to the nation's prosperity (see Psalm 118:25). Calvin comments, 'God had not promised that his people would be saved in any other way than by the hand and conduct of the king whom he had given them. In the present day, when Christ is now manifested to us, let us learn to yield him this honour—to renounce all hope of salvation from any other quarter, and to trust to that salvation only which he shall bring to us from God his Father.'

The opening words, however, may be better rendered 'Lᴏʀᴅ, save the king!' It is similar to such phrases as 'May the king live' (see 1 Kings 1:25, 31, 39 which is often translated as 'Long live the king'). The final words, reminding us of the opening words of the psalm, are taken as a prayer for God to respond to their request, translating either as 'Answer us when we call' or 'May he (the Lᴏʀᴅ) answer us when we call'.[36]

The final sentence is closer to the opening words of the psalm than appears in most English translations. In place of 'you' (verse 1) we have 'us' which is a fitting ending to a psalm where God's people have been pronouncing a blessing on God's anointed king and so the psalm ends with a direct appeal to God. The 'day of trouble' (verse 1) becomes 'when we call' (literally 'in the day of our calling'). This makes the confident spirit of verses 6–8, as Kidner helpfully comments, 'a matter not of wishful optimism but of realistic faith.'

Subjects of King Jesus, the Messiah, are concerned that the war that still rages, even though the decisive battle has been won at Calvary, will come to a speedy end. The people of God today under the banner of the Lord can often find themselves in an evil day, a day of trouble, and we cannot rest until the last enemy has been finally destroyed. But we bless the Saviour and honour him with our own 'God save the King!' 'Long live King Jesus!'

Psalm 21

Praise at the King's Safety

This royal psalm serves as a sequel to Psalm 20. Petitions offered (20:4–5) have been granted (21:2); expectation has given way to exultation which is 'as it should always be'.[37] There are many word and theme links with the previous psalm besides the now familiar heading 'Psalm of David'. It is possible to view the whole psalm as originally a prayer of thanksgiving offered by King David to God. On the other hand, it could have been written for the people to express praise for what God had done through the king and so it is appropriate that it should belong 'To the Chief Musician' for use in congregational worship. The point is that the destiny of king and people are inter-linked with deliverance due to the power of God. Enveloping the psalm we see king and people praising God's 'strength' (verses 1 and 13) while at the centre point in verse 7 we have the theological heart of the psalm. The psalm must be interpreted in the light of God's promises to David in 2 Samuel 7 and the introductory Psalm 2. David is looking beyond his own era to the time when shadows give way to reality and to what God will do through Jesus the anointed ruler over his people.

Looking back: thanksgiving for answered prayer (verses 1–6)

David refers to himself using third person forms (he, him, his) in his address to God. The people were looking forward to rejoicing over answered prayer for the king's deliverance (20:5) and now that victory is a reality, the king is overjoyed and this composition is with a view to his subjects joining him in praise to God. It is the 'strength' of the 'LORD' (Jehovah/Yahweh), often associated with God's rule (Psalm 29:1), that has given the king this deliverance (verse 1).

God has given him 'his heart's desire' (verse 2) in answer to the prayer of 20:4 where a similar thought is expressed even though the wording is different. What the king had wished for has been granted (see Psalm 2:8–9). God, his strength and salvation, has found the request of his lips and the desires of his heart to be acceptable to him (see Psalm 19:14). David acknowledges that God's encounter with him ('you meet him', verse 3) has been favourable, unlike God's confrontation with the wicked (Psalm 17:13). Just as Melchizedek blessed Abraham after his victory over the kings (Genesis 14:18–20) so God blessed his anointed with 'good' and granted him his royal position, symbolized by the 'crown of pure gold' (verse 3; see Psalm 2:6–7), similar to the golden crown of the Ammonite king that was placed on David's head (2 Samuel 12:30). The Lord was the ultimate king and the earthly representative of God's rule among his people received his royal appointment from God. We can understand why this psalm was chosen to be used in the Church of England on Ascension Day for it certainly anticipates and celebrates the victory of our Redeemer and his subsequent glory.

We can only begin to appreciate the extravagant language of verse 4 as we view it in the context of God's covenant with David in 2 Samuel 7. Prophets like Ezekiel speak of a future David (Ezekiel 34:23; 37:24–25) and such prophecies found their fulfilment in Jesus who is of David's family line and to him the Lord gave the throne of David where he reigns for ever and of his kingdom there will be no end (Luke 1:32–33). David and his immediate successors were shadowy and poor images of this real David (see Psalms 72:17; 89:4; 132:12). Through the deliverance that God has given, the king's stunning importance will be great. God will bestow on him splendour and majesty.

What is said of the king is reminiscent of the promises made to Abraham and his descendants. He has been made 'most blessed for ever' (verse 6; see Genesis 12:2) and these blessings are associated with God's presence (literally 'face') and this is what gives the king such gladness and joy.

A fundamental truth (verse 7)

This verse serves as a concluding comment on what has been said to God about the king and a preparation for what is directly addressed to the king concerning God's activity through him in the second half of the psalm. At this central point, where neither the king nor God is addressed, we are brought to the very heart of the relationship between the two: the LORD's steadfast love toward the king and the king's trust in the LORD. This is also to be the heart of the relationship between God and his people (Psalm 4:5; 17:7).

God's 'mercy' or 'faithful love' pertains to all the gracious blessings highlighted in the previous verses as well as to the promised help given the king in overcoming his enemies in the following verses. By referring to God as the 'Most High' (see Psalm 7:17) David is reminding himself that the 'LORD', the covenant God of Israel, is the transcendent creator God. David can therefore be confident that the king will 'not be moved' or 'shaken' (see Psalms 15:5; 16:8).

Looking forward: assurance of final victory (verses 8–13)

From viewing what God would do for the Lord's anointed one, the psalm moves to showing what the king will accomplish with God's help. While blessings come to the king that will naturally be to the good of his people, curses fall on the king's enemies. The Lord enables the king to 'find' in the sense of to 'reach' those foes who 'hate' him (see 1 Samuel 23:17) and to act powerfully ('right hand') against them (verse 8). With God's help no enemy is beyond the king's reach.

The king, acting as God's agent, will consume all his opponents as if they were burnt up in a 'fiery furnace' (verse 9). It is unfortunate that the translation 'in the time of your anger' (see also the AV) hides the force of the original (literally 'at the time of your face') which suggests the king's 'presence' in judgment, in contrast to God's 'presence' in blessing (verse 6). The king and the LORD are so closely united that the king's wrath and God's wrath are as one to devour the opposition (verse 9). What is spoken of here is revealed to us by Paul and John as the day of the Lamb's wrath when King Jesus will appear in flaming fire to punish with everlasting destruction those who do not know God or obey the gospel (2 Thessalonians 1:7-9; Revelation 6:16-17). The destruction is so complete that such enemies will have no offspring (verse 10). For the ancient Hebrews nothing could be so devastating than to be without children. Victory is described in typical ancient gory terms to make it clear that there would be a total elimination of rebels (see 2 Kings 8:12; Nahum 3:10).

The basis for this complete destruction is that the enemy has threatened to do 'evil' against the king and his people, devising plots that will not succeed because God intervenes through his king (see Psalm 2). He defeats them so that, just as in a battle, the enemy turns to flee when the archers aim their arrows at their faces (see Psalm 7:12–13).

The psalm ends as it began by calling attention to God's 'strength' and 'power' (the same word is translated 'strength' in Psalm 20:6). It is a call to God that is both prayer and praise and when he is raised up in his victorious strength the natural response of God's people is to sing and make music in praise of God. God's power which ought to strike fear into all God's enemies should encourage Christians to sing songs of praise.

God in Christ Jesus won the decisive battle against the enemy at Calvary but the final triumph will come when Christ returns and all enemies are eradicated.

Psalm 22

The King's Sufferings and Satisfaction

This intensely moving psalm is also very carefully constructed. David progresses from a position of utter helplessness and isolation to one of confidence and praise. His own agonizing experience was but a pale reflection of our Lord's sufferings on the cross. But the psalm can also be a model for Christians when they feel overwhelmed, God-forsaken or are undergoing persecution.

Between the two familiar headings 'To the Chief Musician' and 'A Psalm of David' (see Psalm 4) we have a phrase that is difficult to translate and evaluate. It could, as in most versions, be referring to a deer—'Set to "The Deer of the Dawn"' (literally, 'upon the deer of the dawn') in which case it may be the name of an ancient tune. On the other hand, with the ancient Greek Version, it could be expressing the theme of the psalm ('concerning dawn strength') and thus picking up the unusual word for 'strength' in verse 19. Help was often expected at the dawn of a new day (see Psalm 63:1). The title would then be describing the psalmist's eventual change of fortune through the one who is his strength and helper.

The King's sufferings (verses 1–21)

Mental Anguish (verses 1–10)

Lament (verses 1–2)

Psalms 10 and 13 begin in a similar way with the question of why the covenant keeping God is far off and unresponsive. Other psalms will urge God not to forsake his servant (see Psalm 38:21). God has abandoned David to the enemy. There has been no 'deliverance' ('helping'), no response to his lion-like 'roaring' ('groaning') words. Nevertheless, even in this crisis situation David still trusts God and calls out to him as 'my God' (see verse 10), the repetition demonstrating the depth of feeling. The question 'why' is more rhetorical than one expecting a reasoned reply. It gives expression to an experience that is quite unique and inexplicable. Calvin comments that if, in the first part of his conflict in the garden, Christ's sweat was like drops of blood so that he needed an angel to strengthen him, we should not be surprised that in the final suffering on the cross he cried out in deepest sorrow. We are not allowed to forget this sense of abandonment for the verbal form of the adjective 'far' is found in verses 11 and 19.

Unlike verse 1, where the divine name is *El*, the common name for God (*Elohim*) is found in verse 2 (see Psalm 18:6,21). The paradoxical situation is re-emphasised where the personal relationship that exists between David and God is resulting in total silence on the part of God despite David's day and night cries (see Psalm 1:2). Job experienced the same kind of divine dereliction despite his upright character.

Remembering God (verses 3–5)

At this low point David's faith is strengthened by reminding himself of who God is and how in the past he had given his people plenty of reasons to praise him as verses 4 and 5 indicate. He is perhaps thinking of Israel's deliverance from the Egyptians and particularly the song of Moses at the Red Sea (Exodus 15:1–18). They 'trusted' him (notice 'trust' is used three times for emphasis in verses 4–5) and 'cried' to him, in the way David had been doing, and they were 'delivered' (verse 4), they 'escaped' ('delivered', verse 5). God came to their aid so they were not 'ashamed'. The people's praises are full of God and what he has done (see Deuteronomy 10:21) but here it is expressed in an unusual way—God is said to 'inhabit (literally 'dwell/sit') or be 'enthroned on' the praises of Israel'. Kidner questions whether our singing in church is 'a throne for God or a platform for man'.[38] God is described as the 'holy' one (verse 3; see Isaiah 57:15), the transcendent one, who is not limited by circumstances and creaturely weakness. He can act to change David's situation but the problem is that he is not doing so.

Lament (verses 6–8)

From the emphatic 'But you' of verse 3 we have the equally strong 'But I' of verse 6 where David returns to his own situation. He has identified himself with the believing community of the past ('our fathers', verse 4) yet now he is so humiliated and insignificant ('a worm', verse 6; see Job 25:6; Isaiah 41:14) that he is subject to taunts ('reproach'), 'despised' by his people and a laughingstock. With gestures of the mouth and head expressive of their scorn, they mock his faith in the cruel words of verse 8. Those that watched our Lord's crucifixion made similar gestures and gibes (Mark 15:29; Matthew 27:39,43). Their sarcastic comment 'since he delights in him' (verse 8) is particularly hurtful for it would be expected that if God did delight in him then he would not be in his present situation. Again, this is similar to Job's circumstances and those of the Lord's unique Servant (Isaiah 53:2–3). The word for 'trusted' in verse 8 is literally 'roll' conveying the idea of a heavy burden that is rolled over to someone else more able to carry it. Psalm 37:5 and Proverbs 16:3 encourage us to 'commit' or 'roll' such concerns onto the Lord (see 1 Peter 5:7).

Remembering God (Verse 9–10)

David returns to contemplating God's past activity ('But you' or more precisely 'For you') not now for the nation as in verses 3–5 but for him personally. This is especially important in view of the comments being made in the previous lines. He reminds himself of God's providential oversight of his life from the moment he left his mother's womb and fed at her breasts. His awareness of God's care of him from birth belies the jeers of the people and establishes his right to call on him as 'my God' (verse 10, see verse 1).

Enemy Action (verses 11–21)

Cry for help (verse 11)

Taking up the concern of verse 1 that God is 'far from helping' and in the light of God's previous care, David pleads that God would not remain 'far' from him seeing that 'trouble' is near' and there is no one to 'help' him.

Lament (verses 12–18)

Trouble is in the form of strong opponents, as menacing as a herd of bulls or a hungry lion. Have you ever been in a field where cows are grazing? These inquisitive beasts, as soon as they spot you, quickly make their way in your direction and circle you round. How much worse a field of bulls! The cattle and flocks on the fertile plateau, east of the Sea of Galilee, the region now known as the Golan Heights, became proverbial ways to describe the might of enemies (Ezekiel 39:18) as well as the well-fed women of Samaria (Amos 4:1).

Though the language of being 'poured out like water' and of a 'heart ... melted' like hot 'wax' may suggest fear and dismay (Joshua 7:5; 2:11), in this context these images along with 'bones ... out of joint' (verse 14) describe David's extreme physical weakness. He is completely 'washed out' and 'falling apart'. The following verse continues to describe his feeble state. His 'strength' has dried up like a piece of pottery and his 'tongue' sticks to the roof of his mouth; he is parched and unable to speak (Lamentations 4:4; Job 29:10). He has already described himself as a worm (verse 6) and now he expects to lie dead in the 'dust' (verse 15; see verse 29). To be brought to the dust of the ground is the ultimate humiliation, the lowest possible state (see Psalms 7:5; 72:9; Genesis 3:14). What is striking is the direct address to God—'You have brought me ...' (verse 15). For David, God is absent, far off, and inactive yet here he acknowledges God's sovereign control over all that happens. This is something emphasised in the book of Job. Satan was given a free hand by God to afflict Job (Job 1:12; 2:6). Wicked hands crucified our Lord but it was in the plan of God that Christ should suffer.

David's foes ('the assembly of the wicked') are now likened to scavenging 'dogs' ready to lick his blood and devour his carcass (verse 16; see Psalms 59:6; 68:23; 1 Kings 22:38). They mutilate his limbs. The English versions follow the ancient Greek (the Septuagint) in translating 'pierced' whereas the Hebrew text reads 'Like a lion my hands and my feet', leaving us perhaps to provide a suitable verb (see Isaiah 38:13 where Hezekiah speaks of his terminal illness). While the Greek version is amazingly appropriate in describing our Lord's crucifixion the verse is nowhere cited in the New Testament, which should make us reticent in making too much of it.

Stripped of his clothes his emaciated body makes it possible to count his ribs. The greedy assailants look on with delight. David is as good as dead so they use a time-honoured way ('cast lots', verse 18) of disposing of his clothes even-handedly among themselves. All four Gospel writers draw attention to this verse as the soldiers distributed the clothes that Jesus had worn (Matthew 27:35; Mark 15:24; Luke 23:34; John 19:23–24).

Cry for help (verses 19–21)

Again, with an emphatic 'you', David utters a final plea that God would not be 'far' but act quickly to 'help' him even at this late hour (verse 19; see verse 11). For the first time David addresses God by his covenant name 'LORD' (Jehovah/Yahweh), which previously had only been used in derision by the enemy (verse 8). He also calls on God in a unique way as 'my Strength', a similar word to that translated 'deer' in the heading.

Taking up the verb 'deliver' used by his foes (verse 20; see verse 8), David cries out to God to rescue him from death (the 'sword' is frequently used to infer a violent death) and the 'power' of his doglike enemies (see verse 16). There is only one thing left that can be saved and that is his 'precious life' (literally 'my solitary one'). To be saved from 'the lion's mouth' has become a well-known expression in English but here it reminds us of the evil intentions of David's enemies (verse 21; see verse 13). The 'wild oxen'[39] is another animal metaphor for the enemy.

'You have answered me' (verse 21) is separated in some English versions as if this were the moment when God actually intervened and answered David. But in the original there is no evidence for this so that the final line continues the prayer of the first that God would 'answer' him ('Save me ... answer me') right there in the final moments of his life where the enemy seemed all-powerful—'horns' being a symbol of strength. Like Job (see Job 13:3,15–19), David prays in faith to the God who is far off and not answering (see verse 2 where 'not hear' is literally 'not answer'). It is an encouragement to God's people in deep distress to keep trusting and calling out to him though he is silent and the pain or persecution intensifies. Our Saviour endured indescribable suffering on our behalf and 'offered up prayers and supplications, with vehement cries and tears to him who was able to save him from death, and was heard because of his godly fear' (Hebrews 5:7).

The King's deliverance celebrated (verses 22–31)

David was heard because of his godly fear and he encourages all who 'fear the Lord' to join him in giving 'praise' to the Lord (verse 23, 25, 26). Such 'fear'[40] is not slavish but a trustful, loving submission to God that includes awe and respect (see Psalm 33:8). The sudden change, as in Psalm 6, is due to the Lord having heard his cry and not rejected or 'hidden his face from' the 'afflicted' (verse 24; the same word is translated 'poor' or better 'humble' in verse 26; see Psalm 18:27).

Local significance (verses 22–26)

The natural place to express thanksgiving and praise to God is in the assembly of God's people ('congregation' verse 22; see Psalm 1:5; Deuteronomy 31:30), among his brothers and sisters in the covenant. The Old Testament 'congregation' is equivalent to the New Testament term 'church' and the verse is used in reference to Jesus the Messiah and his sufferings for his people. He is not ashamed to call those who belong to him 'brothers' (Hebrews 2:11–12).

Accompanying the praise to God for his saving action David makes his thank-offering. Vows or promises made to God during times of adversity are fulfilled when deliverance comes (verse 25; see Psalm 50:14). One of the purposes of the peace or fellowship offering was to express gratitude and it was the only sacrifice where a part of the offering could be eaten by the worshipper. In fact, as the meat was to be eaten quickly worshippers were urged to celebrate their state of divine well-being with the whole family and the needy (see Leviticus 7:12–18; Deuteronomy 12:12,18).[41] Other humble 'poor' people who have similarly been in desperate straits and have looked to the Lord for help are encouraged to join in the celebratory meal and praise the Lord for his deliverances. A wish is made that they will live long (verse 26; see Psalm 21:4). In reference to the work of Christ on our behalf it is no sentimental toast that one might make at a dinner party such as 'Cymru am byth!' ('Wales for ever!') but a firm reality. Drawing on the benefits of Christ's death we do really live in the fullest sense forever (see John 6:51).

Universal significance (verses 27–31)

There is a cosmic aspect to David's deliverance (see Psalms 2:10–12; 18:49; 72:8–11). The whole world is encouraged to consider the significance of this amazing salvation and be converted and bow in submission and reverence ('worship', verse 27). It is not unusual in the psalms to switch dramatically from speaking about God ('turn to the LORD') to addressing him directly ('worship before you'). The empire that David built up was in many respects a remarkable period in Israelite history when many of the surrounding nations were brought to acknowledge David's rule and authority, but the second half of this psalm like the first half takes us beyond anything David experienced to the one of whom David is but a faint shadow.

The phrase 'families of the nations' calls to mind the promise to Abraham that 'all families of the earth shall be blessed' (Genesis 12:3). When God entered into that special agreement with Israel at Sinai, setting them apart from other nations to be his 'special treasure', he reminded them that 'all the earth is mine' (Exodus 19:5; see Genesis 14:22). It is because he 'rules over the nations' that he chose one nation, Israel, to be the means of bringing light and blessing to the entire world. As a result of Christ's work on the cross people from all nations have turned from idols to serve the living and true God. The Lord is in ultimate control and his rule, seen in the deliverance of which David's experience was symbolic, is one that embraces all nationalities (see Romans 3:29). In the original the exact phrase 'the kingdom *is* the LORD's' occurs in Obadiah verse 21 (see Matthew 6:13).

The psalm moves from racial to social categories by indicating that as the 'poor' worshipped and enjoyed the benefits of this thank offering (verse 26) so too the 'prosperous' are humbled and are brought to 'eat and worship' (verse 29). The final part of the verse is meant to encourage anyone who like David is at death's door, who is in extreme destitution (see verse 15). There is no discrimination in the benefits that Christ has procured (see Galatians 3:28).

The final verses remind us that time is no barrier either. People yet unborn will hear and serve the Lord. There will be a future 'posterity' (literally 'seed'; see Acts 2:39). What was declared at first to his own family in the context of the congregation of Israel is to be declared to succeeding generations (see Psalms 48:14; 24:6). It is God's righteousness that is to be declared, which is here associated with God's deliverance as promised to Adam and Abraham.

Psalm 23

The King of Love

The twenty-third psalm so well-known particularly in the metrical version, 'The Lord's my shepherd I'll not want', is often heard at funerals. But this personal testimony of the Lord's kindness is a piece that can be sung or read at any stage of life. It is a confession of trust in the living and true God who has entered into a special relationship with his people.

The first half of the psalm (verses 1–4) portrays the Lord as a shepherd leading and protecting while the second half (verses 5–6) views him as a generous host providing abundantly and continually. Whatever the picture, the imagery presses home spiritual truth. Like two bookends, the psalm begins and concludes by calling attention to God's special covenant name, 'LORD' (Jehovah/Yahweh, verses 1 and 6), while in verses 4 and 5 he is addressed directly ('you are with me', 'your rod and your staff', 'you prepare', 'you anoint').

The Good Shepherd (verses 1–4)
The scene we might have in our minds from childhood of a shepherd and his sheep may not entirely agree with reality. In the ancient Near East it was a difficult, dangerous and often despised occupation and David had first-hand experience of what it was like. To king Saul he described himself as strong and able to protect his flock from wild

animals although his brothers treated him with disdain (1 Samuel 16:11; 17:28,34–37).

In this psalm David applies Israel's experiences during the wilderness period to his own situation. The 'Lord' (Jehovah/Yahweh) is the name that became precious to Israel from the time of the exodus and Psalm 80 refers to God as the 'shepherd of Israel' who led his people through the wilderness. Moses reminded the people of how Israel 'lacked nothing' all through their desert wanderings and contemplated Canaan as a place where they would 'lack nothing' (Deuteronomy 2:7; 8:9). This is the verb used by David: 'I shall not want' (or better, 'lack nothing'). Israel had sung at the Red Sea of the Lord's leading and guidance (Exodus 15:13) and Psalm 106:8 mentions how God's people were saved 'for his name's sake'. Israel was led by God through a wilderness that is described as a land of 'the shadow of death' (Jeremiah 2:6). In their rebellion against the Lord they grumbled, 'Can God prepare a table in the wilderness?' (Psalm 78:19).

Verse 1 gives us a statement of the Lord's care for David and his people and verses 2–4 then show evidences of his care. Using the imagery of a shepherd David indicates that it is the Lord who causes him to 'lie down', who 'guides', 'restores' and 'leads' him, and who provides him with protection and 'comfort'.

The Lord's care (verse 1)

The image of the 'Lord' as the 'shepherd' of his people was used by Jacob as he blessed Joseph and his sons. He speaks of the God who had 'fed' or 'shepherded' him (Genesis 48:15) and in his parting words to his twelve sons he again refers to God as 'the shepherd' (Genesis 49:24). David strikes this same personal note. He is 'my' shepherd. Even if David is speaking on behalf of the nation the individual relationship is implied. David was a person loved by God and he was certain of God's care—'I shall lack nothing' ('I shall not want'). He spoke from the heart when he later confessed that those who seek the Lord shall 'not lack' any good thing (Psalm 34:10).

Do you know God in this way? Paul could not only write to Christians and speak of 'our God' he could at the same time use very personal language, 'my God'. He was always appreciative of God's good provisions for him and encouraged Christians to rest content in the sure knowledge that 'my God shall supply all your need according to his riches in glory by Christ Jesus' (Philippians 4:19–20).

The kings of Israel were also called to be shepherds of their people and Micaiah prophesied that king Ahab would die in battle and Israel would be scattered on the mountains like sheep without a shepherd (1 Kings 22:17). Ezekiel spoke out against the leaders of his day who acted like irresponsible shepherds having no care for the sheep. By contrast, the Lord is the good shepherd who searches for his flock, gathers them together and feeds them in good pasture (Ezekiel 34). Isaiah looked to the time when the Lord would come and feed his flock like a shepherd and gather the lambs with his arm (Isaiah 40:11). The Persian king, Cyrus, is seen as a type of the Messiah (the Lord's 'anointed') and is referred to as the Lord's 'shepherd' (Isaiah 44:28–45:1).

This background prepares us for Jesus. He saw crowds of people on the hillside and was moved with compassion for them 'because they were like sheep not having a shepherd' (Mark 6:34) and he described himself as 'the good shepherd' who gave his life for the sheep (John 10:11, 14). He is 'that great shepherd of the sheep' (Hebrews 13:20). We are all like sheep who have gone astray (Isaiah 53:6) but it may also be true that you 'have now returned to the Shepherd and Overseer of your souls' (1 Peter 2:25).

The ministerial office in the Christian Church is based on this shepherd image. Jesus is the Chief Shepherd and he calls ministers of the gospel to be under-shepherds, feeding or shepherding the flock of God (1 Peter 5:1–4).

The Lord's provisions (verses 2–3)

1. He satisfies hunger—Unlike in the Welsh mountains where the rainfall is such that the sheep can graze on the same hills the whole year round, the mountains of Canaan provide no year-long supply of fresh grass. The 'green pastures' are a feature of the winter and spring time in Israel. David, however, is able to testify that the Lord's provision is not seasonal. He has amply provided for him whatever the time of year. David is like a sheep lying contentedly in lush pastureland. He is in clover! There is no need to move on. Whatever the outward circumstances, and David had many ups and downs in life, when he was in fellowship with the Lord he was content. This is the contentment that Paul knew (Philippians 4:11). Jesus informs us that through him we are saved and 'will go in and out and find pasture' (John 10:9).

2. He quenches thirst—the 'still waters' are the 'waters of rest'. We are

not to think of stagnant water but of pools formed in the rocks from mountain springs. How refreshing to find cool waters in the shade of the rocks when the sun is beating down relentlessly! The sheep knows it can rest there and drink at leisure. The Spirit directs us to Jesus who relieves the thirsty soul—'And let him who thirsts come. And whoever desires, let him take the water of life freely' (Revelation 22:17; see John 7:37).

3. He revives—he 'restores my soul' means he 'rejuvenates me'. The 'soul' is used for the person. Proverbs 25:13 has a similar phrase for refreshing a person. Tired and weary bodies and spirits are renewed and invigorated through being brought into this restful environment. The Lord refreshed Elijah with good meals and rest before challenging him to return to the fray (1 Kings 19:5-8). Physical restoration is sometimes necessary before spiritual renewal can take place.

4. He prevents from going astray—as the eastern shepherd does not drive his flock from behind but 'leads' them, so the Lord goes ahead of his people. 'My sheep', Jesus said, 'hear my voice, and I know them, and they follow me' (John 10:27). The 'paths of righteousness' are tracks that are straight and dependable, not crooked and misleading. Proverbs describes madam folly's ways as unstable, crooked and devious and leading to death, whereas madam wisdom's paths are upright and good and lead to life (Proverbs 2:10-22). These paths are consistent with God's nature—'for his name's sake'. 'Name' stands for character, reputation (see Psalms 25:11; 109:21). God is always true to himself and what he does is a reflection of his character. He is faithful to his promises.

The Lord's protection (verse 4)

Following on from the previous thought, David acknowledges that when life's way runs through the 'evil' of life-threatening experiences or even death itself, he does not 'fear' for he has the 'comfort' of knowing the divine shepherd is there to protect and guide him. How precious are those words, 'you are with me'! We are urged to be content with what we have for God has said, 'I will never leave you nor forsake you' (Hebrews 13:5-6).

'Valley' refers to those gullies or ravines in the rocky hills and the phrase 'the shadow of death' may be a Hebrew idiom for a valley of deep darkness or a valley where death holds sway. In either case it suggests a place where one is apprehensive of each step. In those narrow chasms wild animals lurked ready to pounce on unsuspecting sheep. The shepherd's 'rod' or club would be attached to his belt to ward off animal attacks and the 'staff' would be in his hand for support. Unlike the hired hand who flees when he sees the wolf coming, our Lord Jesus, the good shepherd, cares for the sheep (John 10:11–15).

The Generous Host (verses 5–6)

Though some have made brave attempts to continue the pastoral scene to the end, it is better to understand a change of image from shepherd to host, from sheep to guest. The mention of a table and house reminds us of the comforts of home.

The Lord's preparations (verse 5)

Probably most of us have, at some time, been entertained by friends to a sumptuous meal. This is the idea in the phrase 'prepare a table' (see Proverbs 9:2). David's friends prepared such a table for him at a time when Absalom, his son became his enemy (2 Samuel 17:27–29). Anointing (literally 'make fat') with 'oil' (see Luke 7:46) and an overflowing 'cup' suggest a joyful welcome and ample provisions. This banquet takes place 'in the presence of my enemies' indicating a victory celebration where David is completely vindicated. The king's opponents are made to witness the triumphant celebrations.[42] It is similar to the description of the enemy nations ashamed of their might, putting their hands over their mouths and licking the dust like snakes as they see God's pastoral care of his people (Micah 7:14–17).

The Lord's pledges (verse 6)

God's attributes of 'goodness and mercy' or 'kindness and steadfast love' are brought to life here and David is assured that instead of wild animals or enemies chasing him, it is these blessings associated with God's covenant promises that will certainly 'follow' (literally 'pursue') him throughout his life. Like servants of the king, they will accompany him to attend to his needs. Those who consider the shepherd image is still in view think of 'goodness and mercy' as a shepherd's dogs running behind the flock to keep the stragglers in check!

The 'house of the LORD' originally referred to any place where God chose to reveal himself to people. Bethel, meaning 'the house of God' was the place where God met Jacob and where he returned to worship years later (Genesis 28:17, 19, 22; 35:6–15). The tabernacle and then the temple were places where God set up home among his people (1 Chronicles 9:23; 2 Samuel 7:13; 2 Chronicles 5:13-6:2). These visual aids for Israel point back to a lost garden temple in Eden and forward to the garden-city temple in the new creation as well as the promises made under the new covenant for this life. With the coming of Christ, there are no special holy places (John 4:21-24) but wherever the church meets in the name of Jesus for communal acts of worship there the triune God ordains to meet with his people by his Spirit (Matthew 18:20). We even have the amazing picture of Father and Son setting up home with the individual believer (John 14:23; see Revelation 3:20).

'I will dwell' follows the Greek version (the Septuagint) of this psalm, while the Hebrew has 'I will return'. Only the priests and Levites were allowed to stay in the temple (1 Chronicles 9:33); king and people of necessity had to come and go. The implication in both texts is that for David the house of the Lord is home for him (see 15:1). For the believer, as Alec Motyer comments, 'when earth's *paths* (2,3), *valleys* and threats (5) are over, there comes the real return home.'

The final phrase, 'for ever' or 'days without end' correctly conveys the point that David is making (literally it is 'for length of days')—the assurance of unending fellowship with God (see 16:11). When children are enjoying themselves they do not want to move anywhere else. Is our chief delight to honour God and enjoy him forever? John picks up the themes from this psalm as he pictures God's redeemed people completely satisfied 'for the Lamb who is in the midst of the throne will shepherd them and lead them to living fountains of waters ...' (Revelation 7:15-17).

As great David's greater son, Jesus could also identify with this expression of satisfaction in the Lord. As well as being divine, he was one hundred per cent human and in his daily life he was as dependent as we are on the sustaining presence and goodness of his Father. Our Saviour who experienced the awesome dereliction of Psalm 22 also knew the blessing of his Father's care.

Psalm 24

The King of Glory

After considering the kind care of the Shepherd King in Psalm 23, David reminds us that this same Lord is the glorious holy one who is over the whole of creation. It presents again truth concerning the Messiah that was first brought to our attention in Psalm 2 and provides a fitting conclusion to the group of psalms that began with Psalm 15.

Though we cannot be sure, the psalm could well be associated with David's capture of Jerusalem and bringing the ark of the covenant into the city to its final resting place in the tent he had pitched for it (2 Samuel 6:12-19; 1 Chronicles 13:1-16:6). There appear to be three sections (verses 1-2, 3-6, 7-10) but only two are suggested by the use of 'Selah' (verses 1-6, 7-10).

Approaching the LORD (verses 1-6)
While the context is Old Testament worship in which the God-given physical objects speak of spiritual realities there is much we can learn about God and our approach to him.

Proclamation (verses 1-2)
Instead of 'The earth is the LORD's', verse 1 begins in the original, 'To the LORD (Yahweh/Jehovah) ...' which emphasises more strongly the

truth of the Creator's ownership of the world. Typical of Hebrew poetry the second line parallels the first and makes the first thought more specific. While the 'earth' and its 'fulness' stress that the whole creation belongs to God, it is particularly true of the inhabited 'world' of humans who 'dwell' in it (see Isaiah 34:1; 45:18; Micah 1:2).

Verse 2 presents the basis for God's universal sovereignty. It is 'he', the LORD, who has founded and established the earth in the way we might think of some founder of a city. God created the world and he rules over it. The verse describes poetically what Genesis 1:9-10 and 2 Peter 3:5 present in narrative form. From space we see the earth covered by 'the seas', as well as 'the waters' (literally, 'the rivers') with the landmass rising 'upon' or 'above' them (as in Psalm 8:1—'above the heavens'). The pagan Canaanite world thought of the salt and fresh waters as hostile gods and Baal was celebrated as king for subduing them. Israel was fearful of the threatening, turbulent sea but the people of God could be assured that they were not subject to the whims of competing gods. The living God, Yahweh, who had redeemed them and entered into a special arrangement with them was also the one who had created all things and had gathered the waters together to allow the dry land to appear. With all our sophisticated knowledge we still feel very vulnerable and fearful of rising water whether from rivers overflowing their banks, tidal waves from underwater earth tremors or from rising sea levels through global warming. Though we must not be complacent and are accountable for actions that aggravate disasters we can be assured that our Creator God is in ultimate control and is a very present help in trouble (see Psalm 46:1-5).

The proclamation that the God who created the world both owns and rules it contains a confessional statement that re-echoes words from the time of the exodus. The exact formula, 'the earth is the LORD's', is found on the lips of Moses as he addresses Pharaoh: 'there will be no more hail, so that you may know that the earth is the Lord's' (Exodus 9:29). In his introduction to the Sinai covenant the Lord announces concerning Israel, 'you shall be a special treasure to me above all people, for all the earth is mine' (Exodus 19:5; see also Deuteronomy 10:14). Paul quotes the words of verse 1 in his pastoral advice to converts from paganism. They could eat with a clear conscience food that had been 'offered to idols' and sold in the meat market (1 Corinthians 10:26). It is the sovereign Creator God who owns all things and not the so-called gods of which people are in fear. From this we are encouraged to give thanks every time we come to the meal table for the good gifts that are given us by the Lord (see 1 Chronicles 29:10–13).

Question (verse 3)

If questions are asked about the correct procedure for an audience with a country's ruler it should not be thought inappropriate to ask about our approach into the presence of the one who is the creator and sovereign ruler of the world. The question assumes that though God is high over all he is approachable, so that any Tom, Dick or Hannah can appear before him. It also assumes that though heaven and the highest heaven cannot contain him (1 Kings 8:27) it is possible for finite creatures to come to God. Since the covenant at Sinai was established with Israel God ordained to meet with his people in the holy tent or tabernacle where his special presence was associated with the ark of the covenant. From David's time the ark and the tabernacle (later the temple) were associated with Jerusalem and particularly with Mount Zion, 'the hill of the LORD' (see 2 Samuel 5:7; Psalms 2:6; 15:1). In Isaiah's prophecies as well as the Psalms, Zion becomes symbolic of the coming together of God's true people and of his presence among them, a theme taken up in the New Testament (see Hebrews 12:22; Revelation 14:1).[43]

To 'ascend' and 'stand' are terms expressing a person's approach and acceptance in the worship of God and in the possibility of making requests to him. But though *anyone* can come into God's presence and worship him no one can come *anyhow*. Whether in communal worship or private devotion it must be in a way that is acceptable to God. The Lord's 'holy place' (verse 3) is a reminder that we come before a God who is holy. He is not a part of this world. God's 'terrifying otherness' means that he is distinct and separate in being and character. The Lord God is the most wholesome and perfect being there is. Who can bear to enter the presence of this awesome, ethically pure Being? 'Who among us shall dwell with the devouring fire?' (Isaiah 33:14).

Response (verses 4–6)

The sovereign creator God, the holy one of Israel, the Redeemer of his people, demands, first and foremost, not ceremonial acts but ethical standards such as are presented in the Ten Commandments. There are echoes from both tablets of the law in the response. In word, thought and deed the worshipper is to be upright and genuine, not devious and deceitful.

Four requirements are spelled out (verse 4). This is not an exhaustive list (see Psalm 15 for instance) but they indicate that true worshippers must be people of integrity who are committed to their responsibilities as members of God's covenant community.

While 'clean hands' suggests blameless conduct, 'pure heart' emphasises motives and thoughts that are sincere and innocent (verse 4a). The prophets constantly stress how God rejects religion divorced from behaviour (Isaiah 33:15). He will not listen to those who pray with hands 'full of blood' (Isaiah 1:12-15). Paul directs that 'holy hands' should be lifted up in prayer (1 Timothy 2:8) and speaks with approval of 'those who call on the Lord out of a pure heart (2 Timothy 2:22), while Jesus teaches that 'the pure in heart' are the ones blessed, who will see God (Matthew 5:8).

After the two positive requirements come two corresponding negative ones which highlight forms of deception in relation to God and fellow human beings. Love for God and neighbour is vital for our worship to be acceptable. We cannot deceive God. To 'lift up the soul to' (verse 4b)[44] means 'to set one's heart on' someone or something, or doing something (see Proverbs 19:18). Psalm 25:1 encourages us to 'lift up' our souls to the Lord and trust him. The word translated 'idol' is literally 'emptiness' and is used of futile human help (see Psalm 60:11) as well as of the worthlessness of idols and false gods (see Psalm 31:6; Jeremiah 18:15). God demands our wholehearted worship (Exodus 20:3-6). 'The dearest idol I have known, Whate'er that idol be, Help me to tear it from the throne, And worship only Thee' (William Cowper). To 'swear deceitfully' includes not presenting false testimony in court or more generally giving solemn assurances while having no intention of fulfilling them (see Exodus 20:16; Psalm 15:4).

The psalm reminds us of Jesus' teaching. He insists that if we have offended someone and are conscious of a broken relationship we must immediately take the initiative and seek the forgiveness of the one we have wronged before continuing with our worship (Matthew 5:23-24). James in his epistle warns Christians against hypocrisy and stresses that true religion is more than offering prayers and going to church.

Instead of being 'taken' ('lifted up') by all that is false (verse 4), the worshipper will 'take away' or 'receive' (literally, 'lift up') from God's presence two promises—'blessing' and 'righteousness' (verse 5).

'Blessing' is the opposite of 'curse' and relates to all the good that God has promised in the covenant. The essence of it is expressed superbly in the priestly blessing—experiencing the smile of God and his peace (Numbers 6:23–26). As for the term 'righteousness' there is debate over its use here. Some translate 'goodness' or 'faithfulness'. The term is associated with God's deliverance of his people (see Psalms 5:8; 23:3). There is a perfectly good word for 'faithfulness' in Hebrew if that is what David wished to convey. In this context, 'righteousness' is a law-court term for when a judge pronounces in favour of a person. 'Justification' or 'vindication' would be a suitable translation. The 'LORD' is the Saviour God ('the God of his salvation'; see Psalm 18:46) who has brought deliverance so that blessing and a right standing before God can be received as a gift and not achieved through human activity.

The reply to the question of verse 3 is concluded here, bringing the first part of the psalm to a close. Those who wish to enter God's presence are now described as the 'generation' or 'type of people' (see Psalm 14:5) who 'seek' him in the sense of 'turn to' him. They do not seek false gods or come with pagan attitudes and a hypocritical spirit but turn to the living and true God with a humble, contrite heart.

Another term is used for 'seek' in the phrase to 'seek your face' (verse 6b) with no appreciable difference in meaning. By repeating the idea in the form of a prayer ('your face' in place of 'him') the importance of desiring God and his favour is emphasised. To seek God's face is to set oneself to experience his smile and so to receive his blessing (see verse 5; 27:8–9 with 11:7; 17:15). Despite what God says to Moses about no one seeing God's face (Exodus 33:20) he has provided a way for humans to see God and live. The Old Testament copies and types through the tabernacle worship give way to the reality in Jesus Christ who not only reveals the invisible God by 'tabernacling' among us (John 1:14–18) but enables sinful creatures to enter God's holy presence and to experience the smile of his face in blessing and peace (Hebrews 9:24; 10:19–22; 4:16).

It is clear in the psalm that David is describing the true worshippers of God, who worship God in spirit and truth. The same distinction that Paul makes between the merely natural and the true descendants of Israel (Romans 9:6–7) is emphasised here. In the original, the name 'Jacob' appears at the end of the sentence and some translations make sense of it by adding 'God of Jacob'. But just as 'those who seek your face' parallels 'those who seek him' so 'Jacob' is best seen as parallel with 'This is the generation of'. It is those who belong like Jacob to the true people of God who are the ones blessed by God. These are the true Israelites 'in whom there is no guile' (see John 1:47). 'For we are the circumcision, who worship God in the Spirit, rejoice in Christ Jesus, and have no confidence in the flesh' (Philippians 3:3).

The LORD approaching (verses 7–10)

This part of the psalm takes up many of the themes from the song that Israel sang after their deliverance from the Egyptians (Exodus 15:1–18). In that song it is prophesied that the Lord would bring his people to the promised land and that a mountain sanctuary would be established where the LORD would make his earthly residence (Exodus 15:17). That mountain is Mount Zion in the heart of Jerusalem.

In this section we move from the worshipper approaching the presence of the Lord on Zion's hill to the all-conquering LORD entering Jerusalem and the tabernacle under the symbolism of the ark of the covenant. Jerusalem had been a Jebusite city which David had taken and made his capital. In Abraham's day it had been under the leadership of the priest-king Melchizedek (Genesis 14:18). It was here that God finally chose to make his home among his people, a faint reminder of a lost presence in the Garden of Eden but anticipating the final rest in the new creation when God will reside among his people forever (Revelation 21–22). It is also prophetic of our Lord's ascension to the right hand of the Father after his victory over sin, Satan, death and hell.

The proclamation (verses 7,9)

The call goes out to receive 'the King of glory'. Like the Hebrew phrase 'the place of his holiness' which is translated 'his holy place' (verse 3) so here we should read 'the glorious King'. The poetic language addressed to the gates and doors seeks to convey the greatness of the King and may express a call to look with expectant joy (see Luke 21:28). The entrances to the city and sanctuary must give every indication of welcoming its king with open arms. Gates must proudly hold their heads up high, ancient doors must not hinder the progress of the glorious victor. He must not be dishonoured by having to stoop to enter.

But the 'everlasting doors' are suggestive of something more than an earthly city and sanctuary. Along with the 'gates' they point to a heavenly reality of which people like Abraham and Jacob had some knowledge. Abraham looked for a heavenly city (Hebrews 11:10) while Jacob spoke of his experience at Bethel as 'the gate of heaven' (Genesis 28:17). These verses direct us to Jesus' entrance into the heavenly sanctuary (Hebrews 9:24; see Ezekiel 44:1–2).

The proclamation is repeated to emphasise the importance of the person, with only a slight change in the form of one verb from 'be lifted up' (verse 7) to 'lift up' (verse 9).

The question (verses 8a,10a)

The force of the original suggests, 'Who is this whom you describe as the glorious king?' Only in this psalm is the phrase 'King of glory' found. David was the earthly king whom God had appointed to reign over his people. He had been given honour and importance. Is there someone else more glorious seeking special entrance? If there is, then his identity must be revealed.

The response (verses 8b,10b)

The question is answered abruptly and forcefully—'the LORD ... the LORD' (Jehovah/Yahweh). Attention is drawn particularly to the LORD as king in Book 4 of the Psalter (see Psalms 90–106). He is described in warlike terms as 'strong and mighty' and 'mighty in battle' (verse 8b). David probably has in mind the song of Moses which speaks of the LORD as 'a man of war' who had decisively defeated the Egyptians and who 'shall reign for ever and ever' (Exodus 15:3,18).

The question is repeated[45] for dramatic effect to highlight the climatic description, 'The LORD of hosts' (verse 10b). This is a phrase we find in Romans 9:29 and James 5:4. It has military associations in that 'hosts' means 'armies' and often appears where God is seen as head over the angels or stars (see 1 Kings 22:19; Genesis 2:1). Only rarely is it used of Israel's armies but a significant passage is where David confronts Goliath with the words, 'I come to you in the name of the LORD of hosts, the God of the armies of Israel, whom you have defied' (1 Samuel 17:45). From the contexts in which it is used the phrase speaks of the all-powerful God, which is why some English versions translate 'The LORD Almighty'.

'LORD of hosts' brings us back to the beginning of the psalm with the thought of the Lord's universal sovereignty. He who is the

Creator-Redeemer, the mighty God and universal sovereign is the one proclaimed as 'the King of glory' (verse 10b). Creation reveals the stunning splendour and greatness of the LORD (verses 1-2; Psalm 19:1) and in his temple all cry 'Glory!' (Psalm 29:9). This is the one whom Isaiah describes as 'the King, the LORD of hosts' (Isaiah 6:5). Significantly, John adds that Isaiah saw the glory of Jesus and spoke about him (John 12:41).

It is not a coincidence that among the Jews this psalm was appointed for use on the first day of the week.[46] It finds fulfilment in the resurrection of Christ and his ascension to God's right hand. The original creation, when God formed and filled our world, commenced on the first day of the week and the resurrection and glorification of Christ on the first day of the week is the beginning and guarantee of the new creation when the King's stunning grandeur and importance will be fully disclosed. It comes as no surprise either that Jesus the Messiah can be given the name that is above every name—'LORD' (Yahweh/Jehovah; Philippians 2:9-11; see Isaiah 45:21-25; Joel 2:32; Acts 2:21-22; 16:31; Romans 10:9-13).

Psalm 25

An Alphabet of Prayer

We have many ways to try and remember things. One method is to organise what we want to memorise with the aid of letters of the alphabet and that is what seems to be happening here. This prayer belonging to the David collection ('Of David') is so arranged that verses begin in turn with different letters of the Hebrew alphabet (see Psalms 9-10), though in this case the scheme is not strictly followed. Two letters are left out ('*Waw*' and '*Qoph*'; see Psalm 119) while two verses are given the same letter '*Resh*' ('Reflect' or 'Look on my affliction' verse 18; 'Reflect on' or 'Consider my enemies' verse 19) which draw attention to David's lament over his sins and his enemies, matters that trouble him throughout the psalm (see 2,7,11,20,22). The final letter of the alphabet introduces verse 21 while the last verse begins with a letter that has already been used, the letter '*Pe*'. The choice seems purposeful (see Psalm 34), for the letters beginning the two halves of the twenty-two letter Hebrew alphabet (*Aleph* the first letter and *Lamedh* the twelfth) together with the final '*Pe*' spell out the consonants of the verb 'to learn' or 'teach'. The arrangement of the Hebrew letters thus emphasises another important concern, one that is significant in Proverbs: the need for God to 'teach' him the right way (see verses 4-5,8-9,12).[47] It also draws our attention to the first, middle and last lines of the psalm where prayer is directed to the LORD God, with a trusting spirit (verses 1–2a), seeking personal pardon (verse 11) and the redemption of his people (verse 22).

Reading this psalm in translation means we do not have the original helps to memorise it but it is one that we would do well to remember as we come in prayer to God. It is like other wisdom psalms that speak of fearing God, of trusting him and of the need to be guided by him (see Psalms 1; 34; 119). The psalm comes from David's own personal experience but the last verse reminds us that as Israel's royal representative he can speak for the nation. Its alphabetical arrangement encourages the people of God in turn to memorise it and use it in their personal devotions.

The psalm's special alphabetical layout also means we should not expect the material to have any neat sub-divisions. However, as if to help us look at the psalm in sections, David begins and ends the first and third sections by directly addressing God (verses 1–7,16–22), whereas for the most part the central section speaks of God indirectly (verses 8–15).

Looking to the Lord (verses 1–7)

The opening words 'I lift up my soul' (verse 1) recall 'lifted up his soul' in the previous psalm (Psalm 24:4). David's 'whole being' is set on the LORD (Yahweh/Jehovah) his God. Outward expressions of devotion such as the lifting up of our hands or eyes in prayer are useless rituals if we do not have that inner desire for God.

Shame (verses 2–3)

With enemies who have betrayed his trust seeking to discredit him for no reason, he appeals to the Lord with confidence that he and all who trust God will be vindicated. While the word 'trust' occurs only in verse 2, David's complete reliance on God is evident throughout, especially in the use of the verb 'wait' (verses 3,5,21). It does not mean passive resignation but eager expectation. It is a hope that is sure and certain because it is based on God's promises. On many occasions before he became king, David learned the secret of patiently waiting God's timing for him to take the throne. A promise had been made and it was not for him to go ahead of God even though he had numerous opportunities to kill Saul the anointed leader (see 1 Samuel 26:7–11).

How often is it the case that those who testify to God's care of his people feel embarrassed and humiliated in the face of enemy taunts when severe troubles bring no obvious relief from God! As in Job's case, his friends turned against him, arguing that he was being punished for gross sins. The enemies in David's situation were more often than not people who had once been close to him. But they had turned against him and were gloating over his predicament. To 'deal treacherously' (verse 3) means to act deceitfully. In the light of the covenant references (see verses 10,14) these enemies were probably people who had shown by their actions their unfaithfulness to God's covenant with Israel and their un-brotherly spirit within the covenant community. Instead of the true covenant people of God under the leadership of their king being humiliated and embarrassed, the prayer is that those who have broken their covenant obligations may be disgraced.

Guidance (verses 4–5)

There follows this prayer for guidance—'Show me' (literally, 'Make me to know'), 'teach me', 'Lead me' ('Cause me to walk'), 'teach me'. The word for 'lead' belongs to the same word family as 'way' or 'road' so that the psalmist is asking for help to travel the road set out in God's law. Whatever personal guidance we may desire as believers our fundamental need is that our daily conduct should be true to the will of God revealed in his written Word. God's 'ways' and 'paths' are associated with God's law, God's instruction (see Psalm 119). When Israel made the golden calf at the foot of Sinai, Moses described the incident as a turning aside 'from the way which the Lord had commanded' (Deuteronomy 9:16). God's Word instructs us in the way that we should go (see 2 Timothy 3:16).

While 'your truth' (verse 5) may be another term for God's word it is possible that it means God's faithfulness, his truthfulness, so that David is appealing for help to do God's revealed will on the basis that the Lord is a dependable God. This thought carries on into the next sentence where David appeals to God his saviour ('the God of my salvation'). He has experienced God's faithfulness and saving mercy in the past and with these strong arguments prays that God will come to his aid that he might live that life of obedience to God's word. David is not being over-dramatic as with one verb after another he calls out for God's help. Here is a humble believer aware of his need, of enemies that seek to shame him and of testing experiences that can destabilise and easily drive him off course, yet looking expectantly and continually to the Lord—'on you I wait all the day' (verse 5).

Remember (verses 6–7)

We can appreciate why his cry to God in the previous stanzas is so urgent as he now confesses past failures. The enemy can tempt the believer to despair when present difficulties are assumed to have arisen because of former sins. Long forgiven and forgotten sins begin to play on our minds and consciences and we are ashamed and begin to think that God has left us. Comfort comes from reminding ourselves of God's grace as we plead on the basis of past expressions of his kindness and unfailing love.

'Remember' is the key verb. First of all, David appeals once more to the Lord's nature that remains unchangeable ('from of old'). He cries to the Lord to 'remember' his 'tender mercies' (see Psalms 40:11; 51:1) and 'loving kindness' (often translated 'mercy' as in verse 7; see Psalm 5:7). They speak of the Lord's 'compassion' and 'steadfast love'. These are two characteristics associated with God's gracious activity with regard to his people, expressed especially at the time of the exodus, when he entered into that covenant with them and gave them many precious promises.

Next, he prays that the Lord would 'not remember' his youthful 'sins', whether inadvertent ones or 'youthful lusts' (see 2 Timothy 2:22), or 'his transgressions' by which he means perhaps more recent, wilful acts of rebellion that are playing on his mind (see Psalm 51). As Spurgeon comments, 'David would have his sins not only forgiven, but forgotten.'

Finally, he prays, 'remember me'. There is a 'you' in the original which is difficult to convey in modern English. Perhaps 'You yourself remember me' catches the sense (see the Authorised Version 'remember thou me'). He asks that God would deal with him in line with the Lord's steadfast love ('your mercy'). His plea rests not on any merits of his own but solely on the Lord's 'goodness'.

When Moses asked to see God's glory, the Lord proclaimed his name: 'The Lord, the Lord God, merciful and gracious, long-suffering, and abounding in goodness and truth ...' (Exodus 34:6–7). It is on the basis of this revelation echoed in this petition that David is able to pray and ask God's forgiveness (see Psalm 103). The cross of Jesus impresses upon us even more clearly God's covenant goodness and love in forgiving and forgetting as we humble ourselves and confess our sins (see 1 John 1:9).

God's covenant love (verses 8–15)

Having drawn attention to God's character, David now stops to reflect on these attributes in the following verses. It serves as a kind of hymn of praise. He draws in people like himself who recognise they are failures. They are sinners, but they are sinners who have repented; they are the 'humble poor' who believe and seek to live as true members of God's covenant community, showing God the respect of which he is worthy. Do you belong to this community?

There are two parts to this section, each ends on a personal note (verses 11 and 15). Both halves speak of God's covenant and of being taught by him.

The ways of the Lord *(verses 8–11)*

The Lord, the redeemer of his covenant people acts toward them in a way that is consistent with his character. He is 'good'. Absolute goodness is found in God alone as Jesus insisted (Mark 10:18). He is also 'upright' as Moses indicated in his song (Deuteronomy 32:4). Unlike crooked and twisted Israel (Deuteronomy 32:5), the Lord is completely straight in his dealings with us. Again, unlike us, he is good in that he is kind and understanding toward those who are opposed to him.

How amazing! He teaches 'sinners', people who are in rebellion against his rule. He instructs them concerning his revealed will. This is how we become Christians in the first place. We hear or read God's Word in the gospel. The good news concerning Jesus Christ is God's way for us, in fact, Jesus is the only way to God and eternal life (John 14:6). Apollos had been instructed in 'the way of the Lord' but Aquila and Priscilla explained to him 'the way of God' more accurately (Acts 18:24–26). The early disciples of Jesus in Acts are often referred to as 'followers of the Way' (Acts 9:2; 19:9,23; 22:4; 24:14,22). It is 'the way of salvation' (Acts 16:17). There are only two ways, the way of life and the way of death (see Deuteronomy 30:19; Proverbs 2; Psalm 1; Matthew 7:13–14).

Sadly, we still sin as believers and yet the Lord continues to show kindness. He leads (or 'guides'; it is the same verb in verse 5) those who have a 'humble', repentant spirit, and 'teaches' them in the way that is right ('justice', verse 9).

The psalm continues to give expression to the Lord's good and upright nature. Two terms closely associated with God's covenant are 'mercy' (or 'steadfast love'; see verse 6) and 'truth' (or 'faithfulness'). They sum up 'All the paths of the Lord' (verse 10), in other words, all the ways the Lord has dealt with his people since entering into that special agreement with them at Sinai. With those who keep the covenant requirements ('testimonies'), God remains true to his promises. As Spurgeon crisply states, 'Keepers of the covenant shall be kept by the covenant'.

Within the context of God's undying love for his people there is 'pardon' for covenant members who confess their sins (verse 11). David pauses at this point and recalls again his sins (see verse 7), recognising the serious nature of his 'iniquity'. He is guilty of 'great' sin (see Psalm 19:13), and he cries out to the one who alone can grant the remission of sins. He pleads the Lord's reputation—'For your name's sake' (see Psalm 23:3). This is his nature; his name is 'merciful and gracious, long-suffering and abounding in goodness and truth ... forgiving iniquity ... by no means clearing the guilty' (Exodus 34:5-7). The sacrificial offerings pointed to the righteous way God had in mind for guilty sinners to be pardoned. They pointed to Christ's death on the cross where he bore the punishment of all who look to him for salvation.

The blessings of the Lord (verses 12–15)

These verses describe the benefits that come to the humble penitent people who are concerned to follow God's ways rather than the rebellious road to destruction. These are now described as those who 'fear' God, a description that envelops this second part of David's hymn in praise of God (verses 12,14). The fear of the Lord is the beginning of wisdom and knowledge (see Psalm 111:10; Proverbs 1:7). It expresses not a state of terror or anxiety but an attitude of reverence, love and trust, a desire to please and serve him and not to defame his name.

The question 'Who is the man who fears the LORD?' (verse 12) is not answered by giving further descriptions of the godly (see Psalm 24:3-6), but indirectly through recounting the blessings that come to them.

The first blessing is the type of guidance that really matters. We are encouraged to believe that when we submit to his revealed will in the Bible, the Spirit of God will help us make right decisions. Some take God as the subject of 'he chooses' (verse 12) but as in Psalm 119:30 it refers to the choices made by the one who reveres God. The meaning is that God will so teach his people that they will make choices that are consistent with their commitment to the Lord. Many believers are often worried whether they have made the right decision from various good options, especially when the going gets tough, instead of realising that God desires them to live with that choice to his glory. Our concern should be that when decisions are made they are in line with what God has taught us in his Word by his Spirit.

A further blessing associated with God's covenant promises both to Abraham and the Israelite nation relate to life in the land of promise. The good LORD (verse 8) promises 'good' ('prosperity', verse 13). All kinds of material and spiritual good are included. Those who seek the Lord 'shall not lack any good' (Psalm 34:10). The peaceful, contented life is portrayed in the old Sinai covenant in very concrete down-to-earth terms, where each person in the country lives safely 'under his vine and his fig tree' (1 Kings 4:25; Micah 4:4). It also includes the joy of knowing that through their offspring the future inheritance in Canaan ('inherit the earth')[48] is assured (see Genesis 17:8; Deuteronomy 4:1). The covenant blessing of peace and prosperity associated with Canaan becomes a token or type of the eternal security associated with the new earth. For Abraham, Isaac and Jacob, Canaan was the physical guarantee of that future 'earth' (see Hebrews 11:8-10,13-16). It is developed by Jesus in the Beatitudes (Matthew 5:5) and by Paul in his quotation from the Fifth Commandment (Ephesians 6:1-3) and in his reference to Abraham's offspring inheriting the whole world (Romans 4:13).

The final blessing takes further the blessing of verse 12. The Lord's 'covenant' blessings include his 'secret' counsel (verse 14). The Lord's 'secret counsel is with the upright' (Proverbs 3:32). Later, the same word is used to describe the confidences that David shared with a close friend who turned traitor (Psalm 55:14). God shares his mind and purpose with those who reverence him. Abraham is called God's friend (1 Samuel 41:8; 2 Chronicles 20:7; James 2:23) and becomes one of the Lord's confidants (Genesis 18:17). Similarly, Jesus calls his disciples 'my friends', promising to make known to them the Father's mind if they do his commandments (John 15:14-15). By his Spirit the Lord reveals to us from the Bible the thoughts he has concerning his people, to give them 'a future and a hope' (Jeremiah 29:11).

Being in such a blessed and privileged position means that David can look up to the Lord with confidence and expectancy (verse 15), assured that he will deliver him from present hostile opposition and lead him on into a glorious future. The 'net' is a favourite figure of speech taken from the hunting world to describe the crafty plotting of an enemy (verse 15; see Psalm 9:15). Like verse 11, this part of the psalm ends on a more personal note (verse 15) and prepares us for the return to prayer in the closing section.

Seeking the LORD's look (verses 16–22)
With his eyes ever toward the Lord (see verse 15) David continues his prayer which now takes on a more urgent note. Like David we are to pour out our cares and concerns knowing that the Lord cares for those who love him (1 Peter 5:7) and is the only one who can save us from ourselves and our foes.

> What a friend we have in Jesus
> All our sins and griefs to bear ...

David's concerns
There is a build-up of words to convey David's situation. He speaks of being lonely ('desolate') and weak ('afflicted', verse 16) especially as the enemies are numerous and powerful (see verse 19), in 'deep anguish' ('an enlarged heart of trouble') and feeling pressured ('distresses') (verse 17), and in 'affliction' and 'pain' (verse 18).

The causes of his concern
These troubles have two main causes—his 'sins' and 'enemies' who have a violent hatred of him (verses 18b–19). These are two specifics that still trouble the believer. Personal sin afflicts God's people and can be the cause of suffering though not always, as we know from Job's experience. Satan and all his dark powers also attack with malicious hatred and Job certainly felt that.

David's fervent cries
Because we are not fighting against 'flesh and blood' but principalities, powers and the 'rulers of darkness' (Ephesians 6:12) the same fervency in prayer is needed that we find in David's appeal to God. He calls out:

1. 'Turn ... and have mercy (verse 16). Literally he prays 'Face toward me ... and be gracious to me', which is a very graphic way of expressing the need of God's unmerited favour (see Psalm 4:6) and is reminiscent

of the priestly benediction, 'The Lord make his face shine upon you and be gracious to you' (Numbers 6:25).

2. 'Bring me out' (verse 17).[49]

3. 'Look ... and forgive' (verse 18). Here the more usual word for 'forgive' (literally 'take away') is found in place of the less common word used in verse 11 ('pardon'). Sin is likened to a burden too heavy to bear, a picture taken up by John Bunyan in his famous *Pilgrim's Progress*.

4. 'Consider' (verse 19), which in the original is exactly the same word as in the previous verse. David prays first for God to 'look' at his trouble in terms of his sins and what they have caused and then to look at his enemies who have caused him more trouble.

5. 'Keep ... and deliver me' (verse 20).

6. 'Let me not be ashamed' (verse 20).

As the psalm draws to a close we are reminded of David's first concerns—'ashamed' (verse 20; see verses 2–3), 'trust' (verse 20; verse 1–2) and 'wait' (verse 21; see verses 3,5). The word for 'trust' here means to 'seek refuge in' (see Psalm 2:12), a more graphic way of expressing the usual word found in verse 2.

Perseverance and hope

Although there are psalms that appeal to David's own 'integrity' and 'uprightness' (see 7:8; 26:1,11; 36:10), that is far from David's mind in verse 21. As a repentant sinner before God he is not pleading anything in himself. As the second half of the verse suggests he is not trusting to his own human qualities but those divine characteristics that act like bodyguards to preserve him through all his troubles. He has already testified that the LORD is 'upright' (verse 8). These two divine attributes guarding God's servant remind us of 'goodness and mercy' in Psalm 23:6 and God's light and truth in Psalm 43:3. Waiting for God does not mean forlorn inactivity but a sure hope in God's ability to fulfil his promises enabling the believer to go forward confidently.

The LORD's redeemed people

This final verse is not an added extra by a later editor, but part of the psalm's original design as we saw from the irregularities of the alphabetic pattern. There are times when David speaks for his LORD, the Messiah, as in Psalm 22. On other occasions he can speak on behalf of the LORD's people, the Israel of God, as indicated in the closing verse of this psalm. God's covenant applies to all God's people and what was experienced in the life of David was expressive of the sufferings, longings and hopes of the whole Israel of God whether in Old Testament or New Testament times. The individualism seen in so much of the modern western world and that has infiltrated large sectors of the church is foreign to the biblical perspective. We are reminded that we belong to the whole family of God.

David's 'troubles' (verse 17) are the 'troubles' of all God's people (verse 22). Israel's troubles include sin and its effect and all the continuing activities of the 'snake' and his offspring (see Genesis 3). We can say therefore that the 'redemptive language may anticipate Psalm 130:7–8'.[50] It looks with anticipation to the final day of redemption when all our troubles will be finally removed and God's people will be saved to sin no more. God's people are already redeemed by the blood of Christ but we wait expectantly for the redemption of our bodies and the renewal of all things.

Psalm 26

An Appeal to the Supreme Court

This psalm is not the plea of a self-righteous person. It is not like the prayer in Jesus' parable of the Pharisee and Tax Collector where Jesus criticises those who trusted in themselves that they were righteous and despised others (Luke 18:9-14). David is not seeking to exalt himself nor is he showing an arrogant spirit toward others. It is similar to Psalms 7 and 17 in that it urges God, in its opening words, to act on David's behalf and vindicate him (see Psalms 7:8; 17:1-2) and David's quiet confidence in God and plea for God to redeem and be gracious fits well with the previous psalm (verses 1,11; Psalm 25:16,22). Unlike Psalm 25 with its confession of past sins, the stress in this psalm is on David's moral and religious integrity. There are echoes of Psalm 1 in verses 4 and 5 and it calls to mind the kind of people who can approach God in worship as in Psalms 15 and 24. David's openness to God's scrutiny is reminiscent of Psalm 139. The reference to God's dwelling place prepares us for further links with the sanctuary in the following two psalms (verses 6-8; see Psalms 27:4-6; 28:2).

In Psalm 25 David is afraid of being put to shame and asks the Lord to teach him his ways and to lead him in God's truth whereas in this psalm he is able to confess that he has walked in that truth.

Plea for vindication (verses 1-2)

David has nothing to hide as he comes before God in prayer. He has a clear conscience and is prepared for God to examine him. The psalm suggests that accusations have been made against David just as they would be made against the Messiah himself. Other psalms indicate how foes were continually making false allegations. David therefore makes this plea for God to 'judge' ('vindicate') him and 'redeem' him (verses 1,11). These are not the words of a proud, self-satisfied and self-confident person. As in Psalm 7:8 we are to think of a courthouse scene where David is appealing to a judge, who has all the evidence, to decide in his favour. Jesus also looked to God his Father to vindicate him (1 Peter 2:21-23). True Christians in all ages have also had false charges made against them but we are to follow the example set by our Lord and so can turn to God using these words of David.

David makes three statements to back up his plea. First, he claims to have 'walked in my integrity'. The word 'integrity' is often translated 'blameless' (see Genesis 17:1). David is not claiming sinless perfection but he is indicating that he is living an honest life where there have been no obvious moral blemishes. In addition, he has 'trusted in the LORD' which suggests that he has looked to the Lord and not to other gods or to his own military might in time of need. The third verb 'slip' is not a common word (see Psalms 18:36; 37:31) and suggests that the path through life is tricky and therefore it is easy to lose one's footing. To be forewarned is to be forearmed. (see Psalm 17:1-5) .

Such claims concerning his moral integrity and religious devotion to God are open for God to investigate. Three further verbs are used in the request for God to test him. David prays that the Lord would 'examine' in the sense of to test for purity as gold is tested (see Zechariah 13:9). He then asks the Lord to 'prove' him suggesting that God would test him as he did Abraham (Genesis 22:1). Finally, he asks the Lord to 'try' him in the sense of to refine his inner self ('mind', literally 'kidneys', and 'heart'; see Psalm 7:9) as precious metals are smelted in the fire for impurity (see Psalms 12:6; 139:23). By asking God to test him in this way he is really saying: 'Lord, you know all things, you know that I have been faithful to you'. It reminds us of Peter's response to Jesus' searching questions: 'Lord, you know all things; you know that I love you' (John 21:17).

Basis for vindication (verses 3–8)

God's 'unfailing love' ('loving-kindness' but often translated 'mercy')
and 'truth' (or 'faithfulness') form a pair that are closely associated
with God's revelation of himself at the time of the exodus (Exodus
34:6; see Psalm 25:10). God calls his people to show the same moral
characteristics (Proverbs 3:3; 16:6). They stand in contrast to the
selfishness and infidelity of the wicked.

David's moral commitment (verses 3–5)

Having God's steadfast love ever before him inspires him in his own
loving commitment to God to go on living in a way that follows in
the path of God's truthfulness and reliability (verse 3). This means on
the negative side a refusal to be drawn into the thinking and lifestyles
of the wicked. As in Psalm 1 a sharp distinction is made between
people like David who walk in God's paths of truthfulness and the
'wicked' (verse 5) who are also described as 'idolatrous mortals' (verse
4; literally 'men of vanity' or 'emptiness'; see Psalm 119:37), 'hypocrites'
(or 'deceivers') and 'evildoers'. He will not 'sit' with them in the sense
of enjoying their company. Those who are committed to God and find
their home among God's faithful people will be resolutely opposed to
the 'congregation of evildoers' (verse 5; see verse 12; Psalm 64:2).

While we are to mix with non-Christians to bring God's love to them,
this must be accompanied by a decisive repudiation of their immoral
lifestyles and a refusal to participate in their worldly way of thinking
and acting. We are to be like Jesus who was in the world but not of it.
He came alongside people and was concerned for their eternal well-
being.

David's religious commitment (verses 6–8)

As he comes before God to the tabernacle he professes his innocence
in words reminiscent of the 'clean hands' of Psalm 24:4. There was a
hand-washing ceremony ordained by God in situations that demanded
public declarations of personal innocence (Deuteronomy 21:6; see
Matthew 27:24). We also find that the priests were required to wash
their hands and feet before fulfilling their duties in the tabernacle
(Exodus 30:17–21). These ceremonial rituals provide the imagery for
David's words here but it does not mean that he literally washed
his hands in a special ceremony (see Psalm 73:13). His hands are
not stained with the blood of innocent people and so he can

approach God's altar to offer his sacrifices. These thank offerings are accompanied by words of testimony to God's goodness but he also takes the opportunity to tell of God's awesome deeds, especially those connected with the exodus (see Psalm 9:1).

From hating or opposing the congregation of the evildoers he declares his love for God's 'habitation' (verse 8). When not used of God's heavenly or earthly home or of God as his people's refuge (Psalms 68:5; 71:3; 91:9), the term refers to an animal's den (Jeremiah 10:22). David's love for this special 'house' is because of its association with the revelation of God's stunning greatness. The 'glory' that was revealed to Moses on Mount Sinai descended on the tabernacle in the wilderness as it was later to do when Solomon's temple was completed (Exodus 33:18-34:8; 40:34-35; 1 Kings 8:11). It is not so much the 'place' itself that David loves as the God whose presence is associated with it. The word for 'dwells' (literally 'dwelling place' or 'tabernacle') is akin to the later Jewish term 'shekinah' used to convey the revelation of this divine glory. John expresses the reality to which the glory cloud pointed when he relates how the 'Word became flesh and dwelt (tabernacled) among us' (John 1:14).

Plea to be spared the fate of the wicked (verses 9-11)
David returns to prayer as he considers the fate that awaits 'sinners' and those who shed innocent blood. It may well be that David has been accused falsely of belonging to such a group who hatch plots and use bribes to achieve their ends (verses 9-10). Again he protests his innocence and confesses his determination to continue in the path he had been following—'I will walk in my integrity' (verse 11; see verse 1). He throws himself completely on God's unmerited favour ('be merciful' or better 'be gracious') and prays that he would 'redeem' him by acting like a next of kin to rescue him from his plight.

A statement of confidence (verses 12)
This verse along with verse 11 brings us back to where David started in verse 1 and forms a frame around the psalm. It also completes the link with Psalm 1 in that we have had references to walking and sitting and now David speaks of standing (Psalm 1:1). He is assured that the God who has kept him will not allow his feet to stumble. By living in the way that God has directed he knows that he stands on level ground and can worship the Lord on bended knee ('bless') in

the great congregation (the plural word 'congregations' is a Hebrew way of describing greatness and fulness) with no hidden secrets or unconfessed sins. God grant that in our communal worship we are not hypocrites.

Psalm 27

Messiah's Confidence and Concerns

This is another of those memorable psalms that Christians have found so comforting in times of distress and discomfort. It forms one of a clutch of 'of David' psalms (Psalms 25–28)[51] which combine expressions of trust (verses 1-6) with calls for help (verses 7-14). As with the previous psalm it delights in God's house (verses 4-5; see Psalm 26:6-8) and recognises the importance of the 'level' place (verse 11 see Psalm 26:12). The unique feature of this psalm is that instead of expressions of confidence following the pleas for help, the opposite is the case. This has led some to think that two separate psalms have been united (see Psalms 9 and 10). On the other hand, key terms and phrases appear in both halves suggesting that the psalm was one from the start. The expressions of assurance in the first part do not mean that all David's concerns have melted away and made him self-reliant and that is why he continues to makes his requests known to God.

Confidence in the LORD (verses 1-6)

Oxford University, from at least the second half of the 16th century, has had as its motto the opening words of this psalm, indicating the close association between the revelation of God through his Word and the pursuit of knowledge.

The build-up of words expressive of God's goodness along with the rhetorical questions in verse 1 encourage David to go forward with confidence. 'The LORD is my light' (verse 1) for he is the one who dispelled the dark forces of evil associated with David's enemies and the threat of war (see verses 2–3 and 2 Samuel 22:29). 'Light' is here almost synonymous with 'salvation' (see Isaiah 49:6) and speaks of blessing, joy and life that deliverance from enemy attack or physical illness and death brings (see Psalm 18:28; 56:13; 97:11). 'God is light' (1 John 1:5; Psalm 104:2) and the Bible associates God's light with the glory of his presence and grace (Isaiah 9:2–7) to guard, guide and give light to his people (Exodus 13:21–22; 14:19–20; Isaiah 42:16). It also expresses the glorious purity of his moral holiness (Isaiah 4:3–6; 6:1–5; 1 Timothy 6:16), and the revelation of his truth (Psalms 19:8; 119:105,130; Proverbs 6:23; John 12:35–36). Darkness, on the other hand, signifies judgment, error, ignorance and evil, and is often associated with suffering and death (Exodus 10:21–23; Job 18:5–6; Isaiah 8:19–22; Zephaniah 1:15; John 3:19–20). Jesus said, 'I am the light of the world. He who follows me shall not walk in darkness, but have the light of life' (John 8:12). It is 'the God who commanded light to shine out of darkness who has shone in our hearts to give the light of the knowledge of the glory of God in the face of Jesus Christ' (2 Corinthians 4:6).

While 'salvation' in the Old Testament often concerns the rescuing of God's people from physical deliverances of various kinds, there is a more fundamental and ultimate end in view, namely, the rescuing of a world estranged from God. Great though the deliverance of God's people from Egyptian slavery was, it was but a preview and foretaste of something bigger and more wonderful that would undo the work of the snake (see Genesis 3:15). Isaiah makes this clear in the second half of his prophecy where he also introduces the Lord's unique Servant Israel, as the world's Saviour from the consequences of its sin (see Isaiah 49:3–6; 52:13–53:12; John 1:29). Such truths come to the surface from time to time in the Psalms not only in those passages where sin is confessed and forgiveness granted but where God's servant David becomes a type of the future Suffering Servant.

The Lord is not only his 'light' and 'salvation', David can also say he is 'the strength of my life' (verse 1). 'Strength' translates a term meaning 'refuge' or 'stronghold'. It implies a place of safety, such as an impregnable rock (see Psalm 31:2) especially in time of war. The word is sometimes translated 'fortress' (see Jeremiah 16:19). David looked for such places when he hid from Saul in the Judean wilderness. Similar metaphors are used in Psalms 9:9 and 18:2 with reference to the Lord's protection of his servant. It is possible that David is thinking here of God's sanctuary as the stronghold (see verse 5).

'Whom shall I fear? ... of whom shall I be afraid?' (verse 1) are questions that David puts to himself for encouragement. Through the Lord's saving, keeping power there is no one to fear. Paul employs similar language to assure believers (Romans 8:31–36). It is good to talk to ourselves in this way to strengthen our faith when we feel dispirited.

There is a further build-up of terms to describe David's 'enemies' in verses 2 and 3. They are the 'wicked', those spoken of in earlier psalms, who have no fear of God and are intent on harming the righteous. David describes them graphically as those who 'eat up my flesh' (verse 2) like wild animals devouring their prey (see Psalms 7:2; 14:4; 17:12). They are like an 'army' besieging a city or engaging in full-scale 'war' (verse 3). David is 'confident' that such 'foes' will not ultimately prevail. His enemies 'stumbled and fell' in previous encounters on account of the Lord's deliverances and he therefore will have no 'fear' however many forces are arrayed against him in the future. David's confidence does not lie in his own abilities or even his own trusting nature but in the living God who acts on behalf of his people.

Our trust is in the same God who acted at Calvary 'that we should be saved from our enemies and from the hand of all who hate us' (Luke 1:71). We are assured that sin shall no longer have dominion over us, that Satan will be crushed under our feet shortly and that 'we are more than conquerors through him who loved us' (Romans 6:14; 8:37; 16:20). James Hannington, the first bishop of Equatorial Africa, on the day before he died a martyr's death, wrote in his journal: 'I am quite broken down and brought low. Comforted by Psalm 27.'[52]

David's confidence is further explained in verses 4 to 6 indicating how the Lord is his stronghold (see verse 1).

'One thing I have desired of the LORD, that will I seek' (verse 4) expresses the psalmist's single-minded aim to know God's special presence and his protective care.

Jesus replied to an anxious Martha, cross at her sister for listening to Jesus instead of helping, 'you are worried and troubled about many things. But one thing is needed, and Mary has chosen that good part ...' (Luke 10:41–42).

David's one all-consuming ambition is spelled out in words

reminiscent of Psalm 23:6. In place of 'goodness and mercy' David desires
to dwell in the LORD's house 'all the days of my life' (verse 4). Whether
the reference is to the tabernacle/temple at Shiloh or in Jerusalem,
David's longing cannot be taken in an entirely literal way. Only those of
the tribe of Levi had the right to live at the place where God ordained to
be especially present among his people under the symbolism of the ark
of the covenant. Though David longed to be present as often as possible
in the Lord's earthly palace that would have been impossible twenty-four
seven. We must therefore understand his language to include a figurative
sense. He desired to enjoy fellowship with God wherever he was but
naturally when he was prevented from attending the tabernacle he
longed to be there too (see Psalms 42:1–4; 63:1–2).

His desire was to gaze at 'the beauty of the LORD' (verse 4). The word
for 'beauty' is a noun meaning 'desirableness, pleasantness'. It is only
found elsewhere in Psalm 90:17 and Zechariah 11:7,10. Moses wished to
see God's glory and the LORD made his 'goodness' to pass before him by
proclaiming his attributes of steadfast love, grace, patience, faithfulness
and justice (Exodus 33:19–34:7). In our own private devotions as well as in
communal worship, is this our over-riding desire, to view our God as he
has revealed his nature and character so spectacularly in the gospel and
particularly in Jesus the unique Son of the Father (John 1:14,18)?

The tabernacle construction had a beauty of its own, likewise
Solomon's temple and later, Herod's temple with which our Lord's
disciples were so impressed (Mark 13:1–2). The pictures, images, altars
and vestments that are often seen in church buildings, meant sincerely
as aids to worship, have a distracting effect as the Reformers were quick
to point out. Calvin reminds us that the earthly tabernacle was made
according to a divine pattern shown to Moses at Sinai (Exodus 25:40).
David encourages us to look with the eye of faith to that spiritual temple
and true worship that Jesus spoke of to the Samaritan woman (see John
4:21–24). The Word, the sacraments and the communal prayers are the
outward ornaments now approved by God under the new covenant by
which the people of God worship together.

The third part of David's desire was 'to inquire in his temple' which
probably means his concern to know God's will. It was the high priest's
ephod containing the Urim and Thumim that often enabled David to
ascertain the guidance he needed during the period when Saul sought
to kill him (see 1 Samuel 23:9–12; 30:7–8).

With the Lord so precious to him, he is assured of the protection to which he has already referred in the opening verses. The Lord provides safety for his people 'in the time of trouble' (verse 5; literally 'in the evil day'). For our 'evil day' we have 'the whole armour of God' (Ephesians 6:13) whereas David speaks of three ways in which God protects him. First, he speaks of God concealing him in his 'booth' ('pavilion') as Jochabed hid her son Moses or Rahab the two spies (Exodus 2:2–3; Joshua 2:4).[53] Then he thinks of God hiding him under the 'covering' or 'secret place' of his 'tabernacle', almost like a place of asylum as when Adonijah fled from Solomon to the horns of the altar (1 Kings 1:50–53). Finally, David sees himself lifted up 'high upon a rock' for safety which takes us back to the Lord as his 'stronghold' (verse 1) and to the idea of the Lord as his 'rock' (see Psalm 28:1). This final image may not be so unrelated to the previous ones when we consider that the tabernacle was associated with the hill of Zion (see Psalms 3:4; 61:1–4).

Knowing this kind of protection David has his head 'lifted up' above all his enemies (verse 6; see Psalm 3:3) and with shouts of joy and triumph (the emphasis of the verb is on shouting) can offer sacrifice in God's tabernacle, singing and making music to the Lord. As God's people today we are to sing and make melody to the Lord as we offer our sacrifices of praise and thanksgiving (Ephesians 5:19–20; Hebrews 13:15). Just as victory shouts and songs were sung after the defeat of Pharaoh's forces so we find when all the enemies of God and his people have fallen, heaven exults with a loud voice (Revelation 19:1). We can lift up our heads even when the times are perplexing and people are fainting with fear and foreboding (see Luke 21:28), because we have 'fled for refuge to lay hold of the hope set before us' (see Hebrews 6:18).

Calling to the LORD (verses 7–14)

Having fortified himself with many reasons for confidence, David now utters this cry for help in a time of great need. The opening words introduce his prayer, pleading that God would first 'Hear' his cry, then 'Have mercy' and thus 'answer' him (verse 7).

'Seek my face' (verse 8; see Psalm 24:6) is God's invitation to all his people (see Authorised Version 'Seek ye …') which David repeats back to God before declaring 'Your face, LORD, I will seek'. From the time of Moses the Lord had encouraged his people to seek 'admission to his presence for the purpose of asking a favour' (Alexander; see Deuteronomy 4:29). 'True prayer is never a presumptuous approach to God, but rather a response to His gracious initiative.'[54]

The second line of verse 9 helps to clarify the first line and both express powerfully the hope of acceptance and favourable action (see Psalm 4:6b). The pictures are familiar to us. When someone's face turns from us it means the person is displeased with us. Or perhaps we have had the experience of being dismissed from the presence of someone angry with us. Recognising that the Lord has been his help in the past he appeals to his saviour God (see Psalm 18:46) not to 'leave' or 'forsake' him. Can you say with David that God is 'my help' and 'my salvation'?

When parents, whose natural instincts are to care for their offspring, forsake their children, it means total abandonment (see Psalm 38:11). With verses 4 and 5 in mind David is assured that 'the LORD will take care of me' (verse 10) or better 'the LORD will take me in'. The Lord's loving care of his people is over and above the best that human parents can show (see Psalm 103:13; Isaiah 49:15). This is of particular relevance to converts to Christ who have been ostracised by their families and denied access to their own homes.

The LORD's way, in this context, is not his revealed word as in Psalm 119 but his providential guidance leading David in a 'smooth', level way (see Psalm 26:12) as distinct from a rough and dangerous one. David does not wish his 'enemies' (literally 'my watchers') to gloat over any falls. How often is it the case that committed Christians are particularly watched by the ungodly who are frequently the first to pour scorn on Christians when they do not live up to expectations. How we need to pray like David that such enemies will not have any cause to sneer and dishonour our Saviour.

David's enemies are now termed 'my adversaries' (verse 12) who are more specifically called 'false witnesses' whose testimonies ('will' or 'heart's desire') could result in a death sentence. Luke describes Saul's persecuting zeal as 'breathing threats and murder against the disciples of the Lord'. Nehemiah also had to contend with false accusations from enemies like Sanballat (Nehemiah 6:5–9). What has been true of God's people through the ages comes to a head in the experience of the Lord himself (see Mark 14:55–59).

The final confession of trust is incomplete but what is missing is clearly implied as the English translations make clear—'I would have lost heart' (verse 13; see Psalm 119:92 for the complete sentence).[55] The effect is to make the abbreviated statement 'unless I had believed ...' even more emphatic. We could then translate as: 'I certainly believe I will see ...'. 'In the land of the living' (see Psalm 52:5; Isaiah 53:8) has reference to this earthly life as opposed to 'the land of darkness and the shadow of death' (Job 10:21). David is confident he will survive physically to see what the eye of faith desired (see verse 4), namely, 'the goodness of the LORD'. God's 'goodness' (see Psalm 23:6) includes earthly and spiritual blessings that flow from God's gracious nature associated with his covenant name—'the LORD' (Jehovah/Yahweh).

The final exhortation (verse 14) is not an address to others for the verb is in the singular, unless we assume that it is a call to the nation collectively. The psalm closes as it opened with David, ever aware of his frailty, encouraging himself in anticipation of further troubles. He is not gritting his teeth, convincing himself that he is prepared for whatever may happen next with Stoic determination. The repetition of 'Wait on the LORD' indicates David's own powerlessness but also where his faith and hope rest. In the light of past gracious interventions by God, he urges himself to be of 'good courage' (see Deuteronomy 31:7) assured that the Lord will strengthen him. The Lord himself states, 'In quietness and confidence shall be your strength' (Isaiah 30:15).

Learning from Jesus

The experience of David expressed in this psalm is God's word to us. First, we see David as a type of Christ. The psalm points us to the relationship that Jesus had with God his Father, his complete trust in him and his desire for him. The prospect of God hiding his face from him and of experiencing his anger was one over which Jesus agonized in Gethsemane. Like David he 'offered up prayers and supplications with vehement cries and tears to him who was able to save him from death, and was heard because of his godly fear' (Hebrews 5:7). Though false witnesses spoke against him and he was delivered into wicked hands, Jesus was not delivered over to their will. He suffered and died according to God's will, was cut off from 'the land of the living' yet rose triumphant and exalted (verse 12-13; see Isaiah 52:13-53:12; Acts 2:23-24). All through his life and death Christ waited for the Lord to vindicate him.

In all this we are taught how to trust the Lord in the ups and downs of life, confident that the Lord will never let us down.

'Fear Him, ye saints, and you will then
Have nothing else to fear'.[56]

Psalm 28

Messiah's Supplication and Song

I n this last of a group of psalms headed by 'of David' (see Psalm 26) and linked by word associations to the previous two, confidence *follows* David's cries for help, unlike Psalm 27 where the opposite is the case. The psalm's change of mood half way through is a feature of these biblical prayers. The assurance that God has heard his 'supplications' is similar to Psalm 6. David's personal needs in the first half of the psalm are seen by the end to be part of a much bigger concern that involves God's people as a whole. As in the previous psalms David's experiences become symbolic of the more intense trials and difficulties that Jesus endured so that his words can be more readily appreciated on the lips of the Saviour. It is also true that David's prayer is one that believers can make their own.

Appeal to the LORD (verses 1-5)

We do not know the nature of his distress, but the sense of urgency is apparent as David calls out to the Lord for help.

The silence of God (verses 1–2)

David seeks an audience with the LORD (Yahweh/Jehovah) but he seems to be getting nowhere. 'Rock' is an old name for God (see Deuteronomy 32:4; 1 Samuel 2:2; Psalm 18:2; 62:6) and suggests both power and reliability. But this firm foundation of all his hopes is 'silent' (see Psalm 35:22). It adds to his anguish. If God refuses to answer, the psalmist will become 'like those who go down to the pit' (verse 1; see Psalm 22:29 'go down to the dust'; Job 7:9 'goes down to sheol'). The word 'pit' can mean a hole in the ground, a cistern or a dungeon (Leviticus 11:36; Isaiah 24:22) but often it is associated with death or 'sheol' (see Psalm 30:3). David pictures himself as being in the realm of the dead where all is silent (see Psalm 94:17; 143:7). It speaks of death under the wrath of God (see verse 3; Psalm 88:6-7; Isaiah 14:15; Ezekiel 32:23,29; Luke 16:26). The sense of God-forsakenness is similar to Psalm 22:1, something our Lord experienced during those three hours of silence and darkness.

Whether in a standing or kneeling position, hands raised in supplication[57] is expressive of a humble, self-despairing heart cry for God to favour him (see 1 Timothy 2:8). His prayer is directed to the earthly replica of God's heavenly home. It is described as the 'holy sanctuary' (verse 2). This is not related, as was thought, to God's 'word' (as in Authorised Version 'oracle') but is a reference to the inner part of the tabernacle/temple, 'the holy of holies' (1 Kings 6:5,16; 7:49; 8:6,8; 2 Chronicles 3:16). In Solomon's dedicatory prayer over the newly erected temple he calls on the Lord to hear the prayers directed toward this place of worship (1 Kings 8:30,48). This is what we find Daniel doing in exile even when the temple had been destroyed (Daniel 6:10). By his atoning death on the cross, Christ has put an end to the need for an earthly place of sacrifice, and we now look to him who has entered the real inner sanctum.

A cry for justice (verses 3-5)

As in Psalm 26:9, David is concerned that justice is seen to be done. He does not belong with the hypocrites and those who do evil (see Psalm 26:4-5) and therefore he does not wish to be dragged away to the fate that the ungodly deserve (verse 3; see 'pit' in verse 1). The word for 'wicked' is sometimes translated 'ungodly' as in Psalm 1. They are associated with the 'workers of iniquity' (verse 3) who are the enemies of God and his people. Sometimes they can appear friendly but they harbour evil intentions (Psalm 12:2). The Lord speaks of such people, and prophets like Jeremiah often suffered under their deceitful practices (Jeremiah 9:8; 42:1-6; 43:1-3).

David was always reticent to take the law into his own hands or to seek personal revenge. Once he was tempted to be vindictive in the case of Nabal who treated him harshly when he asked for food (1 Samuel 25:2–35). Here David hands the matter over to the Lord who said, 'Vengeance is mine, and recompense' (Deuteronomy 32:35). The threefold use of 'according to' (verse 4) indicates his call for the punishment to fit the crime. This is also true of the phrase 'render to them what they deserve' (verse 4). It is to the God of justice and fairness that he looks and that is where we must turn when righteous anger burns at the injustices and evils of our day. In the same way Jesus encourages those who trust him to look to the Lord for justice and vindication (Luke 18:1–8). We are urged to 'repay no one evil for evil', in so far as it depends on us to 'live peaceably with all', and never to avenge ourselves but to leave it to the wrath of God (Romans 12:17–19).

The activity of the hypocrites ('their deeds') and 'the work of their hands' are contrasted with the 'the operation ('the work') of his hands' and 'the works ('the deeds') of the LORD' (verses 4–5).[58] Actions reveal much about the kind of person doing them. Jesus said that by their fruits the false are known (Matthew 7:15–20). Israel was punished on account of their evil deeds, which revealed they had forsaken the Lord (Deuteronomy 28:20). We shall all be judged by our works (Matthew 16:27; Revelation 20:12–13) but we cannot be saved by our works (Ephesians 2:8–10). We are saved by God's good work in Christ. Having no 'regard' for 'the works of the LORD nor the operation of his hands' (verse 5), particularly in redemption and judgment, only adds to their guilt.

These ungodly people who should know better deserve to be destroyed, never to be seen again and David is assured that this will be so—'He shall destroy them and not build them up again' (verse 5). The verbs 'destroy' (literally 'tear down') and 'build up' are found together frequently in Jeremiah (see 1:10; 24:6; 31:28; 42:10; 45:4). But whereas the Lord through Jeremiah holds out the possibility of building up again what was torn down, no hope is offered here. There is a final day of judgment when the wicked will be for ever put down. At his Second Coming the Lord Jesus will be revealed 'in flaming fire taking vengeance on those who do not know God, and on those who do not obey the gospel of our Lord Jesus Christ. These shall be punished with everlasting destruction ...' (2 Thessalonians 1:7–9). While the day of grace is still with us we are urged to turn to God and trust his Son,

Jesus the Messiah, who alone can deliver us from the wrath to come
(1 Thessalonians 1:9:10).

Praise and prayer (verses 6–9)

An abrupt change of mood occurs at this point. Some have wondered
whether David has received a prophetic word but this need not be the
case. Already he is certain that the ungodly will eventually be punished
(see verse 5 and Psalm 1:6). He now has that inner conviction from God
that he is not silent and has heard David's prayer.

Thanksgiving for answered prayer (verses 6–7)

'Blessed be the LORD' (verse 6) is the first of many such expressions in
the psalms calling for reverent, submissive worship (see Psalm 31:21).
The phrase is used to bring the first four sections of the Psalter to
a close (Psalms 41:13; 72:18; 89:52; 106:48). To 'bless' implies bowing
the knee in submissive worship (see Psalm 16:7). The grace that he
has pleaded for in verse 2 ('Hear the voice of my supplications') he
is assured will be granted (verse 6: 'he has heard the voice of my
supplications').

His trust is in the Lord, whom he describes as 'my strength' (verse
7) and 'my shield' (see Psalm 3:3). Having experienced the Lord's 'help'
he not only trusts but 'exults' or 'greatly rejoices' and gives thanks to
him with his 'song'. There are echoes of Moses' song at the Red Sea
deliverance (see Exodus 15:2–3). 'My heart' (verse 7) is used twice to
express that his whole being is taken up with God unlike the wicked
who 'speak evil in their hearts' (see verse 3).

Prayer for God's people (verses 8–9)

The experience of answered prayer leads David to pray for his people.
The Lord who is his strength is 'their strength' too.[59] He is not only
David's 'shield' but his 'saving refuge' (verse 8; literally, 'the stronghold
or fortress of salvation'; see Psalm 27:1). We are also reminded that
David is the Lord's 'anointed' (verse 8; see Psalm 2:2).

As the Lord's appointed ruler of his people, David acknowledges
that God is the ultimate ruler and deliverer of his people. In place of
the curses that 'the wicked' deserve (see verse 4) he calls for blessing
on God's people whom he describes as his special possession ('your
inheritance', verse 9; see Psalm 33:12; Exodus 34:9; Deuteronomy 9:29).
'It is as right to pray for the overthrow of the wicked as it is to pray

for the blessing of the church.' (Motyer). In both instances our chief concern must be for God's honour not our selfish satisfaction.

The prayer recalls again expressions relating to the exodus and the wilderness by calling the Lord their strength, their salvation and his people his inheritance. The final petition introduces a pastoral note that is again reminiscent of the exodus experience. The Lord is not only David's shepherd (Psalm 23:1) he is Israel's shepherd too, and as he carried them ('bear them up', verse 9) through the wilderness (see Exodus 19:4; Isaiah 63:9) so David prays that he will continue to do so for ever.

Isaiah prophesied the coming of the LORD who would 'feed his flock like a shepherd ... gather the lambs with his arm, and carry them in his bosom' (Isaiah 40:11). This is our good shepherd who is both the Lord's anointed and David's Lord and ours. He is the God-Man Christ Jesus who prayed with strong cries and tears, who looked to God for vindication when he was taken away with the wicked and experienced the ultimate curse for the sake of others, who gave thanks that his prayers were heard and continues to intercede for and uphold his people for ever.

Psalm 29

The Voice of the Victorious King of Glory

Even with all our scientific knowledge there is something terrifyingly awesome about an electric storm. Against the background of Canaanite Baal worship to which Israel was so frequently attracted, David demonstrates God's rule over the forces of nature by his powerful word. He is the supreme judge and the one who blesses his people. We are urged to acknowledge his stunning importance. As in Psalms 8 and 19, the LORD (Jehovah/Yahweh), the God of redemption, is the one whose glory is revealed in his creation.

The poem picks up words and ideas from the previous psalm. Not only does it end in a similar way with strength and blessing for God's people (see verse 11 and Psalm 28:8-9) but 'the voice' of David's pleas for mercy set against the background of God's silence (Psalm 28:2,6) is answered by the sevenfold thunderous 'voice of the Lord' (see verses 3-9).

Call to worship (verses 1-2)
This 'Psalm of David' opens with an example in Hebrew poetry of climatic or staircase parallelism, where the first line is held in suspense until another line or lines add the crucial point. The first line is 'Give

to the Lord ...', with a second line providing a further step to complete the thought 'Give to the Lord glory and strength' (verse 1).

In what way can 'glory' and 'strength' be given to 'the God of glory' (verse 3) who gives strength to his people (verse 11)? 'Give' is used in the sense of 'ascribe'. By recognising and praising God's splendour and might that God 'is pleased to interpret as a gift to him' (Matthew Henry). In addition, any glory, honour, influence and power that human rulers or heavenly beings may have must be acknowledged as coming from God. This is the idea in the vision of the kings of the earth bringing their glory and honour into the heavenly city (Revelation 21:24).

The call to worship is addressed to the 'mighty ones' (verse 1). This might be the correct understanding of the Hebrew phrase 'sons of gods' (*elim*), although most commentators now suggest 'heavenly beings'. Angels seem to be in mind when the phrase occurs again in Psalm 89:6. It is similar to 'sons of God' (*elohim*) in Job 1:6; 2:1; 38:7 where it certainly means the divine beings that surround God's heavenly throne. We have seen how the term for God or gods (*elohim*) can be used of angels in Psalm 8:5. One other possibility is that it refers to human rulers who have their angelic counterparts in the heavenly realm (see Psalm 82:1,6 and perhaps Genesis 6:2,4; Isaiah 14:4–20; Daniel 10:13,20)—what Paul describes as the principalities and powers, both good and bad (Ephesians 1:21; 3:10; 6:12). Whether human or supernatural, everyone, including those in positions of authority, must bow to the supreme ruler and acknowledge his worth (see verses 9–10).

The 'glory due to his name' (verse 2) is that which belongs to him as God. The stunning splendour and importance of the one great Reality must be rightly appreciated, confessed and celebrated. All that God has revealed of his nature and character in his word and works displays his glory. Recognising and expressing this in prayer and song is part of true worship (see Psalm 5:11 for God's 'name'). All earthly and heavenly power is urged to lay aside pride and self-importance and honour God in a way that he deserves.

The term for 'worship' (verse 2) in the original means 'bow down', 'prostrate oneself'. People of the East, even today, show respect by bowing low in the presence of someone special. Jacob bowed himself to the ground seven times as he approached his brother Esau and Jacob's sons did the same when they came before their brother Joseph in Egypt (Genesis 33:3; 42:6). While a literal bowing to the ground in God's presence may be in mind here, it is the respectful, submissive attitude of mind and heart that pleases God. A head bowed in prayer can be an appropriate symbolic gesture. The fundamental moral code, however, forbids bowing down to any carved image or human made to represent God (Exodus 20:4–5).

The call is to worship the LORD 'in the beauty of holiness' (verse 2). There is division of opinion over the meaning of this phrase. Some understand it to refer to special clothes ('holy attire') worn by those officiating in the tabernacle (see Leviticus 8:13). If that is so, David makes use of this association to emphasise the need for worshippers to come before God with clean, pure lives as the Book of Leviticus teaches. It is the kind of beauty that Peter encourages wives to exhibit before their husbands (1 Peter 3:3–4).

On the other hand, the context suggests that it is God's holy splendour that is in mind. As we are to bestow on him the glory of his name so we are to worship him in the majesty of his holiness. God is most holy; he is the most wholesome, pure being there is, set apart from everything and everybody else. When we visit great palaces like Hampton Court or Versailles we see the splendour in which rulers of the past lived. The Queen is still referred to as Her Majesty to emphasise her special status. God is the most majestic person of all and this must be remembered by all in authority. The sight that Isaiah had of the LORD and the heavenly worship emphasised God's transcendence, uniqueness and magnificence. It brought his servant to bow low in deep humility and penitence (Isaiah 6:1–5). While the whole of our lives is to be a daily offering of worship to God, there is a place for individual and communal special acts of worship where we join the heavenly beings humbling ourselves before this majestic, holy God. The Lord's Day provides a special opportunity for collective acts of worship in anticipation of the final Day of the LORD.

The words of this call to worship appear again in Psalm 96:7–9 only there they are addressed to people the world over (see also 1 Chronicles 16:29; 2 Chronicles 20:21).

The voice of the LORD (verses 3–9)

This splendid poetic description of a violent thunderstorm (verses 3–4) and its devastating effects (verses 5–9) conveys something of the awesome nature of the living God. As Psalm 19 makes clear God speaks in the whole of creation and yet, as Calvin puts it, David deliberately selects those works of God that will awaken the drowsy and 'drag them, as it were, in spite of themselves, humbly to adore him'. Martin Luther tells of being struck down by a bolt of lightning. He was so terrified by the storm that he vowed he would give up law and become a monk if his life was spared.

The powerful, majestic, 'voice of the LORD' is likened to thunder (see Psalm 18:13). In days before aircraft and gunpowder, thunder would have been the loudest sound known. This is the God who gave the Ten Commandments in the context of thunder and lightning. It so terrified the people that they pleaded with Moses, 'You speak with us, and we will hear; but let not God speak with us, lest we die' (Exodus 19:16–19; 20:18–19). The people thought it thundered when the Father answered Jesus' prayer in John 12:28–29 (see also 1 Samuel 2:10; 7:10).

'Glory' encloses this section of the psalm (verses 3,9) and reminds us of the 'glory' that is to be given to God (verses 1–2). The LORD is the 'God of glory' (verse 3; Acts 7:2; see 'King of glory' in Psalm 24:7–10).

The 'waters' (verses 3) may refer to the Mediterranean Sea from where the storm began before it engulfed the whole land of Israel (verses 5–9). There may also be an allusion to the waters of the great Flood (see verse 10; Genesis 7:6–7,10) or to the time of creation when 'the word of the Lord' gathered the waters of the sea together (see Psalm 33:7; Genesis 1:2,9). In the myths of the Ancient Near East, the gods had great difficulty controlling the original waters. Earthly and heavenly powers must acknowledge the Lord's sovereignty. It is the Lord, not Baal the Canaanite god of weather, who has absolute control.

In the Psalms 'waters' can also be used for any experience that tends to overwhelm God's people (see Psalms 18:16–19; 46:3). Comfort comes through knowing that the one whose voice is 'over the waters' (verse 3) has promised that 'when you pass through the waters, I will be with you; and through the rivers, they shall not overflow you' (Isaiah 43:2).

There is no need to suppose that the metaphor changes from a thunderstorm to an earthquake in verse 8. The storm that rolls in from the sea (verse 3) first hits land in the north. Those majestic tall cedars are uprooted and the massive 'Lebanon' mountain range and 'Sirion' (the name used by the people of Sidon for Mount Hermon (Deuteronomy 3:9) appear to skip like calves and young oxen (verse 6) as they are lit up by the forked lightning ('divides flames of fire', verse 7). It moves south across the country to the 'wilderness of Kadesh' (verse 8). The ground seems to shake with the noise of the thunder and wind, causing frightened animals to give birth prematurely and stripping trees of their leaves (verse 9).

God's 'temple' or palace (verse 9), in this context, is not any earthly structure in Jerusalem but either God's heavenly home or perhaps the whole created order. There are indications that the earthly tabernacle/temple was viewed as a model of the cosmos. The temple was to be a 'symbolic reminder to Israel that God's glorious presence would eventually fill the whole cosmos.'[60] As Psalm 19 speaks of the heavens declaring the glory of God so here perhaps all ('everyone', literally, 'all of it') of creation is moved by God's majesty to cry in ecstasy, 'Glory!' (verse 9). Spurgeon writes: 'Here is a good precedent for our Methodist friends and for the Gogoniants (*Gogoniant* is the Welsh for 'glory') of the zealous Welsh'.

Even today a thunderstorm remains impressive and awesome. 'What a monstrous thing is it', writes Calvin, 'that while all the irrational portion of the creation tremble before God, men alone, who are endued with sense and reason, are not moved! Moreover, though they possess genius and learning, they ... shut their ears against God's voice, however powerful, lest it should reach their hearts.'

The God of judgment and salvation (verses 10–11)

The reference to the waters in verse 3 reminds David of the 'Flood' (verse 10). In the original the word for 'Flood' is only used of the great deluge in Noah's day. Despite the devastation and loss of life, at no time was anything out of control. The LORD 'sat' or 'was enthroned' over the Flood. The God who at the first divided the waters and set boundaries between land and sea, brought the earth back to its initial watery state as a punishment for human rebellion (Genesis 1:2; 7:10–12). At the same time he saved Noah and his family. This is the LORD (Jehovah/Yahweh) who is seated as 'King for ever'. The God whose voice is heard in the storm still rules the elements and this is a warning to the ungodly but it is also a comfort to the godly.

The psalm ends by assuring God's people that the sovereign Lord is well able to protect them ('give strength') and 'bless' them with a state of well-being ('peace'). Our Lord Jesus is both 'mighty God' and 'Prince of peace' (Isaiah 9:6).

When we come together to worship is our first concern to get something for ourselves from God or to give something to God? The call at the beginning of worship is to give to God but it ends with God giving and blessing his people. We join with all heaven in giving praise to God and it is as we give of ourselves to God that blessing flows.

Psalm 30

From Sadness to Gladness

Why do you want to live? Is it to please yourself or to honour God? David prayed that he might live and bring praise to his Lord. The psalm expresses heartfelt thankfulness for the Lord's deliverance in answer to prayer.

The reference to David in the heading should be separated from 'house'. Literally 'of David' is 'belonging to David', as we find in Psalms 25–28. This one is specifically a 'Song' relating to the 'dedication of the house'. It could refer to David's palace but more likely to the LORD's house, and this is why most modern versions translate it as 'temple'. It could have been composed at the time when David set up a new tent for the ark of the covenant in Jerusalem (see 2 Samuel 6:16–17). Perhaps a more likely occasion is the one recorded in 2 Samuel 24 and 1 Chronicles 21. David's sinful action in taking a census of the people resulted in a plague that killed thousands. The place where the plague was stopped and sacrifice offered was chosen as the site for the future temple. David however could already refer to the place as 'the house of the LORD God' (1 Chronicles 22:1) in a way similar to Jacob's recognition of God's presence at Bethel—'This is none other than the house of God' (Genesis 28:17).

The Jews later used the psalm at the Festival of Dedication (*Hanukkah*; see John 10:22) which celebrated the restoration and cleansing of the temple in 165 BC after its desecration under Antiochus IV Epiphanes.

It is a typical thanksgiving psalm, in which David is very appreciative of the Lord's kindness toward him in sparing both him and the rest of Jerusalem's inhabitants from the deadly plague. There are similarities of thought and expression between this psalm and Psalm 6 giving the impression that the prayer of the earlier psalm is answered here.

Praise (verses 1–5)

The psalm begins on a very personal note (verses 1–3) but soon the community of the faithful is called to join in the praise (verses 4–5).

Like water drawn from a deep well (see Exodus 2:16,19) so the LORD has 'lifted' David up from deep trouble (see Psalm 40:2). David in turn 'exalts' the LORD (verse 1). The LORD, of course, is high and lifted up already but David lifts him high both in his thoughts and in his praises. No doubt there were numerous Saul supporters who would have taken the opportunity to gloat ('rejoice') at any misfortune David experienced. But David 'cried out' to the LORD (Jehovah/Yahweh) 'my God' and he restored him. Verse 3 indicates that he had been drawn up from a near death situation. In view of his allusion to drawing water in verse 1 the 'pit' (verse 3; see Psalm 28:1) is an appropriate term. Both 'grave' ('*sheol*') and 'pit' are associated with death and the 'healing' may well refer to recovery from a deadly physical illness. On the other hand, David could well have been thinking of his own mental and spiritual sufferings (see Psalm 147:3) on account of his sin and the resulting plague that had affected so many of his people.

David calls on God's faithful people to add their praises (verses 4–5). God's 'saints' are those members of the covenant community who show loving commitment to the Lord and his people (see Psalm 4:3). The Hebrew term (*hasid*) found here was later used of those Jews who stood out against Greek oppression and joined Judas Maccabeus in liberating the people from oppressive rule. They were called the Hasidim. Hasidic Judaism today is a mystical, pietistic branch of Orthodox Judaism founded in the 18th century.

The 'remembrance of his holy name' (verse 4) is literally 'the memorial of his holiness'. It is God's holiness, which sets him apart and is associated with his name Jehovah/Yahweh (see Exodus 3:14–15), that is to be mentioned in the thanksgiving. This particular celebration of God's holiness arises from the forgiveness and restoration David has experienced (see verse 5). The comparisons are quite superb. Put more literally verse 5 reads: 'For there is a moment in his anger but a life in his favour; in the evening weeping lodges but at morning joyful cries ring out'. If the census is the background (2 Samuel 24) then we have an example of David and the people experiencing God's anger. For God's people there is a lifetime of God's grace with momentary expressions of God's anger. David is not minimising God's displeasure at human sin but expressing the amazing wonder of God's love. We do not deserve any kindness from God yet he is so gracious toward his people. Weeping from hurt, sadness and concern is like a night lodger. A new day brings ringing cries of triumph and joy. (see Psalm 126:5–6). The apostle Paul takes these thoughts further and speaks of 'our light affliction, which is but for a moment, is working for us a far more exceeding and eternal weight of glory' (2 Corinthians 4:17).

Confession (verses 6–7)
David now reveals the circumstances that led to the experience of God's anger. His statement in verse 6 does not necessarily suggest complacency and self-confidence. It could be taken to refer to the ongoing confidence he had in God and verse 7a would suggest that David was aware that it was the Lord who had established and strengthened his kingdom, making him secure on Mount Zion. If this is so, then God's anger resulting in the hiding of his face, as in the case of Job, was inexplicable and troubling, even if short-lived.

Most commentators, however, consider that David has been too self-confident, despite his awareness of God's help, and this was certainly the case when he held the census. God showed his displeasure ('hid your face', verse 7b) in the troubles caused by the plague. It is true that we can be too complacent with self-confidence and yet piously attribute our good fortune to God.

Prayer (verses 8–10)
The experience humbled David and caused him to plead with the Lord not to let him die. Notice the intensity of his appeal—'Hear, O Lᴏʀᴅ, and have mercy on (or more accurately, 'be gracious to') me; Lᴏʀᴅ, be my helper!' (verse 10). There are expressions in this psalm similar to those that Hezekiah used later in his testimony after recovering from his near-death illness (Isaiah 38:17–19). David argues boldly with God. If he dies ('my blood', verse 9) and is among the dead ('I go down to the

pit'; see verse 3) he will no longer be able to give thanks ('praise') to God and proclaim his faithfulness ('truth') in this world. 'The best pleas in prayer are those that are taken from God's honour' (Matthew Henry).

God's initial curse on account of human sin brought the original couple and their offspring back to 'the dust' (verse 9; see Genesis 3:19). Human beings are body and spirit and when they die their bodies lie silent and cold in the grave. Death is the unnatural separation of what belongs together. For humans to be bodiless is likened to them being naked (2 Corinthians 5:1–4). The emphasis on the body in the Old Testament is significant and counteracts not only later Greek ideas but such modern views concerning spirituality that disparage the importance of each individual's body. While Old Testament believers certainly did not have the light that Christians today enjoy in view of Jesus' resurrection and New Testament teaching, it would be wrong to read too much into David's statements here and in other Old Testament passages. This psalm is not giving instruction concerning the afterlife. It is about this life; it is about living for God and praising God in the body here and now. If you are lying dead you cannot sing and dance any longer.

Testimony (verses 11–12)

The whole psalm is really a testimony expressing thanks for God's help in deliverance, but in these closing verses it is even more prominent. David returns to the theme of praise with which the psalm began (see verses 1–5). God has answered his prayer: his 'sackcloth', the outward symbol of his 'mourning' (see Esther 4:1–4), has given way to 'dancing', the expression of 'gladness' (verse 11; see verse 5b). David describes this transformation in graphic language. It is as if the Lord himself had taken off the sackcloth and clothed him with joyful festive robes. At the destruction of Jerusalem by the Babylonians in 587 BC, dancing was turned into mourning and joy ceased (Lamentations 5:15).

God had a purpose ('To the end that') in completely reversing David's situation. Instead of being at a point where he would be 'silent' in the grave, unable to give thanks and declare God's faithfulness (verse 9), David is able, with the whole of his being ('glory'; see Psalm 7:5; 16:9), to 'sing praise' and 'give thanks' to the Lord always (verse 12). 'Man's chief end is to glorify God and to enjoy him for ever' states the Westminster Shorter Catechism and it is for this purpose we have been redeemed, to bring glory to God. In view of God's mercies to us we are to present our bodies as living sacrifices (Romans 12:1). 'Let us continually offer the sacrifice of praise to God, that is, the fruit of our lips, giving thanks to his name' (Hebrews 13:15).

The psalm also points us to David's greater Son, Jesus the Messiah. He was not self-confident but always lived in dependence on his Father. Yet he experienced God's anger on account of our sins. He endured a night of weeping, went down to the pit and was heard. He was raised from Sheol to bring praise to God and he calls his people to join him in recounting the triumphs of God's grace and the silencing of his foes.

Psalm 31

In God's Hands

Here is another psalm where David prays for deliverance from enemies and emphasises his need for God's protection. The psalm may well have been a favourite of Jonah and Jeremiah judging by some of the phraseology they use (verse 6 and Jonah 2:8; verse 13 and Jeremiah 6:25). It closely parallels Psalm 22, where 'To the Chief Musician' was last found. Both psalms were in our Lord's thoughts and quoted by him as he hung on the cross, which is why so many of God's people through the centuries have used them especially when facing persecution and death. John Huss the Czech reformer (1371–1415) recited Psalm 31 as he was led to his fiery death. In the reign of Queen Mary, while Bishop Hooper awaited execution for his faith, he encouraged his wife to read Psalms 6, 22, 30 and 31 for their lessons of patience and consolation.

The way the psalm is constructed is similar to the previous one. The first part could stand complete on its own (verses 1–8; see Psalm 30:1–5) with the second part adding more detail only this time in the form of a lament before ending on a positive note (verses 9–24; see Psalm 30:6–12).

Confidence (verses 1–8)
David is concerned about enemies who are trying to catch him out and

put him to shame. As in many of the psalms it is difficult to pinpoint the circumstances, which has made it all the easier for others to use just as it is. Some think David wrote it while fleeing from Saul at the time of the treachery by the citizens of Keilah (1 Samuel 23:1–13). Others consider that it dates from the period of Absalom's rebellion.

Prayer (verses 1–6)

The psalm commences with a declaration of reliance on God, reminiscent of the way previous psalms open (see Psalms 7:1; 11:1; 16:1; 25:2). David's appeal for deliverance is based on solid arguments associated with the LORD, the covenant-keeping God. This gives Christians encouragement to use such arguments in prayer.

1. 'Let me never be ashamed' (verse 1)—The implication is that the shame of abandonment and defeat would reflect badly on God. Perhaps David is already feeling some shame because of what the enemy is doing so he urgently calls for God to hear and act quickly ('deliver speedily' verse 2).

2. 'Deliver me in your righteousness' (verse 1)—As Calvin reminds us, God has committed himself to his people so he cannot deny himself. God proves himself to be the righteous God he is by keeping faith with his people. God's righteousness, in this context, means acting in a way that is true to his righteous character and that involves being true to his covenant promises to save his people and defeat their opponents.

3. 'Be my rock ... For you are my rock ...' (verses 2–3)—He calls on God to be to him now what he knows him to be. It is as if he said, 'You are my rock, therefore be my rock'. There is a build-up of terms to express the protection and safety that God gives to those who seek refuge in him: 'my rock' (verse 2; see Psalms 18:2,31,46; 28:1); 'refuge' (or 'strength', 'stronghold'; see verse 4 and Psalm 27:1); 'a fortress of defence' (literally 'a house of fortresses'); 'my rock' or 'my crag' (verse 3; a different word from verse 2; see Psalm 18:2); 'my fortress' (see Psalm 18:2).

4. 'for your name's sake' (verse 3)—David again appeals to God's character, that he would be true to what he has revealed of himself. The implication is that if God did not rescue him the Lord's reputation would be at stake. Verse 3 closes with a reminder of the Lord as a good shepherd, whom David can ask to 'lead' and 'guide' him (verse 3; see Psalms 23:2–3 and 25:11). At the exodus Moses sings of the Lord leading

and guiding his redeemed people by his strength to the safety of God's mountain.

5. 'you are my strength' (or 'stronghold', verse 4b; it is the same word translated 'refuge' in verse 2)—David argues again on the basis of what God has been to him.

6. 'O Lᴏʀᴅ God of truth' (verse 5)—There is a further appeal to God's character and David's confidence is grounded in God's ability to save. In contrast to trusting in worthless idols (verse 6) it is to the real, faithful God that David entrusts ('commit') himself. This is not fatalistic resignation but an affirmation of faith. David's 'spirit' is a reference to his life and he expresses a sure hope that he will be rescued ('redeemed' or 'ransomed'; see Psalm 26:11) from his present trouble.[61]

Whereas David committed himself to God and experienced deliverance from death, Jesus entrusted himself to God in death and was delivered from the final enemy by his resurrection from the dead. He is the perfect example for believers (see 1 Peter 2:21–23; 4:19). The verse teaches us the way to live and die well.

Following Jesus' quotation of verse 5 in his final prayer on the cross (Luke 23:46), we hear echoes of it in Stephen's dying words (Acts 7:59) and from many more of God's people down the centuries as they faced death. John Knox heard the early Scottish Protestant, George Wishart, pray 'Father of heaven, I commend my spirit into thy holy hands' before he was burnt at the stake. Knox himself, as he lay on his bed dying, was often heard repeating to himself, 'Come, Lord Jesus; sweet Jesus, into thy hands I commend my spirit.'

7. 'I have hated ... But I trust ...' (verse 6)—In David's final argument, which is an emphatic expression of loyalty to the Lᴏʀᴅ, (Jehovah/Yahweh), he contrasts his opposition to those who cling to worthless idols with his own affirmation of trust in the Lᴏʀᴅ. Gods other than the Lᴏʀᴅ are described literally as 'vanities of emptiness' ('vain idols'; see Jonah 2:8). The gods of the nations, represented by images or idols, are 'vanity', insubstantial like vapour (see Deuteronomy 32:21; Jeremiah 10:15); they are 'emptiness', 'nonentities', and create false hopes (see Psalm 24:4; Jeremiah 18:15; 1 Corinthians 8:4–6). In some quarters it may be politically incorrect to describe other people's objects of worship in these terms but the truth remains, there is only one real, living God. 'But the Lord is the true God; he is the living God and the everlasting King' (Jeremiah 10:10; see 1 Thessalonians 1:9). To 'hate', as

in other biblical contexts, is a strong image for to 'love less' (see Genesis 29:30-31; Deuteronomy 21:15-17; Luke 14:26) and David wishes to make it clear that these idol worshippers were no friends of his and that he was in no way tempted to worship their gods.[62]

Praise (verses 7-8)
As so often when, in distress, David petitions God, he can look forward to a positive outcome. He declares that he will rejoice and be glad (see Psalm 9:2) in the Lord's unfailing 'love' ('mercy', verse 7). As at the time of the exodus (see Exodus 3:7-8), David is assured that the Lord had 'seen' ('considered') and 'known' (see Psalm 1:6) his affliction ('trouble') and distresses ('adversities' or 'troubles'; see Psalm 4:1) and would come to his assistance, not allowing him to be delivered into the power of the enemy. It was the kind of situation David was in at Keilah (see 1 Samuel 23:11). But instead of being 'shut up' in enemy hands, God enabled his feet to stand in a 'wide place' (verse 8; see Psalms 4:1; 18:19,36). How many have cried to the Lord in similar tight situations and have known the relief of being given space again!

Complaint (verses 9-18)
Having expressed his confidence in final deliverance, David now turns to recount the awful condition he is in. Phrases from this lament are used by Jeremiah who found himself more than once in a similar state. We are also reminded of Job's mental anguish.

Expressing his feelings (verses 9-13)
It is at this point, not at the beginning as in Psalms 4:1; 6:2, that David pleads for God to 'be gracious' to him ('have mercy on me', verse 9). He describes his 'trouble' (the plural form of this word is used in verse 7, 'adversities') in language reminiscent of earlier laments, particularly Psalms 6:6-7 and 22. First he relates how his troubles have affected him personally (verses 9b-10) using metaphors associated with physical suffering. Not only his 'eye' but also his whole person 'wastes away with grief' (verse 9b; see Psalm 6:7). His 'grief' is more than sorrow. The word suggests that indignation is mixed with it. Sorrow ('grief' but not the 'grief' of verse 9) and groaning ('sighing', verse 10) are expressive of the deep feelings he was enduring at this particular time in his life.

While the Hebrew text refers to David's 'iniquity' (or 'guilt', verse 10), the ancient Greek version, the Septuagint, translated two centuries

before Christ came, has 'weakness' thus making it easier to apply the
whole psalm to Jesus as the 'man of sorrows'. However, Jesus, who
knew no sin, did become 'sin for us', says Paul. Sin was imputed to
the sinless Saviour. They became his ('my iniquity') and he bore the
punishment. The English bishop and scholar, George Horne (1730–
1792), warns, 'If sin was punished in the innocent Lamb of God, let us
not expect that it should be unpunished in us, unless we repent'.

David's description of his predicament (verse 11) is even more
applicable to Jesus who was despised by his foes and deserted by his
friends. He was considered to be a spent force, a 'yesterday's man',
perishing like a broken clay jar (verse 12). The 'slander' of people like
Shimei and the 'counsel' of those like Ahithophel against David (verse
13; see 2 Samuel 16:5-13,20-23) point us forward to the conspiracy that
led to Jesus' death. Christians can expect similar treatment from the
ungodly world.

Confession and petition (14–18)
Following David's lament he now returns, as in verses 1–5, to declare
his trust in Israel's covenant keeping God ('LORD' verse 14) and that
encourages him to plead with God for deliverance from his enemies
and those pursuing him. As he does so he acknowledges that his
'times', meaning the future and all the circumstances and events
of his life are under God's control (verse 15; see 1 Chronicles 29:30).
These words, 'My times are in your hand', were particularly helpful to
Geoffrey Bull (1921–1999), a Scottish missionary to China and Tibet,
while enduring brain-washing at the hands of Chinese Communists.

David's prayer, 'Make your face shine upon your servant' (verse 16),
echoes the priestly blessing (Numbers 6:25; see Psalms 4:6; 27:8-9). On
the basis of God's 'steadfast love' ('mercies') he pleads for deliverance.
Again as in verse 1, David looks to the Lord to respond to his cries
so that he will not be shamed. He looks to God to shame his wicked
foes. David prayed that Ahithophel's counsel would be turned into
foolishness and God answered his servant. When Ahithophel saw that
his advice was not followed he committed suicide (2 Samuel 15:31;
17:14,23). In this he foreshadowed Judas the betrayer of Jesus.

In verses 17-18 we are reminded of the contrast between the 'wicked'
and the 'righteous' (Psalm 1). The Lord's people, those who are right
with God, when they are under threat, are encouraged to pray for the
defeat of their foes. Like David, Christians are not to take revenge but

to pray to the God whose right it is to punish the wicked (1 Samuel 26:10-11; Romans 12:18-21). When we pray, 'Your kingdom come ... Deliver us from evil' this is what it will mean in concrete terms: the enemies of God's people will be finally destroyed. That does not stop us also from praying *for* our enemies that they will have a change of heart. Our Lord prayed for his enemies on the cross but the day is coming when he will appear in glory as the universal judge to punish all who remain in rebellion against God and his people (2 Thessalonians 1:4-10).

Confidence and courage (verses 19-24)

David extols the 'goodness' of God. It is 'laid up' ('hidden' or 'stored up') and 'prepared' ('done') for those who 'fear' ('revere') and 'trust' or 'rely on' God. This is something that all can see ('the sons of men', verse 19). God's goodness includes sheltering his people from 'the plots of man' and hiding them in a shelter ('pavilion') from 'accusing' or 'contentious tongues' ('strife of tongues', verse 20). Again, this verse expresses more concretely what it means for God to be David's 'rock of refuge' and 'fortress of defence' (verse 2).

David's strong conviction issues in reverent worship—'Blessed be the LORD' (verse 21; see Psalm 28:6). God has shown the 'wonder' of his 'steadfast love' ('marvellous kindness') toward him when he was like a besieged city (better than 'strong city'), hemmed in on all sides, not knowing where to turn. He describes how he reacted. In his alarm (rather than 'haste', verse 22; see Psalm 116:11) he had said, 'I am cut off from before your eyes'. The situation is similar to David's position in Psalm 22:1 where he is cut off from God. As then, his predicament did not prevent him from crying out to God and God heard his 'plea for grace' ('supplications').

From expressions of worship King David turns to address the congregation of God's people as together they wait for God's deliverance. There are good grounds for those committed in love to the Lord ('saints' verse 23; see Psalm 30:4) to continue to love him by dedicating themselves to his service. The Lord is committed to his people, preserving the faithful and justly punishing ('fully repay') the one who acts with pride (see Proverbs 16:18; 29:23).

David's final exhortation is for his people to 'be strong' ('be of good courage', verse 24; see Psalm 27:14). Though the phrase 'he shall strengthen your heart' is dear to many of God's people, the original is more accurately translated 'let your heart be valiant/take courage'. They are called to strengthen themselves in the Lord as they wait for God to act. The verb 'hope' or 'wait' is almost equivalent to 'trust'. Those who wait on the Lord shall renew their strength (Isaiah 40:28–31). The Lord Jesus is our great example as he endured such suffering at the hands of his enemies, he trusted God and waited for God to vindicate him. Christians, experiencing great hardship and harassment from the enemies of Christ, can draw comfort both from the psalm and the life of our Lord as they eagerly wait for the hope of the coming glory (Romans 8:18–25).

Psalm 32

A Pardoned Sinner's Testimony

This well-loved psalm may have been composed after David's eventual repentance over the Bathsheba incident (2 Samuel 12 and see Psalm 51). David's testimony is expressed in such a way as to instruct and encourage others to experience the joy of God's forgiving grace. Augustine, the famous North African bishop and theologian of the late fourth and early fifth centuries, is said to have had this psalm written up on the wall in front of him during his final illness. By that time the psalm had become the second of the church's seven 'penitential psalms' (see Psalm 6 for the first). But in place of sorrow for sin it is the happy position of a pardoned penitent that is expressed here.

It is the first of thirteen psalms with the heading 'Contemplation' or 'Skilful' (*maskil*) that has been traditionally translated 'Instruction' (see Psalms 42, 44–45, etc.). While the meaning of the term is unknown it may be related to the verb 'instruct' which occurs later in the psalm at verse 8. While all the psalms are instructive our attention is particularly drawn to this one in which it is understood, as Augustine puts it, 'that not by the merits of works, but by the grace of God, man is delivered, confessing his sins'.

While the beginning and end of the psalm speak more generally (verses 1–2,9–11), the central part expresses the personal experience of the psalmist (verses 3–8). There are a number of triple expressions like 'transgression forgiven', 'sin covered' and 'not impute iniquity' (verses 1–2) and 'I will instruct you ... teach you ... guide you' (verse 8) throughout the psalm that emphasise the points being made (see also verses 5,11). The word Selah is also found three times at appropriate points where a musical interlude or pause allows for further reflection (see Psalm 3:2,4,8).

Privilege (verses 1–2)

It is not the righteous person of Psalm 1 who is congratulated but a repentant sinner who has received God's forgiveness (see Psalms 1:1; 2:12 for 'Blessed'). This is a wonderfully privileged position to be in—O the happy state of such a person!

Three terms are used to describe the nature of sin: 'transgression' denotes wilful rebellion against authority; 'sin' is the most general of the words but it describes a failure to reach a set target; 'iniquity', sometimes translated 'guilt', suggests perversity or deliberate waywardness and its consequences. Unless we understand sin's true character we shall not appreciate how amazing is God's forgiveness.

Three terms are also used for the pardon received and they give further insights concerning sin. The first term, 'forgiven', suggests that the rebellion is 'lifted' from the rebel who finds it too heavy to carry. Sin is like a burden that weighs a person down. John Bunyan knew this and wrote of it in his classic work *Pilgrim's Progress*. He depicted Christian with his burden of sin and guilt coming to the cross where it rolled from his back and disappeared. 'There he is', said John the Baptist as he saw Jesus coming toward him, 'God's Lamb who takes away the world's sin' (John 1:29). In response to David's confession of sin the prophet Nathan replied, 'The Lord has taken away your sin' (2 Samuel 12:13).

God's pardon also means that sin is 'covered' (see Psalm 85:2). Sin is offensive to God. It is like an ugly mess that needs to be properly hidden and not just brushed under the carpet Only God can adequately cover our sin. David tried to hide it himself and it did him no good (see verses 3–5a). Christ's atoning sacrifice, to which the tabernacle sacrifices pointed, is the means by which sin is permanently dealt with. Can you sing meaningfully with Charles Wesley: 'Plenteous grace with Thee is found, Grace to cover all my sin?'[63]

The third way which expresses God's pardon of sin states that the

LORD (Yahweh/Jehovah) 'does not impute iniquity'. God no longer reckons guilty those who are perverse, wayward sinners. They are counted among the righteous. This is the teaching of Paul concerning the justification of the ungodly and he uses these verses along with Genesis 15:6, where the word 'impute' first occurs, to support his argument (Romans 4:4-6). The three terms for sin and its forgiveness together emphasise the completeness of God's pardoning grace.

There is no 'guile' in such privileged people. They have ceased deceiving themselves, God and other people about their moral failure and rebellion. Donald Williamson, a pastor in California, uses the illustration of those belonging to Alcoholics Anonymous where each member introduces themselves by name and adds 'I'm an alcoholic'. He adds, 'What would happen in the church if we all used the same kind of pattern to introduce ourselves, "I'm Don, I'm a sinner"?' It also means that the confession involves true repentance.

Relief (verses 3-5)
From his own experience David illustrates the kind of situation that existed prior to the forgiveness described in the opening verses.

Sinful silence (verses 3-4)
What misery he endured before he confessed and received God's forgiveness! While there is 'a time to keep silence and a time to speak' (Ecclesiastes 3:7) it is never right to keep 'silent' when it comes to unconfessed sin. The silence of an unrepentant spirit is not a happy state. Perhaps we all have known the turmoil within when we have kept quiet and failed to own up to some misdemeanour at home or in school. Living with guilt and seeking to stifle the conscience can affect our bodies. Using poetic language reminiscent of the previous psalm he speaks of how his 'bones grew old' and of 'groaning' all day (verse 3; see Psalm 31:10). In addition, he considers his physical weakness to be a judgment from God—the heavy hand of God was upon him (verse 4). As the hot summer sun drains the body of moisture so the psalmist felt spiritually and physically dehydrated. Similar corrective judgments by God brought sickness and death to certain members of the Corinthian Church (see 1 Corinthians 11:30-32). We are urged not to 'despise the chastening of the Lord nor detest his correction; for whom the Lord loves he corrects' (Proverbs 3:11-12).

Penitent pardoned (verse 5)

The three terms for sin of verses 1 and 2 appear again along with three verbs that express David's penitent spirit: his 'sin' is 'acknowledged'; his 'iniquity' is 'not hidden' (or 'covered'; see verse 1); and his 'transgressions' he will 'confess'. It is a comprehensive confession (see Psalm 51:1-2 for more details) and as we saw in the opening verses it leads to a comprehensive forgiveness. Instead of keeping silent and trying to hide his sins he comes clean and confesses not to some intermediary but directly 'to the LORD'. Wonder of wonders, without further ado, he gained the Lord's forgiveness! It is the word 'carried' ('forgave'; see verse 1) that is again used to express God's pardoning grace. No specific sins are mentioned because all the emphasis is on the importance of confessing and experiencing the blessing of being forgiven.

The truth of this psalm is summarised by Solomon: 'He who covers his sins will not prosper, but whoever confesses and forsakes them will have mercy' (Proverbs 28:13). We are also encouraged by John's words, 'If we confess our sins, he is faithful and just to forgive us our sins and to cleanse us from all unrighteousness' (1 John 1:9).

Protection (verses 6–7)

This encouragement to pray to the Lord is addressed to God but it is for the benefit of the 'godly' (sometimes translated 'saints'), those committed to the Lord and his people (verse 6; see Psalms 4:3; 30:4). David's own experience of the Lord's complete protection—notice another triad of phrases in verse 7—provides evidence of the promise that when troubles arise they will 'not come near him' (verse 6). The Lord is his hiding place; he is the one who will 'preserve me from trouble' and will 'surround me' with victorious shouts (verse 7). The distress is likened to 'a flood of great waters' that was once a harmless stream or wadi. But however menacing it will not be overwhelming. Trouble is not always due to sin but when it comes for whatever reason, and particularly where sin is unconfessed, it is important not to keep silent but to 'pray' to the Lord while he gives the opportunity—'in a time when you may be found' (verse 6; see Isaiah 55:6). Instead of being engulfed by an enemy's 'words of hatred' (Psalm 109:3), God's people will be surrounded by 'joyful shouts ('songs') of deliverance' (see verse 11) presumably from fellow worshippers. We also know there is joy in heaven over one sinner who repents (Luke 15:7,10).

Guidance (verses 8–10)

God's promise (verse 8)
The Lord replies directly to David in verse 8 and through him to all God's people as the command in verse 9 is in the plural. Three verbs reminiscent of the wisdom teaching of Proverbs are used to indicate God's ability to keep members of his covenant community from falling into sin. God is a teacher who promises to 'instruct', to 'teach' the way in which the godly should go and to 'counsel' or 'advise' ('guide') them. Attached to these promises of divine instruction is an added bonus. Rather than 'guide you with my eye' the original suggests being 'under God's watchful eye' so that he may protect, care and observe our every move.

God's warning (verses 9–10)
The irrationality of sin makes us like stubborn untrained animals that need to be constantly restrained or 'they will not come near you' (verse 9). Failure to obey the Lord, and especially in this context, to come near and confess sin with a repentant spirit, leads to God's heavy hand (see verse 4). Such discipline is probably included in the 'sorrows' referred to in the proverbial saying of verse 10 (see Proverbs 26:3). Though there are exceptions as other psalms will indicate (see Psalm 73:3), as a general rule of thumb in this life, a refusal to repent and seek forgiveness from God, so typical of the 'wicked', only leads to pain and misery. But everyone who 'trusts in the LORD', and in particular, prays, making confession of sin (verses 5–6), will be surrounded, not only with joyful shouts (verse 7), but by God's 'steadfast love' ('mercy'). The covenant-keeping God is committed to those who are committed to him.

Joy (verse 11)
This calls for a final comprehensive expression of praise: 'Be glad', 'rejoice' and 'shout for joy' (the same verb is used in verse 7b). This threefold call is made to those who can be described as the 'righteous' ones, those who are 'upright in heart'. They are 'righteous' through no activity of their own but on account of God's grace in not reckoning their sin against them (verse 2). Despairing of themselves all their trust is in the Lord.

Psalm 33

Praise God—The Creator, Sovereign and Saviour

Here is a psalm to lift our spirits and to remind us that God rules the world and that he cares for those who trust him. This anonymous psalm is a fine example of a hymn of praise to the LORD (Jehovah/Yahweh). Following the introductory psalms (Psalms 1 and 2), this is the second of the two psalms in Book 1 with no heading (see Psalm 10) and probably owes its present position to the way its opening line takes up the theme of Psalm 32:11. The introductory call to worship (verses 1-3) is followed by good reasons for praising God (verses 4-19) and closes with a confession of trust and prayer (verses 20-22). Our faith is strengthened as we contemplate who God is in our praises. Adoration also encourages petition.

Call to Praise (verses 1-3)
The exhortation displays the poetic skills of the psalmist. Not only are the three verses parallel to one another but each verse contains synonymous parallelism. The call is addressed to all who are 'righteous' and 'upright', in other words, to those who, acknowledging they are sinners, know God and his forgiving grace and are committed to him (Psalms 1:6; 7:10; 32:11). The call is to 'Rejoice in the LORD' (verse 1). It

is the same 'ringing cry' of joy found in Psalm 32:7,11. Such 'praise' from God's people is 'fitting' ('beautiful') especially given what we are told in the following verses about God.

The 'Praise' at the beginning of verse 2 means to 'acknowledge', either in the sense of 'confessing' sin (see Psalm 32:5) or as here, 'giving thanks' (see Psalm 7:17; 30:9). In fact, God is glorified when we acknowledge our sins as well as his gracious gifts (see Joshua 7:19). The psalmist encourages God's people to 'sing' and to 'play' (literally 'touch' in the sense of to 'pluck' strings) the musical accompaniment but it is emphasised three times that all is to be directed to 'the LORD', 'to him' (verses 2-3), not for the satisfaction and entertainment of the worshippers.

This is the first reference to musical instruments in the psalms (see Psalm 150 for a full list and treatment of the subject). It is difficult to distinguish between the harp and the lyre. Both were stringed, free standing or arm-held, instruments. The worshippers are called to 'make melody' with the 'harp' (or better 'lyre') and 'an instrument' ('harp') 'of ten strings' (see Psalm 144:9), and to do so 'skilfully' with 'shouting' ('shout of joy'; see Psalm 27:6; Numbers 23:21). Not the sort of singing most modern Western traditionalists would allow in public worship! When Saul asked for someone who could play the harp well (the same idiom as here), David was employed (1 Samuel 16:16-17). The 'new song' need not necessarily have been an original piece but old words heartily sung in the light of new experiences of God's activity (see Psalms 40:3; 96:1; Isaiah 42:10). Christians, as members of the new covenant and belonging to the new creation are encouraged to sing songs relating to the defeat of sin and Satan through the atoning work of Christ (Revelation 5:9; 14:3) and to do so with grace, 'making melody in your heart to the Lord' (Ephesians 5:19-20; Colossians 3:16).[64]

Causes for Praise (verses 4-19)
The reasons for the call to worship are set out. They are based on:

God's Character (verses 4-5)
Various moral qualities of God are highlighted. The Lord is 'upright' (Psalm 25:8) and his 'word' is 'upright' ('right'). The same term translated 'upright' is used of his people in verse 1. God's 'word', which is the expression of his will, is straightforward. We are assured that his promises will not deceive. His 'work' is closely associated with his

'word'. The parallel line speaks of the 'faithfulness' or 'truth' of his every 'work', which means that he always carries out what he promises. What is more, because he is the perfect standard of what is right and fair (see Psalm 36:6), 'he loves righteousness and justice' (verse 5). He is committed to acting in this way himself (Psalm 103:6) and seeing right conduct and fair decisions especially among his people.

God's 'goodness' or 'steadfast love' was particularly evident in Israel but is here described as filling the earth (see Psalm 119:64). His faithful love is another element in God's nature that demonstrates his glory, a glory that fills the whole earth (see Isaiah 6:3). One expression of that loving commitment visible to the whole world is the rainbow arch. It speaks of the gracious promise he made to Noah and every living creature with a view to fulfilling that initial promise of victory over the snake (Genesis 9:8–17). But as Paul argues, the whole world is without excuse in that God's eternal attributes are clearly to be seen in creation itself (Romans 1:20–21). The ultimate expression of God's stunning greatness is Jesus Christ who is the very embodiment of God's steadfast love for Gentiles as well as Jews (John 1:14; 3:16). New Testament believers have more than enough reason to praise God.

God's Creative Power (verses 6–9)
The psalmist alludes to the Genesis account of creation as he presents a second motive for praise. The effectiveness of the 'word of the LORD' (verse 6), already mentioned in verse 4, and emphasised again in verse 9, is displayed in the 'work' of creation (see Genesis 1:9,11, etc. 'Then God said ... and it was so'). 'By faith we understand that the worlds were framed by the word of God ...' (Hebrews 11:3). The heavenly 'host' refers to the stars and planets (Genesis 2:1). While 'breath' parallels 'word' we must not lose sight of its significance. Creation is by God's potent power (Job 33:4) as well his authoritative word. The 'breath' or 'spirit' of God was active along with God's spoken word: 'And the Spirit of God was hovering over the face of the waters. Then God said ...' (Genesis 1:2–3). Word and Spirit, along with the Father, as the New Testament makes clear, are the three Persons of the one true God.

In place of the stately prose account of God's division of the waters in Genesis 1:6–10 we have this highly poetic picture of the Lord's complete mastery of the seas and ocean depths, what seems so terrifyingly uncontrollable. Similar language is used to describe the 'heap' of water of both the Red Sea and Jordan crossings (Exodus 15:8;

Psalm 78:13; Joshua 3:13,16).[65] Just as God's miraculous activity at the Red Sea brought dread to the surrounding nations (Exodus 15:14-15) so the whole inhabited world should 'fear' and 'stand in awe' of God and his creative power (verse 8). We are reminded of the reaction of the disciples when Jesus calmed the storm. Greatly fearing they said, 'Who can this be, that even the wind and sea obey him!' (Mark 4:41).

Again reminiscent of Genesis 1 it is emphatically stated that it is God and he alone who has brought all things into being ('he spoke and it was', verse 9). It 'stood' means that when God commanded, it appeared, it was created.

God's Control (verses 10–12)
Another reason for praising God is that he who can create a universe from nothing and order the unruly waters can frustrate the plans and schemes of nations (verse 10; see Isaiah 44:25). On the other hand, God's plans can never be thwarted (verse 11: see Isaiah 44:26-28; 46:10-11). Isaiah also speaks to the same effect when he writes, 'The word of the Lord stands for ever' (Isaiah 40:8; 55:11).

How privileged ('Blessed'; see Psalm 2:12) Israel was to have the 'LORD' (Jehovah/Yahweh) as their God! God chose them above all the other nations to be his special possession (verse 12; see Psalm 28:9). Moses had already reminded Israel of how privileged they were in having the LORD God so near to them (Deuteronomy 4:7-8). He also indicated that it was not because they were any better than any other nation that God had set his love upon them but purely out of unmerited divine love and to keep his promise to Abraham (Deuteronomy 7:7-8). How blessed are all God's people the world over—a chosen generation and a holy nation—'who once were not a people but are now the people of God' (1 Peter 2:9-10)!

God's Care (verses 13–19)
Possibly the psalmist may have had the Tower of Babel incident in mind as he introduced the final reason for praising the Lord (see Genesis 11:5). The cause for praise follows the form of the previous section (verses 10-12). First, the psalm mentions God's relationship with the entire human race ('all the sons of men', verse 13) as well as with each one 'individually' (verse 15; see verse 10).[66] It closes with the benefits that come to God's people (verses 18-19; see verses 11-12), and

these are given added force by what is said about the futility of all that
the world looks to for deliverance (verses 16–17).

The anthropomorphic language of God looking, seeing and
watching, far from implying that God is not all-knowing and needs
to discover what is happening, emphasises God's complete awareness
of all human activity. The threefold 'all' in verses 13–15 underlines the
point. As the creator of their 'hearts' (or 'minds') he can discern what
people are thinking and planning. While humans look 'at the outward
appearance the Lord looks at the heart' (1 Samuel 16:7).

The triple 'all' (verses 13–15) is matched by the threefold 'great' in
verses 16–17 (translated 'multitude' in verse 16a). All that the ancient
world considered great and powerful is highlighted—the king and
his great army, the warrior and his great strength, and the war horse
and its great might—by themselves they are not capable of bringing
success. The implication is that only the Lord can give victory and
therefore our trust must be in him alone. The best that this world can
offer is useless without him for it is he who gives power and ability to
humans.

What a blessing to know that God's watchful care ('the eye of the
LORD', verse 18; see Psalm 32:8; Deuteronomy 11:12) is over those who
'fear him' (see Psalm 25:12), on those people of his who 'hope' in his
unfailing love ('his mercy')! They need not fear any nation however
powerful and threatening. The care that God has for his people extends
to delivering and preserving them from every kind of circumstance
however grave. The synonymous parallelism, a special feature of this
psalm, presents such a situation where God's people might be under
siege and threatened with starvation: 'deliver ... from death', 'keep ...
alive in famine' (verse 19). A most notable example was when Syria
besieged Samaria in the time of Elisha the prophet (2 Kings 6:24–7:20).

Confession and expectation (verses 20–22)

Having shown how great the Lord is, the psalm concludes with three
verses that express his people's joyful trust in God and a closing prayer
that they will continue to experience his steadfast love ('mercy'). Words
used in the previous section reappear in this closing confession. The
life ('soul') of the covenant community that the Lord saves from death
(verse 19) now 'waits' for the Lord who is their 'supportive shield' ('help
and shield' verse 20). God assured Abram with the words, 'I am your
shield', Genesis 15:1; see Psalm 3:3; 18:2). They have trusted one who

in previous actions has revealed himself as the unique awesome God that he is ('his holy name') and so they can be joyfully confident as they look to the future (verse 21; see 'rejoicing in hope' Romans 12:12). The faith implied in their 'hope' (verse 22; see verse 18) does not take God's help for granted but prays that his 'faithful love' ('mercy') will continue to be 'upon' them, in proportion to their faith ('just as we hope in you' or 'in keeping with the hope we have', verse 22). 'This passage gives us another very sweet consolation, namely, that if our hope faint not in the midst of our course, we have no reason to fear that God will fail to continue his mercy towards us, without intermission, to the end of it' (Calvin).

Psalm 34

The King's Song and Sermon

Here is a testimony to God's deliverance that includes both praise and instruction. Like so many of the psalms in Book I, it bears witness to God's intervention in times of danger and distress. The psalm is a stimulus to Christians to share their experiences and what they have learnt with fellow believers for their own encouragement and comfort.

Along with Psalm 56 it belongs to the time when David, in seeking to escape from Saul, took refuge in the Philistine city of Gath where Achish was the ruler. David soon became very afraid of the king and deceived him by faking insanity[67] and eventually made his escape (1 Samuel 21:10–22:1). In the psalm heading, the Philistine king is called 'Abimelech'. The most plausible suggestion is that, like the term 'Pharaoh', the name 'Abimelech' (meaning 'my father is king') was a royal title given to Philistine rulers among whom was Achish of Gath.

Perhaps the dynastic title rather than the personal name is used in the heading to remind us of the incidents in Genesis when both Abraham and Isaac were afraid of earlier Philistine Abimelechs and tried to deceive them (Genesis 20 and 26). Instead of being deceitful and lying, this psalm encourages God's people in fearful situations to act more honourably. Are there occasions when you are gripped by fear and are tempted to take irrational and unbecoming action? Take to heart this wonderful psalm and act upon it!

This again is a well-constructed poetic piece in the form of an acrostic, an A to Z psalm very similar in structure to Psalm 25.[68] Another feature of this psalm is the repeated use of 'all' clustered toward the beginning (verses 1,4,6 and translated 'any' in 10) and end (verses 17,19,20 and translated 'none' in 22: 'all those who take refuge in him shall not be condemned').

Telling out God's greatness (verses 1–3)

The psalm opens with David's resolve to praise God 'continually' and reveals his desire that others will have their spirits uplifted and be able to join in. While the word 'bless' is often used of being blessed by God with gracious benefits, here it has the more literal sense of 'bow the knee' in homage (see Psalm 16:7). Both knee and 'mouth' combine in the adoration and praise of the Lord (verse 1).

In fact, David is wholly committed ('soul' verse 2) to praising God. Instead of praising himself and his achievements (see 1 Kings 20:11; Jeremiah 9:23) it is the Lord who is the object of his boasting. Quoting Jeremiah 9:24 Paul makes it clear that the only ground for boasting is 'in the Lord' (1 Corinthians 1:31).[69] Instead of being sickened as we often are by human boasting, those like David, described as the 'humble' (see Psalms 9:12b; 25:9), listen in and themselves are 'glad' (verse 2).

He invites them to join in the worship—'with me ... together' (verse 3). But how can they 'magnify' (or 'make great') and 'exalt' the Lord and 'his name' when he is already lifted up and great? They do so by personally acknowledging who God is and what he is like. Declaring publicly in worship what God has revealed of himself also enables others to become aware of God's greatness. As a telescope does not change the heavenly body but serves to make it bigger to the observer so our praises do not alter God but help to magnify to us and others just how great he is.

Testifying to God's goodness (verses 4–10)

David now relates how the Lord has acted toward him for the encouragement and help of others.

The testimony (verses 4–6)

To 'seek' God is often used for worshipping God especially at a place of worship (see Amos 5:5–6; Psalm 24:3–6) but here it means coming to God in prayer and David records that God responded by rescuing him 'from all my fears' (verse 4). He repeats his testimony in verse 6 where 'cried out' parallels 'sought', 'heard' parallels 'heard' (literally 'he answered' in verse 4), 'saved' parallels 'delivered' and 'troubles' (or 'distresses'; see Psalm 4:1) parallel 'fears'.

He describes himself as 'This poor man', meaning not only that his situation puts him in a weak physical position but that he is aware of his poverty of spirit (see Matthew 5:3). He belongs to the 'humble poor' who, despairing of self, rely on God. The word 'fears' (verse 4) means 'terrors' (Psalm 31:13). It is used to describe the God-forsaken state of the wicked (Isaiah 66:4). David not only feared Saul at this time but also the dreaded Philistines and despite his own foolishness the Lord delivered him from his enemies so that the source of his 'fears' were removed and this in turn removed his feelings of dread.

A general comment in verse 5 separates the two verses of testimony and it has the effect of underlining David's experience. Others have 'looked to' the Lord as David sought help from the Lord. As a result their faces did not blush with shame or their colour drain from them through fear. Instead, they were 'radiant' (verse 5), similar to the way a parent's face lights up at the sight of a lost child (see Isaiah 60:5).

The appeal (verses 7–10)

David's exhortation to others is introduced with the encouraging statement that the Lord's 'angel' acts like a protective shield ('encamps around') to deliver his people (verse 7). This is another way of saying that the Lord himself comes to the rescue as in the previous verses. The 'angel of the LORD' is, as one commentator has put it, 'God himself localised in time and space' (see Genesis 31:11–13; Judges 6:11–24).[70] Before the Son of God became incarnate as the man, Jesus the Messiah, the LORD was seen by the Old Testament people in human form. He appeared to Joshua as the Commander of the Lord's army (Joshua 5:13–15). Elisha's servant was given visible proof of the Lord's supernatural protective presence when the Syrians besieged Samaria (2 Kings 6:15–17).

Those who look to God for help, who seek him in prayer, are the ones who 'fear him' (see also verses 9–10). This is not the terror of verse 4 but the reverential awe that is characteristic of 'humble poor' believers. The 'fear of the LORD' is one of the themes of this psalm.

Before urging God's people to 'fear the LORD' (verse 9) David gives a general invitation to share in the experience of how 'good' the Lord is (verse 8). People are called to judge for themselves what was to become a confession of faith, namely, that the 'LORD is good' (see Psalms 100:5; 106:1; 107:1; 118:1; 136:1). Oh the happiness and good fortune of everyone who 'trusts' or more literally 'takes refuge in' the LORD (see verse 22; Psalm 2:12)! Peter uses the language of David as he encourages Christians to feed on the gospel word (1 Peter 2:3). But the ultimate purpose is that we might enjoy the Lord himself.

The true people of God are called 'his saints' (verse 9; see Psalm 16:3). This phrase, 'his holy ones', which sometimes refers to heavenly beings (Psalm 89:5,7) in this instance has the same meaning as 'saints' in the New Testament (see 1 Corinthians 1:2). It refers to those who belong to the holy God. They have been chosen by God, set apart for God and called to live distinct, morally holy lives. Due to the pressures of the ungodly world and their proneness to give way to temptation, God's people constantly need to be encouraged to remain true to the Lord. The command to 'fear the LORD' (verse 9) is given not only because genuine, reverent commitment to God is what is due to him but because 'it is the surest method of securing their own safety and supplying their own wants' (J. A. Alexander). Despite being strong and nimble, young lions can lack food. They symbolise the self-sufficient who resort to their own devices. But God's people, his saints, the ones who 'seek the LORD', will not lack 'any good thing' (verse 10; see a similar contrast in Isaiah 40:30–31). 'Every good and perfect gift is from above and comes down from the Father of lights ...' (James 1:17). David 'sought the Lord' (verse 4) and the evidence of his goodness is there for everyone to see—God rescued him from a dangerous situation enabling him to escape to the cave of Adullam (1 Samuel 21:12–22:1). It is a clear encouragement to all God's people not to 'seek' or have recourse to other gods in times of distress but earnestly to look to the Lord for help. God calls to his wayward people, 'Seek me and live; but do not seek Bethel ... Seek the Lord and live' (Amos 5:4–6).

Teaching God's wisdom (verses 11–22)

The 'fear of the LORD' (verse 11) that has been mentioned in the previous section (verses 7 and 9) now becomes the focus of attention. We are instructed in how and why the Lord should be revered.

Instruction (verses 11–14)

Typical of the way instruction was given in the courts of the Ancient Near East and like a father with his sons, David invites his students ('children', literally 'sons') to listen. It is similar to the call in Proverbs 4:1 and 5:7. Unlike pagan wisdom teaching, Old Testament wisdom begins and ends with the 'fear of the LORD' (verse 11; see Job 28:28; Proverbs 1:7; Ecclesiastes 12:13). This is the wisdom that brings health and strength, plus a long and secure life in the land (see Proverbs 1:33; 3:1-10; 9:10-11). But what does it mean to fear the Lord in practice? The answer was first given by Moses and repeated by David and Solomon. Living in reverential awe of God involves obeying his commandments (Deuteronomy 6:2,24; Proverbs 4:4-5; Ecclesiastes 12:13), 'for this is your wisdom and your understanding' (Deuteronomy 4:6).

The question posed by David is one that most people then and now would desire to answer in the affirmative—do you want to live a long and enjoyable life?[71] What David is asking, like Old Testament wisdom teaching generally, lies within the context of God's covenant with his people where the LORD's 'good' things included very down-to-earth items like having many children and much livestock and produce. But it did not stop at that for they would also know the spiritual blessing of the Lord walking among them and being special to them (see Leviticus 26:3-13; Deuteronomy 28:1-14; Psalm 4:6-8).

The answer to the question, as we saw above, shows the close connection between the fear of the Lord and keeping his commandments. Typical of wisdom teaching, a life honouring to God covers both speech and action. The tongue must be kept under control, a matter to which both Proverbs and James give special attention (see Proverbs 12:17-20; 17:4,7; James 3:1-12). 'Lying lips are an abomination to the Lord' (Proverbs 12:22) and 'a righteous man hates lying' (Proverbs 13:5). Such deceit must not be found in our relationship with God (see Psalm 17:1) nor with others.

To 'depart from evil' (verse 14) is included in the meaning of wisdom and Job is a prime example of the wise person (Job 1:1; 28:28). The positive side to this is to 'do good', the kind of 'good' that is desired for oneself ('see good', verse 12). The same contrast is presented by the prophets: 'Cease to do evil, learn to do good' (Isaiah 1:16-17); 'Seek good and not evil ... Hate evil, love good' (Amos 5:14-15).

To 'seek peace' and to 'chase after it' ('pursue it', verse 14) means a commitment to living in harmony with God, oneself and others that produces a state of well-being. Those who are at peace with God are called to 'pursue the things that make for peace' and as far as humanly possible to 'live peaceably with all men' (Romans 14:19; 12:18; see Hebrews 12:14).

The New Testament encourages us to see that the blessings that come from God include physical as well as spiritual benefits in this life. The life of the believer, however, is also seen to reach on into the eternal realm that includes living in a new creation where there is no more curse. David was aware as much as the apostle Peter, who quotes these verses (1 Peter 3:10-11), that this life will always include suffering and hardships, nevertheless, as Edmund Clowney comments, the blessing of the Lord will make days of suffering 'good days' for his people. And he gives the example of a 'good day' in the book of Acts where we find Paul and Silas in prison with their backs bleeding and their feet in the stocks, singing psalms at midnight.

Encouragement (verses 15–22)

The remainder of the psalm teaches God's saints truths about the Lord for their comfort and encouragement. Typical of wisdom teaching (see Proverbs 10:6-7) those who revere the Lord are now called 'the righteous' (verse 15,19,21; see Psalm 1:5) whereas those who hate the righteous are the 'wicked' (verse 21; see Psalm 1:1). Notice how God's covenant name 'the LORD' (Jehovah/Yahweh) appears in almost every verse of the psalm (1-4,6-11,15-19,22). This is the God who makes promises to his people and keeps them. It also means that there are warnings for the wicked and that God carries out his threats too.

The threats:

1. God's face is set in anger against the wicked. It results in the memory of them being eliminated from the earth (verse 16).

2. God's justice will be done (verse 21)—We reap what we sow. While the righteous are delivered from many 'evils' ('afflictions' verse 19), just one 'evil' (verse 21) can 'slay' the wicked. God pronounces them guilty and worthy of punishment ('condemned'; see Psalm 5:10).

The promises:

1. God's care (verse 15)—He watches over his people (see Psalm 33:18) and is attentive to 'their cry' ('cry for help'; see also verse 17 where a different verb is used: 'cry out').

2. God's deliverances (verses 17 and 19)—David again refers to the cries of his people and brings to mind his testimony in verses 4 and 6. As David was saved from 'all his troubles' so God will deliver the righteous 'out of all their troubles ... out of them all'.

3. God's presence (verse 18)—He comes near to save the 'contrite' (literally 'the crushed in spirit') and the broken hearted. These are terms that describe penitent sinners (see Psalm 51:17; Isaiah 57:15).

4. God's protection (verse 20)—'He guards all his bones'

5. God's justifying grace (verse 22)—Unlike the final state of the wicked (see the parallel in verse 21), those who are 'his servants', who 'seek refuge' ('trust'; see verse 8) in the Lord, will be redeemed and not treated as guilty.

Jesus, who was himself meek and humble in heart (Matthew 11:29), could appreciate the truth of this psalm and John records how verse 20 found its fulfilment when the Roman soldier who pierced his side did not break his legs to hurry death as he had already given up his spirit (John 19:30–36).

Psalm 35

A Righteous Cause

What a situation to be in! Allegations have been made by people you have helped in the past and which you know are untrue. Unfortunately, if the issue were to come to court there might be enough circumstantial evidence presented to convict you and if that happened you know it would mean your ruination. That is the kind of situation in which David found himself. The psalm may have drawn on David's experiences when relentlessly pursued by Saul and especially the pressure he was under when he had the opportunity to take Saul's life. On that occasion David pleaded his innocence and said, 'Let the LORD judge between you and me, and let the Lord avenge me on you. But my hand shall not be against you ... Whom do you pursue? ... Therefore let the LORD be judge ... and see and plead my case, and deliver me out of your hand' (1 Samuel 24:12-15).

It is placed after the only other psalm to mention 'the angel of the Lord'. But whereas in this psalm 'the angel' is called to pursue the trouble-makers to their damnation (verses 5-6), in the previous one 'the angel' protects and delivers from trouble (Psalm 34:7). It is the enemy that needs to be shamed in this psalm (verse 4) while in the previous psalm shame is removed from the faces of God's people (Psalm 34:5). The 'lions' are also mentioned in both psalms (34:10;

223

35:17). As Psalm 34 ended with lawcourt language ('condemned' and 'not guilty') so this psalm opens with a concern for justice and is the constant theme throughout.

David's lament in verses 11–18 is surrounded by pleas to God for vindication against his accusers.

Plea for vindication (verses 1–10)
The way in which the prayer is set out is similar to the closing section (verses 19–28) with wishes and vows following petitions.

Petition (verses 1–3)
Though battlefield language is used—'fight ... shield (verse 2; the small, light shield as in Psalm 3:3) and buckler' (a large shield that protected the whole body as in Psalm 5:12. Goliath's armour-bearer carried one in 1 Samuel 17:7,41),[72] 'the spear' (verse 3; a short wooden shaft with stone or metal head used at close range or thrown; see 1 Samuel 20:33; 26:8)—it is general opposition and especially a legal fight that is uppermost in mind throughout the psalm (see Psalm 109:3). 'Plead my cause ... with those who strive with me' (verse 1) would be better rendered 'Contend ... with those who contend with me.' David's God, the LORD (Yahweh/Jehovah), is asked to match David's opponents, contention for contention, fight for fight. He wants his God to act as a defensive shield (see Psalms 3:3; 5:12) and to 'stand up' (verse 2) for him, to take the offensive and 'stop' (verse 3) his pursuers.[73]

In the final line he asks for personal assurance of God's salvation— 'Say to my soul' (means 'Say to me', verse 3). The Lord reminds Israel that he is their saviour who promises to 'contend with him who contends with you' (Isaiah 49:25–26). 'Salvation' has physical as well as spiritual dimensions (see Psalm 34:6). If you know for certain that the God who has made great and precious promises is your salvation what more do you need?

Wishes (verses 4–8)
The imprecatory language, in which David calls down curses on his foes, is similar to that used in previous psalms (see 5:10;10:2). If David is to be saved then his enemies must be defeated. He makes his complaint to God and looks to God to take vengeance and to vindicate him. Again, we are reminded of the times when David had the chance to kill Saul but he left it to the Lord to deal with him in his own time

(1 Samuel 24 and 26). We are encouraged like David to pour out our concerns to God and not to take the law into our own hands.

There are four curses in verses 4-6. They call for those who would seek to be rid of David and plan his downfall to be shamed and humiliated (verse 4a), defeated ('turned back') and confused (verse 4b), blown away like husks of grain with the Lord's angel driving them (verse 5), and having to make a run for it, slipping around in the dark, with the Lord's angel in close pursuit (verse 6). As the enemy has pursued David (verse 3) so David wishes the same treatment for his enemy.

If the angel of the Lord is not your deliverer he will be your downfall. We are reminded of the Lord's warning to Israel, 'I send an Angel before you to keep you in the way and to bring you into the place which I have prepared. Beware of him and obey his voice, do not provoke him, for he will not pardon your transgressions, for my name is in him' (Exodus 23:20-21). This same Angel is revealed to us as the Lord Jesus who comes to be glorified in his saints and who will also take vengeance on those who do not know God or obey the gospel (2 Thessalonians 1:7-9).

There are more curses in verse 8 where David calls for his enemy to fall without warning into the kind of hunter's trap that they have set for him ('net ... hidden', see verse 7). Twice for emphasis David states that the enemy's action was 'without cause' (verse 7; see verse 19). The rest of the psalm will indicate how unjust are his enemy's allegations.

Vows (verses 9–10)

To be assured that God is his salvation (which also means dealing with the enemy) results in a 'soul' that is 'joyful' (verse 9; see verse 3). 'All my bones' (verse 10), like 'soul', is an emphatic way of referring to one's whole being. The confession of verse 10 begins using words reminiscent of Moses' song at the Red Sea 'LORD, who is like you' (Exodus 15:11). Not only does God deliver defenceless Israel from the might of Egypt but the 'poor and the needy' (verse 10) from the grip of powerful and ruthless people within the community. Like the term 'poor' (see Psalm 34:2), the 'needy' are the 'godly' (see Psalm 69:33) who are sometimes but not always in need of material help (see Psalm 12:5).

Plight of the sufferer (verses 11–18)
In place of curse this section is dominated by lament which leads to prayer and then to the prospect of praise.

Lament (verses 11–16)
The lament of verse 7 is expanded here and it is clear that David not only had to contend with Saul but there were probably many enemies at court who did not wish him to succeed.[74] The legal language returns. These violent people ('Fierce witnesses' verse 11; see Psalm 27:12) have taken their stand before a judge and accusations are made of which David has no knowledge. Their treachery is cruel and their ingratitude inexcusable. In place of David's own sympathy for these people when they were in trouble and whom he had regarded as if they were close family—which he spells out in verses 13 and 14—they have repaid him 'evil for good' so that his 'sorrow' (verse 12; literally 'childlessness for my soul'; see Isaiah 47:8) is like one who has lost children. He expressed his sorrow by wearing sackcloth—like a hair shirt uncomfortable next to skin—fasting and beating his chest as he prayed like the penitent tax collector (Luke 18:13; see Nehemiah 2:2).

Behind his back ('I did not know', verse 15) his accusers have been vicious and relentless in their verbal attacks, expressing their hostility by gnashing their teeth (see Psalm 37:12; Acts 7:54) in the company of profane ('ungodly' verse 16) mockers.[75]

Petition (verse 17)
David appeals to God in his distress, addressing him not by his covenant name 'Lᴏʀᴅ' (Yahweh/Jehovah) but 'Lord' or Master, the one who has sovereign oversight. The phrase 'how long' is typical of the psalms of lament (see 6:3; 13:1)[76] and here it expresses David's frustration. For how long can God go on seeing this injustice and not intervene? So he pleads that God would 'rescue' (literally 'restore') his 'precious life' (literally 'my only one'; see Psalm 22:20) from the enemy's destructive activity which he likens to an attack by young 'lions' (see Psalm 34:10).

Vow (verse 18)
His anticipated response to God's intervention (see verses 9–10) will be one of thanksgiving 'in the great congregation', perhaps at one of the important tabernacle festivals like Passover or Tabernacles. The public

act of worship by a vast congregation ('many people') in praise of what God has done will have the effect of witnessing to God's goodness (see Psalm 22:22–25; 26:12).

Plea for vindication (verses 19–28)

David continues to pray for victory over those who have become his enemies, ever keeping before him the desire that through it God will be honoured.

Lament (verses 19–21)

The lament in verses 20 and 21 arises out of his desire to see an end to the gloating by those who are 'wrongfully' his foes. They have rejoiced in his adversity (see verse 15) and hated him 'without a cause' (see 7:4; 25:3), narrowing ('wink') their eyes in a malicious, antisocial manner (verse 19; see Proverbs 6:13).

The reasons why these enemies must be silenced are introduced with the word 'For' (verse 20). They do not speak 'peace' (so putting themselves at odds with God who delights in the 'peace' or 'prosperity' of his servant; see verse 27) and disturb the 'quiet' people of Canaan with lying words (verse 20). The 'quiet in the land' (verse 20) is a unique expression in the Bible and probably refers to those who quietly go about their daily affairs endeavouring to be faithful to the obligations of God's covenant.

As they pull faces with their eyes so these foes do the same with their mouths (see Isaiah 57:4) in order to ridicule David. The hurrahs express their joy at seeing the distress they are causing.

Petition (verses 22–25)

But David's enemies are not the only ones who 'have seen' (verse 22; see verse 21). David cries to the LORD (Yahweh/Jehovah) who sees not only his trouble but all the actions of the enemy (see verse 17; Psalm 10:14) and he prays that God will no longer be a silent and distant witness (see Psalm 28:1). His prayer becomes even more urgent as he calls on God to 'stir' himself, to wake up (verse 23; see Psalm 7:6) and speak out on his behalf. He does not think of God as literally needing to be awakened in the way that Elijah mocked the prophets of Baal (1 Kings 18:27), but he uses this vivid anthropomorphic language to express more forcefully his desperate appeal for help. The lawcourt scene is again very obvious with the use of 'my vindication' (literally 'my judgment/justice') and 'my cause' (same word as verse 1, 'contend for me') in verse 23, and 'Vindicate me' or 'Establish justice for me' (literally 'judge me', verse 24; see Psalm 26:1).

He appeals to God's character 'according to your righteousness' (verse 24) in the same way that Abraham recognised that God, the judge of all the earth, would 'do right' (Genesis 18:25). In the present context the plea is that God would do the right according to the covenant relationship that exists between God and David and then the enemy will have no grounds to gloat ('rejoice') any more (see verses 15,19 and Psalm 30:1). The implication is that David is innocent of all the accusations that have been made and so the enemy must not have the satisfaction of seeing their evil desires fulfilled and so pronounce him finished ('swallowed up', or 'destroyed', verse 25).

The boldness of expression in these verses arises out of David's close relationship with the one whom he calls 'my God', 'my Lord' (see verse 17) and 'O LORD my God' (verses 23–24). Do you possess that personal relationship with the one true God? Have you that freedom in prayer? Thomas, when he saw the risen Lord Jesus, exclaimed, 'My Lord and my God' (John 20:28).

Wish (verse 26–27)

It is not personal vindictiveness but the cause of truth and justice that concerns David. Echoing the words of verse 4, David prays that his enemies who have gloated over his calamity and acted proudly ('magnify themselves') will be shamed, confused and humiliated (verse 26). At the same time he is concerned that all who 'delight in' ('favour') David's 'righteous cause' (verse 27, literally 'my righteousness' or 'my justification') will give a 'ringing cry of joy' and 'be glad' (the same word translated rejoice' or 'gloat' used of the enemy; see verses 15,19,26). Instead of the enemy magnifying themselves through their malicious acts it is the Lord who is to be 'magnified' (see Psalm 34:3) by those people of God in the community who love justice. Those who 'favour' ('delight in') David's 'righteous cause' speak of the Lord who 'has pleasure in' ('delights in') the 'peace' ('prosperity') of his servant. While the enemy gloated over David's 'hurt' or 'calamity' God delighted in his welfare, his 'prosperity' (Hebrew *shalom* 'peace' or 'well-being').

Vow (verse 28)

David promises to witness with audible words (literally, 'my tongue shall mutter', see Psalm 1:2) to the 'righteousness' on which he has grounded his plea (see verse 24) as he praises God 'all the day long'. That divine attribute is the fixed standard by which everything is measured and it works to put things right. In delivering David from his enemies, God is doing exactly that. David's vindication or justification is his righteousness and is evidence of God's righteousness. In the context of God's covenant with Israel that means that God is being true to his word, to deliver the humble poor and to bring low the haughty (see 1 Samuel 2:4-8; Luke 1:51-53). Does your justification by God so thrill you that you cannot help talking about God's amazing righteousness all the day long?

David's experience in this psalm anticipates the greater injustice suffered by Jesus the Messiah who was hated without cause (John 15:25; Psalm 69:4), treated wrongfully by those for whom he had been concerned, and then had wrongful allegations made against him by false witnesses. But as David looked for God's justice so our Lord committed himself to this same righteous God and he was justified or vindicated by his resurrection (1 Timothy 3:16; Romans 1:4). And the Christ who died for our sins was raised for our justification too (Romans 4:25). Our Saviour went further than David, for he willingly received the ultimate curse that all haters of God and his people deserve so that all who repent and trust his saving work might no longer be under that curse but know the blessing of God—peace with God, the peace of God that passes all understanding and everlasting well-being.

Christians can expect persecution, but Jesus urges us, like David, to pray that God's will might be done on earth and to commit ourselves into God's hands asking him to deliver us from evil. We look forward to the day when all Christian believers will be finally vindicated on that day of resurrection and judgment.

Psalm 36

Human Arrogance and Divine Grace

This poem reminds us of Psalm 2 and assures the godly that despite the proud plans of the wicked they can look with confidence to the Lord. There are three main sections: The schemes of the ungodly (1-4); the character of God (5-9); the cry of the godly (10-12).

To the familiar heading is added a phrase describing David as 'the servant of the LORD' (see Psalm 18). It speaks both of the person's exclusive allegiance to God and of the protection that the person can expect from God. The formula is often used in reference to Moses and it became in Isaiah's prophecy a way of describing Israel as a nation and especially Israel's representative, 'the Suffering Servant' who would bring universal blessing. Sometimes God addresses individuals like Moses, Caleb, David and Job as 'my servant' (Numbers 12:7; 14:24; 2 Samuel 3:18; 7:5,8; Psalm 89:3,20; Job 1:8; 2:3; 42:7).

The schemes of the ungodly (verses 1-4)
David is given ('within my heart') a prophetic word ('An oracle') concerning the 'transgression of the wicked' which he wishes to share. In 2 Samuel 23:2 David is aware of the Spirit of the Lord speaking through him (see Acts 2:30) but unlike the prophets who proclaimed

directly a word of judgment on the wicked, this is more like an 'insight' into the mind of those who are opposed to God.

They are wicked and devise their evil plans because they are in rebellion against God. Not only is there no humble respect for and dependence on God that a godly fear generates (the 'fear' that is the beginning of wisdom), but they are brazenly unafraid of God in the sense that they do not even tremble like the demons before the king of terrors. Such ungodliness naturally leads to unrighteousness which the rest of the section proceeds to depict. The particular acts of evil in which people engage is due to their relationship with God being all wrong.

Those who are in rebellion against God have such an inflated view of themselves they cannot appreciate sin for what it is nor hate it. This is the most likely meaning of the difficult original (verse 2). There are echoes of Psalms 1 and 2 in the verses that follow. They distort the truth with their wicked words and because they lack that wisdom which comes from above they are unable to do good. In the quiet of their bedroom they plan wickedness and as they are committed to a way that is not good they do not despise what is evil. This is the ungodly, unrighteous world of human beings, living without thought for God or what he counts as good, ever seeking their own selfish ends no matter who they trample on and destroy. Where is God in all this if there is one? Paul includes the second half of verse 1 in a series of Old Testament quotations to back up his argument concerning the plight of human beings in sin (Romans 3:18).

The character of God (verses 5–9)

How different is the LORD to these arrogant humans! David does not, like Paul, speak of the wrath of God already revealed against such ungodly, unrighteous people. Rather, he emphasises God's love and care for all who put their trust in the LORD. God, in fact, goes out of his way to 'preserve man and beast' (verse 6b). How reassuring it is to be reminded that God is there and that he remains true to character! First, the infinite nature of God's steadfast love, faithfulness, righteousness and judgments are highlighted from highest heaven to the deepest sea. This is followed by a testimony to the benefits that come to those who trust themselves to this God and draw on his resources.

God's 'mercy' is his steadfast love; his 'faithfulness' means he can be trusted, fulfilling all his promises as well as carrying out all his threats.

The LORD's 'righteousness' and 'judgments' mean that he will always act in accord with his own upright standard of what is right and fair.

God's character is experienced—his loving commitment to his people is something very precious. Like chicks under the protection of mother hen's wings so the godly can find protection in the Lord (verse 7). Jesus wept that so many of his own nationality were refusing to come under his care and saving grace.

They are treated like honoured guests 'abundantly satisfied' (literally 'watered fully', verse 8) with the very best ('fulness', literally 'fatness') that God's house provides. There is a never-ending supply in the Lord's delightful river. The word for 'pleasures' or 'delights' (verse 8) is the name of the area where the original garden was situated—'Eden', a place with plenty of water. For people used to drought and desert conditions the idea of rivers and fountains speaks of vitality and fruitfulness.

Light and life (see verse 9) are often found together in the Bible. God's first creative word is 'Let there be light' and he subsequently filled the earth with life. With regard to creation Jesus, as the Word of God, 'was life and the life was the light of men' (John 1:4; 5:26). Later in John's Gospel, light and life are associated with the salvation that he brings. The Lord is the source of all life, natural and spiritual ('the fountain of life'; see Jeremiah 2:13; 17:13; John 4:14; 7:37–38). Experiencing God's light dispels the darkness associated with human sin and ignorance. Not only are there echoes of the creation narrative but we find John also using both the symbolism of water and light to convey something of the satisfying splendour of the new creation (Revelation 21–22).

The cry of the godly (verses 10–12)

In the light of this confession of God's character David returns to the present situation where the ungodly behave with arrogant pride. He has no desire to become like the wicked but he is aware of his own frailties and the enemy's strength. His plea is therefore that all who know God and are upright in heart might continue to experience God's faithful love ('loving-kindness') and 'righteousness' (verse 10). He is given assurance that however troublesome and overbearing the ungodly presently are, they will not finally succeed. They are to lie 'fallen', 'cast down', unable to rise (verse 12). That will be the end of all opposition to God and his people. As John puts it 'Babylon the great is fallen, is fallen' (Revelation 18:2). The next psalm will express in more detail what will happen to the ungodly.

Psalm 37

Don't Fret

We can easily get upset and angry when we see how those who have no thought for God seem to thrive and go unpunished. This psalm is to calm our nerves and encourage us to put our faith in God. It is similar to the teaching we find in the wisdom books of the Bible and the opening words are almost identical with Proverbs 24:19. What is introduced in Psalm 1 is developed here and is a reminder that despite the difficulties experienced in so many of the psalms in this first book, we are encouraged to view life as a whole from the right perspective.

This is another acrostic psalm where each of the letters of the Hebrew alphabet are used in turn to begin a new stanza (see Psalms 9-10; 25; 34).[77] Apart from verses 14-15 and 25-26 each stanza consists of four half lines (equivalent to two verses).

Being an alphabetic psalm it does not have any clearly marked sections of thought but the repeated phrases 'cut off' (verses 9,22,28,34,38) and 'inherit the land/earth' (9,22,29,34) do suggest a means of dividing the contents into five sections.

Exhortations and Encouragements (verses 1-11)

The psalm opens with a call urging us not to get heated with rage—a much stronger idea than that conveyed by the word 'fret' (verse 1).

Have we had the experience of boiling inwardly with no opportunity to let off steam against those who have caused the anger? The word only occurs at the beginning and end of this first section (verses 7–8) and in the corresponding verse in Proverbs 24:19. We are not to get worked up or 'envious' concerning those described as 'workers of iniquity' and 'evildoers'. They are referred to later as the 'wicked'. They may use the right terminology and be ever so religious but as Jesus reminds us, they do not do God's will but practise lawlessness (Matthew 7:23).

Why must we cool down? David encourages us to believe that like the fresh green grass in springtime on the hills of Judea that soon withers and fades with the heat of the sun, so these evil people flourish only for a brief moment. Instead of eyeing the wicked (of whom he will have more to say later) and getting riled needlessly, our attention is directed to the Lord. This will bring our blood pressure down! We are urged to 'Trust in the LORD and do good' (verse 3) and enjoy the benefits of God's 'faithfulness' in the promised land, to 'delight' in the Lord and 'commit' (literally 'roll upon Yahweh') our lives to him for he will see to it that our requests are realised ('he will give you ... he shall bring *it* to pass', verses 4–5). The Lord will bring about a judicial decision of a right standing for his people ('your righteousness ... your justice', verse 6) as clear as the midday light. In other words, the Lord will vindicate his people for all to see. Just as God the Father vindicated Jesus by his resurrection to glory, so all God's people will be vindicated at the general resurrection.

The second half of this section (verses 7–11) repeats the concerns of the first half. This time the positive command to trust comes first—'Rest' or 'Be still' and 'wait patiently' for the 'LORD'—followed by the call 'do not fret' over anyone who succeeds in 'schemes' or plots that ride roughshod over others (verse 7; see verse 12). We are warned to refrain from getting all worked up within ('anger', 'wrath') for such fretting will result in more evil, such as taking the law into one's own hands instead of looking to God to take vengeance (verse 8).

The end of the wicked person is again stressed while the humble believer ('the meek' verse 11) can look forward to the future with confidence. Evildoers will, in 'a little while' (verse 10), be 'cut off' (verse 9), a term that is used frequently in Leviticus for direct punishment from God that includes death and disinheritance. On the other hand, those who look to the Lord to come to their aid will 'inherit the earth' (or 'land', verses 9,11); those who 'delight' themselves in the Lord (verse

4) will 'delight' themselves in the 'abundance of peace' (verse 11). The land promised to Abraham's descendants is a reminder of the paradise lost through sin and a type of the new earth to come. Peace involves security and well-being. There are many throughout history who have coveted land and succeeded in taking it by force. How privileged are God's people for in the end, as our Lord indicates, the 'meek shall inherit the earth' (Matthew 5:5; Isaiah 32:16-19).

The righteous and wicked contrasted (verses 12–22)

A new section opens with the seventh letter of the Hebrew alphabet. Here we are taught that the attempts of the wicked to oppress the righteous ultimately come to nothing. In the New Testament James deals with the non-Christian rich who were exploiting the poor righteous believers and encourages them by indicating that God will deal with the oppressors (James 5:1-11).

While the 'wicked' person 'plots' (see the noun 'schemes' or 'plots' in verse 7; Psalm 31:13) against the righteous and menacingly 'gnashes at him with his teeth' like a snarling wolf (see Psalm 35:16), the Lord has them in derision for he is in ultimate control and will punish them in due course (see Psalm 2:4; Psalm 59:8). The following stanza (verses 14-15) has an extra two lines in verse 14 to emphasise that the weapons used with deadly intent by the wicked against the righteous, who are described as 'poor', 'needy' and 'upright', rebound to their own hurt and loss.

Verses 16-19 remind us of the wisdom books of the Bible, especially the 'better than' proverbs (see Proverbs 12:9; 15:16-17; 16:8, etc.). The 'wicked' enemies of the righteous may be 'many', 'wealthy' ('riches'; literally 'abundance') and powerful ('arm' can suggest strength), but this will not last, for 'arms' as well as 'bows' can be 'broken' (verse 17: see verse 15). While the 'righteous' may not have much, it is enough if they have the Lord upholding them.

The righteous are termed 'the upright' (verse 18) or more accurately 'the blameless'. They are like Job who, while not sinless, displayed no obvious moral defects. These people's lives are known to the Lord (see Psalm 1:6). Unlike the wicked whose days are numbered (verse 13), the godly live out their days and their inheritance is eternally secure. When times of trouble come, when for instance famine strikes, they will not be ashamed for they will have plenty to eat (verses 18-19). The wicked, on the other hand, described as 'the enemies of the Lord' (verse 20) will 'perish'. Like pleasant pastureland that is soon burnt by sun or fire they will be quickly consumed and vanish like smoke (see verse 2).

The final proverb of this section (verse 21) contrasts the ultimate prosperity of the righteous who are able to show mercy and give generously (see verse 26) and the poverty of the wicked who are unable to repay their debts. It is a reminder of the promise to a faithful Israel: 'For the LORD your God will bless you ... you shall lend to many nations, but you shall not borrow' (Deuteronomy 15:6). The contrast is emphasised in the closing lines (verse 22) between the 'blessed' by God who 'inherit the earth' (see 11) and those 'cursed' who are 'cut off' (see verse 9).

Exhortations and Encouragements (verses 23–29)

Like the first section, these verses urge the righteous to live godly lives by reminding them of their position and security. The 'steps' refer to the whole course of life which God has 'ordered' and 'he delights' to execute the plan he has formed (verse 23). But David also knows that the godly can 'fall' but they will not be hurled down and perish like the wicked for the Lord 'upholds' them (verse 24; see verse 17). The verb 'to hurl' is used by the prophet Jeremiah to describe the punishment of being cast out of the land of promise (Jeremiah 16:13; 22:26,28) and is appropriate in this psalm where the opposite of inheriting the land is to be cut off, which involves having no inheritance in the land. It is a lovely picture that is painted of the Lord's care and support of his people—upheld by 'his hand'. Isaiah assures and comforts his people with the thought of God upholding his people with his 'righteous right hand' (Isaiah 41:10).

The situation depicted in verses 21–22 is reiterated here in verses 25 and 26 with the added illustration from experience. David in his mature years can say that throughout his life he has not, generally speaking, seen the righteous finally and utterly forsaken (although for a time it might seem so; see Psalm 22:1) nor their offspring begging for food. Rather they have been in a position to show mercy and lend to others and enable their offspring to prosper too.

It is emphasised again that to 'dwell' securely in the land (verses 27, 29) is the sure and certain hope of those who turn aside from evil and do good (see verse 3). On the other hand, the offspring of the wicked will be 'cut off' (verse 28). The wicked have no posterity through whom they can dwell for ever in the land, whereas the righteous have a future in the land through descendants that are blessed (verse 26). Enveloped in this hope is the truth concerning the Lord's preserving grace in verse 28. Far from abandoning (see verse 25) his 'saints' (see Psalms 30:3; 31:23; 32:6) he keeps them for ever. The Lord loves to make decisions that are fair and right ('justice'). No one need fear to trust him for we are not ruled by impersonal arbitrary forces but by a God who is committed to carrying out what he has promised.

The righteous and wicked contrasted (verses 30–34)

Again this short section ends with the righteous inheriting the land and the wicked 'cut off' (verse 34). We are given more information about the righteous. They speak 'wisdom' and 'justice' (see Proverbs 1:2–3), and because they have made God's law their own, it has affected their way of life. They have not slipped morally from the right path (verse 31; see Psalms 18:36; 26:1). The wicked on the other hand 'watches' the righteous with the intention of seeking an opportunity to kill him (verse 32). But again we are encouraged to believe that the Lord will not abandon ('leave', verse 33; see verse 28) the righteous to the power of the enemy nor allow them to be defeated in court. It reminds us of Romans 8 where no charge can be laid at the feet of those who are in Christ.

In the light of all this, the righteous are encouraged again to 'wait on the LORD' (verse 34; see verse 9) and keep true to God's way until the time of vindication and exaltation when they will enjoy the benefits of their inheritance. Then they will see what the Lord already sees (verse 13), namely, the wicked 'cut off' (verse 34; see Isaiah 66:24 for the righteous looking at the end of the wicked).

Consider the end (verses 35–40)

What is predicted in the previous verse is backed up from experience (see verse 25). David had seen a wicked person, terrifyingly powerful ('in great power', verse 35), who seemed to flourish like the righteous in Psalm 1. He spread himself like 'a native green tree' and yet he passed away. He was simply not there any more—the 'behold' (verse 36) conveying the idea of surprise. Though David looked for him he could not be found. Lloyd-Jones could say: 'I was never worried for a second about a man like Hitler; it was enough for me to read the thirty-seventh Psalm.'[78]

What happens to people who are 'blameless' (verse 37; see verse 18) and 'upright'? We are encouraged to 'Mark' ('watch') and 'observe' ('see') such people and our own conclusions will be those of David that 'there is a future for the man of peace' (rather than 'the future of that man is peace', verse 37). Such a person behaves in a way that encourages good relationships with both God and humans. On the other hand, 'transgressors', those who rebel against God and encourage trouble, will be destroyed at once. The 'future' of such wicked people will be 'cut off' (verse 38). Psalm 73 will remind us again of the fate of the ungodly. There the psalmist almost stumbled as he saw the prosperity of the wicked but recovered himself when he considered their end.

The psalm closes by emphasising in language more typical of David's poetry that the deliverance of God's people comes from the Lord who is their 'strength (or better 'stronghold') in time of trouble' (verse 39; see Psalms 27:1; 28:8; 31:2,4). He is the one who helps and delivers them from 'the wicked' not because of their good deeds or because they try to save themselves, as in the popular saying 'the Lord helps those who help themselves', but because they have taken refuge in ('they trust') the LORD (verse 40).

Psalm 38

Sin and Suffering

This is a very intense and urgent appeal from a distressed and humbled David. It calls to mind Job's situation but without the confessions of sin (see Job 30). Traditionally, this lament is seen as one of the seven 'penitential psalms' (see Psalm 6). To the familiar heading 'A Psalm of David' is added a phrase that occurs again as a title only in Psalm 70: 'To bring to remembrance' or 'to commemorate'. While some associate it with the 'memorial offering' (see Leviticus 2:2; 24:7), in the contexts where David uses the term, it suggests bringing his plight to God's remembrance. It may therefore be a special term to describe the lament, one of the three main types of psalm that the Levites were appointed to use in the sanctuary, the other two being thanksgiving and praise (see 1 Chronicles 16:4).

Opening plea (verse 1)

David's opening cry invoking God's special covenantal name 'O LORD' (Jehovah/Yahweh) is similar but not identical to that in Psalm 6:1. God is depicted as a father or teacher who 'rebukes' and 'chastens' his people rather than a judge who punishes the wicked. David is a believer; he loves God and is loved by God. But believers like David still sin and like a father who disciplines his children so the Lord disciplines those whom he loves (Proverbs 3:11-12; Hebrews 12:5-11). All sin is an

240

affront to God and is treated with the utmost seriousness. Emphasis falls on the 'wrath' of God and his 'hot displeasure' and they describe his settled opposition toward all who rebel in any way against his authority. David is aware that God is justified in chastening him but he prays that he would now no longer experience God's burning anger. It is on account of Christ's atoning death on the cross that God's wrath is appeased for all God's people who like David place their trust in God's saving provision.

Sin and Suffering (verses 2-10)

Physical and mental suffering is here acknowledged to be a divine punishment for sin where in the parallel line of verse 3 both God's 'anger' or 'indignation' and David's 'sin' are seen as reasons for his lack of wholeness and well-being ('soundness' and 'health',[79] verse 3). Jesus implies a link between sin and suffering in the case of the disabled man whose sin he pronounces forgiven (Mark 2:1-12). Paul can likewise see a connection between the wrong behaviour of the Corinthian Christians over the Lord's Supper and the sickness and death of some of their number (1 Corinthians 11:29-30). However, not all personal suffering is to be viewed as a direct result of some particular sin. The book of Job and Jesus' teaching make that clear (John 9:3) but David confesses that in his case it is true. While not jumping to immediate immature conclusions, Christians ought to reckon with the possibility that their illness has a disciplinary function on account of their waywardness. Perhaps among the Puritans it was overdone but we find the godly Matthew Henry using his frequent ailments to consider his life and to encourage him to be more zealous for his Lord. God's 'arrows' (see Psalm 7:12-13) and his heavy 'hand' (see Psalm 32:4) express graphically how the punishment was felt (verse 2). The reference to his 'flesh' and 'bones' (verse 3) describes David's entire being especially as it affected his outer person.

David's attitude to his sin (verses 4-6)

The next two verses concentrate on how his sin has affected him, thus taking up the thought of verse 3b, 'because of my sin'. It is not only the effects of sin but the sin itself that is disturbing him. His 'iniquities' or 'offences' have overwhelmed him like huge waves and have burdened him like a heavy load (verse 4). In verse 5 David views his sin as 'foolishness' (a term we usually associate with Proverbs, see especially

Proverbs 14) and the resulting ill-health smells ('foul' is literally 'stink') and looks revolting, being described in terms of a severe skin disease (see Isaiah 1:6). For a believer, sin is irrational and sheer stupidity.

David's sufferings (verses 6–8)

In these verses the lament continues to describe David's sufferings. He is bent over and humbled by the suffering and is like someone in mourning (verse 6; see Psalm 35:14). Instead of the normally healthy, fatty 'loins' (or waist; see Job 15:27) there is loathsome fever and no 'soundness in my flesh' (verse 7; the last phrase repeating the first part of verse 3). He is greatly 'numbed' ('feeble') and crushed ('broken' as in Psalm 51:8,17) and his voice, like the roar of a lion (see Isaiah 5:29 and Psalm 22:1), gives expression to his bodily, mental and spiritual anguish (verse 8).

David's cry to God (verses 9–10)

At this point David calls out to God, this time (see verse 1) using the term for ruler, 'Lord' (verse 9). Although he is aware that he deserves what he is experiencing of God's righteous indignation, he confesses that his whole being is an open book before God. The unspoken 'desire' of his heart as well as the audible 'sighing' or 'groaning' (see Psalms 6:6; 31:10) are not 'hidden' from the Lord (verse 9) just as Israel 'groaned' under Egyptian bondage and their cry was heard by God (Exodus 2:23–24). Verse 10 brings this section to a close by summarizing his state: his pounding heart, his strength evaporating, and the light that is expressive of life gone from his eyes.

Response of Friend and Foe (verses 11–16)

Up to this point only God and David have been in the picture but now others are added. When help is needed most, those near and dear to him keep their distance. Paul experienced the loss of support from friends when he needed them most (2 Timothy 4:9,16). Here David's close associates treat him like someone unclean. His condition is described in verse 5 in terms reminiscent of the skin diseases associated with the leprous conditions set out in the Mosaic law (see Leviticus 13). Interestingly, David refers to his affliction as a 'plague' (verse 11), a word that appears sixty-six times in Leviticus 13–14 with reference to unclean conditions in human skin, leather goods and house walls.[80] In those instances there is no thought of divine punishment but here, as with the plagues of Egypt, the context suggests the plague or attack is a judgment from God. It also provides opportunity for enemies to move in to lay traps using threats and deception to destroy him (verse 12; see Psalm 35:4). There were those like Saul at the beginning of his public life and Absalom his son in later life who were out to 'seek' the life of David (1 Samuel 20:1; 2 Samuel 16:11).

David's reaction (verses 13–14)

To all this provocation David's response in verses 13-14 is to react as if he has not heard ('deaf') and like one who could not speak ('mute'). The phrase 'does not open his mouth' prepares us for Isaiah's similar description of the Suffering Servant's silence in his affliction (Isaiah 53:7). By not responding to the enemy, David's faith shines out. He can keep silent because his 'hope' is in God or he 'waits for' God (see Psalms 31:24; 33:18), who will 'answer' (rather than 'hear').

David's cry to God (verses 15–16)

This assurance is expressed, as in verse 9, in David's cry to God, in which he addresses him first by his covenantal name 'O LORD', then as sovereign 'O Lord' and finally in personal terms, 'my God' (verse 15). His refusal to answer back and his patient acceptance of his situation is not because he has become insensitive to his enemy's intentions. They are out to gloat when his 'foot slips' (literally, 'when my foot moves'; referring to his present sufferings; see Psalm 15:5) and to use the occasion to exalt themselves. He looks to the Lord alone to vindicate him. The history of David's associations with his enemies provides many examples of his quiet confidence in God rather than in rash action. Jesus urges Christians to turn the other cheek (Matthew 5:39) and the same spirit is taught by the apostle Paul (Romans 12:14,17).

Sin and Suffering (verses 17–20)

David returns to his earlier thoughts (see especially verses 2-5). The first part of verse 17, 'For I am ready to fall', reads literally, 'For I am established to stumble' which probably means that David is confessing that he is 'prone to stumble' either in the general sense of being prone to afflictions (see Psalm 35:15) or in this context of moral failure that has resulted in 'anguish' (more literally his 'pain') that may unbalance him completely. There is a more direct public confession of wrongdoing in verse 18: 'For I declare my iniquity'. This is coupled with evidence of a penitent spirit, implied in his anxiety or 'anguish' over his sin.

David's powerful enemies are mentioned again and this time it is clear that there is no justification for their hatred (verse 19). Those who are opposing him are using the occasion of David's present situation to reward his previous 'good' toward them with evil (verse 20). Again, we see this in Saul's attitude although David always tried to serve him well.

Closing plea (verses 21–22)

The psalm closes as it began with an urgent plea to God. The intensity of his prayer is seen in the fourfold call: 'O Lord', 'O my God', 'O Lord' and 'my salvation' (see Psalm 27:1). 'David's capacity to wait God's time … owed nothing to a placid disposition or to a situation well in hand, but everything to the God he knew by name … as Master and Saviour' (Kidner). The sense of abandonment ('do not forsake me'; see Psalm 27:9) and isolation from God ('be not far from me'; see Psalm 35:22) coupled with his call for God to hurry to his aid underline David's desperate state. Familiar expressions are used but we are especially reminded of Psalm 22:1,11,19. The God who is perfectly just in punishing sinners and disciplining his people is also amazingly gracious to save and forgive the repentant.

We have seen how David's situation can be readily applied to the Christian, but it cannot go unnoticed how certain verses are strikingly similar to the experiences suffered by Jesus. Because of David's confession of sin, however, commentators and preachers have been reticent to apply the psalm to Christ. But taking our cue from psalms quoted in the NT that definitely point to Christ, and in which David acknowledges personal sin we see this psalm also as prophetic. What David the man of faith experienced as a sinner becomes prophetic of what our Lord the sinless one endured on behalf of sinners. He who 'knew no sin became sin for us'. He became the sinners' substitute and therefore experienced the ultimate wrath of God that sinners deserve. In his physical situation on the cross he was to all intents and purposes cursed by God in the eyes of the Jews and the worst of criminals in the eyes of the Gentiles. He experienced abandonment by those near to him (Matthew 26:56) and on the cross in the ultimate sense of God-forsakenness (Mark 15:34). His friends stood afar off gazing at his crucifixion (Mark 15:40–41; Luke 23:49). Before Jew and Gentile authorities he held his peace and gave no answer (Matthew 26:62–63;

Luke 23:9; John 19:9). He was the real Servant of the Lord who kept his mouth shut and was led like a lamb to the slaughter. They hated him for no reason (John 15:18–25). In fact, they hated him more for doing good. Instead of retaliating he committed himself to him who judges justly and looked to God to vindicate him (1 Peter 2:23; 1 Timothy 3:16). This is our Saviour who is also the supreme example to Christians experiencing personal trials and persecutions (1 Peter 2:21).

Psalm 39

Aliens and Foreigners

In this psalm there are a number of resemblances to Psalm 38. It opens with a determination not to speak in the presence of enemies (verses 1-2, also verse 9; see Psalm 38:13-14), it acknowledges that personal sin is the reason for the divine 'plague' that has afflicted him (verses 8,10; see Psalm 38:11) and it looks in hope to the Lord (verse 7; see Psalm 38:15). Though it has these features common to the lament it belongs more to the wisdom psalms and there are obvious similarities to the Books of Job and Ecclesiastes.

Between the now familiar introductory phrases 'To the chief Musician' (see Psalm 4) and 'A Psalm of David' (see Psalm 3) is added 'To Jeduthun', a name that occurs again in Psalms 62 and 77. In this heading it could mean that the chief musician is named—'Belonging to Jeduthun, the chief musician'. Jeduthun, along with Asaph and Heman, of the tribe of Levi, had charge of the music in God's house and under king David's supervision (1 Chronicles 16:41; 25:1-6). He is also described as the king's seer, prophesying with a harp, in hymns of praise and thanksgiving to God (see 1 Chronicles 25:3; 2 Chronicles 5:12-14; 35:15). The position is similar to that of Miriam who was called a prophetess when she led the women in song (Exodus 15:20). We also read of prophets with musical instruments whose prophesyings seem to be of a more unusual order involving no specific word from God,

246

and similar to what Saul engaged in under supernatural influence (see 1 Samuel 10:5–6,10–11; 19:20–24).

Here is a prayer in the wisdom tradition that challenges all believers to wake up to the effects of God's curse resulting from the original disobedience in the Garden—'in the day you eat of it you shall surely die' (Genesis 2:17; see also Genesis 5:5,8,11,14,17,etc.).

The Build-up to Prayer (verses 1-3)

Different interpretations have been put forward concerning these opening verses. Some see David training himself to exercise patience with Stoic resolve, 'trying to beat sin by disciplined silence' even when he should have spoken 'good' words (verse 2).[81] For others, David's attempts at self-discipline failed and he eventually gave vent to ill-advised complaints to God (Calvin).

It is better to see these abrupt introductory lines as not dissimilar to David's situation in the previous psalm. He resolves not to be provoked into making unguarded comments in the presence of 'the wicked' (verse 1; see Psalm 38:13–14) and though he has some success at first, in the end his emotions get the better of him but his outburst is not directed to any person but to God. We all know what it is like to dwell on an issue that troubles us so that it begins to make us boil inside.

David's 'ways' (verse 1) refer to his behaviour and in this instance to the things he speaks. He does not wish to sin by charging God with wrong (see Job 1:22). The phrase 'from good' (verse 2) could mean that David held his peace 'with no good result ('to no avail', see English Standard Version) or 'from saying anything good' (see New International) or perhaps 'beyond what is good', meaning that he kept silent more than was good for him (Goldingay). This is why he becomes more hot and bothered. There is a time to be silent but also a time to speak (Ecclesiastes 3:7). David, like the Suffering Servant, is right to be silent in the face of enemy provocations (Psalm 38:13–14; Isaiah 53:7) but to bottle up one's emotions and lose inward peace is not good. In avoiding 'sin with my tongue' (verse 1) he is sinning in his heart. Paul urges Christians, 'Be anxious for nothing, but in everything by prayer and supplication, with thanksgiving let your requests be made known to God; and the peace of God, which surpasses all understanding, will guard your hearts and minds through Christ Jesus' (Philippians 4:6). In the end this is what David does, he addresses God. Instead of 'musing' or muttering quietly to himself (see Psalm 2:1), 'I spoke with my tongue' (verse 3).

The following verses present the great ache of David's heart which he now offloads onto God. It also reveals his faith in the God who is right to punish sin but who also pardons and delivers from the full consequences of our wrongdoing.

The Prayer (verses 4–13)
There are natural breaks in what David expresses to God, marked by the repetition of 'Certainly/Surely every man is vapour' (not so obvious in English translations!) and by the use of 'Selah' (verses 5,11; see Psalm 3). The final verse ends with the same thought of a life soon gone and is 'no more' (verse 13). Two sections of the prayer also begin by addressing God using his personal covenant name 'LORD' (Jehovah/Yahweh; verses 4 and 12). The middle section uses the term 'sovereign' ('Lord'; verse 7).

Human frailty (verses 4–5)
The fragile, fleeting nature of human life is what concerns David, a fact impressed upon him personally through his present sufferings (see verse 10). He prays for the humility to acknowledge and accept ('make me to know ... I may know, verse 4) the unwelcome fact of how transient ('my end ... the measure of my days') and 'frail' his own life is. A similar prayer is found on the lips of Moses who saw a whole generation die in the wilderness (Psalm 90:12). There is great excitement when someone lives for a hundred years with pictures in the local paper. But David confesses that however old he might live it is 'as nothing' (verse 5) in God's estimation, a few 'handbreadths'. This same measure is called 'four fingers' in Jeremiah 52:21, since it stood for the width of the hand minus the thumb.

The important additional point that is made in verse 5 is that it is God who has made his life so brief ('Indeed, you have made ...'). And this is not only true of David because of his own circumstances, it is so in the case of 'every man' (literally, 'all humanity'), even those in their 'best state' (literally, 'standing firm'); those in the prime of life who appear strong and healthy are but 'vapour'. The fact that the whole phrase is repeated in verse 11 (it literally reads, 'Surely all humanity is vapour') means we are to take this truth to heart.

The word translated as 'vapour' or 'breath' (see Isaiah 57:13) appears again in verse 6 where it is given a figurative meaning: 'in vain' (or 'for nothing'). In the Old Testament it is the metaphorical understanding of 'vapour' that predominates. Breath or vapour is used particularly to convey the idea of transience. On a cold misty day you often see people's breath like little puffs of smoke that disappear in a moment. Though 'vapour' can be used in some contexts for what is weightless, without substance and futile, such as the worship of idols (see Jeremiah 10:3,15; 16:19), that is not the sense here. It is the fleeting nature of human life that is in mind (see also Psalms 62:9; 144:3-4). It is a theme constantly brought to our attention in the Bible from Isaiah 40:6-8 to James 4:14, 'For what is your life? It is even a vapour that appears for a little time and then vanishes away'. The same truth is pressed home by the Preacher's twelve-chapter sermon on his text 'Vanity of vanities ... all is vanity' (Ecclesiastes 1:2; 12:8). In that sermon, where the word for 'every' or 'all' and the term 'vapour' (often translated 'vanity') occur many times, the Preacher's point is not that all is useless and without meaning (as regrettably it is often translated) but that the whole earthly existence is transitory. The name given to Adam and Eve's second son, Abel, is the very word we have here for 'vapour' and prophetic of a life cut short through his brother's murderous action.[82]

Hope not despair (verses 6-11)
The two parts of verse 6 could well be the conclusion of the previous section with the identical emphatic start to the lines—'Surely' in the original is the same word as 'Certainly' (verse 5)—and underlining yet again life's transitory nature. But taking verse 6 as the opening of the second section of David's prayer, reminds us that there is no real change in his thinking from the beginning to the end of this section with regard to the brevity of life in this world. Like the Preacher who closes his sermon as he began with 'all is vapour', so David ends as he began repeating the refrain with which he closed the previous section, 'Surely every man is vapour'.

The first part of verse 6 expands on the truth that all humans are mere vapour by describing a man as living like a 'shadow' (literally, 'image'; see Psalm 73:20). There is an air of unreality about human life in this world. There is no substance to it. Though there is plenty of bustling activity ('busy themselves') such as you find in city centres it is all a 'vapour' ('in vain'), because it is so insubstantial and transient. People 'heap up' things like storing away grain (see Genesis 41:35) or hoarding money (Job 27:16) and yet do not benefit from it all. The

Preacher sounds a similar note (see Ecclesiastes 2:18–21). Despite all our feverish efforts we cannot be sure who will enjoy our hard-earned wealth. In his parable of the rich fool Jesus warns those who are concerned about earthly treasure but are not rich toward God (Luke 12:13–21).

The renewed stress on the brevity of human life (verse 6) leads to this 'And now', in which David confesses anew his confidence in God—'My hope is in you' (verse 7). There is nothing one can 'wait for' or 'look to' with certainty in this world apart from God. The prayer continues with the plea that God would rescue the psalmist not only from his sin and guilt but, more particularly in this context, from the trouble he is experiencing (see verse 10) as a direct result of all his 'transgressions' (verse 8) or, to be more precise, all his rebellious activity against God. David has been severely disciplined by God but he prays that it would end so that he might not be exposed as an object of ridicule by the 'foolish' who blaspheme (verse 8; see Psalm 14:1). It is interesting to note that although he had sinned grievously, he does not consider himself as belonging to the 'wicked' fools (see verse 1). It is because he belongs to the company of those who are committed to God that he is able to pray in the way he does.

It is because God has brought about David's crisis situation (the emphasis is on the 'you') that he has kept 'mute' (verse 9; see verse 3) in silent submission. There is no justification for changing the exact verbal form from the past 'I was mute' (verse 3) to the present 'I am mute' and to suggest that from 'obstinate suppression' David now displays 'filial submission' (Alexander and see ESV).

Conscious of the Lord's 'plague' (verse 10; see Psalm 38:11), this 'blow' (literally 'hostility') of God's hand that has consumed him, he prays more directly for its removal (see verse 8). From his own personal afflictions in verse 10 David moves back in verse 11 to a general statement about God disciplining people on account of sin, dissolving to nothing 'his beauty' (the things that make him desirable, such as his strength and health) as a 'moth' destroys a garment. This part of the prayer then ends appropriately by repeating the words from the close of verse 5—'Surely every man is vapour'.

Plea for relief (verses 12–13)

Up to this point the psalm has taken the form of a meditation on the frailty of human life prompted by his own calamitous circumstances, with a call to rescue him from his plight. Now we are introduced to the kind of pleas associated with the beginning of a psalm—'Hear my prayer (verse 12; see Psalm 4:1) ... Give ear to my cry' (see Psalm 5:1). His 'tears' express the earnestness of his supplications (see Psalm 6:6) pleading that the God who has this special relationship with his people ('LORD') would not be 'silent' at his distress call (see Psalms 28:1; 35:22). The argument he uses to draw God's attention returns to the theme of the transitory nature of human life, only this time he uses expressions familiar from the writings of Moses.

A 'stranger' would be better translated 'resident alien', one who is a foreigner living more or less permanently in the land but with no right to possess any of it. A 'sojourner' or 'temporary visitor' is one whose stay in the country is generally much shorter. Both terms are brought together to describe Israel's position in Canaan. They are tenants in a land that belongs to the Lord (Leviticus 25:23). Israel was urged to show love and care toward such vulnerable people as the resident alien and temporary visitor, remembering that they were once in such a position in Egypt (Leviticus 19:33–34). David uses this terminology to argue that God should act similarly toward him. By adding 'as all my fathers were' David is probably thinking of Abraham who introduced himself to the 'sons of Heth' as a resident alien and temporary visitor (Genesis 23:4; see also 47:9) and as it states in the New Testament, he 'sojourned in the land of promise as in a foreign country, dwelling in tents with Isaac and Jacob' (Hebrews 11:9).

The Chronicler includes a prayer of David that echoes what is expressed in this psalm. At the very point where David's reign reaches a climax he confesses how transient this life is even at its best, but that all is a gift from God. 'For we are aliens and pilgrims ("temporary visitors") before you, as were all our fathers; our days on earth are as a shadow and without hope' (1 Chronicles 29:15). All our living and enjoyment in this world must be seen as something God allows us for a limited period, for some longer, for others shorter. Do we appreciate that in this world we are like guests in someone's home? Even if we have inherited or bought our own house we cannot stay there permanently. Illness and death in the family bring home to us the reality of what David is saying. It is wisdom to remember these things.

The final verse ends as the other sections have ended, with the prospect of departing from this earthly scene, of being 'no more' (verse 13; Job 7:8)[83] as far as living in the world is concerned (see Genesis 5:24).

It does not mean ceasing to exist altogether. David's final appeal does not mean that he is no longer interested in God's gracious presence (see Psalm 27:9). Like Job, David's concern is that God would remove his angry gaze associated with the discipline that has made him so aware of his mortality (see Job 7:19; 14:6), and would grant him a little respite ('regain strength' or 'brightness' or 'smile') before he departs this life (Job 10:20–21).

While this psalm arises out of David's particular circumstances the main point it addresses is true for all of us in this world. It is not the subjective reaction of a depressed person but expressive of an objective reality that is depicted in the early chapters of Genesis (2:17; 3:3:16–19; 5:5,8,11,14, etc.), by Ecclesiastes (6:12; 12:1–8), Isaiah (40:6) and by the New Testament apostles (Romans 8:18–25; 1 Peter 1:24–25; 2:11; James 4:14). The wise woman of Tekoa certainly impressed the truth upon David when she confronted him with the words, 'for we will surely die and become like water spilled on the ground, which cannot be gathered up again' (2 Samuel 14:14). The smell of death lies over the whole of creation as a result of that initial rebellion in God's garden (see Psalms 90:7–12). We are all sinners and we all deserve this death sentence. Even with the clarity and fulness of revelation that Christians enjoy through the coming of the Lord Jesus Christ and his triumph over sin and death, we are not exempt from the initial effects of Adam's sin. We are all part of a human race of sinners under God's curse that in this world includes pain, sorrow and death.

Of course, there is still much we do not understand. Why should a recognisably good person like Job receive so much trouble? But through Christ we look forward with Abraham to 'a better country', to a new creation, to the resurrection of the body and to the end of the curse (Hebrews 11:13–16; Revelation 21:4; 22:4). In Christ, as far as the heavenly city is concerned, we can say with Paul that we are no longer strangers and aliens but permanent citizens (Ephesians 2:19). We can also pray for recovery from illness and trouble that we might serve him better while we have breath, and can thank God for all the good things he allows us to enjoy to 'brighten up' life's 'little day'. The Preacher encourages us during our fleeting lives (not 'meaningless' or 'useless', as it is often translated), to make the most of these good gifts from God (Ecclesiastes 2:24; 3:12–13,22; 8:15; 9:9).

Psalm 40

Past Blessings, Present Need

It is both encouraging and humbling to read or to hear of the experiences of those whose lives have been wonderfully changed by the power of God and who have committed themselves in selfless service to the Lord who has saved them. In this psalm we have a segment of David's 'spiritual autobiography'[84] in which he reveals his commitment to share the good news of God's salvation with others. David uses the memory of God's goodness to him in the past (verses 1-10) to plead for his help in the present (verses 11-17). The waiting on God, the cry for deliverance, the presence of enemies, all in the context of personal sin, connects it with the previous three psalms. In fact, the psalm brings together phrases and concerns found from Psalm 30 onward and particularly Psalm 35.

The way the psalm moves from praise and proclamation to prayer and lamentation reminds us of Psalm 27. Although the final section (verses 13-17) appears again as Psalm 70, we must not think that the verses have been tagged on here. The two parts belong together as is seen from the subtle word links. From the heading ('To the Chief Musician ... of David'), which is exactly the same as in Psalms 13, 19-21 and 31, it is clear that David's personal experience was meant to be used by the 'great congregation' of God's people.

Testimony (verses 1–3)

The 'waiting' that David has referred to in previous psalms (37:9,34; 39:7) is emphasised here, using a familiar Hebrew idiom first found in Genesis 2:17. Like 'surely die' (literally 'dying you will die') we have here 'waited patiently' (verse 1) or 'simply waited' (literally 'waiting I will wait'). He resorted to no other avenues; he simply persevered in waiting for his covenant keeping God ('Lord') to respond. But what is only hoped for in the previous psalms is actually experienced. The Lord 'inclined' or 'bent down' to hear David's 'cry' (see Psalms 17:6; 31:2; 39:12), like someone leaning forward to catch what is being said.

As in Psalm 30:1–3 David testifies to God's action in delivering him from what appears like a near death experience or a situation that had brought him extremely low mentally and spiritually. The deliverance is highlighted by the contrasting states. He has been brought from 'a horrible pit' (literally 'noisy pit'; see Psalm 65:7) and from 'miry clay' (see Psalm 69:2,14) and has had his feet placed firmly on 'rock' (verse 2; see Psalms 18:2; 31:3). After such an experience his 'steps' would need to be steadied (see Psalms 17:5; 37:31). Jeremiah was literally put into a pit where he could easily have drowned as he sank into the slimy mud at the bottom (Jeremiah 38:6). Any kind of disaster is for David a death-like experience. The image of a 'pit' is used to describe the grave and especially to denote the state of the wicked—'death under the wrath of God' (Motyer; see Psalms 28:1; 30:3). Our salvation not only involves deliverance from the realm of sin and Satan and the pit of destruction, but positively it means being securely established in Christ. Our Lord Jesus Christ knew what it was to wait patiently until he was brought out of his 'pit' experience on behalf of sinners.

As a result of the divine rescue David can sing again. He can utter a 'new song' (verse 3; see Psalm 33:3; Revelation 14:3) in the form of 'praise'. It could well have been a freshly composed piece but not necessarily so, for former compositions can be applied to new situations, as is the case when we use the psalms in our devotions. This praise is to 'God' not humans and the plural 'our' leads David to encourage others to 'see' and 'fear' ('be in holy awe of'; see Psalms 34:7,9; 52:6) the 'Lord' and to 'trust' him (see Psalm 26:1). Is our praise of God infectious, encouraging others to an appropriate response when they see our enthusiasm?

Affirmation (verses 4-5)

Arising out of his personal situation David makes this general declaration concerning the 'blessed', happy position (see Psalms 1:1; 34:8) of people who place their confidence in this covenant God ('LORD') rather than in those who 'have regard for' ('respect', literally 'turning to'; see Psalm 25:16) 'the proud'[85] or who 'turn aside' from the good way to 'lies' (verse 4). The psalmist is probably thinking of false gods (see Leviticus 19:4) as well as humans who exalt themselves to godlike positions. In support of this affirmation verse 5 declares before God ('O LORD my God') that what has happened to him is but another demonstration of God's purposeful ('your thoughts'), 'wonderful' activity toward his people (see Psalms 9:1; 92:5). The 'us' clearly shows he is thinking more generally of the innumerable saving works of the Lord that makes an orderly list impossible, they 'cannot be recounted to you in order'. John reckons at the end of his Gospel that there were so many other things that Jesus did the world itself would be unable to contain the necessary books (John 21:25).

Commitment (verses 6-8)

David returns to his own situation and to the response that he needs to make to God's activity in his life. How is he to express his gratitude? The normal response would be to offer animal sacrifices (1 Samuel 11:15; Psalms 107:21-22; 116:17). But here David does not rush to make the usual thank-offerings. He mentions in verse 6 four of the five main kinds of offering: 'sacrifice' is often used for thank-offerings associated with the peace or fellowship sacrifices; 'offering' can be used as a general word for sacrifice, present or tribute but specifically for the grain or cereal offering; the 'burnt offering' was given particularly as a propitiatory sacrifice to appease the divine wrath, while the purification or 'sin offering' had an expiatory function for cleansing from sin's impurity.[86]

The point that David is making is that obedience to God is more important than mindless sacrificial rituals. Such offerings are worthless when divorced from a willing submission to God and his will. Saul offered many such sacrifices after his victory over the Amalekites but he had flouted the explicit command of God. Samuel's immortal words are probably on David's mind here: 'Has the Lord as great delight in burnt offerings and sacrifices as in obeying the voice of the Lord? Behold, to obey is better than sacrifice and to heed than the fat of rams'

(1 Samuel 15:22). Successive prophets emphasised the same message (see Isaiah 1:11–17; Jeremiah 6:19–20; Amos 5:21–24; Hosea 6:6; Micah 6:6–8).

'My ears you have opened' (verse 6; literally 'you have dug') is not an allusion to the ceremony of boring through the ear of a willing slave as a symbol of lifelong service (see Exodus 21:6 and NIV's 'my ears you have pierced'). David uses very graphic language to describe the way the Lord has prepared him for responding to God's will. He speaks as if the Lord has dug the holes in his skull for his ears so that he can hear clearly! It reminds us of what the Servant of the Lord said: 'The Lord God has opened my ear; and I was not rebellious, nor did I turn away' (Isaiah 50:5). Like Isaiah's willing response to God's call, David cries out excitedly, 'Here I come' ('Behold, I come', verse 7; see Isaiah 6:8). He delights to do whatever his God desires ('I delight to do your will, O my God', verse 8; see Psalm 1:2). God's 'law' or instruction he has made his own; it is 'within' as part of his emotional makeup (see Psalm 37:31; Deuteronomy 6:6; Proverbs 3:3). David is dedicated to obey God sincerely and it is a characteristic of all those in the new covenant (Isaiah 51:7; Jeremiah 31:31–34). Christians are urged to offer their whole selves as living sacrifices to God (Romans 12:1–2). The Lord's written revelation is described as 'the volume of the book', 'the Scripture scroll' (verse 7), a probable reference to the Mosaic Law Book and particularly to that portion that deals with the duties of an Israelite king (Deuteronomy 17:14–20). David appreciates that it 'concerns' him or is 'about' him ('of me', verse 7; see 2 Kings 22:13) as king.

Instead of 'ears you have dug' the pre-Christian Greek translators who produced the Septuagint (LXX), as witnessed in the Hebrews 10:5 quotation, substituted 'a body you have prepared', understanding the body part to stand for the whole physical frame, which is a very legitimate interpretation. As in other passages of the Septuagint Version, this rendering lent itself more easily to viewing the verses as a prophecy concerning Christ. Jesus said that Moses 'wrote of me' (John 5:46). What we see in God's servant David, a man after God's own heart who would do all God's will, is but a shadow of what was perfectly displayed in Christ, the obedient servant of the Lord (see Acts 13:22–23). Our Saviour also offered the real sacrifice to which the old sacrificial system pointed, making those blood offerings forever obsolete (Hebrews 10:1–18).

Proclamation (verses 9–10)

Not only does David respond by offering his whole being in glad surrender he is also keen to preach the gospel, the 'good news' (see Isaiah 40:9) 'of righteousness in the great congregation' of God's people, perhaps at festival time (verse 9; see Psalm 22:22-26). The righteous God 'sets things right' (see Psalm 35:24) through his wonderful works. David makes a point of emphasising before God ('O LORD, you yourself know') that he has resisted the temptation to say nothing. He has not restrained his lips, or kept God's righteousness 'hidden' within him, neither has he 'concealed' from the people God's loving commitment and truth (verse 10; Psalms 5:7; 19:9). He has declared those characteristics of God so closely associated with his covenant promises (see Exodus 34:6-7; Psalm 36:5-6) and which have been demonstrated freshly to David in the deliverance he has experienced. The character of God is revealed in even stronger colours in the saving work of Christ on the cross, where wrath and mercy meet.

Supplication (verses 11–17)

David's plea in this section reminds Christians that though they have cried to God for help in the past and known the blessing of deliverance and forgiveness they can come again and again to the Lord in prayer. We need not be reticent to apply to him again and at the same time to acknowledge the wonders of God's previous activity in our lives.

Introduction (verse 11)

This verse could be a statement of confidence ('You will not withhold your tender mercies from me ...'; see English Standard Version) or a prayer ('Do not withhold your tender mercies from me'). There may be deliberate ambiguity in David's words but it does provide the basis for his lament in verse 12 and his pleas in the remainder of the psalm. He draws attention again to God's 'covenant love' ('loving-kindness') and 'truthfulness' ('truth') that can 'preserve' him from danger and trouble (Psalms 31:23; 32:7). God's 'tender mercies' or 'compassion' presents another feature of his character not previously mentioned (see Psalms 25:6; 103:4). As David did not 'restrain' ('withhold'; verse 9) his lips so he expects God not to 'withhold' (same word as in verse 9) his compassion in his present predicament. Jesus revealed the heart of God when on numerous occasions he was 'moved with compassion' at the condition of the people and acted to bring relief and salvation (see Mark 1:41; 6:34; 8:2).

Lament (verse 12)

As God's 'wonderful works' could not be 'numbered' so David now speaks of 'innumerable' troubles that have come at him from all quarters and which he admits are the consequences of his own sins, a factor that connects this psalm with Psalms 38 and 39. He is so overwhelmed by his sins that he cannot 'see' ('look up' is wrong; see Psalm 38:4) and his 'heart fails' (literally 'my heart has left me'; see Psalm 38:10). All Christ's sufferings and the punishments he endured were not on account of his own personal sins. Only in the sense that he stood in the place of sinners can this part of the psalm be applied to our Saviour. He was made to be sin who knew no sin (2 Corinthians 5:21).

Cry for deliverance (verses 13–17)

The recollection of the Lord's previous activity encourages David to make this urgent plea for 'help' and quick action ('make haste', 'do not delay', verses 13 and 17; see Psalm 22:19). He uses God's covenant name twice in verse 13 and again in verse 17 along with the personal 'my God'. What he wishes on enemies, who gloat over his troubles and are bent on destroying him, is for them to be shamed (verses 14–15; see Psalm 35:4,21,26). For the believer it is Satan the accuser who enjoys seeing a Christian fall and in trouble. It hurts especially when his earthly followers draw attention to Christians who have become morally compromised. Our enemy the devil seeks to condemn and destroy us. But our Saviour has gained the victory over sin and Satan so that with Paul we can confidently call out, 'Who is there to condemn?' It is Christ who died and is risen. No one can lay any charge (Romans 8:31–39).

The desire to see people 'rejoice' and praise God with such words as 'The LORD be magnified' (verse 16; see Psalm 35:27) is a way of emphasising what he wishes to see in his own experience. He is a believer who seeks God for help and delights in his saving activity ('love your salvation') wherever it is seen. In contrast to God's greatness, David expresses his own 'poor and needy' state (see Psalm 35:10) and his desire for God, his 'help' and 'deliverer', to think of a way of rescuing him from his present trouble ('thinks', verse 17; see verse 5). There is no 'yet' or 'but' in the original which suggests the line is not a statement but a prayer wish following the ones in verse 16—'may the Lord think concerning me'. 'The Christian', states H. L. Ellison, 'is never in greater peril than when he speaks as in Revelation 3:17.' It is 'the poor in spirit' who are in reality the blessed and privileged people (Matthew 5:3).

Psalm 41

Trouble, Treachery and Triumph

This psalm ends a long run of psalms associated with David and it follows quite naturally those that have preceded (see especially Psalms 35–40) where the problems of sin and suffering, illness as well as deception by trusted friends again surface. The exact heading appears in Psalms 19–21 and 31[87] and the first of the concluding doxologies (verse 13) marks the close of Book One of the Psalter. As Book One began with a beatitude (Psalm 1:1) so this final psalm begins in the same way ('Blessed', verse 1). The psalm opens (verse 1–3) and closes (11–12) on a positive note while the lament in the middle section begins and ends with the cry 'Lord, be merciful to me' (verses 4 and 10).

Affirmation (verses 1–3)

'Blessed' as in Psalm 40:4 must not be confused with the word for 'blessing' or worshipping God. It describes the happy, fortunate state of the godly and is never used of God. Our attention is drawn to the privileged position of the person who 'considers the poor' (verse 1). A different word for 'poor' is found here from that in Psalm 40:17 but it conveys the same idea. It covers people with any kind of weakness or suffering as well as those with little or no standing in society (Genesis 49:19; 2 Samuel 3:1). As for the verb 'consider', this is often found as a wisdom word (see Proverbs 1:3; 10:5,19; Daniel 12:3,10) with the idea of 'acting wisely'.[88] The implication in the term is that there is a definite policy to help the weak of society rather than an off-hand approach. Israel as a nation was specially directed to care for the weak and vulnerable of society (Deuteronomy 15:7-11) and Christians are not allowed to forget their responsibilities particularly toward believers in need (Acts 11:27-30; Romans 15:26; Galatians 2:10; James 1:27).

Those who have mercy on the poor find happiness in the promised land ('blessed on the earth', verse 2; see Psalm 37:3,9,11; Proverbs 14:21) as the opening line has asserted and indications of what that good fortune in the land might mean are presented here. When 'trouble' overtakes those who have been considerate to the weak, when 'enemies' are in control (see Psalm 27:12) and 'illness' strikes, the Lord will come to their rescue to 'deliver', 'preserve', 'keep ... alive' (see Psalm 22:29), 'strengthen' and 'sustain' (verses 2-3). In affirming in each of the first three verses what the covenant God of Israel ('LORD') does for the righteous, David also briefly addresses God ('you will not deliver him to the will of his enemies', verse 2; 'you will sustain him ...', verse 3).

In this fallen world where those who love God and desire to do his will suffer all kinds of trouble whether due to their own personal folly or not, it is most assuring to know that they are not forgotten by God who works all things for our good and his glory (Romans 8:28). This is the privileged position of God's people.

Lament (verses 4–10)

What has been asserted in verses 1-3, probably with David's own situation in mind ('bed of illness', 'sick-bed' verse 3), is now personally applied where in the original the 'I' of 'I said' (verse 4) is emphasised—'I myself said'. His appeal to the covenant God to be 'merciful' (better translated 'gracious'; see Psalm 4:1) means in this context to 'heal' him (see Psalm 6:2) of whatever has laid him low. Bodily disease affects the whole person or 'soul' and is made worse by the consciousness of sin (see Psalm 38:1-5). All sin is fundamentally rebellion against God hence David's confession, 'I have sinned against you' (verse 4; see Psalm 51:2). It is often viewed as a disease that needs healing (see Isaiah 1:4-6).

The reaction of David's enemies to his weak state (verses 5-9) is the very opposite to that of the one blessed in verse 1. Theirs is no wise, considered response nor do they try to follow God's gracious treatment of the weak. They have already concluded that David deserves the worst of punishments, to be condemned to death and forgotten ('his name perish', verse 5; see Psalm 9:5). Like Job's comforters they come to visit and end up speaking empty words (Job 2:11; 16:2–3). Whatever tittle-tattle they can gather they use outside in the street to spread malicious gossip. The term 'iniquity' (verse 6) describes the 'harmful material' gathered by the enemy.

David found his servants whispering about the death of his son, not wishing to speak openly to him about it until he challenged them (2 Samuel 12:19). Here he is conscious of enemies who 'whisper' among themselves about him and plot or 'devise ... hurt' or 'harm' (literally 'evil', verse 7) against him. The verb 'whisper' is sometimes used for incantations (see Psalm 58:5) and the associated noun can refer to snake charming (Ecclesiastes 10:11). If this is the background here then these enemies are suggesting that their magic has inflicted on him ('clings to him'; literally 'poured in him') 'an evil disease' (literally 'a thing of Belial'; see Psalm 18:5; 2 Corinthians 6:15), a devilish condition from which David will never recover (verse 8).

To cap it all, David's trusted friend ('familiar friend', verse 9; literally 'man of my peace'), with whom he had enjoyed companionship over a meal (see Jeremiah 38:22; Obadiah 7), has betrayed his trust. We can only guess what the idiomatic phrase 'has lifted up his heel against me' (verse 9; literally 'he has made great against me a heel') means exactly. The verb 'lifted up' ('made great') suggests that the traitor has 'acted proudly' (Psalms 35:26; 38:16). The 'heel' reminds us of what happened at the birth of Isaac's twin sons, Esau and Jacob and of the pun on Jacob's name: 'the deceiver' and 'heel' (Genesis 25:26; 27:36; Hosea 12:3). The phrase might mean that David's former friend has proudly tricked and taken advantage of him. The most obvious example of this in David's life was during the revolt by his son Absalom when Ahithophel the king's top confidant turned traitor (2 Samuel 15:12,31; 16:23).

This verse is quoted by Jesus concerning his betrayal by Judas, one of the twelve disciples chosen to be closely associated with him (John 13:18). David's experience in this incident again previews the sufferings that our Lord faced especially those leading up to his sacrificial death on the cross and prior to his victorious resurrection and ascension.

Verse 10 of our psalm returns to the plea of verse 4 that David's covenant God would be gracious to him and this time he speaks of being raised up, a most appropriate request in view of the enemies' hopes that he would 'rise up no more' (verse 8). At first sight the motive for his restoration 'that I may repay them' seems out of keeping with David's usual response of leaving God to deal with his enemies. According to an ancient Jewish interpretation David is thinking of repaying evil with good along the lines of Proverbs 20:22. It is better, however, to understand with Calvin that as king and judge David had the responsibility under God of pronouncing 'the appropriate punishment on wrongdoers' (see Psalm 31:23).

In this respect David, as a type or model of Christ, presents us with two complementary aspects of Christ's person and work. The one most often brought to our attention is of the Lord's Servant who despite great provocation and injustice prayed for his enemies (Luke 23:34) and committed himself to God whose prerogative it is to take vengeance (1 Peter 2:18-23). However, the other truth concerns the coming again in glory of the risen ascended Lord to take vengeance (2 Thessalonians 1:7-8). These two truths are held in tension and Psalm 2 has given us the clue to understand how both are to be accepted. Though the enemies considered he would rise no more, God has exalted his anointed one and calls his enemies to bow in submissive repentance and faith before the Son, otherwise they will experience his wrath (Psalm 2:10-12). Christians are called to follow Christ in not repaying evil for evil (Romans 12:17-21). But in leaving God to repay our enemies we are looking to the day of reckoning when perfect justice will be done and the blood of the martyrs avenged through the wrath of the Lamb (Revelation 6:9-11,16-17).

Confidence (11-12)

The psalm ends as it began in confident mood, with David being assured that God is 'pleased' or 'delighted' with him (verse 11). The word is used first of Shechem's affection for Dinah, Jacob's daughter (Genesis 34:19). It is interesting that at the end of Book One we have the same word used of God's delight in the psalmist that is found in the very first psalm of the psalmist's love for God's law (Psalm 1:2). Though David's faith is built on God's word it is certainly encouraged by personal experiences of divine help. God's gracious action toward David will prevent his enemy jubilantly shouting in triumph over his downfall. At heart, David was a man of 'integrity' (verse 12; see Psalm 18:20-24). God was aware of this for he was a man 'after God's own heart'. It is for this reason he has been upheld by God through all his trials and disciplinary experiences (see Psalm 37:23-24). Just as David sets God before him as an object of trust (see Psalm 16:8) so God sets

David before him as an object of the Lord's care. Unlike that of humans God's protection is permanent ('for ever').

Doxology (verse 13)

This final verse of praise to God is probably not part of the original psalm. When all the psalms were put together on one scroll after the return from the Babylonian exile, the prophetic editor responsible for dividing the work into five books, placed a concluding doxology to mark the end of each series of psalms. Thus after the conclusion of the first book we have this burst of praise. With slight variations, we find similar doxologies at the close of books two to four (Psalms 72:18–19; 89:52; 106:48). At the close of the final book and to mark the conclusion to the entire collection we have five Hallelujah psalms (Psalms 146–150). These doxologies remind us that what we read in the individual psalms about God and his relationships with his people demands a response of wholehearted submission to him.

'Blessed' is the translation of a different Hebrew word from that used in verse 1 (see Psalms 16:7; 28:6; 31:21). Normally we think of God blessing humans in the sense of graciously bestowing good things such as his peace (Numbers 6:24–26). We cannot give anything to God which he does not already possess (see 1 Chronicles 29:14) but there is in the word 'bless' more than the idea of praise in which we extol God's character and actions. It involves submissive worship. As we are to give glory to the all-glorious one so we are called to worship the one from whom all blessings flow (see Ephesians 1:3–6). We bless God by wishing him all that is good, praying as we have been taught that God's name would be hallowed, his kingdom come and his will done on earth as in heaven. We bless God by giving ourselves to him in heartfelt devotion. Spurgeon likens his acceptance of such blessing, to us receiving a little present of flowers from children who love us. The God we bless is the one who is in a special loving relationship with his covenant people. The 'LORD God of Israel' is the God and Father of the Lord Jesus Christ. He is worthy of unlimited worship, from eternity past to eternity future.

'Amen' is a Hebrew word that is part of almost every language's vocabulary. It means 'surely', 'certainly'. It was used of the people's 'yes' to God, their acceptance of what he has laid down (Deuteronomy 27:15,16, etc.). We find it used as here in concluding expressions of agreement by the congregation of God's people (see 1 Chronicles 16:36;

Nehemiah 8:6). In the New Testament it is often used as a concluding formula after doxologies to God or Christ (Galatians 1:5; Romans 1:25; 9:5; Revelation 5:14; etc.). Jesus used the double 'amen' to emphatically affirm the truth of what he taught (John 3:3) and he himself is called the 'Amen' because he is the truth as well as the faithful witness (Revelation 3:14; see 2 Corinthians 1:20). It is good biblical practice for the congregation to unite in saying 'Amen' when people have prayed or when the word has been preached (see 1 Corinthians 14:16). Singing 'Amen' at the close of a hymn, once common practice, has gone out of fashion in many Christian congregations.

Book Two

The psalms collected together in this book are divided into two groups: those 'of the sons of Korah' (Psalms 42–49) and those 'of David' (Psalms 51–65,68–70) or 'of Solomon' (Psalm 72) with three anonymous ones (Psalms 66–67,71). A note at the end of Psalm 72 states that 'The prayers of David the son of Jesse are ended' (Psalm 72:20). Lying between these two groups is the first of the Asaph psalms (Psalm 50). Many of the psalms in this book fill out the truth contained in Psalm 2.

The Korahite psalms, like the Davidic ones, refer to enemies and call on God for deliverance. They also draw our attention to Zion, God's city and its place of worship as well as extolling both God as the sovereign over all and his anointed king. Asaph, like the sons of Korah, belonged to the Levite families who had responsibilities for the musical side of the sanctuary worship. It is interesting that one so closely associated with the sanctuary should have produced a psalm directed against false views of sacrifice (see Psalm 50).

The psalms attributed to David generally come from the period when he was escaping from Saul but they begin with his psalm of repentance after his great sin as king of Israel. Again, it is significant that it highlights spiritual sacrifices over animal sacrifice and is concerned with Zion and like Psalm 44 with an exile situation. The Zion theme returns in Psalm 68 while Psalm 69 like Psalm 22 is one that depicts in David's troubles a pale shadow of the sufferings that Jesus endured.

One of the distinctive features of this collection is that when reference is made to the divine being, there is a distinct preference for speaking of 'God' (*Elohim*) rather than 'Lord' (Yahweh/Jehovah). This is particularly noticeable when a comparison is made of Psalm 14 in Book One and the version of it found in Psalm 53.

The message of Book Two is similar to the previous one. God is true to his word and despite evidences to the contrary he does come to the support of his king. It again points us forward to great David's greater Son whose throne endures for ever and who, despite enemy action, will reign supreme and all nations will call him blessed.

Psalm 42

Thirsting for God

These well-loved opening lines introduce us to the second book and continue the concerns and pleas that brought the first book to an end.

Korah, a descendant of Levi and Kohath, became a rebel leader during the wilderness period (Numbers 16:1-40). While he himself was punished his children and their descendants were spared. Like the 'Kohathites', 'the sons of Korah' had important non-priestly tasks, some as gatekeepers, others as singers and musicians, at the tabernacle and temple (1 Chronicles 9:17-19; 6:22-48; 2 Chronicles 20:19). It is no surprise then to find concerns for God's house and city in many of these psalms. At first, these sacred musicians belonging to Asaph, Jeduthun and Haman prophesied in song by order of David. They could therefore be responsible for composing these psalms under the inspiration of the Spirit (1 Chronicles 25:1-6). On the other hand, the personal nature of this psalm suggests that David is the author and that he handed it to these musicians to perform at the sanctuary (see 1 Chronicles 16:7). This is the second of the 'Contemplation' psalms (see Psalm 32 and 'consider' in Psalm 41:1).

Although the traditional Hebrew text and the ancient Greek translation keep them separate, Psalm 43 belongs very closely with Psalm 42. Psalm 43 has no separate heading (see Psalm 10), it has similar 'why' questions (42:9; 43:2) and the same refrain occurs in both (42:5,11; 43:5).[89]

We can identify with the longings and concerns of the psalmist. If for some reason we are unable to meet with God's people for communal worship this should cause us to have similar longings. Yes, we can worship on our own but this must not be thought of as a substitute for meeting together with God's people. We are never meant to be hermit Christians. The psalmist is also experiencing hostility from enemies who are either stopping him from meeting up with the worshipping community or are taunting him because he is unable to go. Some form of persecution perhaps from family members may hinder us from attending a place of worship and this can be frustrating and disheartening. And there are many other ways in which our archenemy the devil can make us spiritually depressed.

The refrain marks off the two sections of the psalm. In each case the lament gives way to personal exhortation.

Lament for the Living God (verses 1–4)

Thirst for God (verse 1–2)

The old metrical version 'When pants the hart for cooling streams', familiar to many, adds the line 'when heated by the chase' which finds no parallel in the text. Rather the picture is of a deer panting during the summer drought for watercourses ('water brooks' verse 1; see Psalm 18:15 'channels of water') that have run dry (Joel 1:20). The 'panting' could suggest the straining of its head to catch the scent of water. It illustrates the psalmist's intense desire for God (see Psalms 63:1; 84:2). David has already spoken of God as 'the fountain of life' satisfying the thirsty (Psalm 36:8–9; see Jeremiah 17:13). Though this is the case there is still a constant need to draw on God. Unlike the gods worshipped by Israel's surrounding neighbours, Israel's God is alive and active. The supposed reality behind the lifeless images is a delusion. There is only one real God and the overwhelming longing of the psalmist is for this 'living God' (verse 2; Joshua 3:10; 1 Thessalonians 1:9).

The living God allows no images of him to be made so that to 'appear before God' or possibly 'see the face of God' (verse 2) means to come to the sanctuary where God has promised to be present (Deuteronomy 31:11; Isaiah 1:12). The tabernacle, and later the temple, was ordained to be God's earthly home among his people. Three times a year the people were directed to 'appear before' the Lord at the central sanctuary (Exodus 23:17–19). Christians now see the face of God in the face of Jesus as he is revealed in the Bible. John speaks of seeing the glory of the only begotten Son who is full of grace and truth (John 1:14). Why do we meet together with other Christians on the Lord's Day? It is good to see each other's faces but is it our chief and overwhelming desire to meet with God in the preaching of his word and at the Lord's Supper? While it is true that the believer can enjoy private experiences of God we are urged not to neglect meeting together (Hebrews 10:25). The term 'soul' (verses 1–2) stands for the whole person longing for God and prepares us for the refrain (verses 5,11).

Taunt of the Enemy (verse 3)

Why the psalmist is unable to attend the sanctuary is not made clear although we have more clues later. The intense longing for God is further highlighted by the grief it is causing. He has no appetite for food. All he can do ('day and night', see Psalm 1:2) is to shed tears (see Psalm 80:5).

As we know from verse 10 it is the enemy who is taunting the psalmist with the question 'Where is your God?' (see Psalm 79:10; Joel 2:17). It has a familiar ring to it. The enemies of God and of his people constantly raise the subject when a tragedy happens—'Where was God in that?' they mockingly ask. The implication is he is either powerless or unconcerned to act. They do not stop to consider other possibilities.

Thoughts of the Past (verse 4)

In his ongoing desperate state, the psalmist does not make things any easier for himself as he deliberately attempts to call to mind (literally 'I will remember'; see Psalm 77:6) happier times and is determined to lay bare his feelings (literally 'I will pour out my soul upon me'; see Psalm 62:8). He is thinking of the festival celebrations such as Passover and Tabernacles when he joined the excited pilgrims shouting with joy and thanksgiving as they processed slowly ('I went with them' does not catch the drama of the original) to 'the house of God'. It must have been something like what is recorded when the ark was finally brought to Jerusalem (1 Chronicles 15:28). There is an unhelpful looking back to the so-called 'good old days' that only makes for more despondency.

Treatment (verse 5)

The psalmist presents us with the cure for his grief ('cast down') and agitated ('disquieted') state. The way out of his spiritual depression is firstly to take himself in hand. He speaks to himself. He has told how he feels in himself (see 'soul' in verses 1–2,4) now he questions himself—'Why ... O my soul'). In a similar position we must do the same. We must not become a slave to our feelings. Instead of allowing 'self to talk', as Lloyd-Jones puts it, we must talk 'to our self'.[90] Secondly, the psalmist urges himself to 'Hope in God' (Psalms 38:15; 39:7). The antidote to despondency is not to listen to self as it reminisces nostalgically on the grand times we used to have in church with our friends but to remember who God is, what he has done and the promises he has made. Finally, like the psalmist we defy self and every enemy and because of our confidence in God we say 'I shall yet praise him' (or 'thank him'; see Psalm 30:4), for his gracious complete deliverance (literally 'the salvations of his face'). God's 'countenance' or 'face' in this context is his favour (see Psalms 4:6; 31:16; Numbers 6:25–26).[91]

Lament for the Giver of Life (verses 6–10)

Again, the psalmist begins by speaking to God (verses 6–7; see verses 1–2), while verses 8–10 parallel verses 3–4 and the section closes with the refrain (verse 11; see verse 5).

Acknowledging God (verses 6–9)

Picking up the words of the refrain in verse 5 ('my soul', 'cast down' and 'within me', verse 6) that reveals he is still downcast, the word 'therefore' indicates that he has begun to learn something from what he has told himself. Instead of calling to mind ('I remember', verse 4) former happy days he is determined to 'remember' God (verse 6). His references to the Jordan valley, the Hermon range from which the Jordan rises and the unknown Mount Mizar (Little Mount) describe an area on the north-eastern borders of Israel (Joshua 13:11). In Israel, this is about as far away as it is possible to be from Jerusalem. It symbolises just how impossible it was for the psalmist to worship at the central sanctuary. When David was forced to leave Jerusalem as a result of Absalom's treason, he headed north and east of the river Jordan and a considerable distance from the capital city (2 Samuel 17:24–27).

The water imagery of verse 7 is probably taken from the sight of the streams of water that plunge down the mountain slopes to form the river Jordan. Of the streams he longs for to quench his spiritual thirst the psalmist only knows those dangerous torrents of water that can overwhelm and drown him (see Jonah 2:3). The 'deep' calls to mind the original waters that covered the earth and that drowned the world. He is engulfed by troubles that God has sent ('your waterfalls', 'your waves and billows'; see Psalm 88:7). This suggests that the psalmist is enduring an enforced exile due to God's disciplining judgments like the one that David experienced when his son rebelled against him.

Despite his distress the psalmist does what he encouraged himself to do in verse 5. He is confident that his God, whom he now refers to by his covenant name 'LORD' (Yahweh/Jehovah, verse 8), 'will command his loving-kindness' ('his steadfast love') continually ('daytime' and 'night'; see verse 3). He will also be able to sing in prayer to the God to whom his life belongs and the one who brings him up from the death-like experience ('the God of my life').[92]

Since the psalmist confidently waits to experience God's faithful love he is encouraged to pour out his troubles to him. With the background imagery of waves of water overwhelming him the psalmist appropriately calls God 'my Rock' (verse 9). There alone lies safety. As in Psalm 22 he appeals to the God who is doing nothing to help him (see Psalm 31:1). As Motyer puts it: 'Faith says "my Rock", experience says "forgotten".' He wears the clothes of a mourner because although he is remembering God, God is apparently forgetting him.

Aware of the Enemy (verse 10)

He also feels a deadly pain ('a breaking of my bones') caused by those who are oppressing him. The tongue can be more cutting than a knife. And so he comes to the point he was in at verse 3 with his enemies taunting him, 'Where is your God?' Are we more pained by the devilish attacks of those who seek to rubbish God in their efforts to destroy our faith than by any physical assault?

Treatment (verse 11)

With the renewed efforts of the enemy of souls we must not lose heart but return to the same remedy that David applied in verse 5. As is often the case with refrains in the Bible, there are slight differences from the earlier words (see Psalm 24:7-10). In place of 'help of his countenance' we have 'help of my countenance' (literally 'the salvations of my face). God is his complete deliverer as verse 8 suggested, lighting up the downcast face. The psalmist counteracts the enemy's scornful questioning concerning 'your God' (verse 10) with the affirmation that God is 'my God'.

Our Saviour, the Messiah, was deeply troubled and tempted like us to get despondent but he did not succumb to sinful self-pity. In the gravest of situations he submitted his own will to his Father's will and trusted him to bring him through the deepest of all sufferings. The psalmist's disturbed, troubled spirit in verses 5 and 6 reflects the experiences of Jesus particularly in the Garden of Gethsemane (Mark 14:34; John 12:27). He was a true human being and 'in that he himself has suffered, being tempted, he is able to aid those who are tempted' (Hebrews 2:17–18).

Psalm 43

Cure for despair

This psalm possesses no heading of its own (see Psalm 10) and because of its clear associations with the previous psalm some scholars view it as a third stanza, with Psalm 42 forming the first two stanzas. However, the traditional text keeps them separate and the ancient Greek translation even gives it a separate heading.[93] Despite the obvious similarities with Psalm 42, the psalm opens on a different note and we must assume that this was a fresh psalm for a different occasion but similar enough for the psalmist to appropriate some of the language of the preceding psalm.

Psalm 43 is a prayer for vindication and restoration. As in the previous psalm, though the psalmist is at present far from the central sanctuary where God promised to meet with his people, he can still call upon him and expect him to hear and answer his cries.

The righteous plea (verse 1)

There is no thought here of the concerns that dominated the lament in the previous psalm. The prayer, using the language of the law-courts, is an urgent appeal to God, the judge, for justice (see Psalms 26:1; 35:1) and deliverance (see Psalm 7) from an enemy that is 'deceitful' and 'unjust'. The singular, 'man', is probably used in place of the plural, although it could refer to the person who is leading the enemy action, such as Absalom. In using the term 'nation' (some versions translate 'people') it is unlikely that one of the surrounding nations is in mind. As Isaiah can speak of his own people as 'a sinful nation' (Isaiah 1:4) so here the psalmist does the same using a word with covenantal associations, 'ungodly' (literally, 'not godly')—those who do not express faithful love, who are not loyal to their covenant commitments (see Psalms 4:3; 37:28).

The reasoned appeal (verse 2)

The psalmist presents reasons in support of his plea with echoes of his lament in the previous psalm. He reminds God that he is the psalmist's refuge ('God of my strength', literally 'God of my stronghold'; see Psalm 27:1).[94] In view of the covenant relationship the psalmist has with God he can expect to be sustained and helped so his questions are entirely appropriate. Why has God 'cast me off' in that justice is not being done? Why is he walking about in mourning clothes because the enemy is allowed to prevail? (see Psalm 42:9).

The ultimate goal (verses 3–4)

The answer to the earnest and confident plea of the psalmist is to be found in the place where God has ordained to make his earthly home and in God's 'light' and 'truth' (verse 3) that act like two guiding messengers (see 'goodness and mercy' in Psalm 23:6). In place of the darkness and misery he is experiencing, he looks for the light of God's favour to rescue him (see Psalms 4:6; 36:9) and instead of the falsehood and unfaithfulness of the enemy he calls for God's truthfulness and loyalty to be in evidence. He pleads for these divine characteristics to be seen in action ('send'), in order to 'lead' him to God's 'holy hill' of Zion (Psalms 2:6; 15:1), like the pillar of cloud and fire led the Israelites from Egypt to God's presence at Mount Sinai (Exodus 13:21; 15:13; 19:1–3).

After David had conquered Jerusalem, the ark of the covenant was eventually brought into the city and placed in the tent that David had erected for it (2 Samuel 6:17). This 'tent' is also called the 'tabernacle' (2 Samuel 7:6), which is the word found in verse 3 ('your tabernacle')[95] and in Moses' description of its dimensions and erection in Exodus (see Exodus 26 and 40).

The 'altar of God' (verse 4) is the bronze altar where the people brought their sacrifices for the priest to offer. Here the psalmist confidently looks forward to bringing his peace offerings as thanksgiving for the deliverance that he has prayed for. It is not the tabernacle or the altar that he is primarily looking to but God himself 'my exceeding joy'. He wishes to praise God in song using the lyre ('harp'; see Psalm 33:2). In the first Book of Psalms God is often addressed as 'O Lᴏʀᴅ (Yahweh/Jehovah) my God' (see Psalm 7:1; 40:5) but in this group of psalms where the name Lᴏʀᴅ is more rare, we have 'O God, my God'.

As Christians we do not go to that temporary symbolic place in Jerusalem to meet God. We come through the real once-for-all sacrificial offering of Christ. 'We have an altar from which those who serve the tabernacle have no right to eat ... Therefore by him let us continually offer the sacrifice of praise to God, that is, the fruit of our lips, giving thanks to his name' (Hebrews 13:10,15). It is a mark of true believers that they desire to have this personal experience of God through Jesus and to rejoice with a most glorious, inexpressible joy (1 Peter 1:8).

Refrain (verse 5)

The closing verse is exactly the same as in Psalm 42:11. Its presence here is a little surprising as the psalmist is much more confident than in the previous psalm. Nevertheless, he still needs to take himself in hand and encourage himself to hold on and wait for the fulfilment of God's promises.

Even when we are in a better state of mind, it is necessary to keep talking to ourselves for our feelings can so easily destabilize us.

Psalm 44

National Crisis

From an individual in crisis in Psalms 42–43, we turn to a nation in trouble. This is the first communal lament where 'we' and 'us' are used. The 'I' and 'my' in verses 4 and 6 may indicate that the king leads the people in this urgent cry for help. Apart from a minor difference in the original the heading is the same as Psalm 42 and like the previous two psalms, God's presence in the past is recalled while his present inactivity is bewildering. There are other links to those two psalms not always obvious in our English versions that show that the three psalms were deliberately placed side by side.[96] As the individual can speak for the community in this psalm, so the personal laments of the preceding psalms could be used by the whole community in times of distress.

Although many including Calvin disagree, David may be the original author and the occasion similar to Psalm 60 when it appears that the Edomites had invaded and inflicted heavy losses on Israel before Joab and his brother Abishai eventually crushed the enemy (1 Chronicles 18:12-13). Other occasions prompting this communal lament might possibly be Joel 1:13-14 and 2 Chronicles 20:1-13. The psalm is applicable to any age and the apostle Paul uses it to warn Christians that loyalty to the Lord will bring persecution (Romans 8:36). As Christ suffered on account of his faithfulness to God so his people must expect similar treatment. The psalm also helps those who cannot understand what God is doing. It encourages God's faithful people to keep trusting and to pour out their concerns and questionings to a covenant-keeping God.

God's past activity (verses 1–3)

It is because the present possession of the land is under threat that the opening verses recall God's work in the conquest of Canaan and the Settlement of Israel in the land. What they have heard with their ears contrasts sharply with what they see with their eyes (see Psalm 48:8 and Judges 6:13). The phrases 'heard with our ears' and 'our fathers have told us' (verse 1) refer to the recounting of the redemptive history of God's dealings with Israel in the sanctuary worship and family instruction (see Exodus 10:2; Deuteronomy 6:7,20–24). Christian parents have a duty to teach their children God's saving activity in Christ and it needs to be prominent in every aspect of communal worship: in song, prayer and preaching as well as at baptisms and the Lord's Supper.

In both parts of verse 2 'them' refers to Israel and a contrast is drawn between what God did to the nations and what he did for his own people. The Authorised and New King James versions do not give the correct sense. While God 'afflicted' (literally 'did evil', meaning 'brought trouble') and 'dispossessed' ('drove out') the Canaanite nations (Deuteronomy 4:38), he 'planted' Israel (see Exodus 15:17) so that they 'spread out' ('cast out' in this context is inappropriate) through the land like the branches of a tree (see Psalm 80:11).

Left to their own devices Israel would not have been able to conquer the Canaanites. What is implied in the previous verses is emphasised in verse 3 that it was the Lord who brought deliverance and settled them in the promised land. Joshua made the point clear in his final sermon to the people (Joshua 24:12). Anthropomorphic language (applying human characteristics to God) is used generously here to press home the personal involvement of God in Israel's conquest of Canaan. God's 'hand' suggests personal action, the 'right' hand the best of his strength (Exodus 15:6,12), his 'arm' his power and the 'light' of his 'face' ('countenance') suggesting his gracious presence (see Psalm 4:6). It was because God 'favoured' them, or delighted in them that he acted on their behalf. It owed nothing to any special qualities in them (see Deuteronomy 7:7–8). Likewise, our salvation in Christ is not due to anything special about us, it is entirely due to God's grace (Ephesians 2:8–9).

Present confidence (verses 4–8)

Reminding ourselves of God's grace and saving activity is an encouragement to faith especially when circumstances are far from easy and it encourages us to pour out our concerns to God. What God was to their ancestors is now explicitly mentioned. Just as kings lead their people into battle God has led his people and he is here acknowledged to be Israel's true king as they face present and future dangers. The earthly ruler speaks for the nation—'You are my king, O God' (verse 4). Though Israel wrongly asked for a king to lead them into battle, the idea of a ruler was built into God's special arrangement with them (see Deuteronomy 17:14–20) and it prepared them for the coming of the Messiah. The Davidic ruler was to represent God's rule over his people (Numbers 24:17). In the God-Man, Jesus Christ our Lord, there are no loyalty divisions to consider, for in honouring and worshipping the Son we do likewise to the Father. The call for 'victories' or deliverance in verse 4 anticipates the pleas at the close of the psalm (verses 23–26). The personal name of the nation's father 'Jacob' is often found in poetry in place of 'Israel' (see Psalm 24:6).

The verses that follow alternate from singular to plural as the royal psalmist emphasises that overcoming enemies is due entirely to God's activity. Israel learned that battles were won not by trusting their own weapons but by having the Lord's presence among them (see Joshua 1:9). Yes, they were called to engage the enemy using their weapons, but fundamentally it is through God's 'name' (verse 5; see Psalm 5:11), meaning that it is through God himself, they are able to gain the victory. The picture we are given in verse 5 is of Israel like a bull or ox that 'gores' ('push down') and 'treads down' ('tramples') and is used to describe God's strength (Deuteronomy 33:17).

If God is the real reason for their victories then it is only natural for them to 'boast' continually (see Psalms 25:5) in what God has done and 'for ever' to 'praise' or 'give thanks' (verse 8). When we hear of an amazing rescue from a collapsed building the person pulled from the rubble cannot thank the emergency services enough for their skill and determination. How poor we Christians are in expressing our appreciation of God's mercy mission to rescue us from sin and damnation!

The opening verses (1–8), however, are not to be treated on their own as a hymn of praise. They are there to form a powerful introductory argument to the following cry of anguish and 'Selah' (see Psalm 3:2) at the end of verse 8 suggests an appropriate pause before launching into the lament.

The lament (verses 9–26)

The 'But' or 'Yet' (verse 9) introduces the contrast with the previous verses. The lament consists of three stages:

The present calamity (verses 9–16)

Far from supporting and helping them against their enemies, God is doing the very opposite. He has not merely left them alone, he has 'rejected' ('cast off') and 'disgraced' them for God is no longer with them in battle (verse 9; see 2 Samuel 5:24). In verses 10–11 defeat has lead to retreat ('turn back') and plundering ('taken spoil'), to slaughter ('like sheep ... for food') and deportation ('scattered ... among the nations'). Even more galling, God has gained nothing from it! (verse 12).

While verses 10–12 show what the divine rejection has brought, the following verses describe the 'shame' they are enduring (see verse 9). They are censured as if they have done something worthy of blame (see Psalm 39:8) and ridiculed; they have become a 'byword' (verse 14; see Zechariah 8:13), a clear example to the surrounding nations of what they should not be like (Deuteronomy 28:37; see Genesis 12:2c), and an object of contempt (see Psalm 22:7). The king especially feels the disgrace and shame (verse 15; see Psalm 69:7).

A perplexing situation (verses 17–22)

God's covenant with Israel at Mount Sinai and emphasised in Deuteronomy 28, was that blessing would come to Israel if they obeyed the commands of the Lord and curses would fall on them if they disobeyed. The history of Israel as portrayed by the prophetic writers of the books of Judges, Samuel and Kings makes it clear that defeat at the hands of enemy nations was entirely due to Israel's unfaithfulness to their covenant obligations. The situation described in this psalm is not so simple. This catastrophe that 'has come upon' them (verse 17) cannot be attributed to the fact that they had 'forgotten' God or had 'dealt falsely' with his covenant. Furthermore, their commitment to God was not a mere external observance but of an inward nature—

'Our heart has not turned back' (verse 18). There is no suggestion of absolute sinlessness but a confession that in their inner attitude and outward action there had been no apostasy. They had not deviated from the way set by God in his law.

The psalmist can therefore see no reason for this awesome divine curse where they are crushed or 'broken' up in a place of total desolation and completely 'covered' in darkness (verse 19). The 'place of jackals' suggests an uninhabited, unclean place (see Isaiah 34:13–14), while 'shadow of death' is expressive of 'deep darkness' (see Psalm 23:4).

God knows exactly what is going on in 'the secrets of the heart' as well as in the outward action of the hands 'stretched out' to a foreign deity (verses 20–21). When the phrase 'search this out' is used of God, we must not suppose, as some now suggest, that he 'does not "automatically" know everything'.[97] This is an anthropomorphic way of emphasizing that God does indeed know exactly what is going on (see Genesis 11:5). To 'forget' the name of their God (see verse 20) is not a case of a simple lapse of memory but an act of apostasy in praying to another god. The opposite of forgetting God's name is to call upon God's name (see Genesis 4:26).

The lament comes to a dramatic climax with this statement that far from suffering such ignominy 'because of' their own disloyalty to God's covenant, it is 'because of' God they are in the awful predicament. The question is, are they being continually killed and slaughtered like sacrificial animals (see verse 11) 'because of' God in the sense of 'for your sake' (verse 22), on account of their commitment to God? Or is it 'because of' God simply in the sense of allowing the enemy to prevail (as suggested in verses 9–14) and refusing to help Israel (see verse 24)? Perhaps both thoughts are present. God has done nothing and so the enemy has been allowed to gain the victory over Israel and their plight has been made worse on account of their loyalty to God. Perhaps they have refused to acknowledge their enemy's gods. The more God's people held true to their covenant obligations and were not idolatrous, the greater the enemy's hostility.

This highly poetic picture of severe persecution or distress (verses 22) was applied by the rabbis to the death of Jewish martyrs. It is used by Paul to indicate that the sufferings Christians experience on account of their faith should be no surprise (Romans 8:36). Christians are called to share in Christ's sufferings that we might share also in his glory

(Romans 8:17–18; see Philippians 1:29). Calvin reminds us that we must always be ready to bear the cross with Christ.

Plea for action (verses 23–26)

In view of the nation's distressing situation, the royal psalmist boldly calls out in verse 23 for God to 'Arouse!' ('Awake') and 'Wake up!' ('Arise'). It is not that God is really asleep as Elijah mockingly said of Jezebel's gods (see 1 Kings 18:27). In fact, Psalm 121:4 states clearly that God 'neither slumbers nor sleeps'. Such anthropomorphic language is used to make this urgent plea to move God to action on their behalf (see Psalm 3:7). The same strong expression 'cast *us* off' (verse 9) appears again with the plea that it would not continue 'for ever' (verse 23).

More anthropomorphic language is found in verse 24—'hide your face' and 'forget'; see Psalm 13:1). The 'hidden face' of God suggests that he has abandoned them in his displeasure (Psalm 22:24: Deuteronomy 31:17). God's people have not 'forgotten' God (see verses 17 and 20) and yet God has forgotten them! With no relief for their 'affliction' (see 25:18) and 'oppression' (see 42:9; 43:2), the agonizing cry goes up, 'Why?' (verse 24).

Again, their desperate straits are described in graphic language that suggests they are at death's door (verse 25; see Genesis 3:19). The final plea in verse 26 is that it is time for God to 'Rise up' ('Arise'), a cry reminiscent of Moses' words as the people set out each day toward the promised land with the ark of the covenant in front of them: 'Rise up, O Lord! Let your enemies be scattered, and let those who hate you flee before you' (Numbers 10:35). Added to this is a call for God himself to be their 'help' and rescue his people as he did at the time of the exodus. The use of the word 'redeem' in this context may also include the idea of 'buying back' what God had sold (see verse 12). As Matthew Henry puts it: 'If he sell us it is not any one else that can redeem us; the same hand that tears must heal, that smites must bind up' (see Hosea 6:1).

The psalm is brought to a powerful conclusion by the appeal, not to any self-righteousness as might be suggested from verses 17–22, but to God's 'steadfast love'—'for your mercies' sake' ('your unfailing love's sake', verse 26). Though the psalmist has no answer to their present crisis his faith shines out brightly. However hard it might be to understand God's purposes, he believes God's revealed word that God is committed to keeping his covenant promises and on that the psalmist rests his plea. We can face such tribulations with the same positive spirit knowing that 'in all these things we are more than conquerors through him who loved us' and that nothing can separate us from the love of God in Christ Jesus (Romans 8:35–39).

Whatever other purposes God has in the sufferings that come to God's people, as this psalm shows and as Job found through all his extreme trials, they do have the effect of bringing believers to seek God more and to call out to him, and that can never be a bad thing.

Psalm 45

The King and his Bride

The marriage of Prince William to Kate Middleton on April 29, 2011 provided the whole world with a spectacular demonstration of a royal wedding. The cameras were first turned toward the handsome figure of William in his smart military uniform and then to Kate and her lovely dress and finally to the bridesmaids and pageboys. What lavish praise was heaped upon the happy couple throughout the day's celebrations!

This psalm is unique in the Psalter in that instead of praising God it is wholly given over to the praise of the king and his bride. It reminds us of the Song of Solomon which is itself unlike any other Old Testament book.

In addition to familiar phrases such as 'To the Chief Musician' and 'A Contemplation of the Sons of Korah' that we find in this part of Book Two (see Psalm 42), the heading includes 'Set to "the Lilies"' (literally 'Upon the Lilies' or 'Anemone'; see Psalms 69 and 80—the Hebrew term, *Shoshannim*, gives us the English name Susan), suggesting the tune to which it was sung, and 'A Song of Love' makes clear the psalm's subject matter.

Introduction (verse 1)

The psalmist indicates how he is moved to utter this special poem

('composition'; literally 'works') 'concerning' a king.[98] His 'heart is
overflowing', it is 'astir', 'bubbling up' like boiling water with a 'good
theme' (literally 'a good word'; see Jeremiah 29:10; 33:14). His tongue
is like the pen of a 'rapid writer' ('ready writer'). The same phrase is
used of Ezra but there it means 'skilled scribe' (Ezra 7:6). This unique
introduction presents the psalmist as a prophet, inspired to utter this
God-given message. It is reminiscent of the introduction to David's
final testimony: 'The Spirit of the LORD spoke by me, and his word was
on my tongue' (2 Samuel 23:2).

Praising the royal groom (verses 2–9)

The king is directly addressed and in a similar way to the Song of
Solomon, comment is made on his physical appearance—'the most
handsome of humans' (Songs 1:16; 5:10) who has the gift to speak
well—'grace is poured upon your lips' (verse 2). While the Bible
emphasises that good looks are not everything and that God is more
concerned about moral and spiritual qualities (see 1 Samuel 16:7;
1 Peter 3:3-4), it does not despise outward form and beauty. It was
expected that a king would be outstanding in physical form. Saul, we
are told, was a tall, handsome man (1 Samuel 9:2). David is especially
noted for his handsome appearance (1 Samuel 16:12; 17:42) and his son
Absalom impressed everyone by his good looks (2 Samuel 14:25).

The film 'The King's Speech' has drawn attention to the importance
of a king being able to speak with authority if people are to be gripped
by his words. This king did not need human assistance to speak.
'Grace' could mean that the king had been given divine ability to speak
fluently as well as referring to the wise and winsome words that poured
from his mouth (see Proverbs 22:11; Ecclesiastes 10:12; 1 Kings 10:8).
Having such qualities already indicates God's blessing but, reminiscent
of David's prayer that blessing upon his dynasty would continue (see
2 Samuel 7:29), the psalmist assures the king of on-going blessing from
God not only in the sense of an enduring dynasty but of continual
satisfaction in the presence of God (see Psalm 16:11). The king 'after
God's own heart' is 'blessed ... for ever' (see Psalm 21:6; 2 Samuel 7:29;
1 Chronicles 17:27).

The mighty warrior (verses 3–5)

Like British Prince William arrayed in military uniform on his wedding
day so we have the Davidic king, the 'mighty one' or 'warrior', urged

to display the symbols of power and victory—his 'sword' at his side, and 'glory' and 'majesty' (verses 3) like medals of service. These latter items are ones that normally characterise God (see Psalm 96:6) but similar language has already been applied to the king in Psalm 21:5. Isaiah speaks of God's people viewing the Messiah 'in his beauty' (Isaiah 33:17). The king is also urged in his majesty to ride 'prosperously' or victoriously, but not as an oppressor who seeks to gain more territory. It is as a champion in the cause of 'truth, humility and righteousness' that he is to succeed (see Zechariah 9:9 for the king who rides with humility) and his strong right hand is to teach him 'awesome' deeds (verse 4). It is only God who can do such deeds as displayed in Israel's redemption from Egypt (2 Samuel 7:23). The king's 'arrows' are sharpened and ready for use and have done their work in 'the heart of the king's enemies', which means that the peoples are subject to him— they are fallen under him (verse 5; see Psalm 110:1).

The royal court (verses 6–9)

Verse 6 rounds off the military imagery and prepares us for the scene at court. We should not be surprised by this statement addressed to the king: 'Your throne, O God, is for ever and ever'. Divine characteristics have already been applied to him in verses 3 and 4 and all efforts to avoid the obvious are forced and unnecessary. The Davidic king's office is identified with God's rule over his people. As humans were created in God's image to rule over the earth on God's behalf, so the Israelite king was in a special relationship as God's viceroy to rule over God's people. The Davidic ruler sat on God's throne, reigning over the Lord's kingdom (1 Chronicles 28:5; 29:23) on God's behalf (see Psalm 2). Moses became like God to Pharaoh (Exodus 4:16; 7:1), likewise the Davidic king became like God to the people (see Zechariah 12:8). Unlike other ancient Near Eastern cultures however, the Israelite king was never worshipped as a divine being. God's covenant with David (2 Samuel 7:13-17) provides the background to the perpetual ('for ever') nature of this rule (see verses 2 and 17) which finds its complete realisation in Jesus the Messiah.

His 'sceptre' (verse 6), a symbol of rule and authority (Esther 5:2), is one that speaks of the kind of 'righteousness' or better 'upright', equitable rule[99] associated with God, in which the king loves 'righteousness' by doing what is right and rewarding righteous acts, and hates 'wickedness' (verse 7) by making sure that corrupt, ungodly people are punished (see Psalms 11:5–6; 33:5; 37:28).

Now the Davidic king is addressed in such a way that clearly depicts him as a fellow human being distinct from God—'Therefore God, your God' (verse 7b). While there could be a reference here to the Davidic king's actual coronation ceremony (see 1 Samuel 16:13; Psalm 89:20), it is more likely that the anointing 'with the oil of gladness more than your companions' (verse 7) is a figurative way of describing the king's blessed state (see Psalm 23:5) that far outstrips all those in the royal court and indeed all other rulers (see Psalm 21:6).

The anointing imagery is carried over into verse 8 and we are told how the king's clothes are perfumed with aromatic spices of myrrh, aloes and cassia. 'Myrrh' and 'aloes' were used extensively on account of their aromatic qualities by women as well as men (Proverbs 7:17; Songs 4:14). 'Cassia', apparently akin to cinnamon, and 'myrrh' were among the ingredients of the holy anointing oil (Exodus 30:23–33). 'Myrrh' was given to Jesus at his birth (Matthew 2:11) and along with 'aloes' was used at his burial (John 19:39). Not only did the king look splendid but the scent from his richly perfumed robes added to his grandeur.

To add to the occasion and delight of the king ('made you glad'), the music of stringed instruments sounded from 'palace rooms' adorned with 'ivory' (verse 8).[100] We read of Solomon's ivory throne and Ahab's ivory house, not to mention the houses and beds of ivory possessed by other wealthy individuals (see 1 Kings 10:18; 22:39; Amos 3:15; 6:4).

'Kings' daughters' are probably a reference to the royal harem (see 1 Kings 11:3) and they are viewed as the king's 'precious' or 'highly valued ones' (see Psalm 116:15; Proverbs 3:15), often translated as 'honourable women' (verse 9). At the king's 'right hand', in the place of honour (see 1 Kings 2:19), is positioned the king's 'consort', 'the queen' (see Nehemiah 2:6), adorned in the finest gold. Although scholars are at a loss to know where 'Ophir' was, it was renowned for its gold and made Solomon very wealthy (see 1 Kings 9:28; 10:11; Isaiah 13:12).

Praising the bride (verses 10–15)
The mention of the queen in verse 9 prepares for this section where she is addressed as the newly acquired bride of the king. There are no compliments on her appearance as we would naturally expect instead she is presented with sound advice reminiscent of a wisdom teacher with 'daughter' replacing the more common 'son' (verse 10;

see Proverbs 1:8; 2:1; etc.; Psalm 34:11). She is called to pay special attention ('incline your ear'; see Psalm 17:6) to the exhortation. In words that remind us of the first marriage (Genesis 2:24), the new bride is solemnly urged to transfer her loyalties, much as Ruth turned her back on her people and family when she made that famous profession: 'Your people will be my people and your God my God' (Ruth 1:15-16). Rebekah also was willing to leave her country and family to become Isaac's bride (Genesis 24:58).

Though much is asked of her, the king delights in her beauty. As Sarah submitted herself to Abraham, calling him 'lord' (Genesis 18:12; 1 Peter 3:6) so the king's bride is to reverence her husband and be devoted ('worship'; literally 'bow down'; verse 11) to him not only because he is king but her husband. Solomon had foreign wives who did not submit to him and he weakly embraced their culture and religion. Ahab did the same under the influence of his domineering wife Jezebel (1 Kings 11:4; 16:31).

Further advantages in being the king's bride include prosperous nations seeking favours from her and receiving presents from wealthy maritime cities like Tyre—'the daughter of Tyre' (verse 12) being a Hebrew idiom for the city or people of Tyre (see Psalm 9:14).

It is at this point when she is brought to the royal groom that the king's bride, the princess or 'royal daughter' (verse 13; literally 'daughter of a king' with reference the bride's father), is described in any detail, although a brief indication of her dress was given in verse 9. She emerges from 'within' her chamber wowing everyone with her stunning colourful gown[101] 'woven with gold' (verse 13). Finally, the bridesmaids follow (her 'virgin' friends, verse 14) and they all enter with 'gladness and rejoicing' into the king's palace (verse 15).

Concluding address to the groom (verses 16–17)

It was customary to wish newlyweds a prosperous future and numerous offspring (see Genesis 24:60; Ruth 4:11-12). This love song concludes with the wish that the king's dynasty will be permanent and universal. It is addressed to the king and reminds him that however illustrious his background might be it is the future that counts—'Instead of your fathers shall be your sons' (verse 16). A monarch like Solomon can look back at the achievements of king David but he is encouraged to look to sons who will share in his universal rule, just as David made his sons 'chief ministers'. Solomon, in fact, divided his kingdom into twelve districts with officers over each (2 Samuel 8:18; 1 Kings 4:7–19).

The closing oracle reminds us that the whole psalm is the inspired utterance of the poet (see verse 1) and it takes up the promise in God's covenant with David (2 Samuel 7:16) that the Davidic name and dynasty will continue. Absalom had no son to keep his name in remembrance (2 Samuel 18:18) but that will not be so in this case. It will lead to people of all nations praising the Davidic ruler for evermore. As God has blessed him 'for ever' (verse 2) so the peoples of the earth are to acknowledge him in thankful praise 'for ever and ever' (verse 17; see verse 6).

Jesus Christ and his people

This psalm has close links with Psalms 2, 21:1–7 and 72 and helps in the interpretation of the Song of Solomon. Though the setting is in the days of a ruling king of David's stock, the psalm presents us with such an astounding picture of a monarch that its true realisation is only to be found in Jesus the Messiah who is of David's royal line. The unique introduction in verse 1 alerts us to view this psalm as pointing beyond an ancient oriental wedding scene. Calvin comments, 'The Holy Spirit is not accustomed to inspire the servants of God to utter great swelling words, and to pour forth empty sounds into the air; and, therefore, we may naturally conclude, that the subject here treated of is not merely a transitory and earthly kingdom.' At best, kings like David, Solomon and Hezekiah are imperfect types of the true 'anointed' one who is in the fullest sense both God and King (see Hebrews 1:8–9 where the quotation is introduced along with the other biblical references to express most clearly the deity of Christ).

What Isaiah prophesies concerning the royal child, Immanuel, who is called 'mighty God' (Isaiah 7:14; 8:8; 9:6; 10:21) is typified in the Davidic ruler (verse 6). Included in the angel's message to Mary concerning the son she would bear is the statement that God 'will give to him the throne of his father David, and he will reign over the house of Jacob for ever, and of his kingdom there will be no end' (Luke 1:32–33), a point stressed in this psalm (see verse 6).

The psalmist's picture of the handsome king who rules righteously (verse 2,4,6–7) is one with Isaiah's prophecy of the messianic king who will be seen in all his beauty (Isaiah 32:1; 33:17). His gracious speech (verse 2) reminds us of the fulness of grace that flows from our Lord

Jesus (John 1:14-17) and of the gracious words that proceeded from his lips (Luke 4:22). The royal warrior theme (see verses 3-5) is taken up in John's vision of the Messiah (see Revelation 6:2) and it is to King Jesus that honour, glory and blessing are given (Revelation 5:12).

As Israel is often depicted as the Lord's bride so the Messiah's bride is the Church which will be presented to him without blemish and spot, wearing white robes washed in the Lamb's blood (Ephesians 5:27; Revelation 7:14), clothed also with fine linen clean and bright which are the righteous actions of the saints (Revelation 19:7-8).

The king's bride was called to renounce her past life, likewise the Messiah's bride must turn her back on her old life in sin and live to the praise of her Lord, submitting to him in everything. Christ's bride is viewed by John as the New Jerusalem to which the kings of the earth bring their glory and honour (Revelation 21:24-26) as our psalm indicates (verse 12). The glad celebrations that surround the bridal party's entrance into the king's palace (verse 13) prepare us for the vision of the heavenly rejoicing at the news that 'the marriage of the Lamb has come, and his wife has made herself ready' (Revelation 19:7). Those who are Messiah's bride become themselves kings (Revelation 1:6) and it is through the Church's witness that people of all nations come to belong to Messiah and praise the King (see verses 16-17). John Ryland's great hymn, 'Let us sing the King Messiah', is an exposition of this psalm. The fourth verse reads:

Majesty combined with meekness,
Righteousness and peace unite
To ensure Thy blessed conquests.
On, great Prince, assert Thy right;
Ride triumphant
All around the conquered globe.

Psalm 46

Security in God

From time to time horrific things happen to stop us in our tracks and make us think of God and eternity. When people are not prepared to stop to listen to what God has to say through his revealed word, the Bible, he will use world events—an earthquake, a tsunami, war, an atrocious terrorist attack—or some tragedy closer to home to challenge us in our busy lives to consider the living God our Creator.

In May 1995, at the fiftieth anniversary of VE Day, marking the end of the Second World War in Europe, the television cameras took us to the Outer Hebrides of Scotland, to Stornoway on the Isle of Lewis. Percentagewise, more men lost their lives in that war from those islands than from any other part of the United Kingdom. An old newspaper reporter spoke of how he saw the men leave on the ferry, no one knowing exactly what they would experience or whether they would return. It was an emotional time as evidenced by the solemn silence of the occasion that was only broken when a church precentor struck up in song the metrical version of Psalm 46 and the whole crowd joined in. The old reporter commented that it was one of the most moving scenes he had ever witnessed. Many of the people who sang knew the reality of the God they were singing about due to the very powerful experiences of the Holy Spirit they had witnessed in the religious revival there in 1934-1939.

This was Martin Luther's favourite psalm. In those days when he was opposed by Pope and Holy Roman Emperor and felt the pressures of his busy, turbulent life almost too great to bear, he would say to his friend Philip Melanchthon, 'Come let us sing the 46th Psalm and let the devil do his worst!' His hymn, *A safe stronghold our God is still, A trusty shield and weapon* is based on this psalm. Here is a psalm to bring comfort and strength to those who put their trust in God and to challenge those who have no time for God.

Many see the victory over the Assyrian army of Sennacherib in the days of King Hezekiah as providing the setting for this psalm (2 Kings 17-18; Isaiah 36-37) but there is no reason why it could not have been composed much earlier during the David-Solomon era and used later during times of crisis in Israel's national life. At a number of points in the psalm we are reminded of phrases from the prophecy of Isaiah and it may be that the prophet knew and made use of the psalm's phraseology in his ministry.

The psalm does not fall easily into any of the recognised categories such as praise, thanksgiving or prayer but it can be included among the 'Songs of Zion' (see Psalms 48, 76, 84, 87, 132) and has links with Psalms 2 and 24. It is clearly divided into three sections with a refrain marking the end of the second and third sections. All three describe upheavals of various sorts but in all circumstances God is seen as his people's safety.

In addition to the regular headings 'To the Chief Musician', 'of the sons of Korah' (the word 'Psalm' does not occur in the original) and 'A Song' (see Psalms 18, 30, 120-134) there is added 'upon' or 'according to Alamoth'. 'Alamoth' means 'virgins' and the exact phrase occurs again in a similar context during the celebrations associated with the arrival of the ark of the covenant at Jerusalem (1 Chronicles 15:20). This would connect the contents of the psalm with the ark as the symbol of God's presence among his people in the heart of David's city of Jerusalem. Although there is no certainty the phrase may well refer to the song's tune or less likely to the pitch of the music.[102]

Confessing God's protection (verses 1-3)

God's people affirm that he is for them a 'refuge' and Books 1 and 2 of the Psalter press home this truth (Psalms 14:6; 61:3; 62:7-8; 71:7) and we are not allowed to forget it in the remaining Books (see for example Psalms 73:28; 91:2,9; 142:5). The verb associated with this noun and often translated 'trust' first appears in Psalm 2:12 where we are assured of the happy state of all those who 'take refuge' in God (see also Psalms 5:11; 7:1; etc.).

God's 'strength' (verse 1; sometimes translated 'power') is also important in the psalms and closely associated with God's protection (see Psalm 28:7–8; 59:16–17; etc.). It is one of God's attributes by which he is able to rule over all (Psalms 93:1; 99:4).

It is one thing to confess and sing of God's attributes when all is well, it is quite another, when our world is turned upside down, to state confidently: 'Therefore we will not fear' (verse 2; see Psalm 23:4). The earth suggests stability (Ecclesiastes 1:4) but it can be 'removed' (literally 'changed'). Earthquakes happen, causing landslides and rock falls that can drastically alter the earth's appearance. It is the sea's raging waters in particular (verse 3) that do great damage not only by tsunamis but by pounding the cliffs in severe storms. As a result, some parts of the east coast of England have seen extensive erosion. These natural occurrences are illustrative of all the upheavals that can disturb and unsettle God's people. Whatever the circumstances, the fear that leads to panic or paralysis has no place, for God is 'a very present' (more literally 'amply found' or 'proved greatly' in the sense of 'amply proved to be') 'help in trouble' (verse 1; see Psalm 22:19).

Experiencing God's presence (verses 4–7)

From fearful destructive waters we are suddenly introduced to a 'river' whose 'streams' or channels 'gladden' God's people (verse 4). It symbolises all that is pleasing, plentiful and satisfying (see Psalms 65:9; 87:7). Unlike so many capital cities of the world both ancient and modern, Jerusalem did not have a pleasant river flowing through its centre. To alleviate water shortage problems in times of siege, Hezekiah constructed a channel to take water from the Gihon spring to the pool of Siloam inside the city walls (2 Chronicles 32:30). The river imagery is used here in association with God's presence to emphasise God's protection of his people (see Isaiah 33:21).

We are reminded of Eden with its river that watered God's garden (Genesis 2:10). It is a picture that takes us through the Bible to the garden city of the new creation with 'the river of the water of life' flowing from God's throne (Revelation 22:1–2; see Ezekiel 47:1–12;

Joel 3:18; Zechariah 14:8). It is that eternal city temple which is spoken of here as 'the city of God' where God has ordained to dwell (verse 4). In the time of David the temple had not yet been built. The ark, the symbol of God's presence, resided in a special tent called the 'tabernacle' (verse 4; see Exodus 40:21; Psalm 43:3) which was erected in Jerusalem (2 Samuel 6:17). It was later placed in the temple that Solomon built (1 Kings 8:6). Jeremiah prophesied a time when it would be required no longer (Jeremiah 3:16-17) and the New Jerusalem is pictured as needing no such edifice for God to dwell with his people (Revelation 21:22). The whole city can be identified as God's holy temple or dwelling place as this psalm indicates and, as Ezekiel prophesies, the city is called, 'The Lord is there' (see Ezekiel 48:35). Jerusalem as it became in the era of David and Solomon is used by psalmist and prophet to symbolise the whole company of God's people with God residing among them. When Samuel was young Israel took the symbol of God's presence for granted and used it like a lucky charm so that God had to teach them a lesson through defeat and humiliation (1 Samuel 4). Jeremiah likewise warned the Jews against treating the temple as if it had magical powers of protection (Jeremiah 7:2-15). When the people of God looked to the Lord of the temple to seek his presence in prayer as Jehoshaphat and Hezekiah did, then God's people were assured of his help and deliverance.

The use of 'Most High' (verse 4; see Psalm 7:17) as a name for God is interesting in this context. The ancient city of Salem (Jerusalem; see Psalm 76:2) was the place where Melchizedek ruled and exercised a priestly ministry on behalf of 'God Most High' (Genesis 14:18-22). It points to God's exalted position and to his sovereign power and authority over the nations (see Psalm 47:2).

The city of God remains; it is not 'moved' or 'toppled' (verse 5) when everything else is disturbed and toppled (see verses 2-3 and 6). We are reminded that in the end-time upheaval with the shaking of the whole creation, the kingdom we are given in Christ is unshakeable (Hebrews 12:27-28). It is not because the city itself is able to withstand a natural catastrophe or enemy attack but solely because of God's presence within her, helping and bringing salvation and hope. The idiomatic phrase 'at the turning of the morning' ('at the break of dawn' verse 5) is used for the moment when the waters of the Red Sea returned, drowning the Egyptian army and bringing deliverance to Israel (Exodus

14:27). The first signs of the morning light came to signify a new beginning and fresh hope (see Psalms 5:3; 30:5).

To emphasise the security of God's people a parallel is drawn between what is observed in nature (verses 2–3) and among the nations (verse 6) with God's city set in between, peaceful and unmoved (verse 4–5). As the waters are not only 'troubled' ('foam'; see Psalm 75:8) but 'roar' or 'rage' (verse 3) so the 'nations raged' (verse 6) and as the mountains 'toppled' or 'were carried' (verse 2) so the 'kingdoms' topple ('were moved', verse 6). The earth that is 'removed' or 'changed' (verse 2) now becomes a symbol for earthly superpowers that 'melt' in fear at the thunderous sound of God's 'voice' (verse 6; see Psalm 18:13; John 12:28–29). Enemies of God's people melt away like the inhabitants of Canaan before Israel (see Exodus 15:15; Joshua 2:24).

The refrain in verse 7 reminds us of the opening confession (verse 1) and the statement concerning God's presence in the city (verses 4–5). It is none other than the 'LORD of hosts' (see Psalm 24:10) who is there for them. For the first time in Book 2 of the Psalter we have a reference to God's covenant name 'LORD' (Jehovah/Yahweh). The addition of 'hosts' underlines the fact that God is the all-powerful ruler of the universe. 'God of Jacob' (see Psalm 20:1; 24:6) in the parallel line again draws attention to God's special relationship with his people. He is 'Immanuel' ('God with us'; see Isaiah 7:14; 8:8,10), who is known to us now as Jesus our Saviour (Matthew 1:22–25). To have the living and true God 'with us' (see Psalm 23:4) is to have the one who is able to deliver in troubled times and to be our 'refuge' or 'stronghold' (see Psalm 9:9), putting his people beyond the reach of any enemy, as the term suggests a different word to the one translated 'refuge' in verse 1.

Acknowledging God's power (verses 8–11)

A call goes out to come and look at the deeds of Israel's covenant God, 'the LORD' (verse 8). It is an invitation to the enemy nations and any among God's people whose faith may be wavering. The outstanding act of God was the deliverance of his people from Egypt, an event that prefigures God's greater work at Calvary. The 'works of the LORD' could also refer to more recent events within Israel's memory just as the Christian Church remembers the great acts of God in times of spiritual revival. For God to bring deliverance to his people often meant appalling devastation ('desolations', verse 8; see Psalm 73:19) for the enemy, as in the case of the Egyptians at the Red Sea. The threat of further war is brought to an end not only by gaining victory over the enemy but by destroying the weapons of war, symbolised in the breaking of bow and spear and the burning of military waggons[103] (verse 9; see Psalm 76:3; 1 Samuel 2:4). These past victories were viewed as foretastes of the end-time day of judgment and salvation, when swords would be beaten into ploughshares and spears into pruning hooks (Isaiah 2:4; 9:4-5; Ezekiel 39:9; Micah 4:1-4). The cessation of war and the establishment of lasting peace for which people long, but is impossible for humans to achieve, is the certain future that the God of peace is working to establish. It is through the prince of peace, who has already won the decisive victory on the cross, confirmed by his resurrection, that this future hope is sure and certain (see Isaiah 9:6-7; Luke 1:31-33; 1 Corinthians 15:25-28).

With these thoughts in mind, God now calls friend and foe to 'stop', 'desist' and acknowledge God for who he is, that he reigns supreme over the superpowers and the whole earth (Isaiah 37:20). This is not a call for quiet reflection at a retreat, as the traditional translation, 'Be still' (verse 10), might suggest, but a summons to hostile forces to abandon their futile attempts to fight against God and his people (see Psalm 2:10-12), and at the same time a call to his people to stop panicking and trust God.

The closing refrain is a fitting response from God's people to the preceding call and it also has the effect of emphasising the confession with which the psalm began (verse 1). Solomon could write: 'The name of the Lord is a strong tower; the righteous run to it and are safe' (Proverbs 18:10).

We do well to listen to the voice of God that we hear in this psalm and to worship him with reverence and awe, 'for our God is a consuming fire' (Hebrews 12:25-29). But what a comfort to be able to say with the apostle Paul, 'If God is for us who can be against us?' (Romans 8:31)!

Psalm 47

Applauding the LORD Most High

'The war to end all wars', that was the misguided thinking of many concerning the Great War of 1914-18. So long as human beings are governed by selfish desires so long will there be war in the home between family members, within neighbourhoods in towns and cities, within nations and between nations. But the search goes on for lasting peace and it is held up before the young as an ideal for which to aim. People still have utopian dreams of lasting peace and tranquillity. Behind all the wars and battles many of which are mentioned in the Bible, there is a deep spiritual war going on. In Genesis 3:15 at the time when the first couple disobeyed God and believed the snake, God instigated this war between the sinister snake and his brood and the woman and her offspring, involving the defeat of the snake but not without cost to the woman's offspring. That snake, seen as God's chief enemy and the real enemy of God's people is later identified as the devil Satan. The Lord Jesus was brought face to face with him in the wilderness and withstood Satan's temptations for him to gain earthly power and influence independently of God. Our Lord's death on the cross is the great fulfilment of that initial promise to the disobedient couple. This was God's way of dealing with the devil's power over a world in revolt against the Lord. As a result of that atoning death, redemption has been won so that people of all nations might be freed from the clutches of the evil one and brought under God's rule. This psalm celebrates that final righteous peace when the whole world acknowledges God's sovereignty. It takes up the previous psalm's depiction of God, exalted among the nations and in the earth.

As is typical of the praise psalms it begins with a call to praise God followed by reasons for doing so (verses 1-5). This process is repeated (verses 6-9) as in Psalms 95 and 100. It is tempting to see the 'Selah' (verse 4) as the marker dividing the two parts of the psalm but this breaks the symmetry between the two sections in which God's exaltation brings each of the sections to a close (verses 5 and 9). Perhaps it is suggesting we take our breath before the important climatic announcement in verse 5.

No new additions are found in the heading only the usual references to the musical director ('Chief Musician'; see Psalm 4), 'the sons of Korah' (see Psalm 42) and 'A Psalm' (see Psalm 3). The psalm takes up themes already mentioned in Psalms 2, 16, and 24 as well as in some of the later psalms (see Psalms 68:18; 110:1).

Praising God's victories (verses 1-5)

Clapping and shouting were expressions of joyful enthusiasm (Psalms 5:11; 98:8; Isaiah 55:12) especially on such occasions as the coronation of an Israelite king (1 Samuel 10:24; 1 Kings 1:39-40; 2 Kings 11:12). Unusual for these hymns the call to praise God goes out to the whole world, to 'all you peoples' (verse 1), not just to Israel.

The reason ('For') why all the nations should praise Israel's God, 'the LORD Most High' (see Psalm 46:4,7-8), is that he is 'the great king over all the earth' and therefore 'awesome' (verse 2). Israel's God is no mere local god. The Assyrian kings gave themselves the title 'the great king' (2 Kings 18:19), but 'the LORD' (Jehovah/Yahweh) is 'Most High' ruling over all so that even superpowers like Egypt and Assyria are under him.

The verbs in the next two verses should not be thought of as referring only to a future day as the New King James Version implies but to what God has done and is still doing. He makes peoples and tribal communities ('the nations', verse 3) subject to ('subdue', see Psalm 18:47) Israel. The phrase 'under our feet' (verse 3; see Psalm 45:5) is an idiom for complete submission and probably arose from the practice of a victorious warrior placing his foot on the neck of a conquered enemy (see Joshua 10:24). The verse is probably referring to the conquest of Canaan under Joshua as well as to the more recent victories of David over neighbouring territories. The Apostle Paul looks forward to the time when the God of peace will crush the great enemy Satan under the feet of God's people (Romans 16:20).

The LORD subdued the Canaanite peoples in order to give the land to Israel as an 'inheritance' (verse 4). We read in Deuteronomy 32:8–9 of the universal sovereignty of the 'Most High' in apportioning the nations their lands and of his special relationship to Israel. The God who loved Jacob and chose his descendants to be his special people (Psalm 28:9; Deuteronomy 4:37–38; Malachi 1:2) also chose their land and loves it (see Psalm 105:11). The 'pride of Jacob' ('excellence of Jacob', verse 4; see Amos 6:8; 8:7; Nahum 2:2; Daniel 8:9) parallels 'our inheritance' and describes the promised land.

Verse 5 recalls the time when Israel entered Canaan and took Jericho. The ark of the covenant, which represented the LORD's presence, went up before them with the sound of the horn (or 'trumpet') and a shout (see Joshua 6). This might suggest that the psalm has in mind God's having 'gone up' (verse 5) to fight for his people as the verb 'to go up' is often used for going to war (see Numbers 13:30–31; Judges 1:1; Isaiah 7:6). On the other hand, 'has gone up' could refer to a victorious return, implying a prior 'coming down' to fight for his people as he did at the time of exodus (Exodus 3:8). This was symbolised by the ark which was brought out and went ahead of the people into battle and was then brought back triumphantly to the tabernacle in the centre of Israel's camp (Numbers 10:35–36).

The 'shout' (verse 5) can refer to the blast of a trumpet (Leviticus 23:24; Numbers 10:5–6) so that 'the sound' (literally 'the voice') of the horn parallels the 'blast' ('shout') of the trumpet. Exactly the same words occur in the description of the joyful celebrations when David brought the ark up to Jerusalem (2 Samuel 6:15). We are reminded of Balaam's prophecy which speaks of the 'shout of a king' in association with the Lord's victorious presence among his people (Numbers 23:21). When Solomon had completed the Temple the ark was brought up to its place in the inner sanctuary with praise and thanksgiving and 'the house of God' was filled with the divine glory cloud (2 Chronicles 5:2–14). Nowhere do we read in the Old Testament of the ark being taken up annually to the temple during the festival of Tabernacles or at the New Year as some scholars maintain.

This psalm depicts God as king and makes no mention of any Davidic ruler (see later Psalms 93–99). Thus all these Old Testament associations prepare us for the truth concerning the deity of Jesus the Messiah. They prefigure God incarnate coming down to do battle against sin and Satan. Through his immaculate life resisting the evil one's temptations and by his going to Jerusalem to be lifted up to die that atoning death on the cross, God the Son as the man Christ Jesus has obtained a moral victory, whereby Satan's dominion over the nations has been broken (Genesis 3:15; Luke 4:5-8; John 12:31-32; Revelation 12:1-12). This victory is confirmed by his resurrection and ascension into heaven where now he sits at God's right hand till all his enemies are under his feet (1 Corinthians 15:25; Ephesians 1:20-23; Philippians 2:9-11; Hebrews 1:3-4).

Praising God's kingship (verses 6-9)

In this second summons to praise God (see verse 1), five times the call is issued to 'sing praises' (verses 6-7). This is to be done with voice and instrument as the verb suggests, and comes from the same word family as 'psalm' (see Psalm 9:2; 30:4). The universal kingship of the LORD, their covenant keeping God, is the special reason for praising him. God, who has been described as *the* great King over all the earth (verse 2) and the king of his people ('our King', verse 6) is again called 'the King of all the earth' (verse 7).

God's personal name, 'the LORD' (Jehovah/Yahweh), is normally used when he is proclaimed as king (see Psalms 93:1; 96:10; etc.). Only here is it declared that 'God reigns' over the Gentile nations (verse 8, but see Isaiah 52:7). Some translate 'God has become king' or 'begun to reign' and see it as an enthronement formula that was part of a supposed worship drama associated with the annual autumnal new year festival. While his kingship was no doubt recognised in worship throughout the year there is no evidence that the Lord was celebrated as ascending in triumph into his holy temple in Jerusalem and enthroned each year. God's 'holy throne' (verse 8) emphasises that his kingship is unique and set apart from all other rule (see Psalm 22:3; 1 Kings 22:19; Isaiah 6:1). The ark with the cherubim over it was the earthly replica of the heavenly reality (Psalm 99:1).

The nobles or 'princes' of the various people groups in the world, also described as 'the shields of the earth' (verse 9; see Psalm 89:18) in that they are the protectors of their peoples, have assembled together and become members of God's people (see further on Psalm 87). The prophets spoke of a time when hostile nations would be one with Israel

(Isaiah 19:24–25; Zechariah 2:11). The phrase 'the people of the God of Abraham' (verse 9) reminds us of God's promise to Abraham that all nations would be blessed through him and that he would be 'the father of a multitude of nations' (Genesis 12:3; 17:4; John 11:51–52). It is by belonging to Christ Jesus that we are Abraham's true descendants (see Galatians 3:14,29). We also recall Abraham's victory over the kings and his contact with Melchizedek, priest of the 'Most High' who blessed Abraham and embraced the God of Abraham (Genesis 14:17–20). The peoples of the world who have become members of Abraham's family can certainly be encouraged to ring out the praises of the Lord Most High.

The second half of the psalm ends like the first half by emphasising that God is 'greatly exalted' (verse 9; see Psalm 46:10). It uses a form of the verb that is translated 'gone up' in verse 5 and presses home to us that God is indeed the 'Most High' over all the nations.

Giving reasons for praise (introduced by 'For' in verses 2 and 7) encourages the people to sing 'with understanding' (verse 7; the same word appears as 'contemplation' in thirteen psalm titles; see Psalms 32; 42; 44; 45; etc.). Singing praise to God must not descend into a mindless act where the music induces ecstatic trancelike states in worshippers. Paul urges the Corinthian Christians to 'sing with the understanding' (1 Corinthians 14:15).

Psalm 48

God's Beautiful City

After the Egyptians surrendered to the Greeks in 332 BC, Alexander the Great founded a new city by the Mediterranean and named it after himself: Alexandria. It became rich and powerful and an important centre of learning, containing one of the ancient world's greatest libraries. After leaving Egypt to continue his military campaigns in the East, Alexander never returned. The city spoken of in this psalm belongs to a greater King than Alexander and unlike the Greek ruler this King is no absent monarch.

The psalm belongs to a group commonly known as 'Songs of Zion' (e.g. Psalms 46; 87; see Psalm 137:3) and encourages us to praise the God of Zion. Psalms 45–48 have a number of items in common especially the kingship theme. The arrangement also shows a link between the divine ruler and his bride (Psalm 45) and the LORD and his city (Psalms 46–48), a link that John also makes in his picture of God's people as both a bride and holy city (Revelation 21:2; see Isaiah 52:1-2; 61:10; 62:5).

When the Jews collected the psalms together into five books and Jewish congregations heard them read or sung in the temple or synagogue after their return from exile they must have interpreted these Zion psalms as pointing to something more glorious than the second-rate city and temple that was built after the Babylonians had

destroyed what David and Solomon had erected. It is true that Jesus'
disciples were impressed with what the Herods had done in extending
and beautifying the Jerusalem temple of their day but city and temple
were destined for destruction in AD 70 as Jesus prophesied (Mark 13:1–
2). Jesus, however, helped his followers to apply temple terminology to
himself.

In the introduction to his Gospel, John identifies Jesus as the true
tabernacle and then records words of Jesus in the following chapter
which he interprets as a reference to Christ's own body. He said,
'Destroy this temple and I will raise it up in three days' (John 1:14; 2:19–
21). The union of believers with Christ in the allegory of the vine and
the branches (John 15:1–16) is a truth that the Apostle Paul elaborates
when he speaks of the Church as the body of Christ, the place where
the Holy Spirit resides (e.g. 1 Corinthians 3:16–17; Ephesians 5:23). Also
important in this context is Jesus' promise of the presence of the Holy
Trinity in the believers' lives (John 14:15–23), something that Paul also
highlights (Romans 8:9–11; 1 Corinthians 6:15,19).

Jesus also urged his followers to be like a city on a hill whose light
cannot be hidden (Matthew 5:14–16). In giving this example, Jesus may
also have been thinking of the prophecies concerning Zion's hill being
so conspicuous that all the nations stream to it (e.g. Isaiah 2:2–5). A
little later he can certainly speak of Jerusalem as 'the city of the great
King' (Matthew 5:35), a clear allusion to this Psalm 48 verse 2. Zion as
a temple-city where God is present with his people is brought to full
expression in John's vision of the New Jerusalem (see Revelation 3:12;
7:15; 14:1; 21:22–23) but it is already developed by Paul in his teaching
on the union of Jewish and Gentile believers as citizens together in
the heavenly city. In the same breath Paul also viewed them as a new
temple where God resides (Ephesians 2:19–22; see Philippians 3:20;
1 Corinthians 3:16–17; 2 Corinthians 6:16).

Though there is fulsome praise of Zion, the psalm makes it clear that
it is God who has made the city the safe and beautiful place that it is.
The psalm may well be constructed with a subtle play on the points of
the compass to emphasise God's kingship over the whole earth.[104]

There are no additional items in the heading to note. What
difference there is between 'song' (see Psalm 30) and 'psalm' (see Psalm
3) particularly when they appear together (see Psalms 65; 75–76) is
uncertain. While 'psalm' is a technical term used in the Psalter to
denote songs sung in worship to the accompaniment of strings, 'song'

is a more general term for any kind of song with or without musical instruments, whether in worship or not (see Amos 6:5). The ancient Greek translation (LXX) adds 'On the second day of the week' and if they were present in the temple on Mondays, as they probably were during the week that led to Good Friday, Jesus and his disciples would have certainly heard the psalm (see Mark 11:1-19).

The Lord praised in his city (verses 1-3)

In place of a call to praise God, the opening line announces the greatness of Israel's covenant Lord and that he is worthy of much praise especially by the worshipping company of God's people in Jerusalem. A sevenfold description of the city is given:

1. 'the city of our God' (verse 1; see Psalms 46:4; 87:3)—It belongs to the Lord, the capital where God has ordained to make his earthly residence among his people, over whom he rules through his anointed king of David's line.

2. 'his holy mountain' or 'hill' (verse 1; see Psalms 3:4; 15:1; 43:3)— Most cities were established on mountains and this was true of Jerusalem. It is 'holy' because God's presence was there symbolized by the ark of the covenant (2 Samuel 6:12), which was later placed in Solomon's temple (1 Kings 8:1-13).

3. 'Beautiful in elevation' (verse 2; see Psalm 50:2)—There are impressive views of the city from the Kidron Valley but observers agree that it is not the highest or most attractive of the Canaan mountains.

4. 'the joy of the whole earth' (verse 2)—The city became famous in the David-Solomon era and people like the queen of Sheba rejoiced at all she saw and heard (1 Kings 10). When temple and city were destroyed by the Babylonians in 586/7B.C. the same hyperbolic language was used to express the tragedy of the judgment (Lamentations 2:15).

5. 'Mount Zion' (verse 2)—Zion was originally the ridge that David conquered and took from the Jebusites and where David brought the ark of the covenant (2 Samuel 5:7; 6:12). Later Zion was used as another name for Jerusalem (see Isaiah 40:9).

6. 'the sides of the north' or 'Zaphon's heights' (verse 2)—The 'sides' refer to the extreme edges or farthest reaches and while it could be referring to the northern extremities of the city, it is more likely that the psalmist is applying to Zion a traditional expression for God's abode (see Isaiah 14:13). The name 'Zaphon' (Hebrew for 'north') was a

northern mountain that the Canaanites associated with their gods, like Mount Olympus was to the Greeks. Prophets and psalmists sometimes employ mythological language to express truths concerning the living God. As one commentator puts it, 'the aspirations of all peoples for a place on earth where God's presence could be experienced were fulfilled in Mount Zion, the true Zaphon'.[105]

7. 'the city of the great King' (verse 2; see Matthew 5:35)—A different word for 'great' is used here from the one in verse 1 and Psalm 47:2 but the idea is similar. While Assyrian kings like Esarhaddon gave themselves extravagant titles like 'great king' and 'king of the world', it is the Lord alone who is entitled to make such claims.

What makes Zion so wonderful is not its physical features but God's presence among his people—'God is in her palaces' or 'citadels' (verse 3; see Psalm 46:5). The city's true fortifications are to be found in the LORD and he has on numerous occasions made himself known as 'her stronghold' ('her refuge', verse 3; see Psalm 46:7,11).

This idealistic picture of Zion is a pointer to something much grander than anything the city achieved even in the best of times. Prophets like Isaiah helped the people in the worst of times to keep singing such songs and looking for their full realization (see Isaiah 2:2–4). That fulfilment began to be seen at Pentecost, when many nations were gathered in Jerusalem, as Luke indicates, and when the gospel went out from that city to all peoples throughout the Roman world (Luke 24:47; Acts 2:5; 8:1,4).

The victorious LORD of hosts (verses 4–8)

This section gives an illustration of God as the 'refuge' or 'stronghold' of his people. The description of the kings (see Psalm 2:1-2) reminds Calvin of the contrast with Caesar's famous words at the conquest of Egypt, 'I came, I saw, I conquered' (*Veni, vidi, vici*). They 'assembled', they 'saw' but, far from conquering, the kings were so 'astonished' (rather than 'marvelled') and 'struck with terror' that they 'took flight' (verse 5; see Psalm 2:5). They were seized with trembling and were in 'pain' like a woman in labour, on the very spot where they expected victory (verse 6). The description of the enemy's reaction when they saw Mount Zion as well as the reference to the 'east wind' (verse 7) recalls the victory over the Egyptians at the Red Sea and the song that was sung (see Exodus 14:21; 15:10,14-16,17). Similar language is also used of the fear that fell on Moab and the Canaanites under Joshua

(Numbers 22:2-3; Joshua 2:9-11). Just as wind and waves can destroy great seaworthy vessels like 'the ships of Tarshish' (verse 7; 2 Chronicles 20:37; Isaiah 2:16-17)[106] so the Lord makes light work of destroying the enemies of God's people.

In the summary statement in verse 8 the psalmist affirms that the reports they 'have heard' about God (see Psalm 44:1) they have witnessed for themselves, and a contrast is drawn between what the kings 'saw' (verse 5) and what God's people 'have seen' (verse 8). The sight that terrified the enemy gives assurance to the citizens of Zion. In view of God's victories over the enemy, 'the city of our God' (verse 8; see verse 1) is now appropriately described as 'the city of the LORD of hosts' (verse 8; see Psalm 24:10). The exodus and conquest of Canaan along with the establishment of Jerusalem as God's city under David produces a confidence in God concerning Zion's future security— 'God will establish it for ever' (verse 8). This was the confidence of which Isaiah could speak (Isaiah 7:1-16) but not the false security that Jeremiah opposed (Jeremiah 7:1-15). The Jerusalem that is below has no future but the heavenly city is the one with firm foundations whose builder and maker is God. This is the city that Abraham was looking for and which will never be destroyed when everything else is shaken to bits (Galatians 4:25-26; Hebrews 11:10,16; 12:22,28). This calls for a moment's pause before proceeding further ('Selah').

The fame of the LORD (verses 9-11)

Within God's 'temple' (or 'palace', verse 9, which is a more suitable translation than 'sanctuary' in a context where the psalm's emphasis is on the Lord's kingship), God's people reflect on his 'loving-kindness' or 'steadfast love' (see Psalm 5:7), that fundamental characteristic of God that accounts for what has been said about God and his city and the assurance they have for the future. Thinking on God's unfailing love and commitment to his covenant promises is something that should be central to our communal worship as we hear God's word, pray and sing and when the ordinances of baptism and the Lord's Supper are administered. Our minds should be continually brought back to the great demonstration of God's unfailing love in the redemption accomplished at Calvary's cross.

In this section that addresses God directly ('O God', 'your') the exodus song is still in mind. It was through God's 'steadfast love' or 'mercy' they were redeemed (Exodus 15:13) and both Egypt and Israel got to know the LORD's 'name' and Israel was able to sing his 'praises' (Exodus 15:3,11). God's 'name' refers to his awesome character and reputation associated with his special personal name 'LORD' (Jehovah/ Yahweh) which, like his 'praises', reach 'to the ends of the earth' (verse 10). Through the missionary expansion, God's fame has spread throughout the world so that in every continent there are those who sing his praises (see Psalm 47:7–9). John heard the symbolic number that represented God's elect people (144,000) but when he saw them they were an innumerable company from every nation and language and they were singing the song of the redeemed on Mount Zion (Revelation 7:4,9–10; 14:1–3).

God's reputation is seen in two specific ways: in his 'right hand' that is 'full of righteousness' (verse 10) and in his 'judgments' (verse 11). God's 'righteousness' in this context speaks of his doing what is right in saving his people and punishing his enemies, while his 'judgments' refer to his just rule, and both can often be mentioned in the same breath as here (see Psalm 97:2). It was this powerful 'right hand' of God that was stretched out to redeem his people in the exodus event (Exodus 15:6,9,12). This 'hand' is always 'full of righteousness', like a king always seen holding the sceptre, for God never ceases to be true to himself in his dealings with humanity. Spurgeon comments: 'Neither saint nor sinner shall find the Lord to be an empty-handed God … to the one, through Jesus, he will be just to forgive, to the other just to condemn.'

These are grounds for praise and why God's people should 'rejoice' and 'be glad' in God's fair decisions including the final destruction of all who oppose him. The 'daughters of Judah' is an idiomatic way of speaking either of the surrounding daughter villages or the young virgin inhabitants, but along with the city itself the psalm is referring to all who by God's grace belong to his special community. They are the ones who have much cause to rejoice and be glad (see Psalm 97:8; Revelation 14:1–4).

The LORD is the city's security (verses 12–14)

This final section returns to thinking about the city itself (see verses 1–3), but again it is with the aim of giving honour to God. There is no evidence that the people engaged in regular ritualistic processions around the city walls as part of their worship. Nehemiah, at the dedication of Jerusalem's wall, took the people around the newly built structure in a procession of praise (Nehemiah 12:27–43) but that was a special one off occasion.

It is probably in their thoughts (see verse 9) that worshippers are invited to take a walk round the city, like tourists, and 'count her towers' (verse 12), give attention to 'her bulwarks' or 'ramparts' that protect the walls, and 'consider her palaces' (verse 13), which is better translated 'pass through her citadels' (see verse 3). Viewing all these impressive fortifications inspires confidence and encourages them to tell their children and grandchildren what all this really means (see Deuteronomy 4:9-10). The psalm does not say 'For this is Zion' but 'For this *is* God' (verse 14). As in verse 3 it is God, their God for evermore, who is the city's real defence. It is he who will be their 'guide', like the good shepherd-king that he is, leading them on in safety (see Psalm 78:52; Isaiah 49:10; 63:14) 'to death', in the sense of 'to the end'.[107]

Zechariah's vision of a man trying to measure Jerusalem encourages us to view this psalm not as something to expect in the present-day earthly city as some suggest,[108] but as a picture of that great holy city, the total sum of God's people from all nations, with the LORD protecting her like 'a wall of fire all around', and her 'glory' (Zechariah 2:1-12; Revelation 21:10-11). The earthly Jerusalem, as God promised, was the scene of the first gospel preaching and where the New Testament Church began and Luke particularly, both in his Gospel and Acts, draws attention to the place of the earthly Jerusalem in the purposes of God but like all the other physical aspects of old covenant worship such as the temple and its ceremonies, the earthly becomes obsolete as it opens out into the heavenly reality.

Psalm 49

'Not Redeemed with Silver or Gold'

This wisdom psalm (see Psalm 37) appeals to all and sundry to listen to truth expressed with musical accompaniment. The theme is the futility of worldly wealth and influence, one that echoes the Preacher's words in Ecclesiastes. It gives warning to the wicked and at the same time brings encouragement to the godly (see Psalm 1).

There are good indications why the 'psalm' is placed after the immediately preceding songs and psalms 'To the Chief Musician' and to 'the sons of Korah'. The links include references to 'peoples' (verse 1; Psalm 47:1), the receiving of divine revelation (verses 3-4; Psalm 45:1) and the thought of death and the hope of morning light (verses 9-12,14; Psalms 48:14; 46:5).

Universal message (verses 1-4)

In these introductory lines a general call goes out to 'all peoples', not only to Israel. Typical of the wisdom teacher (see Proverbs 1:8; 4:1) as well as the prophet (see Micah 1:2) there is a summons to 'Hear' and it is addressed to all who inhabit a transient 'world'—a rare word that denotes the passing world of time rather than its geography (see Psalm 17:14) and appropriate in view of the psalm's message. No one is exempt: 'each and every one' or the commonplace and influential

310

people ('low and high', verse 2)[109] as well as the affluent and oppressed ('rich and poor together') must listen to this important statement. All alike have much in common as the psalm indicates (see especially verse 10).

Using terminology we associate with Proverbs (e.g. 'wisdom', 'understanding' or insight', verse 3; see Proverbs 1:2) the psalmist's mouth gives expression to his heart's meditation. This wisdom message, which he further describes in wisdom language (see Proverbs 1:6) as a 'proverb' or 'instruction' and 'dark saying', here in the sense of a 'difficult problem' (see 1 Kings 10:1), is not his own personal thoughts but a message received by revelation from God. When he calls others to 'give ear' (verse 1) he is only urging them to do what he has done ('I will incline my ear', verse 4). What he himself has heard from God and meditated on he seeks to 'open up' ('disclose') or explain to others.

Prophets were known to 'prophesy' using musical instruments (see 1 Samuel 10:5) but this was probably in the sense of singing praises (see 1 Chronicles 25:3). On one occasion we read of Elisha calling for musicians possibly for the purpose of putting him in a frame of mind for receiving divine revelation (2 Kings 3:15). Here only in the Old Testament do we find instruction being given to the accompaniment of music. In previous psalms the 'harp' (or 'lyre', verse 4) has been used to accompany hymns of praise to God (see Psalms 33:2; 43:4). The psalm encourages us not to despise Christian teaching using spiritual songs. Children's chorus books have been greatly used to introduce gospel truths to youngsters and many of our well-established hymns continue to help in pressing home the Christian message, with their assurances, challenges, warnings and encouragements.

False hopes (verses 5-12)
The question raised in verse 5 expresses an assurance that the righteous have no need to be afraid in 'times of distress' ('days of evil' verse 5) when surrounded by wicked supplanters (literally 'the iniquity of my heels' verse 5 and reminding us of Jacob in Genesis 27:36; Hosea 12:3) who trust in their valuable assets and boast of their enormous wealth (verse 6). But all the money in the world cannot buy long life or finally evade death (verse 7-9). Everyone, as Ecclesiastes even more forcefully emphasises, must face death in the end (verses 10-12).

Rich people in their sailing boats captured by pirates off the east coast of Africa often escape death when the ransom price for their release has been paid. In ancient Israel it was possible in certain legal cases, to pay a ransom to avoid capital punishment (see Exodus 21:29-30). There are indications later in the writings of the prophets that many unscrupulous judges in Israel would take bribe money from influential rich crooks in cases where the death penalty should have been imposed. Poor people in debt slavery could be released with the help of a kinsman redeemer paying a ransom (Leviticus 25:47-49). The point being made in verse 7 is that God cannot be bought off with money.

There are difficulties with the text as a review of various modern translations will show but as our text stands it is saying that no one can save another's life in the community ('*his* brother') or their own (if 'for him' means 'for himself') when God decides their time to die has come. Verse 8 then expands what has just been said by making it clear that the ransom price for human life is far too expensive for anyone to pay even for the richest of people. The phrase 'it shall cease' (verse 8) means either ceasing in the sense of failing to pay the ransom price or ceasing any attempt to pay it. In view of all this there is no possibility of people using their resources in order to live on for ever and not experience death ('see the Pit', verse 9; see Psalms 16:10; 28:1; 30:9). Ezekiel declares that all Israel's gold and silver will be like refuse, of no value and unable to deliver them, in the day of the Lord's wrath (Ezekiel 7:19).

What the wisdom psalmist teaches concerning the reality that faces everyone, is an objective truth that all can see. Death comes to the 'wise' (verse 10)—to those who are teachable, who fear God and seek to do his will (see Proverbs 1:5-7), and equally to the 'fool', that is, to people who have no fear of God, who confidently carry on as if in ultimate charge of their own lives (see Proverbs 1:7) and to the 'senseless', who behave like animals (see Psalm 73:22). All the wealth they have amassed during their lifetime is left to others. Their mistaken assumption ('their inner thought' verse 11)[110] is that their 'houses' (perhaps their summer homes; see Amos 3:15) and their 'dwelling-places' will be theirs from generation to generation 'for ever'. They have made sure they have extensive estates to their name, calling 'lands after their own names' (verse 11). This whole section reminds us of Jesus' parable of the rich fool (see Luke 12:16-21) and the apostle Paul's warning to the rich 'not to be haughty, nor to trust in uncertain riches' (1 Timothy 6:17).

The final verse of this section summarises the sobering point that we all must die. Those we fear and may envy (see verses 5–6) on account of their honourable status and wealth ('honour', verse 12, is from the same word family as 'costly' in verse 8) do not even have enough for 'overnight lodgings' ('does not remain') when it comes to death. In this respect they are no different from cattle ('beasts') that have no bank balance! Both 'perish': humans and animals are 'destroyed' or 'ruined' by death (Ecclesiastes 3:18–21). While Psalm 8 indicates a fundamental difference between humans and animals echoing the truth of Genesis that humanity has been created in God's image to exercise authority over the other creatures, this psalm emphasises that as a result of the initial rebellion we are all subject to the curse of death (Genesis 2:17; 3:19; 5:5,8,11,14, etc.).

Two destinies (verses 13–20)

Typical of wisdom teaching, the psalm turns to consider the fate of the fool and the hope of the wise (see Psalm 1).

The fool (verses 13–14)

The psalm speaks of the 'way' or 'destiny' of those who nurse foolish expectations and their admirers who approve of their sayings. All such people will have a rude awakening. A pause for reflection is appropriate at this point ('Selah'). In his statement of innocence Job indicates that he had not put his hope and confidence in gold (Job 31:24–25), whereas the word for 'foolish' (verse 13) suggests 'foolish confidence'.

Verse 14 has a number of difficult phrases but the general sense is clear. Like sheep destined to be slaughtered (see Psalm 44:11) these self-confident people are appointed (literally 'set') to die (literally 'sheol') which can mean 'death' (see Psalms 6:5;16:10)). They are heading where death will look after them, like a shepherd feeding his sheep (not 'feed on them', verse 14). On the other hand, the 'upright' will soon have the upper hand over these ungodly fools. They will be victorious 'in the morning', the moment when God acts to save his people (see Psalm 30:5). Those who now fancy themselves as role models to be envied and followed will be soon removed by death and all their worldly advantages (literally 'their form' translated 'beauty') will waste away in 'sheol' instead of continuing to enjoy their splendid penthouse suites ('their dwelling' is more literally 'their lofty home').

The wise (verse 15)

Suddenly God is introduced for the one and only time in this psalm. It is as dramatic as the many other 'But God' references in the Bible (see Ephesians 2:4). While no human can redeem either himself or anyone else, God can do the impossible. He only can pay the ransom price to deliver the upright godly from death's power (literally 'the hand of sheol'; see Hosea 13:14). It is God who can certainly 'take' them, as Enoch and Elijah were 'taken' (Genesis 5:24; 2 Kings 2:3,5,9–10; and see Psalm 73:24). Another pause ('Selah') is required here to absorb this wonderful truth.

It is true that in some contexts being rescued from 'sheol' can mean deliverance from present troubles and an untimely death (see Psalms 18:4–5; 30:3) but here the context suggests redemption from the curse of death itself to resurrection light (see Psalm 17:15; Isaiah 26:19; Daniel 12:2). Although Christians can be said to be already redeemed by the blood of Christ (Ephesians 1:7; Colossians 1:14; 1 Peter 1:18–19; see Galatians 3:13) they still await the redemption of the body (Romans 8:23; see Luke 21:28). On the day when Christ returns in glory the dead in Christ will be raised incorruptible and those believers who are alive at the time will be changed and be for ever with the Lord (1 Corinthians 15:52–53; 1 Thessalonians 4:16–17).

Concluding application (verses 16–19)

The wisdom poet has shown conclusively that there are no grounds for being afraid (see verse 5) when people grow 'rich' and the 'glory' or 'honour' of their home and family ('his house' verse 16, or 'household' Genesis 18:19; 35:2) increases. The tragedy of the self-confident, self-satisfied ruthless rich, as this psalm has made plain, is that they must leave everything in which they have trusted. Their 'glory' does not descend after them (verse 17; see Job 1:21; Ecclesiastes 5:15). To the question 'How much did he leave?' the answer is 'Everything!' (Kidner). The pharaohs made great efforts to make sure all their treasures went with them into the afterlife but all to no avail. Paul likewise reminds us that 'we brought nothing into this world, and it is certain that we can carry nothing out' (1 Timothy 6:7).

These rich foolish people spend their lives blessing themselves probably in the sense of congratulating themselves on what they have amassed (literally: 'though in his lifetime his soul he will bless'; verse 18a), like the rich fool in Jesus' parable—'Soul, you have many goods laid up for many years ...' (Luke 12:19). They also enjoy the adulation of their admirers (verse 18b), with no thought of God or of praising and blessing the one from whom all blessings flow. Jesus also had this psalm in mind as he told the story of the rich man and Lazarus in which Abraham says to the rich man 'remember that in your lifetime you received your good things ...' (Luke 16:25).

Again, we are reminded of the end of the foolhardy rich who join their ancestors in their tombs of darkness where 'they shall never see the light' (verse 19; see Job 17:12; Psalm 56:13).

Concluding refrain (verse 20)

The closing lines are very similar to verse 12 and act like a refrain but with a significant variation (see Psalms 24:10 and 42:11 for similar variations). In place of 'does not remain' (*yalin*, 'abide') we have 'does not understand' (*yabin*). In verse 12 the rich and influential think they can beat death with their wealth while here they fail to understand and appreciate what faces them. They are acting like irrational animals that perish without thought and without hope.

This is a powerful message in our materialistic world where 'money talks' and where the young are often encouraged to gain celebrity status and the world's applause. If the rich cannot be saved who can, asked the astonished disciples. Following the psalmist Jesus replied that with men it is impossible but with God it is possible. Jesus said that he had been sent to give his life a ransom for many and by so doing he has obtained 'eternal redemption' (Mark 10:45; Hebrews 9:12; see also Psalm 19:14).

Psalm 50

The Righteous Judge
Cautions his People

It is in the context of God's special relationship with his people that this psalm must be interpreted ('covenant' is mentioned twice in verses 5 and 16). In ancient Near Eastern treaty texts, arrangements were normally made for the periodic reading of the treaty and God made sure that his people remembered the agreement that he had made with them at Sinai. Every seven years, in the sabbatical year for cancelling debts, the law was to be read at the Festival of Tabernacles to the assembled people. At the time when they rejoiced at God's goodness at harvest time and remembered the exodus from Egypt and God's protection of them through the wilderness they were to listen to the covenant obligations (Deuteronomy 31:9-13). It may have been in such a setting that this psalm was composed.

This is the first 'psalm of Asaph', the remaining ones are grouped together in Psalms 73 to 83. 'Asaph' was one of David's chief musicians and composed psalms under the influence of the Spirit (see 1 Chronicles 6:39; 15:17,19; 16:4-7; 25:2; 2 Chronicles 29:30). While the previous psalm is associated with the wisdom books of the Bible this one reminds us of Israel's true prophets and their concerns (see also Psalm 81). When used in the gatherings for communal worship the psalm's preachy, prophetic style served to arouse thoughtless worshippers and to challenge them concerning their covenant obligations. Following the pattern set by this psalm we need hymns that warn and challenge as well as encourage and comfort.

The psalm rounds off the Korah collection (Psalms 42–49), picks up the previous references to 'Zion' and its importance to the whole earth, and prepares us for the first of a fresh David collection with its teaching about sacrifice and heart worship (see Psalm 51:16–17,19).

A solemn summons (verses 1-6)

A call to appear before a judge in a court of law, whether as a witness or defendant, is not one you can lightly dismiss. Here the judge is none other than the living God who is over the whole universe. To add to the solemnity of the summons three different names for God are used— 'The Mighty One' (*El*, the name of the chief god of the Canaanites or the common term for any god in the ancient world), 'God' (*Elohim*, a plural term meaning 'gods' or, as often in the Old Testament, the general name for the true God) and 'the LORD' (Yahweh/Jehovah, the true God's personal name).

The same formation is used twice by the Reubenites, Gadites and half of the Manasseh tribe as they appealed to the all-knowing God at the commencement of their apology to the rest of Israel for their inappropriate action (Joshua 22:22). The first two names could be translated 'God of gods', meaning the 'great God'[III] but the build-up of names emphasises that the sovereign, creator God who is the covenant-keeping redeemer God of Israel (LORD), is the one who speaks, summoning the whole earth to attend the judge's findings.

God makes his appearance from 'Zion', the place where he has ordained to reside on earth and it is described in words reminiscent of Psalm 48:2 as 'the perfection of beauty' (verse 2). Like the bright sun shining out from behind a dark blanket of threatening thunder clouds God 'shines forth' (verse 2; see Psalms 80:1–2; 94:1–2; Deuteronomy 33:2). The splendour and majesty of that eternal light (see Psalm 104:2; 1 Timothy 6:16) appears and he 'will not be silent' (verse 3; see verse 21). The devouring fire (Deuteronomy 4:24; 9:3) and the raging tempest (1 Kings 19:11–12) remind us of God's appearance at Sinai (see Exodus 19:18–19; Hebrews 12:18–21) and the psalmist uses this imagery (see also Psalm 18:7–15) to describe God's coming out of Zion.

The calling of heaven and earth to God's courtroom is not, as in later psalms, to judge the whole world (see Psalms 96:13; 98:9). They are summoned to be present as witnesses to the judge's findings or decision (this is the sense here of 'judge', verse 4) concerning 'his people' (verse 4) who have also been summoned to attend. God's angels are probably the ones called upon to 'gather' them (verse 5; see Mark 13:27). The word 'saints' (verse 5) does not mean they were saintly or especially virtuous. It would be better to translate 'saints' as 'faithful ones' (see Psalm 30:3; the term comes from the same word family as 'steadfast love'). They belong to those who have committed themselves to the special arrangement that God made with Israel at Sinai. There the 'covenant' was 'made' or sealed 'by sacrifice' (verse 5). After the people had promised to obey God's word, sacrifices were offered and half the sacrificial blood was sprinkled on the altar and half on the people (Exodus 24:4–8). It was common in the ancient world for agreements or 'covenants' to be sealed or 'made' (literally 'cut') in this way (see Genesis 15:10,18; Jeremiah 34:18). It indicated the serious nature of the bond; breaking it would mean death. The heavens witness to God's 'righteousness' (verse 6; see Psalm 97:6), to his nature and moral right to be the 'Judge' of his people, and to be the one who rights wrongs. Before we hear the Judge's findings and in view of the awesome nature of the occasion a pause is called for ('Selah').

Judgment begins with God's people (1 Peter 4:17). The spiritual city and temple is purified in this world through the refining flames (see Malachi 3:1–3). Though believers are no longer under 'the terrors of law and of God' but have free access through the blood of Jesus into God's holy presence (Hebrews 10:19; 12:24), 'our God' (verse 3) is still 'a consuming fire', to be worshipped with reverence and awe (see Hebrews 12:28–29). If this is so for the 'righteous' what will become of 'the ungodly and the sinners' who do not obey the gospel (1 Peter 4:17–18; 2 Thessalonians 1:7–8)? There are two charges brought against God's people and underlying both are fundamental misconceptions of God. The first wrong view is that God needs us and our worship while the second false idea is that God is like us, made in our image.

Mindless religion censured (7–15)

Having arrested the covenant community with this graphic courtroom scene, the prophetic psalmist now presents the Judge's accusations. The formula declaring that the Lord will 'be your God and you shall be my people' (Leviticus 26:12; Jeremiah 7:23; see Genesis 17:7–8), so expressive of God's personal relationship with his people, is detected in God's opening exhortation, 'my people' ... 'your God' (verse 7). 'Hear ... O Israel' also recalls God's introduction to the great command to love the LORD with all our beings (Deuteronomy 6:5). This special spiritual relationship is essential to appreciating the charges God makes against his people.

The first accusation concerning ceremonial worship is indirect as there is no explicit word of criticism. In fact, God does not 'rebuke' them for their 'sacrifices' (like the peace or fellowship offerings) and whole 'burnt offerings' (see Psalm 40:6). They were meticulous in offering the required daily sacrifices (Exodus 29:38–42) and were not slow in making their free will thank offerings (see Leviticus 7:11–21). They were 'continually' being offered to the Lord (verse 8).

Blood offerings are no longer required in our worship since Jesus' once-for-all sacrifice at Calvary (Hebrews 10:12). The communal worship of Christians should consist of hymns of praise, spiritual songs, praying, the reading of Scripture, preaching the gospel, teaching God's truth, ministering the sacraments and presenting our monetary offerings.

What was wrong with Israel's worship? It would appear they had a pagan mindset, believing that they were doing God a favour and thought that he actually needed such physical offerings (verses 9–13). Yes, we are to bring what God desires but we are to do so for the right reasons, without ostentation and with sincerity of heart and complete dependence on him (verse 14–15).

God points out in passionate and ironic style that if he were in need of extra blood sacrifices he would not take them from their farmyards, for he owns all the animals of the 'forest' and 'the cattle on a thousand hills' (verse 10). The whole world and all that is in it belongs to the Lord (verse 12; see Psalm 24:1; Deuteronomy 10:14) so if he ever did feel in need of food he would not tell them. Metaphorical language is sometimes used to describe the sacrifices that Israel was to offer God, which if taken literally would indicate that God actually benefited from the food they offered, yet verse 13 makes it clear that he does not gain nourishment from their sacrifices.

This psalm does not give us exhaustive teaching on the purpose of sacrifice.[112] The translation 'Offer to God thanksgiving' (verse 14) might imply that it is a prayer of thanksgiving that is being encouraged rather than an actual blood sacrifice but that is not the case. The people are not being called to stop offering animals but when they do 'sacrifice' ('Offer', literally 'slaughter'), and it is the peace offerings that are particularly in view here, they are to remember that such sacrifices are to be expressions of gratitude to God for favours received or in anticipation of a blessing from God. The people were under no obligation to make, or vow to make, peace offerings but when they did offer them they were to do so with the right attitude. The types of peace or fellowship sacrifices in mind are the 'thanksgiving' and 'vow' offerings (Leviticus 7:11–12,16), where part of the offering was given back to the worshipper to share with family and friends. With such sacrifices 'the Most High' (verse 14, see Psalms 46:4; 47:2) is pleased and in such a relationship where the people are not trying to use sacrifice as a means of bribing God they can confidently look to him in times of distress, and experience the deliverance they seek. Thus Israel will 'glorify', or bring honour to their God (verse 15).

Communal worship is never meant to be a mindless exercise or a way of manipulating God or gaining approval points. Such worship is repugnant to him (see Isaiah 1:12–13; Amos 5:21–24). God does not need us or our money. He is completely independent and self-sufficient. Our worship should not be to gratify self but to honour God (see Hebrews 13:15).

Covenant breakers censured (verses 16–21)

There now comes direct criticism of those who, under a cloak of religious observance are in rebellion against the Lord. The 'wicked' (verse 16; see Psalm 1:4–6) pay lip service to the covenant. Here is the type of person who dutifully offers sacrifice and recites all Ten Commandments (verse 16) but then leaves church and blatantly flouts them (see verses 17–20). Paul may well have had this psalm in mind when he spoke of those in Israel who teach others and will not be taught themselves, who preach the commandments and boast in the law and yet break the law (Romans 2:17–24). The phrase 'my covenant' (verse 16) and 'my words' (verse 17) may well refer to the Ten Commandments (literally the 'Ten Words'), which are also known as 'the words of the covenant' (Exodus 34:28) or simply God's 'covenant' (Deuteronomy 4:13). These hypocrites within God's covenant community 'hate' the 'instruction' (verse 17) given in God's law and treat the commandments with contempt. They are like the 'fools' depicted in Proverbs who despise wisdom and instruction (Proverbs 1:7).

Three of the Ten Commandments are brought to our attention. The way verse 18 is expressed they were not actual thieves and adulterers themselves but took pleasure in associating with them which is what 'consented' means here (verse 18) and enjoyed their company. Being 'a partaker with' (verse 18) is more literally 'throw in your lot with'. These hypocrites get a thrill out of hearing of their exploits in a similar way to those who have their lustful appetites satisfied through feasting their eyes on pornographic material or reading graphic reports of criminal trials. They at the least violate the spirit of the eighth and seventh commandments (Exodus 20:14-15).

They have also broken the ninth commandment that prohibits false witness (Exodus 20:16) in that they have misused their tongues to do evil, to frame deceit and to make false allegations against members of their own family (verses 19-20; see Jeremiah 9:4-5; Micah 7:5-6). We are warned on numerous occasions in the Bible against an uncontrolled tongue and the harm it causes (Proverbs 16:27-28; 18:7; James 3:1-12).

God's silence up to this moment (verse 21; see verse 3) has been misinterpreted. Because he is very patient and has not acted to bring immediate punishment on wrongdoers they have assumed that he condones wrong behaviour. But God is not like us humans and he has now spoken to 'reprove' (verse 21) or 'convict' them by setting out before their very eyes the legal case against them, much as Job sought to lay his case before God (Job 23:4).

Curse and blessing (verses 22-23)

The two sections of the psalm are summarised in these closing verses and they are suggestive of the covenant curses and blessings with which God's covenant with Israel was concluded (see Leviticus 26:3-39; Deuteronomy 28). Psalm 2 likewise ends with warning and blessing.

First comes a word to the people he has addressed in verses 16-21. These people within the covenant community who 'forget God' (verse 22), they are given a wakeup call to think, to 'consider' before it is too late (see Deuteronomy 8:19; Hosea 8:14). God was on their lips when they assembled for worship but in their daily living he was far from their thinking. Hypocrisy is a sin into which all believers may fall. Jesus warns of it many times (see Matthew 12:1-7; 23:1-36).

God graciously warns through gospel preachers before he acts to punish those who treat God with contempt. He is patient and slow to anger but when God's wrath finally falls there is no escape. Divine punishment is likened to a ravenous lion (see Hosea 5:14). God is the only real deliverer and if there is no repentance and we continue to forget God in our daily lives then there is no escaping the punishment that we justly deserve (Hosea 13:6–8).

Then, secondly, comes a word of blessing to the person who 'orders *his* conduct *aright*' (verse 23). These are the ones loyal in practice to the spirit as well as the letter of God's law. This final verse recalls the words that ended God's first charge (verses 14–15). The phrase 'Whoever offers praise glorifies me' would be better translated 'Whoever sacrifices thanksgiving offerings glorifies me' (see verse 14). Those thanksgiving sacrifices associated with the peace offerings that are genuine expressions of thankfulness do bring honour to God. While for the Old Testament people of God worship involved animal sacrifice, for those under the new covenant who are called to worship in spirit and truth (John 4:20–24), God is honoured as we continually bring to him sacrifices of praise 'by him', that is, by Jesus Christ (Hebrews 13:15; Hosea 14:2). These are the ones who will constantly know God as their deliverer ('the salvation of God' verse 23; see verse 15).

This powerful sermon brings conviction, warning and a message of hope. It is the kind of message that needs to be heard when we gather each week for communal worship.

Psalm 51

The Penitent's Prayer

Here is the cry of a repentant sinner seeking God's mercy for forgiveness and restoration.

The psalm begins a series attributed to David that extends to the end of Book 2 (see Psalm 72:20), the exceptions being Psalms 66, 67, 71 and 72. It stands at this point as a contrast to the false views of sacrifice that are attacked in the previous psalm (50:7-15). The heading reveals that it is to be viewed against the background of David's great sin in committing adultery with Bathsheba, seeking to cover it up when she became pregnant and adding to it by organising the death of her husband so that she might become one of the king's wives (2 Samuel 11). David felt no guilt for the dastardly crime until Nathan the prophet was sent by God to awaken his conscience some months later.

His ugly sin involved succumbing to sinful passions and premeditated actions. This is the one of whom God could say that he was 'a man after his own heart' (1 Samuel 13:14). Such sin in a believer though grievous and necessitating severe discipline must be distinguished from sinning with 'a high hand'. David was in a very backslidden state, giving God's enemies cause to blaspheme (2 Samuel 12:14), but he was no apostate (which is what highhandedness means in the Law) and that is clearly seen in his reaction to the prophet's accusing finger, 'You are the man!' (2 Samuel 12:13). The psalm is an expansion of his brief confession to Nathan, 'I have sinned against the LORD' (2 Samuel 12:13).

While the psalm arises out of the king's personal sin and provides every penitent with a pattern prayer, David is not simply a private individual. His sin had its repercussions for the nation as the final verses suggest. The king represented the nation so that the psalm was included in the collection ('To the Chief Musician. A Psalm of David ...') as a corporate expression of the people's plea for divine mercy. In later Jewish worship it was used on the Day of Atonement and from early Christian times it became the fourth of the seven so-called 'penitential psalms' (see Psalm 6).

Plea for forgiveness (verses 1-2)

The psalm opens with a cry for divine 'mercy' or better 'grace' (verse 1). It is the same verb that is used for God's statement to Moses, 'I will be gracious to whom I will be gracious' (Exodus 33:19). Echoing the revelation of God's character to Moses in Exodus 34:5-7 David's appeal is based on God's 'steadfast love' ('loving-kindness') and 'compassion' ('tender mercies'). The word for 'compassion' or 'tender mercies' expresses intense emotion, like a mother's feelings for her child, and is similar to the Gospels' expression when they speak of Jesus being 'moved with compassion'.

In the light of these three words for God's goodness (his grace, unfailing love and compassion), David uses three terms to describe his offence, namely, 'transgressions' (verse 1), 'iniquity' and 'sin' (verse 2). They have appeared in previous psalms (see Psalms 25:7,11) and all three are present in Psalm 32:5. The term 'transgression' suggests wilful defiance; it is rebellion against God's revealed law. While every 'transgression' is sin, not every sin is transgression (Romans 4:15). 'Iniquity' is action that is crooked or wayward and the more general word 'sin' conveys the idea of failure. The three terms together view sin comprehensively.

Thank God that 'where sin abounded, grace abounded much more' (Romans 5:20)! David pleads the 'multitude', the 'abundance' of God's 'motherly compassion' (verse 1) as he calls for God to 'blot out' ('wipe away'), 'wash' and 'cleanse' him. All three verbs emphasise the need for sin's guilt to be removed so that a person can be fit to appear before God. Although the word for 'blot out' is used to denote the removal of a record from a book (see Exodus 32:32; Psalm 69:28) the context suggests the removal of dirt as in Proverbs 30:20 'she eats and wipes her mouth' or as a dish is wiped clean (2 Kings 21:13). It is also used of the Lord wiping away tears (Isaiah 25:8). The second verb 'wash' is one that is employed for pummelling clothes in water (Exodus 19:10; 2 Samuel 19:24) especially when they have become ritually unclean (see Leviticus 11:24-25; 13:6; etc.). With the addition of 'thoroughly' it suggests a washing that is as painstaking as removing ingrained stains from dirty garments. Jeremiah applies the term to indicate how impossible it is for humans to be rid of the mark that sin makes (see Jeremiah 2:22). The verb to 'cleanse' or 'purify' is another common verb associated with the Old Testament purification rituals where some kind of pollution has occurred.

Forgiveness with God must include dealing with the effects of sin. God is of purer eyes than to look on wickedness (Habakkuk 1:13). There can be no fellowship with God while we remain polluted by sin and guilty before our Maker and the God whom we have offended is the only one who can deal with sin's stain and guilt.

Confession (verses 3-6)

David is a repentant man who owns up to his rebellious activity—'For I acknowledge my transgressions ...' (verse 3; see Psalm 32:5). He is convinced of his sin and guilt. There is no merit in acknowledging sin, as Martin Luther was quick to point out. The apostle John states, 'If we confess our sins, he is faithful and just to forgive us our sins and to cleanse us from all unrighteousness' (1 John 1:9). It is wonderful release to have the burden of sin's guilt removed by the God we have offended. But as Matthew Henry comments there is a sense in which it is good for us to have our sins ever before us so that, for instance, the remembrance of past sins might keep us humble and arm us against temptation.

David's despicable actions have brought distress to others and he is not denying how much he has wronged them, but as he indicated to the prophet Nathan, the whole evil episode was an offence against God (2 Samuel 12:13) and he deserved to be punished by God (verses 3-4). Jesus makes the same point in his parable of the lost son, where the repentant boy acknowledges that he has 'sinned against heaven' as well as before his father (Luke 15:18,21). When Potiphar's wife tempted

Joseph to have sex with her he replied, 'How then can I do this great wickedness and sin against God?' (Genesis 39:9).

David recognised that the punishment of his sin was fair and perfectly appropriate. In the purposes of God his sin produces a good purpose—'that (in the sense of 'in order that') you may be found just … (verse 4). God is 'just' and 'blameless' when he sentences and passes judgment ('speak … judge'). Paul uses the Greek translation of verse 4 to make the same point that no one can find fault with God, for he is as faithful in condemning the sinner as in fulfilling his promises (Romans 3:4). In this way confession of sin becomes part of worship, something that is very often missing in many church services. Joshua urged Achan to 'give glory to the LORD God of Israel and make confession to him' and in response Achan began by stating, 'I have sinned against the LORD God of Israel' (Joshua 7:19–20).

David follows this up in verse 5 by indicating that his crime 'was no freak event: it was in character', as Derek Kidner remarks. He is not excusing his sin, blaming it on his parents or on faulty genes— the fivefold use of 'my' in verses 1–3 is proof of that. Neither is he suggesting that his mother was an immoral woman or that conception and birth are somehow sinful as many in the church have misguidedly thought. David is acknowledging that he has a sinful nature. He is stating what the church-going Martyn Lloyd-Jones came to realise when he testified, 'My trouble was not only that I did things that were wrong, but that I myself was wrong at the very centre of my being.'[113] Human depravity is emphasised not only in Genesis 8:21 but Psalm 143:2, Ecclesiastes 7:20 and Jeremiah 17:9.

David has become very open about his outrageous actions and sinful nature and this is something in which God delights. He 'desires' (verse 6) transparency and inward truthfulness, not the pretence and hypocrisy that we find in Psalm 50. Divine illumination ('wisdom') is what accounts for this realistic appraisal of the inner self. If we lack such wisdom ask God to give it (James 1:5).

Plea for cleansing and restitution (verses 7–12)

Cleansing
David echoes his opening plea (see verses 1b-2) by using the terms for cleansing in reverse order—'clean/cleanse', 'wash' and 'blot out/ wipe away' (verses 7–9). But there is a subtle variation here in the

first petition. A more literal rendering reveals that instead of 'from my sin cleanse me' (verse 2b) he pleads 'un-sin me ('purge me') ... and I shall be clean' (verse 7). The verb 'purge' is from the same word family as the term for 'sin' (see verses 2–5). Sin is likened to an infectious disease or a contaminating substance that needs to be disinfected or decontaminated. The verb is found in purification rituals involving 'hyssop' for cleansing 'leprous' houses (Leviticus 14:49,52) and everything and everyone who have become unclean through contact with a corpse (Numbers 19:18–19). Hyssop is a useful means for sprinkling or daubing (Exodus 12:22). The 'leprous' houses were to be sprinkled with blood and water whereas water alone was used to sprinkle uncleanness associated with death.

There is a washing associated with the new birth. Jesus speaks of being born of water and the Spirit. It is interpreted by Paul as the washing of regeneration and renewal by the Holy Spirit (Titus 3:5). The imagery of sprinkled water for inner transformation and renewal is found in Ezekiel where we read 'I will sprinkle clean water on you, and you shall be clean: I will cleanse you from all your filthiness and from all your idols ...' (Ezekiel 36:25–27).

The remaining two petitions pick up the washing metaphors from the opening verses—laundering stained clothes (verses 2,7) and wiping away dirt ('blot out' verses 1b,9). To be washed 'whiter than snow' (verse 7) is a powerful way of conveying glistening purity. God, through Isaiah the prophet, reasons with the people saying, 'Though your sins are like scarlet, they shall be as white as snow' (Isaiah 1:18). Red stains on a shirt or blouse are hard to remove but David is confident that God can shift the stain of sin better than what any washing powder can do for dirty nappies (diapers). Only the red blood of Christ can deal with the red stain of sin. In other words, these stark images point to the atoning death of Christ as the only way sin's polluting and damaging effects can be overcome.

Justification

In every other instance, for God to 'hide' his face (verse 9) is something the psalmist does not welcome for it speaks of divine displeasure (see Psalms 13:1; 27:9). In this case it is part of his plea for forgiveness. David pleads that instead of turning his face away from him in anger God would refuse to see his sins, something God alone can do and does when he justifies the ungodly (Acts 13:39; Romans 3:21–26), and wipes them 'all' away.

The broken bones are figurative of the deep distress he feels arising from God's convicting word and unrelieved guilt (see Psalms 6:2; 38:3,8). The appeal is for God to speak a word that will bring 'joy and gladness' (verse 8) to this broken person. It is the happiness of knowing that his sins have been forgiven (see Psalm 32:1–2) and the assurance of God's presence and salvation (see verses 11–12).

Sanctification

David has been polluted by his sins but these sins are symptomatic of a dirty heart. Only those with a 'pure heart' can come before God and see him (Psalm 24:4; Matthew 5:8). It is only inward purity that makes fellowship with God possible not the external purity rituals of the Old Testament or New Testament sacraments like baptism. This is a gift from God and not the result of human activity (see Acts 15:9). David speaks as one who already knows God's transforming work in his life but his grave sin has brought him to see how deceitful and wicked the human heart is. He therefore prays that the God who has begun a good work within him will do a new miraculous work at the centre of his being (the verb 'create' is reserved exclusively in the Old Testament for God's activity) and 'renew a steadfast spirit within' (verse 10) in the sense of restoring that inner commitment to God and determination to do his revealed will and not to be easily led astray by temptation (see Psalms 57:7; 78:37).

David is aware that he deserves to be banished from God's presence and for God's personal presence, his 'Holy Spirit' (verse 11), to be removed from him (see Isaiah 63:10–11; Ephesians 4:30) as happened to Saul. The former king's confession of sin actually showed no sign of godly contrition (1 Samuel 16:14; 15:30). But David knows that God graciously listens to those who are humble and contrite and who look to God for forgiveness and salvation (Psalm 32:5; Isaiah 57:15–16). His prayer again calls to mind the prophet's words concerning Israel's renewal: 'I will give you a new heart and put a new spirit within you ... I will put my Spirit within you ...' (Ezekiel 36:26–27).

In the final petition 'uphold me *with your* generous Spirit' (verse 12), it is difficult to be certain whether the reference is to God's Spirit or David's. The adjective 'generous', 'willing' is applied to those who brought offerings for the construction of the Tabernacle with 'a willing heart' (Exodus 35:5, 22; see 2 Chronicles 29:31) and the word is used frequently to describe someone of princely or noble rank (see Psalms 47:9; 83:11; etc.). The verb and noun from the same word family also mean to act freely and to give freewill offerings. In every case bar one it is the people who are made willing or give generously so it may well be that David is praying to be upheld with a spirit that is ready and willing to do God's will. The only place where the reference is to God's generosity is in connection with Israel's restoration, 'I will heal their backsliding, I will love them freely' (Hosea 14:4) and it is just possible that the 'your' of 'your salvation' carries over to the next line, as the older versions indicate by the use of '*your*' in italics, so that David is asking that God's gracious willing Spirit would uphold him so that he does not fall and backslide again.

Sin breaks fellowship with God and David is deprived of the experience of God's saving 'joy' (verse 12; see verse 8). Only by abiding in God's love and keeping his commandments can we know that heavenly joy in all its fulness (John 15:9–11).

Testimony to God's grace (verses 13–15)

David is expressing the attitude of a truly repentant person who has known God's amazing grace. Having received so much from God he wants to teach other 'transgressors' (or 'rebels') and 'sinners' (verse 13; see Psalms 22:22; 40:9-10). There is a concern, indeed, a strong determination ('I will') to tell others of God's 'ways', which include his demands as well as his grace (see Psalms 103:7; 145:17). The intended result will be that they, like him, will also turn away from their sins and turn to God (see Psalm 22:27). This is what 'return' or 'converted' (verse 13) means in this context (see Luke 22:32).

The cry of David, 'Deliver me from blood-guiltiness, O God' (verse 14), is not easy to interpret. The word 'blood-guiltiness' (literally it is the plural of blood, 'bloods') is a Hebrew idiom for 'bloodshed' especially for a violent death (see Psalm 5:6) or it can mean the guilt incurred from killing someone or the death penalty for a capital crime. In this context of David's testimony, as John Stott has indicated, it means that, 'although he has indeed been guilty of the blood of Uriah, he is determined that God shall not require at his hand the blood of sinners whom he has failed to warn and teach (cf. Ezekiel 3:16ff. and 33:1ff.)'.[114] This is why David wants to 'sing aloud' God's 'righteousness', in which he is both just and the justifier of guilty sinners who put their faith in God's way of salvation (Romans 3:26) and prays that God would help him to declare his 'praise' (verses 14b-15). We are urged by Peter to declare the praises or goodness of the God who has saved us (1 Peter 2:9).

Sacrifices pleasing to God (verses 16–19)

The 'For' (verse 16) reminds us that this is the essence of what he wished to teach others. The worship of God must begin with 'truth in the inward parts' (verse 6), which is not unlike what Jesus taught (John 4:23-24). There is no suggestion that God is rejecting the forms of worship he himself had appointed through Moses, especially the two regular ways of expressing fellowship and total commitment— 'sacrifice' as in the peace offerings and 'burnt offering' (verse 16; see Psalm 40:6; 50:8). Such blood sacrifices were in God's plan as pointers to our Lord's sacrificial death on the cross. David is implying what the prophets emphasised (see 1 Samuel 15:22-23; Amos 5:21-24; Micah 6:6-8) that expressions of outward worship cannot make up for a heart that is hard and unrepentant and a life lived contrary to God's covenant. Jesus had hard words to say to religious hypocrites using the words of Isaiah, 'These people ... honour me with their lips, but their heart is far from me. And in vain they worship me ...' (Matthew 15:8-9).

Verse 17 is a passage Luther considered to be 'worthy of being written in golden letters'. The 'spirit' and 'heart' of verse 10 are used now to depict a truly penitent person—'a broken' spirit and a heart that is also 'contrite' (literally 'crushed' as in the 'broken' or 'crushed' bones of verse 8 that God has brought about). Calvin comments that the one who has a broken and contrite heart 'has been emptied of all vain-glorious confidence and brought to acknowledge that he is nothing' and in utter helplessness is thrown onto the divine mercy for salvation.

From his own personal situation, David now considers the nation of which he is the leader and representative. His action has repercussions for his people. They share in his disgrace and fall under God's displeasure. David prays that the worshipping community ('Zion'; see Psalms 2:6; 48:1; 50:2) will find acceptance with God ('your good pleasure', verse 18) and experience blessing. To 'do good' in this context is explained in the second line of verse 18. David had built a wall around Jerusalem that we find Solomon needed to repair (1 Kings 9:15; 11:27) but here he prays that God would 'build the walls of Jerusalem', which is a poetic way of asking for the security and prosperity of the city and its people (see Psalms 147:2–3). Christians belong to Mount Zion and have by faith come to the city of the living God and we pray for its prosperity (Hebrews 12:22; Psalm 122:6–8). Isaiah speaks of a strong city with its walls of salvation (Isaiah 26:1).

Self-despairing trust in God for salvation and protection results in communal worship that is pleasing to God—'Then ... you shall be pleased with ...' (verse 19). Such worship meant offering 'sacrifices of righteousness', which, for those under the old Sinai covenant, involved offering in the right spirit the various food and animal sacrifices ordained by God in contrast to those performed in pagan worship (see Deuteronomy 33:19; Psalms 4:5; 50:7–15). They included the 'burnt offering', the most common offering, with the word 'whole' or 'entire' added to indicate that the sacrifice is not only offered up as acceptable to God ('a pleasing aroma') but that the worshipper is preserved alive through this substitute to be wholly the Lord's. The offering of 'bulls' suggests the costliest of sacrifices (see Leviticus 1:3,10,14).

Under the new covenant, Christ has given his whole self for us, as a sweet-smelling sacrifice to God (Ephesians 5:2). David's greater Son brought no displeasure to God but he identified himself with our disgrace and came under God's judgment for the salvation of his people. Praise, thanks and the giving of the whole of ourselves freely and sacrificially from grateful hearts are among the spiritual sacrifices acceptable to God that Christians are urged to offer communally as well as individually (see Psalm 141:2; Hebrews 10:24–25; 13:15–17; Romans 12:1).

Psalm 52

The Wicked and Righteous Contrasted

This psalm begins a series from the life of David when he was being pursued by Saul (see Psalms 54, 56, 57, 59). There are also two earlier ones in Book One: Psalms 7 and 34. It is the first of a small collection of David's 'Contemplation' or instruction psalms (Psalms 52–55; see Psalm 32) and is the second such collection in this part of the Psalter (see Psalms 42–45). Here is teaching that arises out of David's experiences at the hands of his and God's enemies. King Saul along with associates like Doeg are manifestations of the snake's offspring, the 'brood of vipers' (Genesis 3:15; Matthew 3:7; Revelation 12:9), influenced by Satan, the chief enemy of God and his people. Such psalms from David's life are therefore appropriate to be given 'To the Chief Musician' for use by the people of God. David is an example or type of the righteous and Saul and Doeg of the ungodly wicked (see Psalm 1).

The situation

The reference in the heading refers to the narrative in 1 Samuel 21:1–9; 22:6–23. Doeg the Edomite was no simple shepherd but one of Saul's chief men (literally 'the mighty one of the shepherds', 1 Samuel 21:7)

who had been present at Nob when David and his men, on the run
from Saul, sought help from the priests who lived there. When Doeg
disclosed this information to Saul, the king ordered the execution of
the entire priestly settlement including the women and children. The
Israelite soldiers refused such a command but Doeg ruthlessly carried
out the massacre, with the intention, no doubt, of gaining more favour
and influence at court as the psalm suggests.

The accusation (verses 1–4)

The psalm begins abruptly by addressing this arrogant warrior, 'Why
do you boast in evil, O mighty man?' (verse 1). As in Psalm 2 the
question is a statement of confidence: 'what reason have you got
to crow about evil?' The word 'mighty', in some contexts translated
'hero', has been used of the Lord's anointed king in Psalms 24:8; 45:3
(and called 'Mighty God' in Isaiah 9:6) but here it is used for one who
stands in opposition to the Lord's anointed one. He is an antichrist.
Again, with Psalm 2 in mind, such glorying in evil is madness, for what
this warrior has forgotten is God's own commitment to his people—
'The goodness of God *endures* continually' (verse 1) or better 'God's
steadfast love continues daily'. Some modern translations like the
New International miss the whole point of the psalm by accepting the
ancient Greek version, the Septuagint, and adding to the text.

The 'evil' in which the tyrant brags is exposed in the following
verses. He not only uses his tongue to boast of his exploits but to plot
'destruction' (verse 2; see 5:9; 38:12). His 'tongue' is as dangerous as
a recently sharpened 'razor' in the wrong hands, for he is using it to
practise 'deceit' (verse 2). The phrase 'working deceitfully' or 'worker of
deceit' is only found elsewhere in Psalm 101:7 where we are told such
people cannot dwell in God's house (see Psalm 32:2).

The tongue is, as Motyer observes, 'always a primary indicator of
character' and a boasting tongue reveals the 'heart's desire' (Psalm
10:3). As far as moral principles ('good'; see Psalm 53:1) and standards
of truthfulness ('speaking righteousness') are concerned this self-made
man desires all that is bad and false (verse 3). The 'Selah' at this point
may indicate the feeling of revulsion at the description that runs so
contrary to what God's covenant people should be like.

This 'deceitful tongue' (see Psalm 120:2), expressive of the whole
person, desires 'all devouring words' (verse 4). Words are used
to 'swallow' people (see 21:9; 35:25). It is his principal weapon of

destruction. With it he not only boasts but uses it to plot, to lie and to destroy. 'Death and life are in the power of the tongue' (Proverbs 18:21). Christians are warned of its hellish power: It may be 'a little member' but the tongue 'boasts great things'. It is 'a world of iniquity'. 'The tongue is so set among our members that it defiles the whole body, and sets on fire the course of nature; and it is set on fire by hell ... It is an unruly evil, full of deadly poison. With it we bless our God and Father, and with it we curse men, who have been made in the likeness of God ... My brethren, these things ought not to be so' (James 3:5–10).

The sentence (verse 5)
There is a day of reckoning. God will take sudden, decisive action against this man who is a celebrity in his own eyes, who boasts of his wickedness. We are given three word pictures of the tyrant's end. First, like the 'tearing down' of an altar, a building or city wall (see Judges 6:30–32; 8:9; 9:45), God will 'demolish' ('destroy') the warrior 'for ever'. Second, like the snatching of hot coals from a fire (see Isaiah 30:14) God will just as suddenly 'snatch' him away ('take ... away') and 'pull' ('pluck'; see Deuteronomy 28:63) him from his tent ('dwelling place') where he thought he was safe. Third, like pulling up a plant from the soil (see Job 31:8) God will 'uproot' him 'from the land of the living' (see Psalm 27:13; Isaiah 53:8). Such big people have their day and then death takes them. Another 'Selah' is called for, giving us an opportunity to reflect.

The lesson (verses 6–7)
The righteous ones (see Psalm 1:5) see God's action and are filled not with terror but reverential awe ('see and fear', verse 6; see Psalm 40:3. The two verbs sound alike in the original). As in Isaiah 66:24 the righteous 'see' the unending damnation of the wicked of which Jesus spoke (Mark 9:43–48). The sight that issues in 'fear' makes their 'laugh' at the fate of the wicked not malicious but similar to God's laugh in Psalms 2:4 and 37:13. It is not a selfish enjoyment at seeing the enemy destroyed, something condemned and itself deserving punishment (Job 31:29; Proverbs 24:17–18), but it expresses the stupidity of the arrogant warrior. God will catch up with all who practise lawlessness. The laugh is verbalised in the cutting words of verse 7: 'Here is the man ...' The so-called 'mighty' one of verse one is the strong 'man' (the term belongs to the same word-family as 'mighty') who is no match for God. Other psalms indicate that God is the only sure refuge and

strength and that ultimately our trust should be in him. How foolish of this proud person who 'did not make God his strength' or better 'his stronghold', 'his refuge' (see Psalms 27:1; 37:39; 43:2) but 'trusted in the abundance of his riches'. Like Doeg, there have been those who have come to prominence through wealth and then in their thirst for more riches and influence have used deceit and other evil ways to further their ends. Paul instructs Timothy: 'Command those who are rich in this present age not to be haughty, nor to trust in uncertain riches but in the living God' (1 Timothy 6:17).

The last word 'wickedness' (verse 7) is actually the singular of that translated 'destruction' in verse 2. It can either mean that he 'grew strong' ('strengthened himself') in his 'destruction' of others or that he 'took refuge' in his own 'lust' ('wickedness'). Either way the man had gained financially from his evil schemes and deceitful activity. But where did it get him in the end? The same thought is presented to us in Psalm 73 and it also underlines the message of Psalm 49. Obtaining power and wealth through underhand means and making them your trust is utter folly.

The testimony (verses 8–9)

David speaks out of his own situation but also for all the righteous. As in the 'Yet I' of Psalm 2:6 the 'But I' (verse 8) marks a contrast with what has been said in verses 5 to 7. The cocksure mighty one who praises his own exploits and trusts in his wealth is to be like an uprooted tree (verse 5) whereas David is like a long-lasting fruitful tree (see Psalm 1:3), who trusts God and gives thanks to him. The 'olive tree' is one of the most long-lasting trees and highly prized in Mediterranean lands (see Jeremiah 11:16). The 'house of God' (verse 8) could mean the land or people of Israel as God's possession which does provide a good parallel with 'land of the living' (verse 5; see Hosea 8:1; 9:15; Jeremiah 12:7; Zechariah 9:8). On the other hand, it is probably better to see it as referring to the tabernacle at Nob where olive trees may well have been growing in the grounds. But the point of the imagery is to convey the enduring nature of David's position. While Doeg and his ilk are rooted out from their insecure dwellings ('tent', verse 5), those like David flourish in God's house. Both tree and sanctuary reappear later where we read of the righteous flourishing like trees 'who are planted in the house of the Lord ... They shall still bear fruit in old age; they shall be fresh and flourishing' (Psalm 92:12-14). The wicked can flourish like an evergreen tree but they do not last (Psalm 37:35–36) for they are not established in God's house and, unlike David, their 'trust' is not in 'the mercy of God' (verse 8) but in uncertain riches. God's 'steadfast love' ('mercy') takes us back to the beginning of the psalm where the same Hebrew word is used. We can trust 'for ever and ever' (verse 8; see Psalm 9:5) this dependable divine love that 'continues daily' (verse 1).

In the closing verse, despite experiencing the continuing effects of the tyrant's actions, he can with confidence give God 'praise' (verse 9) in the sense of giving thanks (see Psalms 6:5; 18:49). Lasting trust in God's unfailing love leads to eternal gratitude ('for ever') for God's action ('you have done') against the enemy. The action has not yet taken place but David speaks as if it has happened. The thanks are therefore part of the trust, as Kidner observes. He will 'wait on' or better, as William Tyndale has it, 'hope in' God who will act according to his nature. God's 'name' is his revealed character. He is 'good' (see Mark 10:18). This is in marked contrast to the mighty one who loves 'evil more than good' (verse 3). David is prepared to confess his confidence and hope in God not only privately but before God's 'saints'—those committed in love to God (from the same word family as 'steadfast love'; see Psalm 4:3; 30:4; 50:5). In other words he wishes to testify in the place where the worshipping company of God's people meet (see Psalm 1:5).

Here is another forceful reminder of the truth conveyed in the first two psalms. Those who persist in their wicked ways will perish whereas the righteous will flourish (Psalm 1). It also shows the madness of all brutal oppressors like Doeg and Saul who oppose God and his Messiah (Psalm 2). David is not only an example of the righteous but symbolises God's true anointed one. The particular message of this psalm, as the beginning and end emphasise, is that God's faithful love is both 'constant' and 'sufficient even against triumphant ruthlessness' (Motyer).

Psalm 53

The Foolish Condemned,
God's People Restored

A form of Psalm 18 was used by the prophetic author of 2 Samuel 22, similarly, a different version of Psalm 14 has been used here in this second book of the Psalter. Those responsible for the final editing clearly wanted the psalm to be treated independently of the earlier one and to view it in the context of the immediately surrounding psalms.

Psalm 14 was the culmination of a series of psalms where enemies had been mistreating God's people and the psalm indicated that the antagonism stemmed from a society that treated God as an irrelevancy. The present psalm is one of a number that is linked to events in David's early life as depicted in 1 Samuel 21–26.

The Heading
In addition to the regular heading 'To the Chief Musician' and 'of David' that is found in Psalm 14, we find the unusual 'upon Mahalath' used only here and in Psalm 88. 'Mahalath' is commonly associated with the word for sickness or disease (see Exodus 15:26; Proverbs 18:14) and some think of it as referring to the set tune hence the translation 'Set to' or more literally 'According to'. Another suggestion links it with

a musical instrument like a pipe. It is the second in a small series of 'Contemplation' or instruction psalms that appear at this point (see Psalm 52).

The Fool (verses 1–4)

As the previous psalm emerged out of David's reaction to Doeg and Saul (1 Samuel 22) and the following psalm relates to David's experiences in the Wilderness of Ziph (1 Samuel 23:14–29; 26:1–25) so this psalm links up well with the account in 1 Samuel 25:2–42.

The word translated 'fool' (*nabal;* verse 1) is one of the strongest terms employed in the Old Testament to signify godlessness. It was the name of Abigail's husband, Nabal, the man who treated David and his men in a despicable and ungrateful manner. He is described as a 'harsh' and badly behaved person. Not only is he called a 'scoundrel' (literally 'son of Belial') by his servants but also by his own wife who adds, 'For as his name is, so is he: Nabal is his name, and folly is with him (1 Samuel 25:3,17,25). Nabal is all that the Bible means by 'fool'. The fool speaks folly and practises folly by acting counter to what God expects from his covenant people. Isaiah may well have had Nabal in mind when he wrote of the fool who keeps 'the hungry unsatisfied' and causes 'the drink of the thirsty to fail' (Isaiah 32:6–7). Ammon, one of David's sons, also belonged to this ignoble number, as his sister Tamar suggested (2 Samuel 13:13). The 'fool' curses God (Job 2:9–10) and insults his servants (Psalm 39:8). He is typical of the 'mighty one' of the previous psalm. Abigail, Nabal's wife, on the other hand, was a model of the wise godly person who fears God and turns from evil: a woman of good understanding, who gave sound advice and had a generous spirit (1 Samuel 25:3,28–35; see Proverbs 31:10–31).

The actions of the fool are the result of what he thinks and believes 'in his heart'. Just as Enoch 'was not' in the sense of having disappeared from the earth (Genesis 5:24) and David speaks of not being in the world any more (Psalm 39:13) so for the fool God 'is not' as far as his world is concerned. It is not philosophical atheism but the practical atheism that governs the lives of most 21st century Westerners. The situation is a bit like the Deists of the 18th century who considered that God, once he had created everything, left it to tick away on its own without divine intervention. The fool cannot see God intervening in human affairs to punish or to bless. Such people therefore act as if God does not exist.

Sin is the height of folly and David quickly moves to present the general state of humanity in sin. 'The one typical fool', as Spurgeon comments, 'is reproduced in the whole race.' Not only within the community of Israel but generally, as in the days before the Flood, people are 'corrupt' (see Genesis 6:5,11–12) and 'have done abominable iniquity' (verse 1). The much stronger term 'iniquity' or 'wickedness' has replaced the word 'deeds' found in Psalm 14:1. The fool says, 'There is no God'; God says, 'There is none who does good' (verses 1 and 4). The previous psalm indicated how the mighty one not only boasted of evil but loved evil more than good (Psalm 52:3).

Instead of God's covenant name the 'LORD' (Jehovah/Yahweh) as in Psalm 14:2,4,6, this psalm consistently continues with the name found in verse 1, *Elohim* ('God', verse 2). There may be significance in the fact that it results in this divine name occurring seven times in the psalm. Seven is symbolically used in the Bible to convey the idea of completeness. God observes not only the outward appearance but the thoughts and attitudes of the human family ('children of men', verse 2). He looks for any who 'understand' (the same word is found in the heading as 'Contemplation') and 'seek God' (verse 2). This answers some evangelicals who have argued for 'pagan saints', for people who were believers and saved without knowing it or without having received any special revelation from God.

Instead of 'all' or the 'whole' of the human race as in Psalm 14:2 we have here 'every one of them' (verse 3) which makes it clear that every single person belonging to the human race is in the same position by nature. Without God's gracious intervention no one would be saved. They have all backslidden or 'turned back' (verse 3), which replaces the 'turned aside' in Psalm 14:3.[115] While turning aside is bad enough, the situation is now presented as far worse for everyone has moved in a way directly opposed to God. They are morally 'corrupt' or 'rotten'. This verdict is a crushing blow to human pride.

To the phrase 'There is none who does good' (verse 3), repeated from verse 1, and to make the point even clearer, there is added 'no, not one' or more literally, 'there is not even one'. This is the sad state of unregenerate humanity, Israel and the pagan world alike. When the rich young ruler glibly addressed Jesus as 'Good Teacher' he was quickly reminded that no one, only God, is good (Mark 9:17–18).

The question 'Have the workers of iniquity no knowledge?' (verse 4) is like the question at the beginning of the previous psalm. How insane it is for these 'workers of iniquity' to refuse to acknowledge God or worship him![116] As the arrogant bragger 'devoured' people with his words (Psalm 52:4), so here these evil workers ('workers of iniquity', verse 4) 'eat up' God's people like eating 'bread', which is a graphic way of indicating the oppression suffered by the godly at the hands of these unscrupulous people.

The Fool judged (verse 5)

It is here that the difference between the two psalms is most marked. In Psalm 14 the emphasis falls on the Lord's protection of his people, whereas in this psalm the focus is on God's destruction of the fool. As in the previous psalm, it is the God who is ignored or treated as if he has no involvement in human affairs who takes sudden decisive action to punish (Psalm 52:5).

'Those who seemed incapable of fear have now begun to be afraid at last' (J. A. Alexander). One minute such brazen fools had no fears, the next moment they were overwhelmed with terror. Why? 'For God' had struck! Using poetic language reminiscent of the destruction of a besieging army (see 2 Kings 19:35), God is said to have 'scattered the bones' of such fools who encamp against God's people. They will be like the slain on a battlefield, brought to shame and abandoned by God. This is the terrible end of all who do not know God. To be rejected by God is what hell is all about. 'I never knew you; depart from me, you who practise lawlessness' (Matthew 7:23).

The Righteous hope (verse 6)

David and his men were in exile, with the wicked Saul and his supporters ruling in Israel. In addition, the Philistines were a dominant force in the area and eventually succeeded in totally defeating Israel and killing Saul and his sons. God's people as a whole, as Chronicles suggests, were in a situation similar to what happened much later when the Babylonians overran the country. They were in slavery to the Philistines until David was given the kingdom by God and delivered Israel from their enemies (see 1 Chronicles 10).

This is the possible background to David's fervent prayer wish for Israel's 'salvation'[117] It was answered when God used David not only to defeat the remaining supporters of Saul but, after taking 'the stronghold of Zion' from the Jebusites and making it his capital, he dealt decisively with the Philistines (1 Chronicles 11:1–9; 14:8–17). God may seem to be absent or uninvolved but the God of the Bible is the true and living God, who is there and who acts at the right moment in his purposes.

(See Psalm 14:7 for more comment on the text).

Psalm 54

A Prayer for Help

Commenting on the background to this psalm, where David is 'hemmed in on every side by apparently inevitable destruction', John Calvin admires the courage that David displayed 'in committing himself, by prayer, to the Almighty'. He concludes that the psalm teaches us 'that we should never despair of divine help even in the worst situation'.

The series of 'Contemplation' psalms 'of David' associated with the time when Saul was pursuing him continues (see Psalm 52). It is twice recorded how the Ziphites betrayed David's hideout (1 Samuel 23:19; 26:1). Ziph was some twenty miles south of Jerusalem in a most inhospitable region of the Judean mountains. It was a good area in which to escape detection but only if the locals were supportive which in this case they were not, even though they were people of his own tribe. They sent word to Saul, 'Is not David hiding himself with us?' It is Saul who is David's chief enemy but as the history of the period indicates, David did not take it upon himself to kill Saul but committed himself to God as this psalm illustrates. The prayer was given to the 'Chief Musician' to be sung to the accompaniment of 'stringed instruments' (see Psalms 4 and 6). It begins with an appeal to God and ends by giving thanks to him, while at the centre there is David's statement of trust.

Prayer for deliverance (verses 1–3)

The urgent appeal is for God to save 'by your name' (verse 1; see Psalms 20:1–5; 52:9) with 'by your strength' (or 'might') in the parallel line. God's mighty power is one element of his revealed nature, one that is especially important in David's case. The particular salvation David is looking for on this occasion is to be cleared as in a court of law with appropriate action taken against his enemy. The words 'vindicate me' (verse 1, literally 'judge me'; see Psalms 7:8; 26:1) show that he needs God to decide in his favour and to declare the enemy to be in the wrong. Justification involves God deciding in our favour on account of Christ's work, despite the enemy's attempts to condemn us (see Romans 8:31–34).

David calls on God to listen to his prayer ('Hear ... Give heed', verse 2), something that in earlier psalms tends to be the first words on his lips (see Psalms 4:1; 5:1). This is followed by the reasons for the desperate cry. His enemies are called 'Strangers' and 'oppressors' (verse 3), two terms found together to describe ruthless attackers from pagan nations (Ezekiel 28:7; 31:12). These 'aliens in spirit', these 'tyrants' are the types depicted in the previous two psalms who follow their own desires as if God's ways were of no account—'they have not set God before them' (verse 3; see Psalm 16:8). They may be fellow Israelites like Saul or even from the same tribe like the Ziphites but they act like foreigners who are strangers to that special relationship initiated by God (see Isaiah 1:4). The picture that James presents is of a similar kind where the righteous are condemned and murdered by powerful oppressors among them, but they have already been reminded that there is one lawgiver and judge 'who is able to save and to destroy' (James 4:12; 5:1–6). The 'Selah' (verse 3) marks the change from those who give no thought for God to the one who looks to God.

Confession of trust (verses 4–5)

At this point in the middle of the psalm we have this excited expression of confidence in God conveyed by the word 'Behold', which we might capture better by translating 'Here is God who gives help to me!' He is not an absent, inactive God as the fool thinks (see Psalm 53:1) but the sovereign 'Lord' who is the mainstay of his life. The original which is rendered literally as 'with those who uphold my life' (verse 4b) could either mean that God was active with David's men or more probably it is a Hebrew way of expressing emphasis, that God really is the upholder of David's person.

Out of that confidence comes the prayer that God would let the 'evil' that his 'enemies' (literally 'my watchers'; see Psalms 5:8; 27:11) intend for him backfire on them (literally 'return to'; see Psalm 7:16) and that in accordance with God's faithfulness to his covenant promises ('your truth') he would destroy them ('cut them off'; verse 5; Psalms 18:40; 101:5,8). Many consider this to be sub-Christian in the light of Jesus' words and actions concerning loving our enemies and praying for them. But Jesus also spoke of the punishment of evil-doers. We are not to take vengeance ourselves on our enemies but like David to leave the God of justice to punish the unrepentant (Romans 12:19; see Revelation 6:9–11).

Thanksgiving for deliverance (verses 6–7)

Confident of a favourable answer to his cry or in the light of the deliverance he has now received, David promises to offer sacrifice and give thanks to God. 'I will freely sacrifice' (verse 6) could be translated, 'With a freewill offering I will sacrifice to you'. David had made no bargain with God to offer this worship if God delivered him; it was a spontaneous act of gratitude which is precisely what this special type of peace offering was meant to be (see Leviticus 7:11–16). The old covenant blood or food sacrifices are no longer necessary in our worship of God now that Christ has fulfilled them, but every time we bring our praises and prayers in worship we still need to acknowledge that it is only through the atoning sacrifice of Christ we can approach God.

The reference to God's 'name' (verse 6) picks up on the opening cry (see verse 1) and, unusually in this part of the Psalter (Psalms 42–83), the covenant name is actually mentioned 'the LORD' (Yahweh/Jehovah). He is worthy of our worship for he is 'good' (see Psalm 52:9). It is therefore right and proper ('good') that we should praise him.

Like Paul who could say with confidence that the God who had delivered him 'will deliver me from every evil work ...' (2 Timothy 4:17–18), so David can praise the 'name' that 'has delivered me out of all trouble' (verse 7). David's 'eye has seen', not in a gloating way, the enemy defeated (see Psalm 52:6). Concerning the godly, Calvin writes, 'If their satisfaction proceed in any measure from the gratification of a depraved feeling, it must be condemned; but there is certainly a pure and unblameable delight which we may feel in looking upon such illustrations of the divine justice'.

Psalm 55

The Cure for Anxiety

There are no indications in the heading as to the circumstances that led David to compose this passionate plea to God but it has exactly the same introductory titles and directions as the previous psalm. It is the final 'Contemplation of David' in the short series from Psalm 52. There were numerous occurrences, as we have seen, when David found himself betrayed by those he thought he could trust (see Psalms 41:9; 54). The most obvious occasion was when his own son Absalom rebelled against him and his trusted adviser, Ahithophel, betrayed him (2 Samuel 15:1-12). Whatever the original situation, it was later given 'To the Chief Musician' to be sung by the covenant community accompanied 'With stringed instruments'.

The psalm bears witness to the extreme emotion felt by David as he wrote and points us to the deep distress experienced by David's greater Son. At the same time, it provides God's people with an example of how to carry 'everything to the Lord in prayer'.

The lament (verses 1-5)
As often in expressions of grief (see Psalms 5:1; 54:2) the psalmist begins by calling on God to hear his prayer. This is backed up here by urging God not to be like someone who hides from a needy person who wishes to ask a favour ('supplication', verse 1; see Psalms 10:1; Isaiah

58:7). Like Esau's descendants agitating to gain their independence (Genesis 27:40), so David is disturbed ('restless') and 'distraught' ('moan noisily') on account of his 'complaint' (verse 2).

The reasons for his distress arise from the pressure of the wicked enemy's jibes and like the falling of something dislodged so they make 'trouble' (often translated 'iniquity' it can, as here, have the meaning of 'calamity' or 'harm') fall on him and in anger they 'hate' or reveal their animosity toward him (verse 3). David continues to give an account of his inner feelings using graphic language. He speaks of writhing in pain like a woman giving birth and of 'deadly terrors' ('terrors of death'; verse 4) having 'fallen' on him such as were experienced by the people of Jericho (see Joshua 2:9). The effects of the enemy's activity are similar to those felt by the inhabitants of Canaan and its neighbours on hearing of Israel's victory over the Egyptians (Exodus 15:15-16). 'Fear and trembling' have come 'upon' him so that he is 'overwhelmed' with 'horror' (more literally, 'shuddering covers me', verse 5).

The longing (verses 6–8)
Under such pressure and distress, one solution would be to escape just as a dove finds safety in its nightly resting place high up on some rocky ledge in the wilderness (verse 6-7; see Jeremiah 48:9.28). Jeremiah had a similar urge to escape from the adulterers and traitors of Jerusalem (Jeremiah 9:2-3). The strength of feeling that gave rise to this wish leads to a pause ('Selah') before David's urge to flee continues this time under the imagery of running for shelter from a raging storm (verse 8). Taken out of context, Mendelssohn's popular 'O for the wings of a dove' from the second part of his 'Hear my prayer', makes the longing to escape and be at peace seem a right and pleasing thing to do. We all love the quiet life but this is not God's will for his people in this world. It is to fight not flight that we are called, for as Charles Spurgeon comments, 'we have no armour for our backs'.

Further lament (verses 9–15)
From thoughts of escapism David returns to pleading with God for the situation in which he finds himself. The weapon the enemy is using is the tongue to make false allegations and as a result there lurks within David's city 'violence and strife', 'iniquity and trouble', 'destruction', 'deceit and guile' (verses 9-11). He therefore prays that God would 'destroy' (verse 9; literally 'swallow up' as in Psalm 21:9) by dividing

the speech of the enemy as he did at Babel (Genesis 11:7–9). The walls of the city provide no protection from this foe, in fact the enemy lies within the city's open square (verse 11).

David then becomes more personal and actually addresses the chief culprit, 'But you ... a man my equal' (verse 13). We can understand the pain he felt at being betrayed by someone who was particularly close to him. Here was someone he trusted whom he had never suspected. The build-up of expressions to describe that relationship underlines the enormity of the treachery. It is sickening to find a personal friend in whom you confided and with whom you worshipped turning against you in this way. David's experience foreshadowed the behaviour of Judas Iscariot, the ultimate betrayer, one of Jesus' close disciples and all four Gospels make a point of emphasising the fact. On one occasion Jesus said to his disciples, 'Did I not choose you, the twelve, and one of you is a devil?' and the apostle John adds, 'He spoke of Judas Iscariot, the son of Simon, for it was he who would betray him, being one of the twelve' (John 6:70–71).

The call for judgment on the enemy begun in verse 9 concludes in verse 15, with the resumption of the plural 'them' and 'their' to indicate that this was not personal vindictiveness against his friend turned traitor. The intervening verses have provided good reasons why God should act in response to this general uprising against David's rule. David, after all, is ruling over God's kingdom on God's throne in Jerusalem (1 Chronicles 28:5; 29:23). His words must be viewed in the light of Psalms 2 and 45 as pointing forward to the coming Messiah and his rule.

David does not take revenge himself but appeals to God that the enemy would be suddenly taken alive to their graves ('hell' is Sheol the state of the dead; see Psalm 6:5), as happened to those caught up in the Korah rebellion against Moses and Aaron (Numbers 16:31–33).[118] His main motive in calling for this divine punishment is on account of the 'great evil' ('wickedness', the word is the plural for 'evil') 'among them' or 'within them' wherever they stay (verse 15).

After predicting his betrayal, Jesus pronounced a judicial curse on Judas, 'The Son of Man indeed goes just as it is written of him, but woe to that man by whom the Son of Man is betrayed! It would have been good for that man if he had not been born' (Matthew 26:24). It was in God's plan that Jesus would be betrayed but Judas was entirely responsible for his treasonable action.

Confidence and concern (verses 16–21)

An emphatic 'I' opens this section of the psalm ('As for me, I will ...'). David asserts his intention 'to call upon God' (verse 16) and is determined to 'pray and cry aloud' (verse 17, or more literally 'utter my complaint and moan noisily', which picks up the language of verse 2) constantly at all times of the day just as Paul encouraged Christians in their battle against all the tricks of the devil' (Ephesians 6:18). He also expresses his confidence that his covenant-keeping God will deliver him ('the LORD shall save me', verse 16) and 'hear him' (verse 17). So certain is he that he can speak of the deliverance 'from the battle' as if it had already happened—'He has redeemed my soul in peace' (verse 18). Despite the 'many' arrayed against him God has 'ransomed' him safely so that he is in a state of well-being.

David's confidence that God will hear and 'afflict' (verse 19, literally 'answer') the enemy in wrath for what they have done, is based on God's eternal kingship—'he who abides (or better 'sits enthroned') from of old' (verse 19; see Psalm 9:4,11). The 'Selah' at this point suggests a pause before referring to the enemy in whom there is no change of attitude and no fear of God.

The effect of the betrayal by such a close associate has so greatly grieved David that he cannot rid himself of the pain. He comes back to the issue in verses 20 and 21. The outrageous nature of the whole affair is that his supposed friend ('He') has stretched out his hand 'against those who were at peace with him' (verse 20) and violated a sacred and legally binding agreement (literally 'defiled his covenant'). God could not ignore it for it involved something holy that had been defiled (see Psalm 89:31,34). The hypocrisy and deception is graphically portrayed. While his words were 'smoother than butter', and 'softer than oil', his intentions were hostile and meant to maim and kill ('drawn swords', verse 21).

An assuring call (verses 22–23)

David reminds himself of what he has been doing all through the psalm and he urges others like himself who are among the righteous to follow his example—'Cast your burden on the LORD' (verse 22). The word 'burden' means 'lot', 'whatever is given to you'. Instead of bottling up the things that worry us or seeking to get our own back on those who have mistreated us we are encouraged to throw back onto God what he, in his providence, has given us to endure. This is the way to possess a meek and contented spirit, something we see supremely in our Lord Jesus Christ. And the promise is that God will 'sustain you' for he will 'never permit the righteous to be moved' ('be shaken', see Psalms 10:6; 16:8). In a similar way the Apostle Peter writes, 'casting all your care upon him, for he cares for you' (1 Peter 5:7).

While the righteous are held secure, the wicked, like those described in the psalm—'bloodthirsty and deceitful'—will 'not live out half their days' (verse 23) but be brought down by God to the 'deepest pit', literally 'the pit of the pit' (two words with similar meaning; see Psalm 16:10). A similar sounding word for the second of the two terms means 'corruption' or 'destruction'. This takes us further than what was mentioned in verse 15. It is the ultimate punishment of the hell described by Jesus and his apostles that awaits all who neither acknowledge God nor his Son, Jesus Christ.

While sometimes even the best of human beings cannot be trusted, one thing is certain in all the uncertain and disappointing experiences of life, God can be trusted—'but I will trust in you' (verse 23; see Psalm 26:1). Here is the greatest comfort to children and adults who have been abused by close family members or responsible and respected people.

Psalm 56

From Fear to Faith

Concern over the enemy continues in this psalm and despite David's fears there is strong emphasis on his trust in God and his commitment to give thanks to him.

The heading suggests that during the period when David was on the run from Saul he was for a time captured by the Philistines in Gath, one of their main cities in the Gaza region and once home to Goliath. We know he fled there on a couple of occasions and that not all the Philistine leaders were as generous as Achish the king of Gath in their view of David (1 Samuel 21:10-15; 27:1-28:4; 29:1-11). Psalm 34 has a reference to David's first time among the Philistines when he was 'very much afraid' of the king of Gath (1 Samuel 21:12) and David's fears are evident in this psalm (56:3-4,11). The courage he displayed in defeating Goliath was lacking on this occasion and we are reminded of our own weaknesses, that we cannot rely on previous victories and therefore of our continuing need of the Lord's help.

The psalm is the first of a series of five with the heading 'Michtam of David' (Psalms 56-60; see the heading to Psalm 16) and later given to the 'Chief Musician' to be sung in the temple worship. The second phrase ('Set to "The Silent Dove in Distant Lands."') which may refer to the tune is literally 'upon the silent dove of far off' which could mean distant places or people and is certainly applicable to the Philistines who had come via Crete (Caphtor) to Canaan (see Amos 9:7).

Cry and Confession (verses 1-4)

As in so many of these laments, the cry goes out to God that he would 'be gracious' which captures the sense of unmerited, generous favour better than what we generally mean by 'be merciful' (verse 1; see Psalms 4:1; 6:2). This appeal is supported by reasons introduced by 'for'. He has people (the word translated 'man' in verse 1 is poetic for frail humanity), described as 'enemies' (verse 2, literally 'my watchers'; see Psalm 54:5), 'many' of them (verse 2), and they are 'trampling on' or 'panting after' him (the same verb is translated 'swallow up' in verse 1 and 'hound' in verse 2). The fighting is continuous—'all day' (verses 1 and 2, plus verse 5) and his enemies press in on him ('oppresses') like Balaam's donkey pressed the foot of his master against the wall (Numbers 22:25).

'O Most High' (verse 2) translates the word for 'height' or 'on high' (see Psalms 18:16; 92:8). In no other place is it a name for God and it is very unlikely that David is using the term to address God. In this context it is either suggesting that the enemy has the advantage of attacking from 'on high' or less likely, but favoured by some popular translations, it is used figuratively of the enemy acting 'proudly'.

Despite the enemy David professes to God his confidence in him—'I will trust in you' (verse 3; see Psalm 31:6) on the 'day' ('Whenever') 'I am afraid'. The emphasis on God is strong in this psalm—'In God' (twice in verse 4), and it turns into a refrain (see verses 10 and 11). The motto, 'In God we trust', based on verses like this, found its way into the USA's national anthem, *The Star-Spangled Banner* and was first applied to their coins in 1864.

David praises God's 'word'—'(verse 4) which includes all his gracious promises. When translated as 'In God whose word I praise', the need in English to use brackets becomes superfluous. This is the centre point around which the carefully crafted chorus is built—fear-trust-word-trust-fear (verses 3 and 4). In the light of this note of confidence, 'man' (frail humanity, verse 1) and 'flesh' (verse 4), standing for weak, mortal humans, even at their strongest and most powerful are no match against the immortal, almighty God. The prophet, as he shows the folly of not trusting God, declares, 'Now the Egyptians are men, and not God; and their horses are flesh, and not spirit' and later states, 'All flesh is grass ... The grass withers and the flower fades, but the word of our God stands for ever' (Isaiah 31:3; 40:6–8). This is the gospel word that is to be preached (1 Peter 1:4–25).

Complaint and Confidence (verses 5–11)

More details are given of David's situation and it is the way his enemies constantly ('All day') twist his words and plan ('their thoughts') to harm him that grieves him the most (verse 5). Those plans involve 'stirring up strife' ('gather together' is how it is translated in the Greek text), hiding like hunters waiting to ambush and kill him (verse 6). Here David may be thinking of Saul and his men who were ready for him when he escaped from the Philistines (see 1 Samuel 22:6). These enemies of David think that they can also rely on their iniquity to escape punishment.

David therefore appeals to God that he would set things right, that in his righteous indignation he would bring them down (see Psalm 55:23). It is interesting that David uses the more general word 'peoples' (verse 7), meaning people of other races and tribes, which suggests that David is not seeking revenge but seeing his own personal enemies, like Saul and the Philistines, as part of the much wider opposition to God and his true anointed king. The call for vengeance on those who plot evil must be viewed in the light of Psalm 2.

David then focuses on his own situation and with striking metaphors makes a heart-rending appeal that God would take note of his complaint with the implication that he would take action against the enemy. He asks that God would 'number my wanderings' (verse 8), that is that he would 'record' his wandering, homeless situation. He is like Cain in the land of Nod (meaning 'Wandering'; See Genesis 4:16). The second request is that his 'tears' of sorrow (see Psalm 6:6) would be preserved in a 'water-skin' (verse 8),[119] a bit like a meteorologist recording rainfall in a measuring bottle. He wishes to have these matters permanently recorded in a 'book' so that God would remember and that it would move God to act on his behalf. David's cries and tears prefigure those of our Saviour 'who in the days of his flesh, when he had offered up prayers and supplications, with vehement cries and tears to him who was able to save him from death, and was heard because of his godly fear ... learned obedience by the things which he suffered' (Hebrews 5:7–8).

After lament (verses 5–6) and cries to God (verses 7–8) David ends this section with a statement of trust that includes the refrain of verse 4. 'When I cry out' (verse 9, literally 'in the day') picks up the earlier references to 'day' (verses 1 to 3). He is assured that God will 'turn back' or 'defeat' the enemy (see Psalm 9:3) because God is not only on his side ('God is for me', verse 9) but that God is his God as a more literal translation makes clear—'God belongs to me'. Paul could also declare triumphantly, 'If God is for us who can be against us' (Romans 8:31). The refrain interestingly adds an extra line that repeats 'In God whose word I praise' but substitutes 'Lord' (Yahweh/Jehovah) for God (verse 10). Instead of 'flesh' (verse 4) the term 'man' (humankind, *adam*; verse 11) is used. The Lord has promised to be with us so that we can rest content and boldly repeat David's confident words in the face of the stiffest opposition (see Hebrews 13:5–6; Psalm 118:6).

Commitment (verses 12–13)

The psalm ends on a confident note like the close of the previous two psalms (Psalms 54:6–7; 55:23). David has moved from fear to faith so that he can make this forthright commitment to God for the anticipated deliverance. He is under obligation to fulfil the promises or 'vows' he has made to God and in the context of the worshipping community he wishes to come with thank offerings or thankful 'praises' (verse 12; see Leviticus 7:12–15). The reason for David's grateful actions is his expected deliverance from the kind of 'death' and 'falling' (verse 13) the enemy had been waiting to bring about (verse 6). Instead of 'feet ... falling' he can 'walk before God' and rather than in the darkness of death he can walk 'in the light of the living'. To walk about in the presence of God means to enjoy his favour and protection (see Genesis 17:1; Psalm 1:1–3). Light is associated with life and salvation and God is the source of both light and life (Psalm 27:1; see also Psalm 116:8–9). Jesus is the light of the world and he promises that whoever 'follows me shall not walk in darkness, but have the light of life' (John 8:12). We look forward to the day when we shall be for ever in that new world where there is no more curse and no night for the Lord God gives his people light (Revelation 22:4–5).

Psalm 57

Prayer and Praise
to the God of Heaven

J onah gives us a prayer from the belly of a sea monster while 'David' gives us this special psalm ('Michtam'; see Psalm 16) from within a 'cave'. The people of God under the old covenant as under the new were free to call on the Lord at any time and in any place and situation. Like the previous psalm the setting is that period in David's life when he was on the run 'from Saul' as the heading indicates. Among the many caves of the region where David may have hidden we read of the cave of Adullam and one at En Gedi (1 Samuel 22:1; 24:1-3). 'Do not Destroy' (see also Psalms 58-59, 75) has been taken to refer to the set tune for the Chief Musician to use but unlike the previous heading to Psalm 56 there is nothing in the original text to warrant such introductions as 'Set to', 'According to' or 'To the tune of'. In addition to the similar background situation, there are a number of terms and phrases that link this psalm with the previous one. A slightly altered form of verses 7-11 are used later in Psalm 108:1-5.

David expresses great confidence in God as he prays for deliverance so that the psalm concludes with praise. The two halves of the psalm close with a chorus (verses 5 and 11).

Prayer for deliverance (verses 1–5)

The opening plea is identical with that of the previous psalm with 'be merciful to me' (or better 'be gracious to me', verse 1) repeated, revealing the intensity of David's desire. Again, as in Psalm 56:1 the reasons for his plea follow, introduced by 'for'. However, instead of focusing immediately on his troubles as in the laments of the preceding psalms he presents this strong confession of trust in God. He is appealing to God because he 'trusts' (literally, 'taken refuge') in God. The cave might offer some temporary security but his ultimate 'refuge' is God, who is likened to a bird protecting her young under her wings (see Psalms 17:8; 36:7). In a similar way Jesus longed to gather and protect rebellious Israel against whom he had uttered a series of woes (Matthew 23:37). David is seeking shelter there until 'calamities' ('destructions'; see Psalms 5:9; 52:2,7) have passed. Charles Wesley's hymn comes to mind, 'Hide me, O my Saviour, hide, till the storms of life be passed'.[120]

From this confession of trust, David continues with a statement about God that supports and inspires him to continue trusting. His cry is to 'God Most High' (see Psalm 7:17; Genesis 14:22), to the Almighty 'God' (the rarer name for God, *El*, is used in the second line of verse 2) who 'performs for me' (verse 2). The verb for 'performs' means 'to end, bring to an end, complete' (see Psalms 7:9; 138:8) and this could either mean that God finishes what he has begun, as Paul states in Philippians 1:6, or that God will bring the calamities of verse 1 to an end.

Deliverance will come because this God, who is above all other gods, will 'send from heaven'. This is the place where God displays his glory and calls his home but he is not confined there for, as the chorus indicates, he is 'above the heavens' (verses 5,11). David recognises the need for supernatural help to censure ('he reproaches') his enemy, who is described in the language of Psalm 56:1–2 as one who would 'hound' him ('swallow me up', verse 3). A 'Selah' provides an appropriate break before returning to express what God will send. His 'mercy and his truth', in other words his 'steadfast love' and 'faithfulness' (see Psalm 25:10), are vividly portrayed as God's special agents sent to accomplish David's deliverance (see Psalm 43:3). In the same way it is from heaven that salvation from sin and Satan comes. God has done what nothing and no one else could do by 'sending his own Son' (Romans 8:3) who is 'full of grace and truth' (John 1:14). The love of God is seen in this that

God 'sent his only begotten Son into the world' as the 'Saviour of the world' (1 John 4:9-10,14).

David now describes his precarious situation using graphic imagery. His 'soul' (verse 4), by which he means himself and particularly his 'life' is in danger from human beings who act like 'lions' (see Psalm 7:2), who greedily devour like 'fire', and who have 'teeth' like 'spears and arrows' and tongues like sharp swords. As we have noted in the immediately preceding psalms (Psalms 52:2-4; 56:5), the enemy has used slander and abuse to discredit and destroy David. Despite everything, he is able to lie down safely (see Psalms 3:5; 4:8), secure in the knowledge that God is his refuge.

The refrain encourages that confidence (verse 5). It begins by expressing David's desire to see God 'exalted' (see Psalm 21:13). Above his concern to be saved and for the enemy to be rebuked, his overriding passion is that God's glory, the manifestation of his stunning presence, would be seen and acknowledged by all, including the enemies. The word 'above' would be better translated 'over' in this context.

Commitment to praise (verses 6–11)

David continues to describe his dangerous situation but again it turns out to be not a lament but a testimony that issues in praise to God. The imagery changes and David's enemies are likened, as often in the Psalms, to hunters who use nets spread over the pits they have dug to catch their prey. He is 'bowed down' (verse 6) under the weight of the attack yet all changes when the enemy falls into the pit they have dug for him (see Psalms 7:15; 9:15). A couple of occasions are recorded of Saul hunting for David and ending up being caught by David (1 Samuel 24:2-4,14; 26:7-9,20). As so often happens in God's providence, evil brings about its own downfall. Before the psalm continues the 'Selah' probably is there to indicate a way of calling attention to what has just been said or to what follows.

Though he is in the midst of foes with his soul bowed down David's heart is 'firmly established' ('steadfast') unlike rebellious Israel (Psalm 78:37). As in his opening cry (verse 1), the repetition of 'my heart is steadfast' (verse 7) emphasises his loyalty to God. This commitment includes singing and making music with instrumental playing in praise of God ('sing and give praise', verse 7). He refers to his whole being as 'my glory' (verse 8; see Psalms 7:5; 16:9; 30:12) which he seeks to awaken (see Psalm 42:5,11) and urges the instruments—the 'lute and harp' (or 'harp and lyre'; see Psalm 33:2)—that will accompany the singing to wake up so that instead of the dawn waking David it might be the other way round. Centuries later, we read of Paul and Silas in the inner prison at Philippi singing hymns at midnight (Acts 16:25). The psalms often speak of deliverance coming in the morning after the long night of pain and prayer (see Psalms 5:3; 30:5).

David desires to 'give thanks' ('praise') and to 'make music' ('sing', verse 9; translated 'give praise in verse 7) to his 'Lord'. His God is no local ruler and so he wants the whole world to hear his songs of praise ('among the peoples ... nations', verse 9; see Psalm 18:49; Romans 15:9). This is because God's 'steadfast love' ('mercy') and 'faithfulness' ('truth'), which David is assured God will send to save him (see verse 3), are boundless ('reaches unto the heavens ...' verse 10; see Psalm 36:5). This provides a fresh reason for the refrain in verse 11 (see verse 5). David sees his deliverance as having worldwide implications that take us back to God's promises to Abraham (see Genesis 12:3).

The Church has long appreciated the significance of Psalm 57 with the Anglican Book of *Common Prayer* appointing it, along with Psalms 2 and 111, for use during Easter morning worship. David's deliverance from Saul foreshadows the resurrection of Jesus from the tomb and every Lord's Day should be a time when Christians should be eager to wake the dawn with their praises to God and to confess to all that the risen Lord Jesus is the Saviour of the world. Matthew Henry recalls how his father, Philip, would greet his family on the Lord's Day morning with the words: 'The Lord is risen; he is risen indeed'.

Psalm 58

An Appeal to the Judge Supreme

There are no indications as to the background of this intense call for justice but in all other respects the heading contains the same terms and phrases that we find in Psalms 57 and 59. This may suggest that we are to view David's words in this psalm within the context of his experiences during the reign of Saul. Saul's unjust rule, especially as it affected David and his men, is illustrative of all oppressive rule that aims to persecute God's people. The psalm is reminiscent of Psalm 52 for it begins by addressing those in positions of power. It then proceeds to describe them and to pray against them and ends with rejoicing at their downfall. The imagery is most vivid and, to modern Westerners, gruesome but it uses the language of those times to express powerfully the just punishment of all the wicked. There are indications that David may well have had in mind the Song of Moses (Deuteronomy 32:1–43) with its similar language and celebration of God taking vengeance on his enemies.

Accusation (verses 1–2)
There is a problem with the opening line as ancient versions and modern translations reveal. Who is being addressed? Is it 'congregation' (Authorised), 'silent ones' (Revised Authorised), 'gods' (English Standard) or 'rulers' (New International)?[121] The underlying Hebrew

word occurs elsewhere only in the heading to Psalm 56 where it is translated 'silent'. In this context where the parallel line should read 'Do you judge human beings ('the sons of men') uprightly? the first line should probably be, 'Do you indeed speak righteousness in silence?' meaning, 'Do you really deliver right judgments to people by keeping quiet?' The questions are addressed to the powerful corrupt rulers described in verses 2 to 5 who first think up ('in heart') wicked schemes and then implement them ('your hands') on the earth. Instead of dealing out ('weigh out') justice their 'wickedness' is seen in their cruel 'violence' (verse 2; see Psalm 55:9). David here speaks like the prophets who denounced their leaders (see Micah 2:1; 3:1; Amos 5:7). David probably had Saul in mind but his unjust and violent actions were but an example and pattern of all ruthless tyrants including the rich oppressors of James 5:1-6.

Evidence (verses 3-5)

A description of these oppressors is given. David's persecutors belong to that whole class referred to as the 'wicked' (verse 3; see Psalm 1). The seeds of wickedness are there from birth as David confessed in Psalm 51:5 and it is only the grace of God that keeps anyone from the kind of behaviour depicted here. By nature we have all gone astray ('estranged'; see 1 Peter 2:25) and are 'alienated from the life of God' (Ephesians 4:18).

As so often in life, dishonest words ('speaking lies', verse 3) go hand in hand with violence. Their speech has the effect like that of a snake's venom and they are deaf to all pleas and attempts to restrain them just as the cobra or viper is deaf to the voice of the charmers (verses 4-5; see Psalm 140:3). There are echoes of these verses in Romans 3:13 to remind us that we face a 'mirror, not only a portrait' (Kidner).

Condemnation (verses 6-9)

His lament now issues in a prayer for these enemies to be dealt with. They stubbornly refuse to listen to human appeals so David calls on 'God', the covenant keeping 'LORD' (Yahweh, Jehovah; rarely found in Psalms 42-83) to act to disable them. Using language typical of ancient treaty curses in which metaphor and simile are used to great effect David calls on God to render the enemy harmless. First, they are like ferocious lions whose teeth need to be broken to release their prey (verse 6; see Psalm 57:4).

The imagery changes and David wants these vicious oppressors to become harmless like water that vanishes, perhaps as he had seen it soak away into the sandy ground when it is poured out (verse 7a; see 2 Samuel 14:14). Then he thinks of the wicked like broken arrows that can do no damage (verse 7b). Two more illustrations follow in verse 8 where he desires that the enemy will either melt away like a snail whose slimy trail is suggestive of melting away as it moves or be lost as in a miscarriage.

The imagery changes again in verse 9 and although the original is difficult the general idea is clear. David may be using a local saying much like our 'as quick as a flash'. The image is possibly that of cuttings from a thorn bush placed under a cooking pot with dry pieces that burn easily ('burning') to start the fire and green ('living') branches to maintain the heat (see Ecclesiastes 7:6) all to no avail for God will quickly 'whirlwind' them away. On the other hand, the second half of the verse may refer to the 'burning' wrath of God that will swiftly destroy the wicked while they are still 'living' as in the case of the Korah rebellion (Numbers 16:31-33; see Psalm 55:15).

Celebration (verses 10-11)

From the punishment that wicked oppressors like Saul deserve, attention is drawn to the 'righteous' of which David is a type (see Psalm 1). The righteous can 'rejoice' (verse 10) for their trust is in the true God to whom Abraham prayed as the judge of all the earth who will do right (Genesis 18:25). They do not take vengeance themselves but, as the psalm has already indicated, look to God for retribution. He is the final judge who will right all wrongs and punish the wicked. This rejoicing 'must not spring from malice, nor from gratified impatience. It must be that God is honoured, innocence vindicated, wickedness put down, and the cause of truth rendered triumphant'.[122]

The metaphor of washing 'feet (literally 'steps') in the blood of the wicked' (verse 10) was an idiomatic way of expressing total victory over the enemy just as great wealth could be described as 'steps washed in cream' (Job 29:6). A similar picture is presented to us in Isaiah's prophecy of the judgment to come (Isaiah 63:1-6) and the imagery is used by John to depict God's final punishment of the wicked (Revelation 14:17-20; 19:15). The wrath that fell on Jesus at Calvary's cross for every wicked person who repents and turns to Christ will fall on unrepentant sinners on that solemn day of reckoning. We are called to flee from that wrath to come (1 Thessalonians 1:10).

People in general ('men will say' verse 11) will eventually be brought to admit what the righteous have always believed, that justice will prevail despite the power of the oppressors. There is a 'reward' (literally 'fruit', verse 11) for the righteous just as the wicked will eventually reap what they sow (see Isaiah 3:10–11; Galatians 6:7). While our translation has 'Surely he is God who judges in the earth' (verse 11), David actually uses the pagan's own language to express the point concerning divine justice as the following more literal translation shows: 'yes, there are gods judging in the earth' (verse 11).[123]

The joy of God's people over the destruction of the enemies of God and his people 'is a motive that runs through the canon of Scripture ... It begins in the Song of Moses (Deuteronomy 32:43), finds expression in this psalm (Psalm 58:10), is proclaimed in the Prophets (Jeremiah 51:48, against literal Babylon), and reaches a climax in the book of Revelation (18:20, against antitypical Babylon).'[124]

In praying, as Jesus taught, that God's will would be done on earth as in heaven and to be delivered from evil (Matthew 6:10,13) we are praying along the lines of this psalm that justice will be done. The evocative language, reminding us of recent atrocities and especially the unspeakable suffering of God's people at the hands of their persecutors, is meant to stir within us a holy passion to see a just end to such wickedness (see Revelation 6:9–11).

Psalm 59

Our Shield and our Defender

As in so many of the psalms we have been looking at, David speaks as the true representative of his people against the evil intentions of Saul who was out to kill him and endanger the well-being of the nation. In this he reflects Christ and his Church while Saul is a type of all anti-Christian forces. It shares the same heading as the previous psalm but like Psalms 56 and 57 it includes a note that links the psalm to that significant moment in David's life when he began to be hounded by Saul (see 1 Samuel 19:11). Like our Lord Jesus Christ, David waited God's time to be vindicated and this becomes a pattern for his persecuted people (1 Peter 2:21-23).

The psalm depicts in graphic language both the intimidation of David's enemies and the protection provided by David's God. It can be divided into two main parts (verses 1-10 and 11-17), each ending with similar words that act as a kind of double refrain (verses 6 and 14, 9-10 and 17). The 'Selah' at the end of verse 5 and verse 13 suggests a further sub-division.

Prayer for deliverance (verses 1-5)
The psalm begins with the familiar appeal to God for deliverance (see Psalms 7:1; 51:14) from enemy attack. As David's enemies are rising up against him he pleads to the one he later refers to as 'my

363

defence' or 'my high place', that he will be 'set on high' ('defend', verse
1) beyond their reach. David's own house offers no protection from
these murderous people who wish to do him harm. He has given no
cause for these 'mighty' or 'strong' ones to rush to gather themselves
together against him and to lie in wait for his life (see Psalm 35:7,19).
Three terms are used to emphasise his innocence whether in relation
to God or his foes—'transgression', 'sin' and 'fault' (often translated
'iniquity'; verses 3–4a). The blame for this present crisis lies firmly with
the enemy. Jesus was perfectly innocent, having committed no sin at
all and yet the Jewish and Roman authorities gathered together against
him.

The desperateness of the situation is conveyed in the accumulation
of divine names in David's cry—'LORD God of hosts, the God of Israel'
(verse 5). Unusually in this section of the Psalms (Psalms 42–83) God's
covenant name 'LORD' (Yahweh/Jehovah) is found three times in this
psalm (see verses 3,5,8). It is to this God, the God who revealed himself
at the exodus, the God of the heavenly armies of stars and angels
(see Psalm 24:10) and especially the God of his people Israel who had
promised to save them, that the appeal is made for God to 'awake to
help him' (verse 4b, literally 'awake to meet me') and 'to punish all the
nations' (verse 5). God, of course, neither slumbers nor sleeps and sees
everything that happens but David's language conveys the urgency
of his plea and his desire for God to see ('behold' verse 4b) the merits
of his case. Interestingly, David views his personal situation in the
light of God's universal judgment ('punish all the nations' verse 5; see
verse 8). There can be no mercy (literally 'do not be gracious') toward
unrepentant 'wicked traitors' (verse 5b), so different to how humble,
contrite people like David (see Psalm 57:1) are regarded by God. His
prayer is not motivated by personal animosity but sees his enemies as
part of that worldwide conspiracy against God and his anointed (see
Psalm 2). After such a grave prayer the 'Selah' probably suggests pause
for thought.

Picture of the enemies (verses 6–7)
Saul's men were watching his house at night to kill him (1 Samuel 19:11)
and as David prays he likens them to wild dogs roaming the streets
'at evening' looking for their prey (verse 6; see Zephaniah 3:3). The
illustration changes to convey the harm caused by the enemy's words

that are like 'swords' (verse 7; see Psalms 55:21; 57:4). Like the fool of Psalm 53:1 they assume that there is no God listening in.

Confident prospect (verses 8–10)

David, the Lord's anointed one, trusts in the God of Psalm 2 where the same two verbs for God's amusement at the antics of the pagan nations as well as of David's enemies are used—'laugh' and 'derision' (verse 8 and Psalm 2:4; see Psalm 37:13). The situation in which David finds himself is but a small specific example of the universal rebellion against God and the Anointed one of whom David is a type.

David calls on God 'his strength' and 'refuge' or 'high place' ('my defence' verse 9; see verse 1 and Psalm 9:9).[125] Psalms 18:1-2, 28:7 and 46:1 have already acknowledged God as David's 'strength' and all echo the Song of Moses in Exodus 15:2. The enemy may be 'strong' (verse 3) but God is *the* Strong One, so David feels confident to 'wait' or more literally 'watch' for God to take action (verse 9).

In verse 10 David speaks even more personally of his 'merciful God' (or 'unfailing loving God') coming to meet him and show him his 'enemies' (literally 'those who watch me'; see the heading where Saul's men 'watched' the house; Psalms 5:8). Causing him to 'see' his foes ('*my desire*' is not in the original) conveys the same meaning as in Psalm 54:7 where again there is no suggestion of gloating or triumphalism (such expressions as 'gloat' or 'in triumph' are additions to the text found in some modern translations). David can look without fear on his enemies and with relief that God has put things right for his people.

Prayer for retribution (verses 11–13)

From praying for deliverance David now prays against his enemies. As he does so he gives reasons. Ultimately, he has the honour of God in mind as the latter part of verse 13 indicates. David's other concern is for Israel's spiritual good. Though at that time he was not officially king over the nation, as the one set apart and anointed to be the future leader, he acknowledges them as 'my people' (verse 11).

He prays that his foes will not be slain 'lest my people forget' (verse 11). It was a concern of Moses that when God's people were settled in Canaan they might become wayward and forget the Lord (see Deuteronomy 8:11). It was to teach Israel spiritual lessons that the Canaanites were not destroyed all at once (see Judges 2:20-23; 3:1-4). The punishment David calls for is that by God's 'power' they might be 'made to wander' (rather than 'scatter') as happened to Israel for forty years in the wilderness (Numbers 32:13) and as David later experienced during Absalom's treasonable activities (2 Samuel 15:20). Invoking the sovereign Lord as their 'shield', expressive of God's protective care (see Psalm 3:3; Genesis 15:1), he also calls for them to be brought down from their present high position. They needed to be humbled which is exactly what happened to Saul and those associated with him. This is what will happen when God comes in judgment: 'The loftiness of man shall be bowed down, and the haughtiness of men shall be brought low; the Lord alone will be exalted in that day' (Isaiah 2:17).

Verse 12 elaborates on what the enemy are saying in verse 7. They make false accusations on oath ('cursing') and proclaim lies to further their ends. David prays that they will be caught ('taken') in their pride so that those, for instance, who were arrogantly saying, 'Who hears?' (verse 7), will suddenly find out! David is not praying a spiteful prayer but that the 'sin of their mouth' might be punished. God's 'wrath' (verse 13) is his settled righteous reaction to all sin and David's call for his enemies to be finally brought to an end ('consume') and be no more is not personal vindictiveness, as his kindness toward Saul and his family clearly indicate, but that God should be recognised by everyone on the planet ('to the ends of the earth'; see Psalm 2:8) as the ultimate ruler over his people. David made a similar point when he confronted Goliath: 'This day the Lord will deliver you into my hand ... that all the earth may know that there is a God in Israel' (1 Samuel 17:46). The 'God of Israel' (verse 5) is the God who 'rules in Jacob' (verse 13). Both names refer to the father of the nation and are used interchangeably in the psalm to describe God's chosen people (see Psalm 14:7).

Concerning the 'Selah' at this point, Spurgeon comments: 'Good cause there is for this rest, when a theme so wide and important is introduced. Solemn subjects ought not to be hurried over ... Sit thou still awhile and consider the ways of God with man.'

Picture of the enemies (verses 14–15)
Apart from the introductory 'And', David repeats the refrain of verse 6 in verse 14 where David's foes are likened to a pack of prowling dogs scavenging for food. But now there is a change. They are no longer full of their prey and able to belch out taunts and blasphemy (verse 7). Instead, they are hungry, 'they wander up and down' (verse 15; it is the same verb translated 'scatter' in verse 11) searching for food but without

success—'they are not satisfied'. In other words, David already sees his enemies as unable to use him any longer as prey.[126]

Praise for deliverance (verses 16–17)

Before the second refrain (see verse 9) is introduced in a slightly modified and reduced form, David contrasts the 'evening' activity of the enemy with his own 'morning' expressions of praise to God (see Psalm 30:5). He desires to sing of a 'power' or 'strength' (verse 16; see verse 9 and 17) greater than the 'mighty' who have been against him (verse 3) and to give a ringing shout of joy concerning God's 'mercy' or 'steadfast love' (see verses 10 and 17). He also confesses that God is his 'defence' (see verses 1,9 and 17) and a 'refuge' or 'place of escape' in his time of distress.

The concluding refrain brings together again those characteristics of God that he has just highlighted. He addresses God as 'my Strength' using the same word that is translated 'power' in verse 16 and refers to him as 'my defence' and 'the God of my mercy' or preferably 'my steadfast-loving God'. The one noticeable difference from verse 9 is the change from 'for you I will wait' (or 'watch') to 'To you ... I will sing praises'. Instead of watching for God's strength to bring deliverance David is committed to singing psalms of praise to his 'Strength' for God is a safe haven, who loves his people and keeps the promises he has made to them.

There are psalms for all seasons and circumstances. This psalm comes out of a situation of extreme danger. Jesus encouraged his people to pray for their enemies and not to take vengeance and he certainly taught by example as we see from the way he reacted toward those who cruelly treated him and nailed him to the cross. But he also urged his people to pray for deliverance from evil and the evil one and was particularly severe in his condemnation of those who should have known better but were persistent in their opposition to the truth.

God's people must pass through many testing experiences and persecution and instead of taking revenge are urged to pour out their troubles to the Lord. They also have every reason to be cheerful knowing that the Lord is their refuge and strength. 'Is anyone among you suffering? Let him pray. Is anyone cheerful? Let him sing psalms' (James 5:13).

Psalm 60

A Banner of Truth

L ike Psalm 44 here is a cry arising from military defeat but it also includes a message from God that encourages further confident supplication. Amid the many successes that David experienced, it is clear from this psalm that there were significant setbacks. The retrospective reference in 1 Kings 11:15–16 to a possible defeat by Israel during David's kingship prior to Joab's victory over Edom may well be the psalm's setting and the heading, with its references to places identified today as Syria and Northern Iraq, suggests a link with that period when Joab and his brother Abishai were commanding the Israelite forces (see 2 Samuel 8:1–13; 1 Chronicles 18:1–18). The variation in the numbers slain in the 'Valley of Salt'—a place south of the Dead Sea—may be due to references to two different stages in the campaign.

This is the last of the 'Michtam' psalms (Psalms 56–60; see Psalm 16). A new title is introduced, 'For teaching', which only occurs here but it does recall the interesting statement concerning David's lamentation over Saul and Jonathan, known as the 'Song of the Bow'. He gave orders that it should be taught to the people of Judah (2 Samuel 1:17–18). Such poetry is meant to move us emotionally and motivate us to seek God when similar crisis situations arise.

'Set to "Lily of the Testimony"' may refer to the tune to which it was to be sung in the temple worship (see Psalm 45). 'Testimony' may not be part of the tune reference but a separate item, as is suggested in the heading to Psalm 80. Along with 'For teaching' the term 'Testimony' (see Psalm 80) calls to mind the Song of Moses which Moses instructed should be written down and taught so that it 'may be a witness (or 'testimony') for me against the children of Israel' (Deuteronomy 31:19). It was to be a warning to future generations that, if they rebelled against God, disaster would follow. Perhaps this psalm was to have a similar purpose in the life of the worshipping community. Interestingly, verses 5-12 were well remembered and used with minor differences in the formation of Psalm 108:6-13 (the first six verses being almost identical with Psalm 57:7-11).

A lament (verses 1-4)

David does not mention his army's defeat but gets straight to the point. Their plight is due to God. He has 'rejected' ('cast ... off') them (see Psalm 44:9,23), 'broken' them 'down' like making a breach in an enemy's defences (see 2 Samuel 5:20). This is all evidence of God's 'anger' ('displeased' verse 1) and so David pleads, 'restore us again!' which could, in this context be asking God to 'return to us', implying his absence in some way, rather than for Israel to be restored (see Exodus 32:12).

Using earthquake language of land shaking and torn open, David describes how, through the defeat, God has caused their world to collapse and so there is a further plea that he would reverse the damage caused ('heal its breaches', verse 2). He also likens their situation to their forefathers' experience in Egypt when they suffered hardship (see Exodus 1:14; Deuteronomy 26:6) and he describes how Israel ('your people', verse 3) have become like drunkards, 'staggering' ('confusion') from the wine-cup of God's wrath (see Isaiah 51:17).

Verse 4 has its difficulties as the various translations, ancient and modern, indicate. There are two issues: one concerns the meaning of the text, the other concerns interpretation. Many scholars translate 'You have given to those who fear you a banner to be unfurled or to flee to because of the bow'. The question then is whether the verse continues to describe God's judgment of Israel or is a statement concerning the protection that God has given in the crisis. If it continues to describe the effects of God's anger then the verse is suggesting that he has given his people ('those who fear you') a rallying point ('banner') not for victory but for retreat from the enemy archers (see Jeremiah 4:6) or as a rallying banner that exposes them to attack so that they are forced to flee from the 'bow'.[127] Others, however, take it to mean that God in his mercy provides a place of refuge for the godly in Israel.

But the traditional reading 'that it may be displayed because of the truth' has much to commend it. The word for 'truth' in the sense of what is right, only occurs here but a similar form is found in Proverbs 22:21. This 'truth' concerns the rightness and reality of God's promises especially as outlined in verses 6 to 8. In his devastation David calls to mind a word of hope that he had heard previously. God had unfurled a banner for truth's sake or in the cause of truth to which the godly in Israel could rally. It is like the 'pole' (or 'banner') on which was placed the bronze snake and to which the people with snakebites were to look in order to be healed (Numbers 21:8 and see above at verse 2). The 'banner' imagery is used by Isaiah to speak of the coming Messiah: 'And in that day there shall be a Root of Jesse, who shall stand as a banner to the people; for the Gentiles shall seek him, and his resting place shall be glorious' (Isaiah 11:10). God's gospel must be proclaimed that those who humble themselves and trust the Lord might rally there and find healing and safety.

The 'Selah' is well-placed if it is intended to mark a pause for reflection or to prepare for a change of mood.

Pleading the divine promise (verses 5–8)

It is true that there is no expression of guilt in the psalm but unlike Psalm 44 there are no expressions of innocence either and the reference to God's anger suggests that the defeat is due to the nation's sin. David however prays with the encouragements of the previous verse in mind that God would 'save' by his powerful 'right hand' (see Psalm 20:6) and answer ('hear') him in order that deliverance may come to the people of God whom he calls 'beloved' (verse 5; see the heading to Psalm 45). The name was applied to Benjamin (see Deuteronomy 33:12) and formed part of Solomon's other name 'Jedidiah' (2 Samuel 12:25). It is those who are described as 'your people' and who 'fear you' who are loved by him.

David's prayer of faith is based on God's promises to which he now draws our attention. God's people are urged always to remember his 'exceedingly great and precious promises' (2 Peter 1:4). The holy God 'has spoken'. While 'in his holiness' (verse 6) could mean 'in his sanctuary' (see Psalm 150:1) that is not the context here. God has gone on oath; he has sworn by his own holy character to keep what he has promised (see Psalm 89:35; Amos 4:2). God's word expresses in poetry the promise made to Abraham and his descendants concerning land and their authority over the nations (Genesis 12:7; 15:8; 22:17). It was a promise fulfilled first under Joshua when the conquered land was divided among the tribes (Joshua 13-22), then under David (2 Samuel 8:1-14; 10:1-19) and ultimately by David's greater son, Jesus the Messiah, (Micah 5:2-5a; Isaiah 11:1-9; Revelation 21:24,26; see also Psalm 37:11). The repeated 'mine' and 'my' (verses 7-8) emphasise that God is the owner of all the land and remind his people that they are tenants (Leviticus 25:23) and he has the right to allocate and reallocate it as he pleases (see Exodus 19:5; Joshua 19:51; 21:43).

Usually it is enemies who 'triumph' (Psalm 94:3) and God's people who 'greatly rejoice' (Psalm 28:7) but, using the same word in the original, here only is God said to 'rejoice' (or 'exult', verse 6) and he does so over the promised land. In the days of Joshua the land was divided among the twelve tribes (Joshua 13:7; 18:5). 'Shechem' and 'Succoth' (verse 6) represent the two places where Jacob pitched his tent on his return from exile (Genesis 33:17-19), a little preview of Israel's return from exile to occupy the territory under Joshua. These two places also represent the whole land east and west of the Jordan.

In the following verse the whole area is viewed again, this time 'Gilead' and 'Manasseh' denote the east (verse 7; see Deuteronomy 3:12-13) while 'Ephraim' (the dominant tribe in the north) and 'Judah' (the dominant one in the south) represent the west. The latter two names became ways of describing the land and its people especially after the kingdom was divided (Hosea 5:13-14) but here they indicate the special status of God's people. Ephraim is metaphorically described as God's 'helmet' (verse 7, literally 'the stronghold of my head'; see Psalm 27:1) and Judah as his 'lawgiver' or 'staff' (see Genesis 49:10; Numbers 21:18), the one suggesting defence and protection the other authority and rule. God uses his people to rule and protect.

The other hostile nations surrounding Israel are not so honoured. Moab is likened to a basin that slaves used for washing a warrior's feet, while Edom is likened to the slave who has the warrior's dirty sandals thrown at him before the washing takes place.[128] Both illustrations are suggestive of proud nations to the east in subjection to Israel (see Isaiah 16:6-7; Obadiah 1-4) along with Philistia in the west (see

2 Samuel 8 and 10). Concerning the Philistines there is a call for them to show homage—'Philistia, shout in triumph because of me' (verse 8). On the other hand, the words could be a derisive remark—'raise a battle shout against me if you dare'.

A prayer (verses 9–12)

In the light of the promises of God, the prayer continues but with renewed confidence that God is able to give victory against the foe. The reality is that Edom, with its 'fortified' or 'strong city' (see Psalm 31:21) had gained a notable victory over David's army and without divine aid there was no way he could defeat this enemy. Returning to the lament of verses 1–3 God is reminded that he has spurned them and, as Moses warned Israel in the wilderness, he has not gone out with Israel's armies (see Numbers 14:42). They have been abandoned. God's presence has not been there to help them. Unlike Israel in the days of Eli when they looked to the ark as a kind of lucky charm rather than seeking God directly, David cries out for divine help in their distress ('trouble', verse 11; see Psalm 4:1[129]) realising that human help is of no value.

The final verse is a confession of faith in God's ability to give them victory over the enemy—'Through God' they will gain the victory 'for he shall tread down our enemies' (verse 12; see Psalm 44:5; Romans 16:20). This conviction emerges out of the awareness of God's absence during defeat, a humble recognition of the need for divine help, a deep sense of human powerlessness and a strong belief in God's promises. These are points the people of God need to keep in mind as they seek God in days of spiritual declension and when the forces of evil seem unstoppable.

The psalm must be interpreted in the light of the introductory Psalm 2. Edom, as in the prophetic books such as Obadiah, comes to represent, like Babylon does in other Bible books, the ungodly powers of this world that threaten the people of God. Balaam's prophecy speaks of Israel doing 'valiantly' through their kingly representative and possessing Edom (Numbers 24:17–18), while Obadiah prophesies of God's people possessing the land and that the kingdom will be the Lord's. We also have that dramatic and awesome passage of the lone figure of Messiah, the Lord's Servant, approaching from Edom, again symbolic of all God's and his people's enemies. It is a picture of the final defeat of opposition to God. The one who will punish and 'tread down' all his enemies on that final day of the Lamb's wrath is the same Lamb who was slain and himself experienced that wrath when he was crushed and punished on account of God's righteous judgment on human rebellion (Isaiah 63:1-6; 53:5-6,10; Revelation 15-17).

Psalm 61

Long Live the King!

It may well be that this psalm was composed when King David was away on a military campaign that was causing him concern or when he was forced to flee Jerusalem as a result of Absalom's rebellion. As often in the psalms, it opens with prayer and closes with praise. One interesting feature is that the king first prays for himself in the first person ('my', 'I', 'me' in verses 1–5) and then refers to himself in the third person ('the king's', 'his', 'he' in verses 6–7). The heading is very similar to the one found in Psalm 4 except that, unusually, the reference to the strings is in the singular ('On a stringed instrument') and there is no word for 'Psalm' in the original.

Personal Plea (verses 1–5)
Typical of the lament psalms, David begins by crying out for God to listen (see Psalms 5:1–2; 55:1–2) and by implication to answer his prayer but unlike those psalms there is no description of his trouble. 'From the end of the earth' (verse 2) could be metaphorical like the 'horrible pit' of Psalm 40:2 for a near death situation at the mouth of Sheol or for spiritual alienation. But it is more likely that David is speaking about being some distance from home, possibly when he was forced to leave Jerusalem and live east of the Jordan (2 Samuel 17:21–22, 24).

The phrase 'end of the earth' can refer to 'end of the land' (see

Jeremiah 12:12) as moving to Mahanaim certainly was the case in relation to the capital. David was in an exile situation and his 'heart is overwhelmed' (or better 'faint'), which suggests he was thoroughly discouraged and feeling the effects of physical weakness (see Psalm 102). In this situation he calls for God's protection using the familiar 'rock' imagery. God himself is that rock for David (see Psalms 28:1; 31:2). The one who is high also dwells with the humble and revives their fainting spirits (see Isaiah 57:15-16). David prays for God to 'lead' (see Psalm 60:9) him to this safe position. 'We should therefore by faith and prayer put ourselves under the divine management, that we may be taken under the divine protection' (Matthew Henry).

David supports his prayer by reminding God of past protection. God has been 'a shelter' or 'refuge' (verse 3; see Psalms 14:6; 46:1) and 'strong tower' (see Proverbs 18:10). Using the literal language of the original we often speak of someone who has been 'a tower of strength' to us. Do we think of God in this way? Towers were built within the city walls to provide extra protection 'from the enemy' (see Judges 9:51).

Recalling past experiences of God's protection also encourages David to look confidently to the future—'I will abide (sojourn) ... I will trust ...' (verse 4). More picture language is used in which he desires to dwell in God's tent ('tabernacle'; see Psalm 15:1) and to trust in the 'shelter' (or 'hiding place) of God's 'wings' (see Psalms 17:8; 57:1). There are echoes of Psalm 27:4-5 but in this prayer there is even more determination. While David may well have longed to be back in Jerusalem and to attend the place of worship where the ark of the covenant was in the tabernacle (see 2 Samuel 15:24-29), he uses this imagery to speak of fellowship with God and of finding safety in God 'for ever' (verse 4). David is, of course, by his very prayer communing with God but he is missing the visual indications of God's presence associated with the tabernacle and its contents. All those symbolic items have been permanently removed now that Christ has come and fulfilled their purpose. He is the reality to which they point and it is in Christ alone that we can be safe and secure (John 4:21-24; 2 Timothy 1:12). There are times in the Christian's experience when God seems distant and we do need to pray that God by his Spirit would make his presence felt.

The 'Selah' occurs at the point where the prayer becomes even bolder. David brings forward more reasons for his prayer for protection and security as the word 'For' indicates (verse 5; see also verse 3). He is sure that God will hear the promises ('my vows', verse 5; see verse 8) that accompany his prayer and will keep his own promise concerning the inheritance of land to God's humble worshippers, to 'those who fear your name'. It is those who fear the Lord who will inherit the land (see Psalm 25:12–13). Whether David's prayer arose from the defeat he encountered against a combined force of Arameans and Edomites (see the previous psalm) or from Absalom's treason, David has in mind the promises of God proclaimed in Psalm 60:6–8 to which he firmly holds. Land lost to the enemy within or without would be regained and ultimately through Christ, David's greater son, the meek shall inherit the earth (Matthew 5:5). The Christian has a living hope through the resurrection of Christ to an incorruptible inheritance that is reserved in heaven and the promised Holy Spirit is the personal guarantee of the Christian's inheritance (Ephesians 1:13–14; 1 Peter 1:3–5).

Prayer for the royal dynasty (verses 6–7)

With this promised inheritance in mind (see also Psalm 2:8), David continues with good arguments as he prays for the future of the 'king' at a time when he is in danger, especially if the occasion concerned the attempt of Absalom to remove him from the throne. When David refers to 'the king's life' (verse 6) in the third person he is indicating that he is praying not merely for himself but for the ideal king of David's stock along the lines of God's promises to him: 'And your house and your kingdom shall be established for ever before you. Your throne shall be established for ever' and those promises were the basis of his petitions (2 Samuel 7:16, 25–29). David's words concerning the continuance of his kingship remind us of Psalm 21:4 and prepare us for the final psalm of Book Two (Psalm 72:17). This king is to 'abide' (literally 'sit') for ever 'before God' (verse 7; see Psalm 56:13) so David prays that God will appoint ('prepare') those special agents ('mercy and truth' or 'steadfast love and faithfulness'; see Psalm 57:3; Micah 7:20), descriptive of God's commitment to his covenant promises, to 'preserve him'. God promised David that his unfailing love would not depart from him (2 Samuel 7:15) and King Jesus is the true and final realisation of David's dynasty as the angel's message to Mary reveals (Luke 1:32–33; see Romans 1:3–4). He experienced an exile far worse than that of David as his words from the cross reveal (see Psalm 22:1) but God heard him because of his godly fear and enabled him to become the author of eternal salvation to all who obey him (Hebrews 5:7–9).

Jesus encouraged us to pray on the basis of these promises for God's kingdom to come and his will to be done on earth. Through his life and ministry, his atoning death and resurrection, and ascension to God's right hand, Jesus the God-Man is king with 'angels, authorities and powers having been made subject to him' (1 Peter 3:22; see Revelation 1:5). We look forward to the day when that kingdom will be displayed universally and publicly in the grand consummation (1 Corinthians 15:24–28).

Promise to Praise (verse 8)

'So' in view of these amazing divine promises made to David that he has used in his prayer, he is committed to performing the promises (literally 'paying my vows') he himself had made (verse 5), promises that only a king could keep for it involved 'daily' peace offerings of the vow or praise type (see Leviticus 7:12–18). Along with the sacrifices David promises to 'sing praise' (see Psalm 59:17) continually ('for ever') to God, whose revealed nature ('name'; see Psalm 20:1) is worthy of such honour. We likewise are urged to join in public acts of worship and through our Saviour Jesus the Messiah 'continually offer the sacrifice of praise to God ... giving thanks to his name' (Hebrews 10:25; 13:15).

Psalm 62

Truth Concerning God

It is good to take ourselves in hand, especially when we feel threatened or under pressure. David encourages us to talk to ourselves and to remind ourselves of some home truths that we can then share with others. The psalm reminds us of Psalms like 42:5,11 and 43:5. At the same time it gives instruction like the wisdom psalms (see Psalm 37). Only at the close does David briefly address God.

The heading is similar to the one in Psalm 39 except that we have 'on' or 'according to' Jeduthun (not 'To' in the sense of 'belonging to'). This suggests that the psalm is to be sung to music associated with Jeduthun who was one of three leading musicians in the time of David and Solomon (see 1 Chronicles 16:41-42; 2 Chronicles 5:12).

There are close associations with Psalm 61 with the words 'rock', 'refuge', 'strength' and 'mercy' ('steadfast love') all appearing in reference to God (Psalms 61:2-3,7; 62:2,6,7,12). The psalm's strong confidence in God against the background of enemies who are seeking to remove him from his position, couples it to those earlier psalms where Absalom's treason is the probable occasion. Its theme also provides an appropriate link joining Psalm 61 to Psalm 63 where trust in the shelter of God's wings (61:4) gives way to rejoicing in the shadow of those wings (63:7).

One of the striking features of this psalm is the word that appears six times always at the beginning of verses in the original (verses 1,2,4,5,6,9) and is translated either as an assertion by 'truly/surely' or as denoting a restriction by 'alone/only' depending on the context. In this psalm assertions seem to be the dominant idea. The other interesting factor is the close similarity between verses 1 and 2 and 5 and 6. This, along with the two occurrences of the *Selah* (verses 4 and 8), suggest the division of the psalm into three sections. One clear message stands out and is emphasised in each section: the contrast between God and humans as objects of trust.

Quiet trust (verses 1-4)

We might think that confidence in God as 'my salvation' (verse 1) would issue in shouts of joy and praise but instead David is silent toward God (literally, 'Truly to God my soul is silent). Sometimes David kept his mouth shut in case he should make unguarded comments (see Psalm 39:1) but here his silence is a declaration of his complete trust in God as the rest of the psalm reveals. Calvin adds: 'The silence intended is, in short, that composed submission of the believer, in the exercise of which he acquiesces in the promises of God, gives place to his word, bows to his sovereignty, and suppresses every inward murmur of dissatisfaction'.

The 'salvation' spoken of in verse 1 is expanded in verse 2 with familiar terms employed for God—'my rock ... my salvation ... my defence (or 'high place')'—(see Psalms 18:2; 59:1,9,16-17). David is either continuing to confess boldly his faith in God ('Yes, indeed, he is my rock ...') or making the extra point that God alone ('only') is his deliverer. Do we need to choose as both ideas may be in mind? Even though he feels the effects of the enemy's action he will not be 'greatly moved' ('shaken'; see Psalm 37:24).

David now turns in his thoughts to address the enemy and he is probably referring to himself as the 'man' (verse 3) being attacked and pulled down from his position. Though his trust is in God it does not mean he is free of all concern. 'How long?' (verse 3) implies he is enduring an intolerable situation (see Psalm 13:1). The translation 'You shall be slain, all of you ...' (verse 3) gives a warning that the enemy will be destroyed like a wall and fence about to collapse. Another translation which fits the context better continues the question, 'Will all of you murder?' and it is the 'man' himself who is vulnerable and likened to 'a leaning wall' or 'tottering fence' that can be easily pushed over (see Isaiah 30:13). It is typical of the bully to attack the weak. David is aware of his precarious state and that his foes plan to oust him from his 'high position' as ruler of his people. The enemy is two-faced. Using deceit ('delight in lies', verse 4), they show all the outward marks of honouring the king ('bless') but secretly they treat him with contempt ('curse'). Do we honour the Lord with our lips in communal worship and show him disrespect by the way we live? (see Mark 7:6–7).

Trust encouraged (verses 5–8)

David uses the introductory words of the psalm to counter his view of the enemy but this time in place of declaration (verse 1) we have exhortation (verse 5). He urges himself (see Psalm 42:5) to have that same confidence with which he began: to be in silent submission to God, trusting him 'alone'. The reason for this confidence ('for') is that his 'hope' ('expectation') of salvation comes from God (see verse 1; Psalm 37:7). This exhortation issues in greater assurance as he repeats verse 2 in verse 6 without the qualifying word 'greatly'. This refrain is not enough to emphasise his confidence in God's protection and so David continues in verse 7 to confess that his 'salvation' (see verse 1), 'glory', strong 'rock' and 'refuge' is 'in God'. Despite the enemy's attempts to dishonour him God bestows on him the dignity and importance ('my glory') that his office deserves (see Psalms 3:3; 21:5; 45:3–4). God is not only his 'rock' (verse 6) but the 'rock of my strength' (or 'my strong rock'), calling to mind 'tower of strength' (or 'strong tower') in the previous psalm (Psalm 61:3).

The God who is David's 'refuge' (see 'shelter' in Psalm 61:3) is also a 'refuge for us' his people (verse 8). It is with this in mind that he moves from exhorting himself to urging the people to trust in God at all times and to 'pour out' (see Psalm 42:4) their hearts before him as David so regularly does in these psalms.

Jesus Christ would have found great comfort and encouragement in this psalm. What Jesus saw imperfectly previewed in his shadow he experienced in a fuller and deeper way. Our Saviour suffered the greatest dishonour of all from those who should have known better but who instead plotted to have him crucified, the most degrading of all deaths in the ancient world. He could have called on thousands of angels to deliver him yet he silently continued to trust both in the judgment hall and as they nailed him to the tree, waiting on God to vindicate him. His people too shall be glorified in God's good time though they are treated with disrespect and often regarded as the scum of the earth.

Wise counsel and prayer (verses 9–12)

The call for the covenant people to trust God (verse 8) leads David to give them sound advice. He speaks like a wisdom teacher. There are three proverbial sayings in the final verses.

First, humans of whatever status or position in society (see Psalm 49:2) are very fragile and unreliable. People having some power and influence are 'a lie' (verse 9) because they deceive expectations. It is all a delusion. They give the impression to those under them that they are invincible but in fact they also are frail and insecure (see Psalm 39:5,11). There is no substance to human boasting and pretence for when weighed on the scales there is nothing there (see Isaiah 40:15). Put all of humanity together and they are still less than a breath. This is the persistent message of Ecclesiastes and James does not let the boastful business people and bankers forget it either—'For what is your life? It is even a vapour that appears for a little time and then vanishes away' (James 4:13-16).

Second, the main thought seems to be that we are not to have the worldly mindset of those like David's enemies (see verses 3-4). Instead of trusting God (verse 8) they trust in extortion ('oppression') and 'robbery' (verse 10; see Ezekiel 22:29). They set their hearts on increasing their own resources ('riches'; see Psalm 49:6) by whatever means. The verb translated 'vainly hope' is associated with the word 'vapour' or 'breath' (see verse 9) so David is urging us not to become like vapour ourselves through mimicking David's wicked opponents. Jeremiah speaks of those pursuing 'vapour' ('worthless idols') becoming 'vapour' ('worthless idolaters'; Jeremiah 2:5).

Third, a saying is introduced like the graded numerical statements found in the wisdom books. The most common is the 3 and 4 form such as 'There are three things that are never satisfied, four *things* never say, "It is enough"' (Proverbs 30:15-16,18-19, etc.; see also Amos 1:3,6,etc.). There are also 6 and 7 forms (Job 5:19-27; Proverbs 6:16-19). It is a means of drawing special attention to what is said, often to the last item in the series. What 'God has spoken' (verse 11) which has been 'heard' by David, sums up the truth about God presented in the psalm.

Unlike David's foes there is no corruption with the sovereign 'Lord' (verse 12). He can be trusted because 'power' and 'mercy' belong to him. The first characteristic of God, his 'power' or 'strength' (verse 11) picks up the truth conveyed earlier ('the rock of my strength', verse 7), while 'mercy' or 'steadfast love' (verse 12) epitomizes all that David has said concerning God as his refuge and salvation. The final line, 'for you render to each one according to his work' does not introduce a third attribute, the justice of God, as some have thought. As the introductory 'for' suggests, it is statement expressing how the two characteristics of God operate for the comfort and encouragement of those who have been urged to put their trust in God. With humans as Lord Acton's adage states, 'power tends to corrupt and absolute power corrupts absolutely' but with God his absolute power is exercised along with his faithful love to recompense ('render' or 'repay') everyone according to their works (see Deuteronomy 7:9–10; Proverbs 24:12; Matthew 16:27; 2 Timothy 4:14; Revelation 22:12). Paul quotes the words in his argument concerning the justice of God (Romans 2:6). Unlike David's foes, there is no corruption with the sovereign Lord. God's loving power and powerful love mean that he is willing and able to bless those like David who humbly trust him and punish those who, like David's enemies, are intent on fighting against God and his anointed. This is what is emphasised in Psalms 1 and 2.

As David presents these fundamental truths concerning God he moves from proclamation to prayer just at the point where he speaks of God's faithful love—'Also to you, O Lord, belongs mercy' (verse 12). Is the truth about God merely head knowledge? Have you been so moved by the truth and experience of God that speaking about him encourages prayer to him?

Psalm 63

Desiring God

How concerned are we to experience the living and true God and to have fellowship with him? For John Calvin, the theologian of the Protestant Reformation, Christian doctrine was never divorced from practical piety and it was the Psalms that most stirred him to know God better and to submit to him in reverence and love.

David, who describes himself as 'the king' in verse 11, is 'in the wilderness of Judah' probably during the period of the great rebellion under Absalom (see 2 Samuel 15–18). He has been forced to flee from Jerusalem and from the visible symbols of God's presence at the tabernacle. Besides this common background Psalms 61 to 63 form a kind of trilogy with similar themes and language being used.

Thirsty for God (verses 1–2)
Difficult circumstances draw some people to seek God while others become more entrenched in their opposition to God. David had on numerous occasions enjoyed experiences of God when he worshipped at the Jerusalem 'sanctuary' (verse 2) and this was why David desired God with such intensity. Augustus Toplady, the writer of the well-known hymn, 'Rock of Ages', wrote in his memoirs: 'Surely O God, I could not long after thy presence, if I did not know the sweetness

of it' and he could testify to times when he was 'favoured with some comfortable glimpses of my heavenly Father's countenance.'[130] David's present desire for God was not a new experience but perhaps more intense on account of his situation. Do we have such desires every time we come together in communal worship to recount God's saving work and hear his word?

The verbs translated 'looked' and 'see' (verse 2) do not necessarily mean he saw visions (see Psalms 27:4; 42:2) but worshipping at the tabernacle with the ark of the covenant as its most important object, representing God's 'strength' ('power') and the stunning importance of his being ('glory'), involved reliving the exodus and entry into Canaan when God's awesome presence and mighty acts were revealed to Israel and the nations. The ark is referred to as God's 'strength/ power' (see Psalm 78:61) and 'the ark of your strength' (2 Chronicles 6:41; Psalm 132:8). When the ark was captured by the Philistines it was an indication that God's 'glory' had departed from Israel (1 Samuel 4:21–22). That exile situation prefigured the time when Ezekiel saw God's glory depart from the temple prior to the fall of Jerusalem into the hand of the Babylonians. Unlike the people of Eli's time (and of Ezekiel's concerning the temple) who had a superstitious view of the ark and its presence at the head of their army, David looked for God himself and with the eye of faith saw beyond the ark to the reality of God's 'strength' and 'beauty' in his heavenly sanctuary.

It is interesting that David told Zadok and Abiathar the priests to return to Jerusalem with the ark and not to follow him and his supporters to the wilderness (2 Samuel 15:23–29). All the physical circumstances including the loss of the ark and his weary condition in the wilderness of Judah expressed something of David's spiritual state. He was literally 'in (not 'like' as some translate') a dry and thirsty (weary) land' (verse 1) and was himself 'weary' (2 Samuel 16:14) but his earnest cry expresses his yearning for God. He addresses the unique majestic 'God' (*Elohim*) in a personal way as 'my God' (*El*). While the verb 'to seek early' indicates eagerness and determination we should not be too ready to dismiss a more literal understanding of seeking at daybreak, especially in view of David's meditations through the night (verse 6). The ardour of his search involves his whole being, 'soul' and 'flesh'. Similar longings for God are expressed by the sons of Korah (Psalms 42:1–2; 84:2).

Satisfaction in God (verses 3–8)

These verses divide into two neat parts. The 'lips' (verses 3, 5), expressive of David's whole being, mark out the first part of his worship (verses 3–5). His lips 'laud' or 'commend' ('praise', verse 3) and with his mouth he utters 'praise' (verse 5). It is David's testimony that God's steadfast love ('loving-kindness', verse 3) is more satisfying than all the blessings that make life peaceful and secure. David's complete satisfaction in God is likened to a guest joyfully praising the host after eating a full-course meal of the choicest foods available (verse 5; see Genesis 45:18). When denied these benefits, as David certainly was in the wilderness, he was still assured that all was well because of God's gracious faithful love toward him, a love that is ultimately responsible for every blessing. For Paul, life was Christ and death gain (Philippians 1:21).

Desiring and knowing God and being conscious of his power (Psalms 61:3; 62:11), glory and faithful love (Psalms 61:7; 62:12) leads David to worship God. When Moses prayed to see God's glory, it was God's attributes that were proclaimed and this led Moses to fall to the ground in worship (Exodus 33:18–34:8). David offers 'praise' to God (verse 3) and wishes to 'bless' God (verse 4; see Psalm 16:7) throughout his life (see Psalm 61:8) by giving him the honour and respect that is due to him. When David writes, 'I will lift up my hands in your name' (verse 4) his raised hands toward heaven were an outward indication of his inward desire to worship, calling on the God who had revealed himself to him (see Psalm 28:2; 1 Timothy 2:8). Physical expressions of worship without the inner reality are of no value to God. At the time of Israel's defeat before the Babylonians, the people were urged to lift up their hearts as well as their hands to God in repentance (Lamentations 3:41).

David's satisfaction in God is now viewed from a different angle (verses 6–8). A new self-contained sentence begins with 'When' (verse 6).[131] By referring to 'the *night* watches' of ancient times, where for military and civic guards the night was divided into three (see Exodus 14:24; Judges 7:19; 1 Samuel 11:11 where two watches are mentioned), David indicates how long a night could seem as he lay awake on his bed. But instead of thinking about the enemy, he makes a point of turning his thoughts to God and no doubt recalling what he has mentioned earlier about God's power, glory and faithful love. While for the wicked God is 'in none of his thoughts' for David it is the reverse.

God is in all his thoughts and just as the righteous meditate on God's law (Psalm 1:2; 119:148) so he mulls over those thoughts of God.

As he remembers each occasion of God's help in the past this encourages him to see himself as a vulnerable chick happily running for cover under the 'shadow' of mother hen's wings (verse 7; see Psalm 61:4 where 'shelter' is used) in order to express his joy. To raise shouts of joy ('rejoice'; see verse 5 where the same verb is used 'joyful') means he feels safe and satisfied under God's protective care.

John Newton captures the message of these lines when he writes of his Saviour:

> His love in time past
> Forbids me to think
> He'll leave me at last
> In trouble to sink;
> Each sweet Ebenezer (stone of help)
> I have in review
> Confirms His good pleasure
> To help me quite through.[132]

His 'soul' or whole being (verse 8), that had yearned for God (verse 1) and was satisfied with God (verse 5) is one that is devoted to God alone and is being upheld by God's powerful activity ('your right hand'; see Psalm 18:35; Isaiah 41:10). To 'follow close' (verse 8) or 'cling' like a dry tongue sticks to the roof of the mouth (Lamentations 4:4), is used figuratively in many parts of the Old Testament for loyalty to the Lord rather than following after other gods (see Deuteronomy 4:4; 2 Kings 18:6).

Confident of victory (verses 9–11)

It is with this renewed confidence in God that he now turns to consider the enemy that has forced him into the wilderness. Filling our minds first with thoughts of God is the best way to tackle the troubles of life. The references to the defeat of David's enemies are placed at the beginning and end of this final section of the psalm while at the centre the king and his people gladly boast in the God who has given the victory.

David is assured that those who seek to destroy the 'life' (literally 'soul') of such a person who has found full satisfaction in God and is devoted to God, will themselves be destroyed. Similarly, influential people plotted to 'destroy' Jesus (Mark 11:18). They will 'go into the lower parts of the earth' (verse 9; see Psalm 61:2) which is a descriptive way of speaking of death. The king is confident of victory in the final battle against his enemies. His foe will 'fall by the sword' (verse 10; literally 'pour him into the hands of the sword', an idiom that suggests a combination of violence and betrayal; see Jeremiah 18:21) with their bodies lying on the battlefield a prey to wild animals, the 'jackals' being the final scavengers.

As in Psalm 61:6 David refers to himself as 'king' (verse 11), drawing our attention to its messianic significance (see Psalm 2:6). The gladness implicit in his earlier joyful shouts (verses 5 and 7) becomes explicit when he states that he will 'rejoice in God'. It is 'in God' he rejoices not in his own resources or military might. The people who belong to the king also join in praising or boasting in God ('glory'). They are described as 'everyone who swears by him' which in other contexts means swearing oaths in God's name but here it is more natural to take it as referring to the king. In 2 Samuel 15:21 Ittai swears by David as well as by God: 'As the LORD lives, and as my lord the king lives'. While his loyal people join with the king, whose mouth is open, in praise to God (verse 5), the 'mouth' of his enemies 'who speak lies' (verse 11; see Psalm 62:4) is 'stopped'. This forceful image suggests something like the shutting of the Thames barrier to prevent a tidal surge flooding the city (see Genesis 8:2).

The psalm encourages Christians in all the difficult experiences of life particularly in our warfare against the world, the flesh and the devil to gain strength and confidence through meditation on God and the remembrance of who he is and what he has done. But we are also assured by looking to our Saviour, King Jesus, 'who for the joy that was set before him endured the cross, despising the shame ...' (Hebrews 12:2). His triumph over Satan, sin, death and hell is our triumph and because of him we can boast in God our Saviour. All who stubbornly oppose the Messiah and speak blasphemy and lies will be silenced and find themselves with the great deceiver in the lake of fire which is the second death (Revelation 20:10–15).

Psalm 64

Oppressed but not Cast Down

This 'Psalm of David', belonging to the collection associated with 'the Chief Musician' (see Psalm 4), is concerned with the verbal attacks of the enemy hinted at in the final line of the previous psalm (Psalm 63:11). David's situation again seems to be the conspiracy associated with his son Absalom (2 Samuel 15-17). The previous psalm focused on God with the enemy only briefly mentioned, but here it is the reverse. Nevertheless, both psalms close by praising God.

Petitioning God (verses 1-2)

Typical of the laments that we find in the psalms (Psalm 61:1), David calls on God to listen to his pleas and act. The translation 'meditation' (verse 1) does not capture the idea of the word in this context. It can mean 'complaint' (see Psalm 55:2) or 'troubled thoughts' (Kidner). He prays for protection ('preserve') for the terrifying threats ('fear') of the enemy are real. They are 'evil-doers' ('wicked'), 'workers of iniquity' (verse 2; see Psalm 28:3) who are secretly plotting against David and gathering together as a 'mob' ('insurrection'; the same word as a 'throng' in Psalm 55:14) so he needs to be concealed ('Hide me'). We are reminded of the plots and united action against the LORD and his anointed in Psalm 2:1-2.

David's opening prayer encourages Christians to pour out their concerns to God in prayer.

'Have we trials and temptations,
Is there trouble anywhere;
We should never be discouraged:
Take it to the Lord in prayer'.[133]

Enemy action (verses 3–6)

Further details are given of the enemy's activity. In his trouble with Saul as with Absalom's rebellion, David finds that the enemy's use of words is one of their chief weapons. Their tongues are sharpened like their swords in order to wound (verse 3; Psalms 52:2; 57:4; 59:7) and their 'bitter words' (verse 3) do their work like well-aimed poisonous arrows (see Psalm 58:7). Their slanderous deadly attacks come unexpectedly with stealth. They act like hunters lying in wait in the shadows ready to shoot at the righteous (see Psalm 11:2), who are described here as 'blameless' (verse 4). David is not suggesting he is without sin but indicating there is no obvious defect of character to account for what they are saying and doing (Job 1:1,8).

The enemy 'encourage themselves' (verse 5, literally 'strengthen for themselves') in their evil plots, boastfully proclaiming the secret snares they have laid, believing that they have a free hand and are accountable to no one (verse 5; see Psalm 10:13). This is why they have no 'fear' (verse 4) for they believe that no one, not even God is interested in what is happening (see Psalms 10:11; 59:7). They are plotting and scheming acts of wickedness ('iniquity') that they believe contain no obvious flaws ('perfected' verse 6; the same verb is translated 'blameless' in verse 4). David adds an ironic comment to the effect that the human mind and heart are so deep that they consider their plans are bound to succeed (verse 6).

We cannot but be reminded of the 'bitter words', the plotting and scheming and underhand methods employed against our Lord. Under a cloak of piety and loyalty to Caesar they drew together a mob to have Jesus destroyed, using false witnesses and other deceitful practices.

God's counteraction (verses 7–9)

At this point there is an abrupt change and David confidently speaks of how the tables are turned on the enemy. Using the language of the previous verses the God who was thought to have no interest dramatically intervenes. Just as arrows were to be shot suddenly at the blameless so God 'suddenly' shoots an 'arrow' at the enemy (verse 7; compare verses 3–4). The plots that their 'own tongue' have devised will bring disaster on themselves and far from their former admirers being drawn to them it will result in their gazing at them in terror ('see them', verse 8; see verse 5) and fleeing away just as Israel fled when the earth opened to devour Korah and his fellow conspirators (Numbers 16:34).[134] While David's foes have no fear, God's activity will result in a general 'fear' or proper reverence for God, when they realise that he is the absolute ruler and judge of all. They will 'declare' and 'wisely consider' the wonderful and powerful work that God has done (verse 9). Similarly, after the third plague, Pharaoh's magicians were brought to acknowledge, 'This is the finger of God' (Exodus 8:19). There is a cosmic, end time dimension to these psalms where God's authority and powerful acts are universally recognised ('All men' or 'all humanity', verse 9).

Praising God (verse 10)

The turn-about that is seen between verses 3–6 and 7–9 is matched by the complete change in David's thinking from his lament in verses 1–2 to his glad spirit at the close of the psalm. He speaks as a representative of all the 'righteous' (Psalm 1:5–6) and 'upright in heart' (see Psalms 7:10; 36:10) who have been in danger from the enemy. All such people can 'be glad' (the same word translated 'rejoice' in Psalm 63:11a; see Psalm 32:11) in the 'Lord' (Jehovah/Yahweh). They can 'trust' or, more literally, 'take refuge' (see Psalm 2:12) in the God who revealed himself so wonderfully at the time of the exodus and 'glory' in him (see Psalm 63:11).

As in Psalm 2 we have another glimpse at the folly of those who gather together like an angry mob to plot against the Lord's anointed and his people. God has them in derision as he counteracts their seemingly perfect plans and shrewd schemes, turning their own implements of destruction back upon them. The cross, which demonstrated the greatest triumph of evil was turned by God into the greatest triumph of good. True wisdom and happiness is to be found in sheltering in this God who confounds the wise and powerful of this world through what looks like weakness and folly so that we may glory in the God of our salvation: 'He who glories, let him glory in the LORD' (1 Corinthians 1:31).

Psalm 65

Praise to the God of Salvation and Providence

From the evils that have afflicted David in Psalms 51 to 63, the following four 'songs' provide welcome relief. This 'Psalm' given 'To the Chief Musician' for communal worship in the temple is, as the opening line suggests, a 'Song' (see Psalms 18, 30) celebrating God's gracious and powerful activity as well as his kind gifts. Praise has not been missing in the preceding psalms but here this note is sounded from the beginning. We are also reminded of words and themes that have occurred previously including the performing of vows, the worldwide recognition of the true and living God and the blessings associated with God's presence at the sanctuary. The psalm can be included among the 'Songs of Zion' (see Psalms 46, 48, etc.).

Some have seen the victory over the Assyrian army of Sennacherib in the days of king Hezekiah as providing the setting for the psalm (2 Kings 17-18; Isaiah 36-37) but this is 'A Psalm of David' and the situation recorded in 2 Samuel 21:1-14, where national sin lead to a three-year famine, provides the sort of background that gave rise to this composition on behalf of his people. It was only after atonement was made and wrongs righted that God 'heeded the prayer for the land'.

The grace of God (verses 1–4)

All the emphasis falls on God in the first two verses: it is to God that 'praise' is offered or silenced, the 'vow' performed and 'all flesh' come. That emphasis continues throughout the psalm as it recounts God's goodness and grace.

The phrase 'Praise is awaiting you' (verse 1) is literally 'to you silence praise.'[135] From what David goes on to say it is unlikely that we are being urged to praise God silently or that it means silently or quietly waiting for the right time to praise him. The silence probably refers to trustful submission to God (see Psalm 62:1) without sinful murmurings. Praise is to be offered to God with no conflicting sounds or confusing noises either within the individual or the covenant community.

God was associated with 'Zion' (Jerusalem), the hill fort that became the heart of the city established by David as his capital and the place where he brought the ark of the covenant (2 Samuel 5:7; 6:12; see Psalm 2:6). Here the name stands particularly for the sanctuary where the people of God met for worship (see verse 4). The praises of the people are to be brought to the place where God had ordained to meet with them.

Likewise, the communal promise or 'vow' made by David on Israel's behalf is to be paid or fulfilled ('performed') to God at this worship centre. If Israel was being disciplined by God for sin (verse 3) and perhaps suffering one of the covenant curses such as famine (see 2 Samuel 21:1; Deuteronomy 28:23–24) prayers would have been offered and there would have been a commitment to offer peace offerings of the thanksgiving or vow type when those prayers had been answered (verse 2; see Leviticus 7:12–18). This was the one offering where the worshipper could eat part of the animal sacrifice and share it with family and friends. Hannah, Samuel's mother, made a vow concerning her son and when her prayer was answered she offered sacrifice (1 Samuel 1:11,24–28). Vows are often mentioned in this section of the Psalter and especially in the context of thanksgiving and praise (Psalms 50:14; 56:12; 61:5,8; 66:13).

From what is said later in this psalm (verses 9–13; see Psalm 67:5–6), it would seem that prayer had been offered in a time of famine for rain and good harvests and it had been heard and answered in a remarkable fashion. Unlike Baal, the god of fertility, before whom Jezebel's prophets mutilated themselves and called out for him to send rain in the days of Elijah, the true God does 'hear prayer' in a way that all can see. This is an encouragement not only to every person in Israel but the whole of humanity ('all flesh'; see Psalm 56:4) to make the living God the goal of their prayers (literally 'all flesh shall come right up to/as far as you'). This universal note is sounded again in verse 5 and takes up the theme of Psalm 2 (see also Psalm 47). It also formed part of Solomon's prayer at the dedication of the temple (1 Kings 8:41–43). Both John the Baptist and Peter draw attention to the universal scope of the gospel using similar phraseology from Isaiah and Joel (Luke 3:6; Acts 2:17) and it is Isaiah who ends his prophecy with 'all flesh' coming to worship the Lord and to look at the fate of the wicked (Isaiah 66:23–24).

Sin is ever with us and we need forgiveness on a daily basis, but David may have in mind a particular situation where the nation has incurred guilt such as is described in 2 Samuel 21:1. Like Isaiah and Daniel he identifies with his people in their rebellious acts (Isaiah 6:5; Daniel 9:5,11). Such wilful cases of wrongdoing ('Iniquities' verse 3; literally 'words of iniquities') have become much too strong ('prevail') for him, just as the waters 'prevailed on the earth' during the Flood (Genesis 7:24). They are more than he can endure (see Psalms 40:12; 130:3). Only God can adequately deal with sin and its consequences— 'you will provide atonement for them' (verse 3; see Psalm 79:9). The word for 'atonement' (some translate 'forgive') means to 'cover' or 'wipe clean' and is often found in the Law of Moses for the blood rituals ordained by God to atone for sin. Sin makes us unclean and unwholesome but God has provided for the removal of sin's pollution and guilt in the gift his of Son, Jesus Christ. It is significant in this psalm that it is not a priest who makes the atonement as occurs in the laws of Leviticus but God himself (literally, 'you yourself will cover/ purge them') in order that the divine curse might be removed. In commenting on 2 Samuel 21:1–14 Dale Ralph Davis states, 'Atonement is never nice but always gruesome ... Christians must beware of becoming too refined ... atonement is a drippy, bloody, smelly business. The stench of death hangs heavy wherever the wrath of God has been quenched.'[136]

What a privileged and happy position to be in ('Blessed' verse 4; see Psalms 1:1; 32:1)—chosen by God and brought near to God to live in his courts and to be satisfied with his provisions! But only the upright, those with clean hands and a pure heart can live in God's tabernacle and stand in his holy place (Psalms 15 and 24). It is therefore only by God's grace that this privilege is ours. God chose David to be king and brought him near to appear before God in the house of God (Psalms 42:2–4; 63:2). He was God's appointed leader and representative but he also represented the people. The covenant community either with him or represented by him (note the change from the singular 'he may dwell' to 'we shall be') is 'satisfied' with the goodness of God's house, his holy palace (or 'temple'; see Psalm 5:7; 1 Samuel 3:3). It is like being asked to live with royalty and share in the banquets (see Psalms 22:25–26; 23:5–6; 36:8; 63:5). The 'goodness' for Israel would have included the knowledge of forgiveness together with the enjoyment of the fruits of the promised land and the assurance that God's curse had been removed (see verse 11).

It is in Christ Jesus, the specially chosen one who came near with his own precious blood, that true believers are chosen and brought near and given access to the Father to live and dine at his table. They are blessed with every spiritual blessing in the heavenly places in Christ (Ephesians 1:3) and as Isaac Watts poetically puts it, 'The hill of Zion yields a thousand sacred sweets, before we reach the heavenly fields ...'[137] God satisfies our mouths 'with good things' (Psalm 103:5).

The saviour God (verses 5–8)
Answers to prayer are not always to our liking as Habakkuk found. Terrible or 'awesome' things (verse 5) happen but these demonstrations of God's power are never arbitrary for in them he displays his righteous character in putting things right. It is in times of crisis that God's activity creates awe and dread in people. Christ's disciples 'feared exceedingly' when Jesus commanded the wind-storm to cease (Mark 4:41). The events surrounding the exodus from Egypt and settlement in Canaan are described as God's 'great and awesome deeds' (Deuteronomy 10:21; 2 Samuel 7:23). Perhaps a terrifying thunderstorm to end the drought and famine or to scatter Israel's foes is particularly in David's mind (see 1 Samuel 7:10; 1 Kings 18:45).

In these 'awesome deeds' David refers to God, using one of his favourite expressions, as 'God of our salvation' (verse 5; see 1 Chronicles 16:35; Psalms 79:9; 85:4). The God of Israel's 'salvation' (see also Exodus 15:2) is not a local deity but, as anticipated in verse 2 ('all flesh'), 'the confidence' of people the world over ('all the ends of the earth ...'; see Psalms 48:10; 59:13; 67:7). The God who brings terror to his foes also inspires trust. This is why God specially chose Abraham and the nation of Israel in the first place that they might be a light to the nations and that all the families of the earth might be blessed (Genesis 12:3; Exodus 19:5–6; Isaiah 49:6). As part of that aim, God acted on behalf of Israel and gave them the law in order to cause other nations to sit up and admire Israel and respect her God (Exodus 9:16; Deuteronomy 4:6–8).

David then waxes lyrical in this hymn-like piece in verses 6 and 7. It has the effect of further encouraging the peoples of the world to have confidence in God. God's power is over the whole creation, so that the mountains he formed 'by his strength' remain secure by his power. The imagery is that of a warrior 'clothed with power' (or better 'armed with might', verse 6). God is also the one who stills the turbulent noisy seas and their waves just as he did at the time of the Flood (Genesis 7:24–8:3; Psalm 29:3). The 'tumult of the peoples' (verse 7) is often associated with the roar of the waves (see Psalm 46:3,6) and God calms them too. The God who has specially revealed himself to Israel and acted so powerfully in their history is good news for the peoples of the world for he has everything under control (see Psalm 46:10).

To complete this section David turns to speak of those in the 'farthest parts' (verse 8; the same word as 'ends' in verse 5). The 'signs' that exhibit his presence and power and provoke fear are those awesome wonders associated with the exodus from Egypt (Exodus 7:3; 15:14–16; Psalms 78:43; 135:9). Rahab informed Joshua's spies that the people of Jericho were terrified of Israel on account of the tales they had heard about the exodus and the defeat of the Amorite kings on the east bank of the Jordan. What is more she confessed that the LORD God of Israel 'is God in heaven above and on earth beneath' (Joshua 2:9–11). The Philistines had also heard of Israel's God who had 'struck the Egyptians with all the plagues' and they were fearful (1 Samuel 4:6–8). That fear of God can either lead people stubbornly to resist God as was generally the case with the Canaanites and Philistines or to respond in faith like Rahab. East and West, from where the sun rises to where it sets ('the outgoings of the morning and evening' verse 8; see Job 38:19) are brought to respond with joyful shouts.

We see the unseen yet powerful activity of God in the rise and fall of world empires and ruthless tyrants, and we are assured that, as a result of Jesus' death—the most awesome exodus of all God's activities—people of all nationalities are being drawn to Christ and the kingdoms of this world will 'become the kingdoms of our Lord and of his Christ' (Luke 9:31; 22:53; John 12:31-32; Revelation 11:15).

The generosity of God (verses 9-13)

This final section contains some superb poetry and expands on the earlier reference to 'goodness' with which David is satisfied (verse 4; see verse 11). The God who is over the nations to protect his people is also the God who is over creation to provide for their needs. Now that all is well between God and his people, prayer for the land has been heard (2 Samuel 21:14) and, using vivid imagery, a bumper harvest is described.

Rain is one of the most important ingredients to a good harvest and our attention is drawn to it in verses 9-10. The God who controls the roaring seas and waves, is also the God who provides a 'river' (verse 9) or 'channel' that is full of water from the rains. This is the kind of river that gladdens the city of God (see Psalm 46:4; Isaiah 33:21). Unlike Egypt where the Nile overflowed for irrigation, Canaan was 'a land of hills and valleys, which drinks water from the rain of heaven, a land for which the Lord your God cares ... from the beginning of the year to the very end of the year' (Deuteronomy 11:11-12). The rains in the autumn and winter ('the early rain and latter rain' Deuteronomy 11:14; James 5:7) marked out the rainy season (October to May) and were among the important blessings attached to God's covenant with Israel (Leviticus 26:4). The early rains softened the hard soil for ploughing and the later showery downpours kept the soil moist and the crops healthy. People in countries like Britain, where rain is generally plentiful and sometimes the ground is so saturated that vegetables have been known to rot, find it more difficult to appreciate the blessing of rain.

The concluding verses describe the bountiful harvest as God's crowning achievement on a year that has witnessed his goodness and providential care (literally it reads: 'You crown the year of your goodness', verse 11a). God is graphically portrayed in the second half of verse 11 as a farmer with an overflowing cartload of rich grain (literally 'fatness') that drops down onto the tracks ('paths'). The 'pastures of the wilderness' (verse 12) are also renewed with abundant and lush grass and flowers after the rains. Hills, valleys and pastureland are alive and clothed, shouting and singing in joyful praise. They encourage God's people in particular to join in the celebration.

The universal emphasis in the psalm reminds us of God's promise to Noah and all creation: 'While the earth remains, seedtime and harvest, and cold and heat, and winter and summer, and day and night shall not cease' (Genesis 8:22). Paul and Barnabas informed the pagans of Lystra of God's goodness in giving 'rain from heaven and fruitful seasons, filling our hearts with food and gladness' as they urged them to turn from their idols to the living God, the creator of heaven and earth (Acts 14:15–18). How do we show our gratitude to God for all his kind gifts to us? It is one of the marks of humanity's ungodliness and unrighteousness that they do not honour God or thank him but worship and serve created things rather than the creator who is blessed for ever (Romans 1:18–25). But to all who put their trust in the world's saviour, Jesus Christ, there is forgiveness and acceptance into God's presence so that we can rejoice in God through Jesus Christ our Lord.

Psalm 66

Universal Praise for God's Awesome Works

The Westminster Shorter Catechism's memorable answer to the first question concerning humanity's chief purpose is 'Man's chief end is to glorify God and to enjoy him for ever'. Psalm 66 certainly encourages this direction for our lives. The personal element is strong but not at the cost of forgetting the covenant community and the wider world. Biblical religion is concerned about the individual's relationship with God but it is never individualistic.

The 'Psalm' is the second of a group of four 'Songs' (Psalms 65-68) given 'To the Chief Musician' for communal worship at the central sanctuary. It is well placed for it takes up some of the themes and wording of the previous psalm and prepares us for the one following. Some of the important themes it shares with Psalm 65 include praise, prayer heard by God, fulfilling vows and the universal note. Though Psalms 66 and 67 are not attributed to David (Psalm 50 was the last example), by placing them here the final editors wished us to consider them in the context of David's kingship. As for this psalm it could well have been written by David on his return to Jerusalem after the defeat of Absalom.

The psalm divides into two main parts where corporate praise (verses

1–12) gives way to individual thanksgiving (verses 13–20). This has led some to believe that fragments of two psalms have been brought together (see Psalm 108). But it is not unusual for a psalm to move from the singular to the plural and vice versa with the king speaking in the singular as the representative head of his people (see Psalm 65:3–4). The unity of the psalm is maintained by the similarity of language between the two parts (compare verses 5 and 8 with verses 16 and 20). The use of the 'Selah' makes further subdivisions.

Universal Call to Praise God (verses 1–12)

First there is an initial summons to praise, followed by a call to consider God's works and ending with a further summons to praise in the light of what God has done. It begins by addressing people (verses 1–9) and moves to addressing God (verses 10–12).

Calling all to worship (verses 1–4)

The call goes out to everyone on the planet ('all the earth') to give a triumphant 'shout' (verse 1) to God (see Psalm 47:1). This is the same opening as Psalm 100 except that there the personal name for God is used. In addition, the call is to sing with instrumental accompaniment ('sing out', verse 2; see Psalm 33:2) the 'glory' ('honour') of God's 'name'. God is stunningly splendid and therefore praising God must likewise be stunningly splendid—'make his praise glorious' (verse 2; see Isaiah 42:12). We are instructed how to do this by drawing attention to his 'awesome deeds' (verse 3; see Psalm 65:5). Those 'works' are described more fully in the next section.

As a result of the greatness of God's strength the enemies that oppose God and his people are brought to 'submit' or 'cringe' before him (verse 3). While the enemies are forced to submit, the psalmist looks prophetically to the day when 'All the earth' will bow down in heartfelt 'worship' and make music ('sing praises'; see verse 2) to God's 'name' as they have been urged to do in verse 2. The references to 'all the earth' (verses 1 and 4) also recall the exodus theme. It is repeatedly emphasised in the Book of Exodus that Israel's liberation from Egypt was not for their benefit only but had worldwide implications. God's sovereignty in raising up Pharaoh and showing him his mighty wonders was in order that Pharaoh might know that the 'earth' belongs to the LORD, that he is unique in 'all the earth' and that God's reputation might be declared in 'all the earth' (Exodus 9:14,16,29; see also Exodus 19:5; Joshua 4:24).

The end time thrust of these verses looks to the day pictured in the last book of the Bible where the redeemed from every nation worship God and the Lamb and live in glorious light (Revelation 7:9-10; 21:24-26).

Call to witness (verses 5–7)

The people of the world are given more information to encourage them to worship. They are invited to 'Come and see the works of God' and the 'awesome' nature of his dealings with humanity (verse 5; see Psalms 46:8; 65:5-8). Perhaps as they witnessed some of the rituals associated with the main festivals like Passover and Unleavened Bread, they are urged to see for themselves God's fearful acts towards the Egyptians and Canaanites. Mention is made of the crossing of the Red Sea and of the Jordan river (verse 6; see Exodus 14:16,22,29; Joshua 3:5,13,15-17). After the Red Sea crossing the people rejoiced and sang (Exodus 15:1-18) and the psalmist speaking on behalf of his people associates them with that saving experience—'There we will rejoice in him' (verse 6). It is similar to the farmer reciting the confessional statement about Israel's deliverance from Egypt as if he was actually present among them (Deuteronomy 26:5-11). Each generation saw itself as part of the initial group involved in those historical events.

Similarly, Christians identify themselves with Christ in his death and resurrection: his death is their death, his resurrection their resurrection (Colossians 2:20; 3:1,3)—'I have been crucified with Christ ... I live by faith in the Son of God who loved me and gave himself for me' (Galatians 2:20). We call people through the preaching of the gospel and the proclamation of the Lord's death at the Communion Table to 'come and see' the awesome works of God in gaining the victory over the great enemies of sin and Satan, death and hell, bringing redemption for people of all nations who are united to Christ.

The song that Moses and the people sang ended by celebrating the LORD's everlasting kingship (Exodus 15:18) and it is acknowledged here in the statement that God 'rules by his might for ever' (verse 7; see Psalm 22:27-28; Revelation 11:15). That rule involves keeping an eye on the nations (see Psalm 59:5). The final words are a prayer calling on God not to allow the enemies to set themselves up in rebellion against him (see Psalm 2).

Calling all to worship (verses 8–12)

A fresh call, similar to the opening lines of the psalm, summons the 'peoples' of the world (verse 8) to 'bless our God', that is, to give the God of Israel who is the one true and living God, the honour due to him and to sound out his praises. The following verses spell out the reasons why other nations and tribes should join in praising God. Not only has God rescued his people and brought them to Canaan but he has kept them alive in the land or restored them from death-like situations (see Psalm 30:3) and not allowed them to 'slip' ('be moved', verse 9; see Psalm 121:3). In the course of God's care for his people these unpleasant experiences have happened in order to 'test' ('proved') them especially in the sense of being 'refined' like precious metals such as gold and 'silver' are refined by fire (verse 10; see Psalm 26:2). Afflictions are a means by which individuals or the community are purified. God says to Israel, 'I have refined you, but not as silver; I have tested you in the furnace of affliction' (Isaiah 48:10). The genuineness of the Christian's faith is tested through various trials (1 Peter 1:7; James 1:2–3).

The sufferings that God's people have endured are described through a series of graphic images. First, God is likened to a hunter whose 'net' envelops the prey and presses down upon the animal's body (verse 11). Then, God has allowed 'men to ride over our heads' (verse 12a). This may be taken more literally to indicate that God's people have been defeated by 'frail mortals' ('men'; see Psalm 8:4) on occasions. The final picture is of passing 'through fire and through water' (verse 12b; see Isaiah 43:2), symbolic of extreme danger as when an enemy sets a city on fire or when caught by flash floods. Through all these experiences God has brought them out of such trials 'to rich fulfilment' (or 'abundance', verse 12c, translated 'runs over' or 'overflows' in Psalm 23:5).

God's actions through all these difficulties have been like a continual exodus from Egyptian-type afflictions to the blessings of that abundance associated with Canaan. God disciplined Israel and kept them a separated nation to fulfil the promises that he had made to Abraham that through this nation all families of the earth might be blessed. Israel's Messiah who is the Saviour of the world emerges from this background and the people groups of the world are encouraged to acknowledge this and praise God. Jesus said to the Samaritan woman that 'salvation is of the Jews' (John 4:22). Our Saviour himself experienced the greatest affliction of all for the sake of others and came through via the resurrection to be the first of that new creation of glory and blessing. Christians, too, must suffer many trials and tribulations before they enter the future glory of God's kingdom (Acts 14:22).

The King's testimony (verses 13-20)

Here the king begins by addressing God (verses 13-15) and closes by addressing the people (16-20). From the more general celebrations of God's saving activity from the time of the exodus to the beginning of the monarchy period, the focus is on a particular occasion where God brought the people through a testing experience. David speaks for the nation possibly after his return to Jerusalem following Absalom's defeat and death.

Promises fulfilled (verses 13-15)

The king represents the nation as he goes to the tabernacle in Jerusalem with 'burnt offerings' (verse 13). These offerings are in fulfilment of promises ('vows'; see Psalm 22:25) that he had 'blurted out' ('uttered') in his extreme distress ('in trouble', verses 13-14; see Psalm 18:6). The Law of Moses did allow burnt offerings to be made in fulfilment of vows as well as thank offerings of the peace offering variety (see Leviticus 22:18-21). The content of the offerings is spelled out in verse 15. As well as offering 'fat animals' (which are probably the fattened calves) and 'rams', 'bulls with goats' were also added. In the burnt offerings the whole animal, apart from the skin, was burnt on the altar, the smoke ascending as a 'sweet aroma' that appeased God's wrath (see Leviticus 1:3-17; Genesis 8:20-21). These are not the offerings of a private individual. The sacrifices are costly ones, ones that only someone like a king was capable of bringing on behalf of the nation. They are completely burnt up in place of the one who offered them to indicate that the whole of the person's life or of the nation belongs to God. Such blood sacrifices have no place under the new covenant for they are fulfilled in Christ's work on the cross, which was 'an offering and a sacrifice to God for a sweet-smelling aroma' (Ephesians 5:2). The Christian is identified with Christ in that once for all offering and is therefore urged to live as a whole burnt offering for God, dead to this world and its lifestyles (Romans 12:1-2; Galatians 6:14).

Call to witness (verses 16–20)

The final section begins with a similar invitation to the one in verse 5 only this time the call is to 'hear' rather than 'see' and it is made not to the world at large but to the people of God ('who fear God', verse 16; see Psalm 22:23). What they are to hear is the personal testimony of the one offering sacrifice. The following three verses give the substance of the declaration where he states that God had borne witness that he was no hypocrite by hearing his appeals for help and giving attention to his prayer by answering it (verses 18–19). Christ 'offered up prayers and supplications, with vehement cries and tears to him who was able to save him from death, and was heard because of his godly fear' (Hebrews 5:7). He was heard when God raised him from death and exalted him to sit at the right hand of the Majesty on high.

Calvin makes the point that to 'cherish' or 'regard iniquity' (verse 18) 'does not mean to be conscious of sin—for all the Lord's people must see their sins and be grieved for them, and this is rather praiseworthy than condemnable;—but to be bent on the practice of iniquity'. The Lord does not hear the prayer of the wicked, who outwardly may be very religious but whose hearts harbour a rebellious attitude (see Proverbs 15:29; Isaiah 1:15; 59:2; John 9:31; 1 John 3:22).

Whereas the speech of the wicked is characterised by trouble and iniquity ('under his tongue is trouble and iniquity'; Psalm 10:7), the psalmist's speech, in calling out to God, was characterised by extolling God (literally 'exaltation was under my tongue'; verse 17). Directing prayer to the creator God like confessing sin to him is all part of what it means to praise and glorify God (see Joshua 7:19).

The psalm closes appropriately by declaring God to be 'blessed' (verse 20) for not rejecting his prayer or withholding his unfailing love. In the pithy words of Matthew Henry, 'What we win by prayer we must wear with praise.' The concluding note concerning God's 'mercy' or 'steadfast love' is a reminder that 'it is entirely of his free grace that he is propitious, and that our prayers are not wholly ineffectual' (Calvin).

Psalm 67

Blessed to be a Blessing

Is this a psalm for harvest time or for missionary meetings? Both ideas are present but the second is predominant. Jesus used the harvest illustration when challenging his disciples after speaking to the woman of Samaria. He indicated that the fields were already white for harvest and [he] saw his disciples as sent to gather in the fruit. Many of the Samaritans believed in Jesus and confessed that he was 'the Saviour of the world' (John 4:35-42). It is this universal note that is sounded in this lovely and well-loved psalm.

Like Psalms 65, 66 and 68 this is 'A Psalm', 'A Song' and 'To the Chief Musician' but with the added note describing the musical accompaniment, 'On stringed instruments' (see Psalms 4, 6, 54, 55, 61). Like the previous psalm the heading does not refer to David but it may come from the time he was king, as the surrounding psalms suggest, but there is nothing in the text to suggest any particular historical context.

More importantly, this psalm belongs where it does on account of its strong universal emphasis, a theme that has characterised the two previous 'songs' (Psalms 65–66) and continues in Psalm 68.

It would seem the psalmist had the special priestly benediction (Numbers 6:24-26) in mind with its prayer-wish that God would bless the individual Israelite or the nation of Israel as a whole. But the significant thing about this psalm is the way that the blessing is coupled with God's great promise to Abraham that he would not only bless him and his descendants but that 'all the nations of the earth' would be blessed through them as a result (Genesis 12:1–3; 22:18).

The psalm divides into three parts separated by the refrain (verses 3 and 5) with the first (verses 1–2) and third (verses 6–7) acting like book ends to draw attention to the central part (verse 4). In this instance the 'Selah' term (verses 1 and 4) is used for other purposes than literary structure.

Large petitions (verses 1-2)

Firstly, for God's people

The prayer seeks God's blessing on Israel and it clearly echoes Aaron's blessing. As Jesus taught his disciples saying, 'In this manner, therefore, pray ...' (Matthew 6:9) so the Lord taught Aaron and his sons, saying, 'This is the way you shall bless the children of Israel' (Numbers 6:23). The pattern blessing is not followed slavishly by the psalmist and it is interesting that in place of God's covenant name ('Lord', Yahweh/Jehovah), the more general term is used ('God', *Elohim*) as is common in so many of the psalms in this part of the Psalter (Psalms 42–83). In addition, rather than a prayer for others ('you'), the psalmist includes himself with his people ('us'). Three items from the blessing are picked up by the psalmist:

1. 'be merciful' or better 'be gracious' (see Psalm 51:1)—While not the first point in the original blessing this is foundational to every other blessing. We have no claim on God. Whatever God gives us is totally unmerited and so the psalmist begins by humbly acknowledging their need for God to look favourably upon them. God declares it to be one of his fundamental characteristics: 'I am gracious' (Exodus 22:27), and exercises it in a sovereign way: 'I will be gracious to whom I will be gracious' (Exodus 33:19). All Paul's letters begin and end by calling attention to the grace that comes from God the Father and our Lord Jesus Christ (Romans 1:7; 16:20; 1 Corinthians 1:3; 16:23; etc.)

2. 'and bless us' (see Psalm 5:12)—In the Old Testament context, blessing particularly meant fruitfulness in terms of descendants, animals and harvests (Genesis 17:16; Deuteronomy 28:2–13), but these physical benefits were only signs of the more fundamental blessing of fellowship with God—'I will walk among you and be your God, and

you shall be my people' (Leviticus 26:12)—which is the essence of God's covenant relationship with his people. The Church of the Lord Jesus Christ made up of those who look to Jesus alone for salvation is the temple of the living God and the words of Leviticus 26:12 are repeated to encourage believers to live clean and holy lives (2 Corinthians 6:16-7:1; Revelation 21:7). Jesus taught that those who belong to him and remain in him will be fruitful and produce fruit that will last (John 15:5,8,16; see also John 12:20-26). In the new creation there is no more curse (Revelation 22:1-5).

3. 'cause his face to shine upon us' (see Psalm 4:6)—God's 'face' means his presence and the shining face is suggestive of God's favour in bringing benefits, especially in acting to rescue and assist his people (Psalms 31:16; 80:3,7,19). We read, 'In the light of the king's face is life, and his favour is like a cloud of the latter rain' (Proverbs 16:15). When God hides his face it indicates his disfavour or his withdrawal of support (Psalms 30:7; 34:16; 44:24). God's presence (literally 'face') means 'fulness of joy' (Psalm 16:11). This glorious presence bringing salvation is seen in the face of Jesus Christ who is full of grace and truth (2 Corinthians 4:6; John 1:14).

Before continuing, the unexpected 'Selah', far from breaking up the prayer at a crucial point, encourages us to prepare for the momentous direction that it is about to take.

Secondly, for the world

The priestly benediction in the Law of Moses did not go on to indicate a purpose for blessing Israel although God's special dealings with Israel are set against the repeated emphasis in Genesis of God's plans for the whole world. God chose Abraham and his descendants through Jacob to be a light to the nations so that they too might find blessing (Genesis 12:1-3; 28:14; Exodus 19:5-6). The psalmist has taken this to heart and requests on behalf of his people that they might be blessed with divine favour so that the whole world might acknowledge God's dealings ('your way') as revealed in the Scriptures (2 Timothy 3:15). He prays that they will come to appreciate God's purposes and particularly his 'salvation'. Just as material benefits are signs of a special relationship with God so God's acts of deliverance from Israel's enemies point to deeper, more fundamental enemies from which the nations of the world need to be rescued through God's intervention.

Some scholars have suggested, in the light of the harvest theme, that the 'salvation' has more to do with overcoming the forces of nature and maintaining life. If there is a veiled reference to the Flood and its aftermath it can only be to God's covenant with Noah and all creation not to flood the whole world like that again. This commitment must be seen in the context of God's promises to Adam and Eve concerning a special descendant who would be victorious over the snake (Genesis 3:15).

It is the prophet Isaiah who helps to fill out the Old Testament expectation of salvation for the world. The God of Israel is the only saviour of the world and it is through the Lord's Suffering Servant that his salvation will come 'to the ends of the earth' (Isaiah 45:21–25; 49:6; 52:10). Jesus taught his disciples that 'repentance and remission of sins should be preached in his name to all nations, beginning at Jerusalem (Luke 24:47). At the end of his second volume Luke, having shown how Paul reached the capital of the world empire, emphasises the ongoing Gentile mission by quoting Paul's words to the Jews that 'the salvation of God has been sent to the Gentiles' (Acts 28:28).

Joy to the world (verses 3–5)

The refrain or chorus (verses 3 and 5) introduces the central point of the psalm (verse 4) and rounds it off. In Psalm 47, which has a similar universal emphasis, the call was to 'sing psalms' whereas here in the form of a direct prayer, 'all' the 'peoples' of the world are urged to acknowledge God, to give him 'thanks' ('praise'; see Psalm 57:9) for his saving blessings.

Further calls for 'the nations' (or more precisely 'the tribal communities') to 'be glad' and to shout 'for joy' introduce the reason why they should be so happy. God rules with judicial fairness ('righteously'; see Psalm 45:6) and 'leads' ('govern') like a good eastern shepherd (see Psalm 23:3). There is day coming when the kingdoms of this world 'become the kingdoms of our Lord and of his Christ and he shall reign for ever and ever' (Revelation 11:15). That time is associated with the new heavens and a new earth where 'the home of righteousness' will be found (2 Peter 3:13). This is the thrust of the whole Bible. Isaiah again makes it very clear that it is the Messiah of David's line who is also Israel's representative Suffering Servant who will establish justice in the earth (Isaiah 9:6–7; 11:4–5; 42:4).

The 'Selah' (verse 4) again appears after mentioning the good news of God's righteous rule, encouraging the refrain (verse 5) to be seen as more than a repeat performance. There is every reason why the peoples of the world should offer grateful thanks to God.

Universal blessing (verses 6–7)

The theme of the opening lines returns with the prayer—'may the earth yield her increase ...', or statement of confidence—'the earth shall yield her increase', so that having been blessed in this way 'all the ends of the earth shall fear him' (verse 7; see Psalms 65:5; 34:7,9). There is no 'then' in the original and the form of the verb 'yield' (verse 6) is not future but past which is why some translations have 'the earth (or 'land') has yielded its increase'. It is difficult to be certain but sometimes such forms can denote the certainty of a future event. The line is almost identical with the words of Leviticus 26:4 which reads, 'then the land shall yield its produce'.

Whichever way we translate, there is a confident expectancy in these closing verses. Isaiah 55 helps us to see how the harvest theme is transformed into the missionary vision. God's plan is to bless the human race and to bring forgiveness of sins. This is the word that will prosper. The calling is to all to come and eat without money and to delight in the abundance of good things that the Lord's Servant, the Messiah of David's line, has procured through his atoning death. Nations are seen running to Israel to find this blessing. The chapter ends on a note of joy and peace at the prospect of a new creation where there is no more curse.

John Stott has written, 'We shall want God to bless us in order that blessing may come to others; and we shall want blessing to come to others, that ultimately blessing may come to God. Neither our selfish benefit, nor even the salvation of others, will be our consuming passion, but rather the glory of God himself.'[138]

The principle taught in this psalm has been repeated time and again throughout Church history. When God has blessed his people with a spiritual awakening it has led to renewed missionary interest. This happened at the Protestant Reformation when the gospel was rediscovered and it spread far and wide all over Europe. The Great Awakening of the 18th century resulted in the worldwide expansion of the gospel in the 19th century so that today there are people groups all round the globe revering God and offering praise and thanks to him.

Psalm 68

The Triumphant Procession

By common consent this is not an easy psalm to translate or interpret. Spurgeon sums it up as 'surpassingly excellent and difficult. Its darkness in some stanzas is utterly impenetrable ... Our slender scholarship has utterly failed'. As with some other scriptures Matthew Henry observes that here 'there are things dark and hard to be understood.' But the apostle Paul quotes from this psalm when speaking of Christ's ascension and this encourages us to persevere and gain what we can from this intriguing psalm.

It is the last of a series of four entitled 'Song' and is the grand finale to the universal note that has characterised these 'songs'. The heading attributes the 'Psalm' to 'David' for use by the 'Chief Musician' in the central sanctuary. There are clear indications that David, employing unusual words and expressions, composed this magnificent hymn of triumph when the ark of the covenant was brought from Obed-Edom's house to Jerusalem (see 2 Samuel 6:12-19). It would seem that David used the occasion to present a much bigger picture where the progress of the ark represents God's triumphant journey, at the head of his people, from Sinai to Jerusalem.

This will help us to appreciate the general structure of the psalm which divides into two main parts. In the first half the journey moves from the events associated with the exodus and Sinai (verses 1-10) to the conquest of Canaan (verses 11-14) and finally to the ascent into Jerusalem (verses 15-18). The second half, enveloped by the repetition of 'Blessed' (verses 19 and 35) celebrates God's victory over his foes (verses 19-23), and the procession into the sanctuary (verses 24-27), where prayer is offered that the peoples of the world would submit to God (verses 28-31) and the call goes out to all the kingdoms of the earth to make music to the sovereign Lord (verses 32-35).

From Sinai to Zion (verses 1–18)
The first part of the psalm is about God's triumphant journey with his people from Sinai to Jerusalem.

God's presence (verses 1-3)
The opening verses provide the introduction to the psalm and like the close of the previous psalm (see Psalm 67:6) can either be a prayer-wish—'Let God arise ...' or a declaration—'God shall arise ...' It echoes Moses' prayer when the ark, the symbol of God's presence, set out each morning on the journey through the wilderness, 'Rise up, O LORD! Let your enemies be scattered, and let those who hate you flee before you' (Numbers 10:35; Psalm 3:7). God's 'enemies' are 'the wicked' who 'hate' the true God (see Psalm 21:8; Romans 1:30). They are typical of those described in Psalms 1 and 2 and with whom David has had to contend on many occasions. Before the fire of God's holy presence seemingly invincible foes run away for they are as ephemeral as smoke (see Psalm 37:20) and as vulnerable as wax before a fire (Psalm 22:14). While the ungodly 'wicked perish' (verse 2), the 'righteous', those who are in a right relationship to him, have nothing to fear but can 'be glad' (verse 3) and can 'exult' ('rejoice') and 'rejoice exceedingly' (literally 'be 'joyful with gladness') before the presence of God.

God's praise (verses 4-6)
As in the praise psalms we are urged to sing and lift up our voices and extol the God who revealed himself at the time of the exodus under the name of 'I am' (Exodus 3:13-15). The name 'YAH' (verse 4; see verse 18; Isaiah 12:2)[139] is associated with the verb 'to be' and appears at the end of names like Isaiah and Jeremiah and in the expression 'Hallelujah' ("Praise the LORD'). It is a variation on the longer and more common form 'Yahweh' ('Jehovah'). God is not a 'has been' but the ever present one who provides for his people's needs. While the Canaanites spoke

of Baal as the 'Rider of the Clouds' it is in fact the God of the exodus
who 'rides on the clouds' (see Psalm 18:10-19). But the word used here
for 'clouds' or 'heaven' usually means 'deserts' and so there may be an
allusion to the wilderness wanderings.

There are other reasons to sing praises for although God dwells in
the high and holy place ('his holy habitation', verse 5) represented by
the Jerusalem tabernacle, he is no distant, uninvolved God. Like the
ideal monarch of ancient Near Eastern thought, God provides ('father')
and protects ('defender', literally 'judge') all the vulnerable members
of society (see Psalm 10:14,18). The 'fatherless' and the 'widow' (verse
5) are those without a male family head to care and maintain their
rights. God, as head of his people, also provides a home for the lonely
stranger and brings freedom and enjoyment to the captives. As for
the stubbornly 'rebellious' (verse 6), they are left to the sun-scorched
desert. The whole may be a poetic description of the way God came
to his people to 'bring them out' of their captivity in Egypt to the
homeland he had prepared for them, while the stubbornly disobedient
generation was left to die in the wilderness (see Psalm 78:8).

God's provisions (verses 7–10)

Now David addresses God and directly refers to the exodus and
wilderness journey and on through to the land of Canaan. God is
like a warrior king going out at the head of the army. The language
is reminiscent of Deborah and Barak's victory song (Judges 5:4-5). A
pause ('Selah', verse 7) is appropriate at this point before the awesome
'presence of God' at 'Sinai' is emphasised and it is there that this God
entered into a special arrangement with the newly formed nation so
that he is known as the 'God of Israel' (verse 8; see Psalms 41:13; 59:5).
Sending 'plentiful rain' (verse 9) could be a figurative way of speaking
about the heavenly bread Israel received in the wilderness (Exodus
16:4). On the other hand, it could also refer to the life and fertility (see
Psalm 65:9-13) of God's covenant blessings in God's 'inheritance' or
'possession'. This could be the land of Canaan which he gave on loan
to Israel as an inheritance (Psalm 47:4) or a reference to God's people
themselves (Psalm 28:9; Deuteronomy 32:9). The land and its people
without the blessing of water are 'weary' and exhausted but God has
provided from his 'bounty' ('goodness') for Israel, that 'poor', afflicted
'company' ('Your congregation') that had come out of Egypt (Exodus
3:17).

Isaiah spiritualises the blessing of rain to speak of God 'raining down' righteousness so that salvation might spring up from the earth (Isaiah 45:8) and Psalm 72:6 reveals the Messiah himself as coming down like rain showers that enable the righteous to flourish.

God's victories (verses 11–14)

The conquest of Canaan is graphically portrayed in this section and again there are echoes of the victory song of Deborah and Barak (Judges 5). It is made clear that the divine warrior has already given a message of victory—'The Lord gave the word' (verse 11). Our victorious risen Lord Jesus commissioned his disciples with a similar word of victory (Matthew 28:18-20). As the original shows it is a great 'army' or 'company' of women who 'proclaim the good news' (verse 11; see Psalm 40:9; Isaiah 40:9). Women were involved in announcing the victory at the Red Sea (Exodus 15:20-21) and in celebrating David's successes in battle (1 Samuel 18:6-7). It was women who first passed on the good news concerning Jesus' resurrection (Matthew 28:1-8; Luke 24:10).

The women's 'army' relate how the Canaanite 'armies' headed by their kings are in full retreat—'flee, they flee' (verse 12). At home those women looking after their children and the flocks enter into the victory by dividing the spoils of war and they adorn themselves, like the glistening wings of a dove, with the items of silver and gold (verses 12-13; see Judges 5:16,30). A summary statement indicates how the kings in the land were scattered by God 'the Almighty' (*Shaddai*; see Psalm 91:1; Genesis 17:1; Exodus 6:3). The final phrase (literally 'it snows on Zalmon') may be a proverb suggesting perhaps that the rout was as unusual and spectacular as dazzling snow on this dark mountain. 'Zalmon' (linked with a word for 'dark') is a heavily-wooded hill near Shechem (Judges 9:48-49) that is not normally associated with snow.

God's mountain (verses 15–18)

The mention of Zalmon west of the Jordan conjures up in the psalmist's mind this new scene to the east of the Sea of Galilee, to the area of 'Bashan', stretching northward from the Golan Heights to the majestic Hermon mountain range (Psalm 42:6) with 'peaks' of up to 2,814 metres (9,232 feet) which is covered in snow for most of the year. The 'mountain of God' can be taken as a Hebrew idiom for the superlative ('majestic mountain'; see Psalm 36:6) but the present context suggests the literal should be retained.

The pagan Canaanites might have thought that Israel's God would have desired one of these high peaks in the north of the country as the place to live (see Psalm 48:6). Instead, the mountain God has chosen 'to dwell in' is, in comparison to them, the puny hill of Zion, that does not even stand out impressively from the surrounding hills of Judah. Using vivid imagery, the Bashan mountain ranges are pictured as looking on with 'envy' and malice ('watch as an enemy') at the thought of him dwelling on that hillock 'for ever'! But this is the place where the covenant God of Israel, 'the LORD' (Yahweh), has condescended to make his home on earth (see Psalm 132:13–14). He likewise condescends to live with those of a humble and contrite spirit (Isaiah 57:15).

There is a divine principle embodied in the choice of Zion, as in the case of the Lord's choice of David and Bethlehem (1 Samuel 16:11; Micah 5:2; Matthew 2:6). God chooses the foolish, weak, base and despised things of the world to shame the wise and mighty, that 'no flesh should glory in his presence' (1 Corinthians 1:27–29).

The mountain might not seem impressive but God's forces certainly are, like a sea of formidable iron chariots used in warfare (Judges 1:19; 4:13; 1 Samuel 13:5; 2 Samuel 10:18), and this sovereign Lord 'is among them' both to protect (see 2 Kings 6:8–17) and to give victory over his foes (Habakkuk 3:8). It is the God who revealed himself to his people at Mount Sinai who is now present with them in the holy place on Mount Zion (verse 17).

But there is a further truth. The God whose special presence (Exodus 33:12–23) brought his people safely through from Sinai to Zion has now completed his work and as an indication that it is a finished work he returns victoriously to his heavenly home 'on high' (verse 18; see Psalms 7:7; 47:5; Hebrews 1:3). David saw this truth symbolically portrayed under the symbol of the ark as it ascended as in a victory parade to its place of rest in the tabernacle at Zion. The outright victory is conveyed by the picture of taking captive those who had previously captured his people and of tribute being offered to him by former rebels (see 2 Samuel 8:11). The last part of verse 18 is difficult but it may mean that the former rebellious ones come to dwell with 'the LORD God' (literally 'to dwell YAH God'; see verse 4) who also dwells among his people as mentioned in verse 16 (Exodus 29:45–46).

The verses are quoted by Paul in Ephesians 4:8–9. They indicate that God's activity in Israel's history is to be seen as symbolic of Messiah's ministry and these words of the psalm point to Christ's finished work and triumphant ascension. The victorious ascent implies that he was in a conflict situation during his descent as he fought against sin, Satan, death and hell. But Paul's main focus in using the text is to show that in ascending Christ has given gifts to his people (see verse 35), a point celebrated in the second half of this psalm.

Celebration (verses 19-35)

The remaining part of the psalm witnesses the excitement of the procession as it makes its way to the sanctuary and encourages everyone to acknowledge and sing praises to God (verses 19,26,35).

God's salvation (verses 19-23)

Thankful worship is called for—'Blessed be the Lord' (see Psalm 28:6) for he is the 'salvation' of his people (verses 19-20). The accompanying phrases give indications of what this salvation involves and the brevity of the expressions perhaps are meant to convey a variety of ideas.

First, it literally reads 'he loads for us' suggesting either that God 'loads us *with benefits*' (verse 19) or 'carries our burdens' or 'bears us up'. Isaiah speaks of God carrying his people from the beginning of their existence (Isaiah 46:3-4; 63:9) and this fits the present context concerning God's care of his people from Egypt to Canaan. Like an eagle with its young or like a man with his son God has carried Israel (Exodus 19:4; Deuteronomy 32:11; 1:31; see Psalm 28:9). What he did for Israel in its redemptive history he continues doing 'daily' into the future.

Second, the original says 'for the death outgoings or exits' (verse 20) which probably refers to Israel going out or escaping in view of the death in Egypt. The plural 'escapes' suggests that God continually delivers his people from death. It may also be showing that Israel's 'GOD' (Yahweh/Jehovah; verse 20), the sovereign 'Lord', who it is emphasised is the saving 'God' (*El*, repeated three times: 'the God of' ... 'our God' ... 'the God of ...' verses 19-20), is victorious over the Canaanite god of death. The 'Selah' (verse 19) makes sure that we do not rush over these references to God. Our Lord has the keys of Hades and death for he lived and died and is alive for evermore (Revelation 1:18).

The following verses give encouragement to God's people that all God's enemies will be destroyed and no one will escape (see Amos 9:2-3) even if they have fled to the heights of Bashan in the east or to 'the depths' of the Mediterranean 'sea' in the west (verse 22). To 'wound the head of his enemies' (verse 21; Habakkuk 3:13) reminds us of the royal figure who will bruise the head of the snake (Genesis 3:15) and the 'hairy scalp' of the demonic appearance of the long, wild hair of the foe (see Psalm 74:13–14) who continues in its stubborn rebellion ('trespass'). Very lurid language is used, typical of the aftermath of a bloody war, to convey the completeness of the defeat and to indicate that it is God's just retribution on the wicked (1 Kings 21:19; Psalm 58:10). It is similar to the depiction of the final punishment of the ungodly in John's vision (Revelation 14:20; 19:15). Rebellion against the holy God is extremely offensive and deserves the worst of punishments. There is a day of judgment and the gruesome pictures given concerning the doom that awaits the devil and all who belong to him are meant to shock and cause us to flee from the wrath to come into the arms of the one who himself experienced that doom for all who submit to him (Psalm 2:12).

God's procession (verses 24–27)

The scene changes and we are back to the victory parade with the defeated enemies watching God's 'procession' ('goings') as the ark, the symbol of God's presence, was brought into Jerusalem to the sacred tent that David had erected for it (verse 24; see 1 Chronicles 15:1–29). Besides the priests and Levites 'all Israel' were in attendance (1 Chronicles 15:3,28) and this is conveyed by mentioning four of the twelve tribes, two each from the south and north of Canaan. Little Benjamin, the tribe that gained an important position out of all proportion to its size, is in the lead (1 Samuel 9:21). From it came Saul, Israel's first king, and Jerusalem the capital was located there. Judah with its bustling throng ('company') was the dominant southern tribe from which David originated. Interestingly, the dominant tribes of the north, Ephraim and Manasseh, are not mentioned. Instead, Zebulun and Naphtali, two of the most northerly tribes represent the north (verse 27). These are the two in the Galilee region that were the first to fall to Assyria and yet it is prophesied that this despised area associated with the Gentiles will be the first to experience the light of the Messiah (Isaiah 9:1–2; Matthew 4:14–16). The Levites would have led the singing with the music accompaniment but it was not confined to them (1 Chronicles 15:16–24, 28). The girls with tambourines are mentioned to represent all those involved (verse 25; see Exodus 15:20; 1 Samuel 18:6).

David speaks very personally referring to God's procession as the 'goings' of 'my God' and 'my King'. The ark, sometimes called the 'footstool' of the heavenly monarch's throne, represented God's rule among his people. King David is not to be the central focus of the kingdom but the Lord. He therefore calls the various companies or 'congregations' in the procession, all who are the true offspring ('fountain') of Israel (verse 26; Deuteronomy 33:28; Isaiah 48:1), to 'bless God', the sovereign 'LORD'.[140] Jesus Christ fulfils all that the ark signifies. In Christ all the fulness of God dwells bodily (Colossians 2:9). Having overcome the enemy he reigns supreme and by his Spirit he lives among his people. He must be central to our worship and life and with Thomas we cry, 'My Lord and my God' (John 20:28).

God's strength (verses 28–31)

The psalm turns to prayer, urging God to show his 'power' or 'strength' again as he has done in Israel's history (verse 28; see Exodus 15:13), a cry similar to Isaiah's later call that God would put on strength and act as in older times (Isaiah 51:9-11). David then with prophetic insight sees that prayer answered with kings bringing their tribute as a consequence of God's victorious ascent to the heavenly sanctuary, symbolised by the ark's settlement in its earthly replica, the 'palace' (or 'temple'; see Psalms 5:7; 65:4) at Jerusalem (see Isaiah 18:7; Revelation 21:24).

What David is assured will happen, he prays for in his request that God will deal with the powerful foes that are depicted as animals (see Psalms 22:12-13, 16, 20-21). The 'beasts of the reeds' (verse 30) may symbolise Egypt which is later mentioned along with distant Ethiopia (or Cush) as also bringing tribute as a sign of submission (verse 31; see Isaiah 19:21-25; 45:14; Zephaniah 3:10; Zechariah 2:10-13).

God's praise (verses 32–35)

The call goes out again to sing and make music to God, only this time it is universal in view of what has just been prayed, a point worthy of a pause ('Selah', verse 4). All the 'kingdoms of the earth' (see Psalm 46:6) are to worship the one who is not some local god confined to an earthly sanctuary (see Revelation 15:3-4). He is the God whose rule extends to the ancient highest heaven (verse 33; see Deuteronomy 10:14) and it is from there 'his voice' has thundered loudly (see Exodus 20:18-19; 1 Samuel 7:10; John 12:28-30). God's power or 'strength' is to be acknowledged (see Psalm 29:1–2) because not only is 'his strength' revealed in the clouds where his voice sounds out but 'his excellence' or 'dignity' (see Deuteronomy 33:26)—a word often translated 'pride' of those who abuse the righteous (Psalms 10:2; 31:18)—is over Israel. David echoes Moses' song of the one who 'rides the heavens to help' them and 'in his excellency on the clouds. The eternal God is *your* refuge and underneath are the everlasting arms' (Deuteronomy 33:26–27).

David ends by adoring the 'God of Israel'—'O God, you are fearful' (verse 35; see Exodus 15:11; Psalm 47:2). The 'holy places' may indicate God's heavenly and earthly homes and it is from both (literally 'from your sanctuaries') that this powerful God gives strength and power to his people (see Isaiah 40:29–31). 'Blessed be God!' and 'Blessed be the God and Father of our Lord Jesus Christ!' who comforts us and keeps us by his power (2 Corinthians 1:3–4; 1 Peter 1:3–5).

Psalm 69

The King's Sufferings and Joy

This is one of the three most frequently quoted psalms in the New Testament, the others being Psalms 22 and 110. Besides the direct quotations (see John 2:17; 15:25; Acts 1:16,20; Romans 11:9–10; 15:3) there are striking parallels between David's situation and that experienced by our Lord (compare Psalm 69:12,21 with Matthew 27:29,34,48; John 19:28–29). In addition, echoes from the psalm of God's wrath being poured out (verse 24) and of names being blotted out of the book of life (verse 28) are found in Revelation 16:1 and 21:27.

As the Second Book draws to a close we may wonder why the three following psalms (Psalms 69–71) return to the theme of suffering that characterised earlier psalms in the collection. There has been a rising crescendo of universal praise to the God of Israel in the immediately preceding psalms (Psalms 65–68) and Psalm 72 will bring the collection to a close with all nations acknowledging the king of David's line. Why spoil this thread by introducing once more pleas for deliverance from the enemy's cruel threats? It is a reminder to us that the end is not yet (Mark. 13:7-13). The Messiah suffers for his people (1 Corinthians 15:3) and with his people (Acts 9:5). Like the pain a woman in labour suffers while giving birth, so the glory of Messiah's kingdom comes through trials and tribulation.

Besides the familiar heading 'To the Chief Musician' this psalm 'of

David' (see Acts 1:16,20; Romans 11:9), like Psalm 45, was 'Set to "The Lilies"'. As Calvin observed there are close resemblances between this psalm and Psalm 22. It also bears a number of resemblances to Psalm 40 which is interesting in view of the fact that the following psalm (Psalm 70) is almost identical with Psalm 40:13–17. David is a type of Christ but he also speaks for all God's people in their sufferings.

As in Psalm 22 the psalm divides into two uneven sections, with the longer section (verses 1–29) alternating between prayer and lament and the shorter one (verses 30–35) given over to praise and trust. There is a striking correspondence within the first section between verses 1–12 and 13–29 (similar to what we find in Psalm 22:1–11 and 12–21) reinforcing the intensity of the distress and cries for help. Interestingly, it is the call for divine vengeance in verses 22–28 that finds no parallel in the initial twelve verses.

Prayer and lament (verses 1–12)

As Peter, when he began to sink into the boisterous sea, cried out in fear to Jesus 'Lord, save me' (Matthew 14:30) so David, in his extreme distress and danger on account of his 'enemies' (see verse 4), calls out to God, 'Save me' (verse 1; see Psalms 3:7; 6:4; 7:1; etc.). The imagery of being overwhelmed with water has been used before in reference to a strong enemy (Psalm 18:16–17). He also likens himself to someone sinking into mud and water (verse 2), an experience that literally happened to Jeremiah (see Psalm 40:2; Jeremiah 38:6). His intense prayers have gone unanswered so that he is worn out. This weariness is evidenced by his throat parched because of his continual cries to God and by eyes that have become dim through looking expectantly for his God to act, like a watchman staring out all night for signs of movement and who can look no longer (verse 3).

David then describes his enemies as people too numerous to count, who hate him for no reason (see Psalm 35:19), powerful enough to destroy him by 'wrongfully' charging him (verse 4), as Job found his friends doing. They are compelling him to make restitution having falsely accused him of stealing (see Leviticus 6:4–5). Jesus too informed his disciples that they would be hated as the world hated him and by quoting from this verse about the Jews' hatred of him 'without a cause' (verse 4) Jesus condemned them from their own Scriptures (John 15:25).

While David, like Job, would admit he is not sinless, he makes his claim to innocence over the charges made by his foes, and does so with irony as Calvin believes. If guilty deeds and sin's folly are to be found in him then it is God not his accusers who would be the first to know of it. This is a much more forceful way of countering the accusations of his enemies than by making a plain statement that his integrity is known to God. Similarly, there were many who falsely accused the sinless Jesus of sin but he committed himself to God.

David then brings forward further reasons why God should intervene. His plea is fervent as he addresses God as the sovereign 'Lord', the covenant 'GOD' (Yahweh), the divine Warrior ('of hosts') and 'God of Israel'. He shows how these false accusations have wider implications. As king he represents all the godly in Israel who are likewise waiting for or looking to God and seeking help from him. He does not want shame and disgrace ('confounded'), matters that unite this psalm with the following two, to come upon them on his account (verse 6; see Psalms 70:2; 71:1,13).

Not only are his foes' accusations unjust and unmerited, David argues that he finds himself being reviled ('reproach') and put to shame because of his commitment to God (verse 7; see Psalm 44:15,22). The term 'reproach' or 'scathing insults' is a major concern of this psalm (see verses 7,9,10,19,20). How strong is our commitment to God? Perhaps it is because we show so little zeal and fervour for the Lord's work that we suffer little in the way of persecution.

Even family members have turned against him (verse 8). Anger and resentment had already built up among his own brothers before he came to the throne as witnessed by the comments made to him by Eliab, the eldest (1 Samuel 17:28). An example of that commitment and the resulting abuse is his all-consuming 'zeal' for God's house (verse 9). When the ark was brought into the sanctuary at Jerusalem we witness both David's passion for God and his sanctuary, and the antagonism from within David's own household. Michal, the daughter of Saul, indicated by her sarcastic language that she was part of the old guard who opposed God and the man 'after God's own heart' (2 Samuel 6:16–23; 1 Chronicles 15:29). Prior to this there had been an abortive attempt to bring the ark to Jerusalem when we are told that David became angry and afraid of God. This could have well led him to weep and fast (verse 10) in his zeal for God's house and could have given the initial impulse for others to revile him. In despising David they are really out to blaspheme God (see 2 Samuel 12:14). Wearing 'sackcloth' was another expression of his sorrow in connection with his concern for what is right for God's house. But again, his opponents have maliciously twisted his actions, so that he has become 'a byword' (verse 11; see Psalm 44:14). The reaction is the same whether from respectable people who sit at the city gate speaking against him or local drunkards who mock him in their songs (verse 12; see Job 30:9).[141]

The apostle John quotes the first half of verse 9 as an indication that in cleansing the temple Jesus, as 'great David's greater Son', was fulfilling what was anticipated in David's life (John 2:17). Paul uses the second half of the verse as he urges Christians to encourage and help build up weaker members of the church rather than pleasing themselves (Romans 15:3). He takes it for granted that this psalm finds its ultimate fulfilment in Jesus who 'did not please himself' as he willingly went to the cross in obedience to the Father's will (Mark 14:32–42).

Prayer and lament (verses 13–21)

The psalm returns to direct prayer but in place of the brief cry of verse 1 ('save') David makes a sustained appeal to God becoming more intense with every line ('hear', 'deliver', 'draw near', 'redeem', verse 13–18). With all the gossip about him David makes his plea to the covenant keeping 'LORD' (Yahweh/Jehovah) that this will be the 'acceptable' or 'favourable' time, the right moment in God's purposes for him to hear and act (Isaiah 49:8; 58:5). The basis of his trust is the unstinting nature ('multitude') of God's 'steadfast love' ('mercy') and the fidelity of God's 'salvation' (verse 13).

Paralleling the opening lines (verses 1–2) the same vivid imagery is used ('sink', 'mire' or 'clay' as in Psalm 40:2, 'deep waters', 'floodwater overflow', verses 14–15) to describe his enemies ('those who hate me', verse 14; see verse 4). The threat from his foes is deadly and so he cries out that death, here described as the 'pit' of Sheol, will not shut tight its mouth upon him (verse 15). After this description of his desperate state, David appeals to God's revealed character in his desire for God to hear and rescue him. His 'steadfast love' ('loving-kindness') is 'good' (verse 16; see Psalm 25:8). A description of what that 'good' means is given to Moses in Exodus 33:19; 34:6–7 and echoed in the divine characteristics mentioned here. David has confidence in the 'abundance' ('multitude') of God's 'tender mercies' ('compassion') and so he prays that God would 'turn to' him to answer him (see Psalm 25:16).

He then makes the same point by expressing his plea in a negative way—'do not hide your face' (verse 17; see Psalm 27:9).

Often, 'your servant' is a humble way of speaking about yourself in the presence of a distinguished person (Genesis 43:28; 1 Samuel 17:32) but 'servant' is also one of God's ways of speaking about those in a special relationship to him, like 'my servant Moses' (Numbers 12:7). David is given that honour (2 Samuel 3:18; 7:5; etc.). He has made clear the 'trouble' (verse 17) he is in and so the need for quick action is urgent ('speedily'). The note of urgency continues with the plea that at a time when family members have distanced themselves from him (verse 8), the LORD (Yahweh, verse 16), the one who redeemed Israel from Egyptian slavery (Exodus 15:13), would not remain distant but 'draw near' to help. He calls on him to act as a next of kin ('redeem'; see Leviticus 25:25) and 'deliver' ('ransom'; see Psalms 31:5; 55:18) him by paying whatever price is necessary to bring release from his enemies. That release comes through God's stretched out arm (Exodus 6:6).

Do we know anything of this kind of earnest pleading with God? David encourages us to be bold in prayer.

Once more lament returns in the remaining verses of this section (verses 19-21). David comforts himself with this thought that God is not unaware of his plight. The one who is aware of sin's folly in his own people ('you know'; verse 5) is also aware of the treatment David is enduring from his persecutors (verse 19). Terms from the first part of his lament are used again—'my reproach, my shame and my dishonour' (see verses 6,7,10). 'Reproach' or 'scathing insults' has 'broken' and weakened him (verse 20; see Psalm 6:2) and when he looked for sympathy and comfort he found 'none' (see verse 8). Instead of kindness and concern, his opponents showed only cruelty expressed under the graphic image of offering him the most bitter and unpleasant forms of food and drink imaginable—'gall' and 'vinegar' (or 'sour wine'; see Jeremiah 9:15). This is what was literally offered to Jesus before and during his crucifixion (Matthew 27:34,48; Luke 23:36) and the apostle John indicates that this Scripture was fulfilled when as a result of Jesus' cry, 'I thirst', the soldiers gave him sour wine (John 19:28-29). Such psalms as these that Jesus knew from his childhood were very much in his mind and ministered to him as he endured the cross with all its shame, pain and sorrow. His followers must expect no better treatment from the enemies of God and of his Christ. Some

20th century examples include Richard Wurmbrand in Romania under communism and John Sung under the cultural revolution in China.

Punishment and salvation (verses 22–29)

Before David makes a final plea for God to grant him a deliverance (see verses 1 and 13) that will bring him to a place of safety and vindication—'set me on high' (verse 29; see in reference to Christ, Ephesians 1:20-21; Philippians 2:9; 1 Timothy 3:16), he calls on God to punish those who have inflicted such cruelty on him, the representative head of his people. The prayer is made by one who is 'poor and sorrowful' (translated 'grief' in verse 26; see Psalm 40:17) who has no intention of seeking personal revenge but looks to God to deal justly with those who have persistently shown themselves to be implacable opponents of God's anointed and therefore of God himself. It is similar to the cry of the martyrs (Revelation 6:9-10).

Many see here a great contrast between our Lord and David, the one who suffered extreme cruelty from his enemies prayed for their forgiveness while the other calls down curses on his opponents. But there is more to be said. Jesus had not come to condemn the world but to save it and when he read from Isaiah's prophecy about his earthly ministry he stopped before reaching the reference to 'the day of vengeance of our God' (Isaiah 61:1-2; Luke 4:16-21). This did not mean that he objected to that reference or saw the Old Testament passages relating to God's wrath and retributive justice as pre- or sub-Christian. In fact, he indicated that he would himself experience the divine cup of wrath. There were also occasions when Jesus spoke of people being cursed on the day of judgment (Matthew 25:41) and he pronounced 'woes' on the hypocritical religious leaders of his day (Matthew 23:13-36). He spoke of himself as the judge on that last day and both Paul and John see him exercising that function when he comes to take 'vengeance on those who do not know God' and 'do not obey the gospel of our Lord Jesus Christ' (2 Thessalonians 1:7-10; see Revelation 6:15-17; 19:15-16). Motyer has written, 'We who suffer from moral atrophy, who have little capacity for true moral indignation, and who are ever-ready for moral compromise, have no conception what sin really is, how it appears to and offends a holy God and how just is even the most apparently savage retribution'.

This extended list of curses finds no parallel in the first part of the psalm but what he calls for the enemies to receive in punishment roughly follows the kind of treatment he has received from them (see verses 8-12). The imagery is meant to show that the punishment fits the crime and justice is seen to be scrupulously fair and proportionate. God's covenant with Israel also included curses for disobedience that corresponded with the blessings for obedience (Leviticus 26; Deuteronomy 28).

Prayer is offered that: a) they who made David's food and drink bitter (verse 21) will find their table, a place where they normally feel secure, 'a snare' and 'a trap' (verse 22); b) they who brought about physical trouble (verses 3, 14), will likewise be afflicted and their strength weakened (verse 23)—Paul applies verses 21-22 to God's judgment on those Jews who have resisted the gospel (Romans 11:9-10); c) as he had been forsaken by family and friends (verses 8, 20) so they will be left desolate with no one to succeed them (verse 25)—it is a text that Peter sees fulfilled in Judas Iscariot, the archetypal impenitent opponent of God's Messiah (see Acts 1:16,20).

What these curses are really about is the pouring out of God's 'indignation' (see Psalms 38:3; 79:6) and his burning 'wrathful anger' catching up and overtaking them (verse 24). A most startling reason is added for calling down these curses. David's foes are persecuting those like him whom God has 'struck' and they are talking in a derisive way (see Psalm 41:7-8) about the grief of those whom God has 'wounded' (verse 26). There is no indication in the psalm that God has done this on account of any particular sin in David or the godly he represents. On the contrary, it is stated that his troubles are entirely due to his identification with God's cause. How easy it is to judge wrongly and add to a person's afflictions, as Job's friends did when they accused him of some monstrous sin to account for the tragic state in which they found him. There is deep mystery to suffering with no simple answers.

The wording of verse 26 immediately reminds us of Isaiah 53:3-5 where the prophet speaks of the Lord's Servant being a man of 'sorrows' ('grief'), 'stricken' by God and 'wounded'. He was despised for it looked as if he was being punished on account of his own sins but in fact he was suffering 'for our transgressions'.

The curses conclude with a call that the full extent of their crimes will be taken into account and that no forgiveness and righteous standing before God will be theirs (verse 27). In other words he prays that they will have no part with the 'righteous' believing covenant community—their names 'blotted out' from God's register (verse 28).

The idea of a census list of citizens is an old one going back to the numbering of the people of Israel who left Egypt (Numbers 1 and 26). It is Moses who first refers to God's book of destiny (Exodus 32:32–33) in which are found the names of those who belong to him (see Luke 10:20; Philippians 4:3). It is also used to speak of those who belong to the true city of Zion (see Psalm 87: 5–6; Isaiah 4:3). John employs this imagery to speak of the 'Lamb's book of life' (Revelation 20:12,15; 21:27). Those who are truly the Lord's overcome all testing experiences so that Jesus says he will not 'blot out' their names 'from the book of life' (Revelation 3:5). On the other hand, those whose worship is directed to that which is in opposition to God indicate that their 'names have not been written in the book of life of the Lamb' (Revelation 13:8).

Praise (verses 30–36)
As in Psalm 22 there is a dramatic change from lament to praise and with the same certainty that the prayer of the 'poor' is answered (see verses 29 and 33). Like Psalm 22 it also falls into two parts:

Vow to praise (verses 30–33)
He praises the God whose character ('name') has been revealed (see verse 16) in 'song' and shows how great he is by showing 'thanksgiving' (verse 30; see Psalm 34:3). This is more pleasing to the LORD (Yahweh/ Jehovah) than fully grown animal sacrifices with their 'horns and hooves' (see Psalms 40:6; 50:8,12–15).[142] This is not a criticism of animal sacrifice as such for David is zealous for what goes on in God's house, but such open expressions of praise and thanksgiving provide a great encouragement to all the 'humble' people who 'seek God'. To hear what is being said about God revives their spirits. In medieval worship there was a lot to see and smell but the people received no gospel word in their own language to lift up their hearts.

God's grace and kindness are such that he does listen to the cries of the needy and does not 'despise', does not consider worthless, those in an imprisoned situation on account of their zeal for God such as David has depicted in his trouble (verse 33). It could also be a reference to the way God heard the cry of his enslaved people in Egypt (Exodus 3:7–8; Psalm 68:6). As a result of the Jewish Babylonian exile the verse would have taken on new meaning.

Call to praise (verses 34–36)

The praise is to go beyond the universal, which has been a feature of the preceding psalms, and becomes cosmic—the whole created order of 'heaven and earth' and 'the seas' (verse 34). The reason for this extension in the praise, introduced by 'For', is that it goes far beyond David's own personal deliverance (verse 29) to the salvation of 'Zion' and the surrounding land. In Psalm 51:18 David had prayed that God would do good to Zion and build up its walls, here he looks to the ultimate blessing of the new Jerusalem. The desolation associated with the final curse of the covenant (Leviticus 26:31–33), which David has in mind and of which Isaiah prophesied, is not the last word (Deuteronomy 30:5; Isaiah 49:8; 54:3; 61:4). God will gather all 'his servants', those who 'love his name' (verse 36; see Psalm 5:11), and they will possess the land of the new creation and 'dwell in it' (see Isaiah 65:9; Romans 8:18–21; 2 Peter 3:13; Revelation 21:1–7).

Psalm 70

Emergency Call

'Help!' 'Be quick!' 'Don't be long!' often express the desperate plight of those who call the emergency services. It is with that same intense urgency that David calls out to God to rescue him from his perilous state. The opening lines became well-known to generations of worshippers familiar with the old morning and evening Anglican Prayer Book service where the minister prayed 'O God, make speed to save us' and the people responded, 'O Lord, make haste to help us'.

The psalm is almost identical with Psalm 40:13-17 which also belongs to the 'David' collection and given 'To the Chief Musician'. Added to the heading is 'To bring to remembrance' which only occurs elsewhere in Psalm 38 where its use is considered.

The psalm has close links with the previous one where David describes himself in the same humble terms as 'poor and needy' (verse 5; Psalm 69:29,32-33), urgently requesting to be delivered (verse 1; Psalm 69:14) and with a similar desire for quick action ('make haste' verses 1,5; 'speedily' Psalm 69:17). There is a concern in both for those 'who seek' God that they will eventually 'be glad' (verse 4; Psalm 69:6,32). In the one they are referred to as 'those who love' God's name (Psalm 69:36) whereas here they are the people 'who love' God's salvation (verse 4). Psalm 70 can also be seen as an introduction to Psalm 71 which does not have any titles. In fact, some Hebrew manuscripts unite the two psalms. There are many words and phrases that also link these two psalms so that Psalm 70 helps to unite all three (Psalms 69-71) before the final psalm of Book Two.

Please see Psalm 40:13-17 for the explanation of the text. The main differences in the two texts are indicated here. The cries for help (verses 1 and 5) enclose the pleas with regard to two types of 'seeker': those who seek David's life (verses 2-3) and those who seek God (verse 4).

Immediate assistance needed (verse 1)

The urgency of the appeal for help is much more abrupt here, lacking the 'be pleased' of Psalm 40:13. It also substitutes 'God' for 'LORD' (Yahweh/Jehovah) in the opening line which many see as following a general pattern in Psalms 42 to 83 (see Psalm 42). But it is not slavishly adhered to for God's personal name associated with the redemption of his people is not changed to 'God' in the following line. The next three verses give the reasons for the psalmist's cries for deliverance and help.

The ungodly seekers (verses 2-3)

First, David is concerned for himself but it is not a selfish concern for he represents his people, those whom he mentions in verse 4. Three times he prays that the ungodly people who seek the life of the king (see 1 Samuel 25:29) and who humiliate him publicly with their cries of 'Aha!' (see Psalm 35:21,25; Mark 15:29) will be overthrown. 'Ashamed' (or 'shame') and 'confused' ('dishonoured' or 'confounded') in verse 2 are words used about himself and the godly in the previous psalm (Psalm 69:6-7,19) but they are applied here and in the following psalm against the enemy (see Psalm 71:13,24 where 'confounded' or 'confusion' is also used).

Again, the urgency of the plea demands that only essential words are used so the word 'mutual' (or 'together') and the verb 'to destroy' (or 'snatch away') are missing when compared with Psalm 40:14. In verse 3 the verb 'turned back' (see Psalm 6:10) is used instead of 'be appalled' or 'confounded' and 'to me' is omitted in the phrase 'who say to me' (Psalm 40:15).

The godly seekers (verse 4)

David's desires for the righteous are quite different. He describes them as those who seek God (see Psalms 9:10; 10:4; 69:32) and love his salvation. His prayer is that they will 'rejoice and be glad' in God rather than in the enemy's shame. While the ungodly gloat and humiliate the righteous with their repeated 'Aha!', the prayer is that the godly will say continually, 'Let God be magnified' (see Psalm 69:30).

The differences here include the addition of 'and' before 'let those who love your salvation', the substitution of 'God' for the divine personal name as in verse 1 and a slight variation in the term for 'salvation' (from which we get the name 'Joshua'). Christians love the name of Jesus for he is God's salvation. 'Let us love, and sing, and wonder, Let us praise the Saviour's Name' (John Newton).

Immediate assistance needed (verse 5)

It is not a question of wealth, influence or power. This anointed ruler confesses that he is poor in spirit and totally dependent on God. Jesus taught that truly happy and privileged people are those who are poor in spirit and who hunger and thirst after righteousness (Matthew 5:3,6). As David closes by repeating the urgent appeal of the opening lines, there are a number of differences compared with the closing verse of Psalm 40. The phrase 'the LORD thinks upon me' is omitted and 'make haste to me, O God' is substituted and, significantly in these psalms that tend to avoid God's covenant name, 'LORD' (Yahweh) is used again instead of 'my God' (see verse 1).

Psalm 71

Assurance for the Old and Grey

The Christian life does not get any easier with advancing years. Temptations continue and testing experiences of various kinds challenge the believer's faith in God. The psalmist encourages us through all his troubles to take a look backwards to view God's faithfulness and to press on with confidence and be an inspiration to future generations.

There are strong links with the previous psalm with the words for shame, confounded and dishonour appearing again (verses 1,13,24; Psalm 70:2), the enemy described as those who 'seek my hurt' (verse 13,24; Psalm 70:2) and the same urgent appeal 'make haste to help me' (verse 12; Psalm 70:1). But it is unlikely that the two psalms were ever originally united in the way that Psalms 9 and 10 and 42 and 43 were, for they are quite distinct in form and structure. It is probably because Psalm 71 has no heading that the two psalms were closely associated, with David assumed to be the author. There is reference to David's troubles in his advancing years in 1 Kings 1:1 with Solomon eventually being proclaimed king. If this is the background, it would be a most suitable psalm before the final one of Book Two which is attributed to Solomon and where the closing note declares that the prayers of David are ended (Psalm 72:20).

In some respects the psalm contains features typical of the many psalms of lament that commence with petition and sorrow and end on a note of confidence and praise, but this one moves back and forth between cries of help and confessions of trust. The psalm reads like a medley of quotations particularly from Psalms 22, 31, 35, 38 and 40 and in so doing it encourages Christians to use biblical prayers and phraseology and to make them their own as they engage in prayer or compose new spiritual songs.

Petition (verses 1–4)

The opening three verses are almost identical with Psalm 31:1-3 where further comments are found. David's first words show that his prayer arises from an assured position—'In you, O LORD, I put my trust' (or better 'I have taken refuge'). The picture of the Lord being a refuge first appears in Psalm 2:12 and continues throughout the Psalter (Psalms 7:1; 11:1; 16:1; 25:20; 31:1; 141:8; 144:2). In this psalm, associated words such as 'strong habitation' (literally 'rock of dwelling'), 'rock' (or 'crag') and 'fortress' (verse 3) and 'strong refuge' (verse 7) indicate how important this truth was for David in moments of crisis.

The 'shame' that he wishes on his enemies (Psalm 70:2) and that he himself had suffered previously (Psalm 69:7) he prays he will never experience (verse 1). For the Christian, to suffer shame in the cause of Christ is an honour (Acts 5:41) but there are occasions where the enemy's actions in bringing shame on God's people has the knock-on effect of bringing dishonour to God. The most obvious example is Christ on the cross suffering shame and ridicule so that David's prayer was his prayer for vindication and God's glory. Using three different words for rescue, David therefore pleads that God would 'save' him.

Interestingly, it is not God's mercy or grace that he looks to but his 'righteousness' (verse 2), which is another theme emphasised in this psalm (verses 15-16,19,24). God's salvation always accords with his righteous character in that he does and upholds what is right. By this righteousness he delivers the righteous and punishes the wicked. In the gospel the righteousness of God is revealed in such a way that he remains righteous and at the same time justifies wicked, ungodly enemies who put their trust in Jesus (Romans 3:21-26; Isaiah 45:21b).

It is wonderful to have God as a permanently safe place to which we can 'continually' come (verse 3; see Psalm 18:2). Horatius Bonar's poetry comes to mind:

O love of God, our shield and stay
Through all the perils of our way;
Eternal love, in thee we rest,
For ever safe, for ever blest.

Not only is God always available he gives 'commandment' (verse 3) for our safety even as he commands 'victories for Jacob' (Psalm 44:4; see Psalm 68:28). If God commands it then despite what the enemy throws at us we are indestructible till our work on earth is done (Daniel 3:17–18,25). The foes from whose grasp David prays to 'escape' are described as 'wicked', 'unrighteous' (or 'one who acts wrongfully') and 'cruel' (verse 4). David had sons like Ammon, Absalom and Adonijah who were of this sort and showed by their actions that they belonged to the snake's demonic brood.

Confidence and praise (verses 5–8)
The plea is based on a life-time of confidence in the Lord 'GOD' (Yahweh/Jehovah) whom David describes as 'my trust' and 'my hope'. He expands on the phrase 'from my youth' (verse 5) in the next verse where he indicates that God has 'upheld' him 'from birth' and likens his Lord to the midwife who 'took me out' (literally 'cut free', in this context of the umbilical cord) from his 'mother's womb' (see Psalm 22:9-10 for the same idea). With this thought of God's long-term close relationship and support in mind he desires to 'praise' God 'continually' (verse 6). The use of the word 'continually' is another feature of this psalm (see verses 3,6,14) together with 'all the day' (verses 8,15,24).

The term for 'wonder' or 'portent', often in the phrase 'signs and wonders', is used for God's miraculous activity most notably concerning the plagues that struck Egypt (see Psalms 78:43; 105:27). The curses of God's covenant with his people are also described as 'a sign and a wonder' in the sense of a warning to later generations (Deuteronomy 28:46). Is David in his present trouble considered by the 'many' to be an object of astonishment and a solemn warning sign, a typical example of divine punishment (see verse 11)? On the other hand, the immediate context suggests that David has become a signal and amazing example of God's care and salvation. Isaiah and his sons, as well as Ezekiel and Joshua the high priest are used by God as wonders (Isaiah 8:18; Ezekiel 12:6; Zechariah 3:8). Perhaps we should not discount the possibility that while some understood his dire condition as a warning, to others the way God has been his 'strong refuge' has made him an encouraging sign. As leader of his people David desires to witness to God's goodness by praising him, speaking of God's 'glory all the day' (verse 8). The word translated 'glory' is used for the splendour and beauty of priestly and royal robes (Exodus 28:2; Isaiah 52:1) as well as of women's 'finery' (Isaiah 3:18).

Petition and lament (verses 9–13)
Remembering God's support from birth is the basis of David's appeal concerning the end of his life. What he fears most is abandonment, to be cast off and forsaken by God in his ageing years when physical 'strength fails' (verse 9). Generally, an elderly person was respected and valued in the community but in the case of a ruler, any weakness and uncertainty concerning his ability to rule provided enemies with an opportunity to manipulate the situation to their own advantage. These are the circumstances surrounding Adonijah's actions (1 Kings 1; see 2 Samuel 17:1-2). David's enemies have conspired against him, plotting together to 'harm' him (verse 13) by keeping a close watch ('lying in wait', see Psalm 56:6) on him perhaps to assassinate him. They consider that God has forsaken him and so with no one to rescue him they feel justified in chasing and seizing him (verse 11; see Psalm 3:2). In the light of this, David prays to his God ('my God') that he will not remain distant but will come quickly to his aid (verse 12; see Psalms 22:11,19; 69:17; 70:1 and especially 38:21-22) and that his foes will be defeated and shamed (verse 13; see Psalms 35:26; 70:2).

Praise and proclamation (verses 14–18)
The lament gives way to the twin themes of 'hope' and 'praise' on which David does not wish to give up—'continually' ... yet more and more' (verse 14). This praise consists in speaking of God's actions—'your righteousness ... your salvation ... yours only' (verses 15–16)—recalling the beginning of the psalm (verse 2). These acts of deliverance in which he displays his righteous nature are too numerous to count ('I do not know *their* limits' literally 'numbers', verse 15) and David desires 'to go in the strength of' the sovereign 'Lord' and 'God' (Yahweh/Jehovah), meaning that he wants to come into the assembly of God's people to give testimony to the Lord's 'mighty deeds' and to 'make mention of' (or 'commemorate', verse 16) his righteous character as seen in the way he has been true to his promises.

David looks back again over the years from his youth to the present concerning all that he has been taught of God's 'wondrous works' in Israel's history and in his own experience. What he has learnt he seeks to proclaim (verse 17; see Psalm 64:9). In continuing his plea commenced in verse 9 for God not to forsake him in his advancing years, his argument is a strong one and it is made with some earnestness as the repeated 'O God ... O God' indicates. It is not based on self-preservation but that he might continue to be a witness, proclaiming God's 'strength' (literally 'arm') and 'might' for the benefit of present and future generations (verse 18).

Confession and praise (verses 19–24)

This last section is divided into two parts. David first gives a more detailed description of what he wishes to pass on to everyone (verses 19–21) and then the psalm closes with praise (verses 22–24).

David's confidence in God is revealed in this confession of faith (verse 19–21). He begins with one of God's fundamental attributes to which he has already drawn attention—God's 'righteousness' (verses 2,15–16) which transcends human thought (see Psalm 36:5). It is according to this high standard that God acts in salvation and judgment. Next, he refers to the 'great things' God has done (verse 19) which makes us think back to God's 'wondrous works', especially those associated with the deliverance of Israel from Egypt (verse 17). The question 'O God, who is like you?' (verse 19) recalls the Red Sea song which emphasised God's uniqueness—'Who is like you, O Lord, among the gods?' (Exodus 15:11; see Deuteronomy 3:24; Micah 7:18–20). This gives David the assurance that the God who has allowed him to experience many and bitter 'troubles' throughout his life will act again to 'revive' him or to restore him to life from the 'depths' or 'abyss' of the dead. The 'depths of the earth' (verse 20) is used here as a figurative expression for David's life-threatening experience (see Psalm 69:2,14–15).[143] God will do more than revive what he had for he will increase his 'greatness' and in place of trouble he will surround him with 'comfort'.

The psalm concludes with David's vow to give thanks and sing praises with harp and lyre ('lute' and 'harp'; see Psalms 33:2; 57:8). God is described as the 'Holy One of Israel', a divine title used twenty-nine times by the prophet Isaiah (see Isaiah 1:4). It speaks of the 'otherness' of God and of the wholesomeness of his being and moral purity. He alone has the right to be called holy and it is this altogether pure and unique being who has committed himself to his people Israel, those whom he redeemed from Egypt and entered into a special agreement with at Sinai. Again, the song at the Red Sea comes to mind 'Who is like you, glorious in holiness?' (Exodus 15:11)

This God is praised with 'lips' that 'greatly rejoice' and with a 'tongue' that tells (literally 'mutters'; see Psalm 35:28) of God's nature as witnessed both in the salvation of his people and the punishment of his enemies and theirs. God's 'faithfulness' is his truthfulness by which he can be depended on to keep his promises to those who love and obey him and to carry out his threats on those who disobey him. He is the saviour God who has not only 'redeemed' Israel from Egyptian bondage but has done so more recently in the experience of David. Finally, God's 'righteousness' (see verse 1) is again mentioned as it is displayed in answering David's prayers for the shaming of his enemies and for putting things right.

In that Psalm 71 echoes themes and phrases from Psalm 22 we can, through the troubles that afflicted David and from which he was delivered, see shadows of what Jesus experienced when he was greatly troubled even to the death of the cross. When God did not save him from the shame of crucifixion, people assumed that God had finally shown his disapproval of him by deserting him. He was a 'sign', a 'portent' that was spoken against, as Simeon prophesied (Luke 2:34). Yet he was literally revived and brought up from the 'abyss' to be granted 'greatness' and much 'comfort'. It is by the grace and goodness of God that believers are raised from sin and death and look forward to being raised bodily to be with the risen, glorified Christ in the blessings of the new creation.

Psalm 72

Messiah's Universal Reign

There are two well-known hymns based on this psalm:

> 'Jesus shall reign where'er the sun
> Doth his successive journeys run'

by Isaac Watts (1674–1748) and

> 'Hail to the Lord's anointed
> Great David's greater Son!'

by James Montgomery (1771-1854). In both they assume that the psalm is speaking of the Messiah, an understanding that goes back to early Jewish as well as early Church interpreters.

If the previous psalm was composed at a time when intrigue surrounded the succession to David's throne with Solomon eventually being declared king, this psalm which refers to Solomon in the heading, provides a fitting conclusion. The psalm also stands at an important juncture in the whole Psalter. It occurs at the end of Book Two, at the point where the main collection of David's psalms comes to an end (see verse 20). It is the climax to other royal psalms like Psalms 20, 21, 24 and 45, and a powerful reminder of what the

introductory Psalm 2 emphasised—the importance of the special
promises that God gave to David (2 Samuel 7:1–17), promises that
find their ultimate realisation in great David's greater Son, Jesus the
Messiah.

In the Hebrew text, the title is as brief as that of Psalms 35 and
37—'Of Solomon' (see also Psalm 127). Traditionally, it has been
thought to be a prayer that David composed for his son Solomon and
this is why in some Bibles the title reads 'for Solomon'. But as all the
other psalms with this same construction have generally been taken to
indicate authorship there is no reason why Solomon should not be its
author. The final verse of the psalm does not negate this view as David
has been the chief but not sole author of the psalms up to this point
(see Psalms 42–50). Solomon takes up the theme of his father's parting
address where he is promised a prosperous and fulfilling reign if he
remains true to what is written in the law of Moses (1 Kings 2:3).

The psalm, as Motyer has shown, 'fits well with the time and mind
of Solomon'. He could have been praying for himself as the king's son
(verse 1), his empire stretched from sea to sea and to the Euphrates
(verse 8; 1 Kings 4:21; 2 Chronicles 9:26; see Exodus 23:31) and he knew
what it was like to have foreign rulers pay homage to him and to see
the wealth of the nations coming to Jerusalem (verses 9–11,15; 1 Kings
10:1–13,22; 2 Chronicles 9:22–24). His was a time of general peace and
prosperity and he had prayed at Gibeon that he would be given wisdom
to dispense justice and to govern rightly (verses 1–4,7; 1 Kings 3:6–9).
He was a blessing to the Queen of Sheba and she in turn praised his
wisdom and prosperity and the privileged position of his court (verse
17; 1 Kings 10:9–10,13). At the same time the words of the psalm go
beyond the exaggerated comments that poetic licence would allow.
The best of the kings of David's line fall far short of the ideal presented
here. It describes the king that God had in mind all along from that
royal 'seed' that would smash the snake's power (Genesis 3:15) to the
'Messenger of the covenant' who would come to do a refining and
purifying work (Malachi 3:1–3; Matthew 3:11–12). This is the king who
finally fulfils the covenant that God made with David (2 Samuel 7:8–16)
and the prophecies concerning a future 'David' (Isaiah 16:5; Ezekiel
37:24; Hosea 3:5; Amos 9:11).

The psalm begins in verse 1 with the only clear appeal to God. As
for the rest of the psalm it is difficult to know whether to view the
verses as prophecies with the verbs translated 'he will', etc., or as prayer

wishes ('may he', etc.) or a mixture of both with verses 2–7 and 12–14 as prophecies and verses 8–11 and 15–17 as prayers. The whole psalm can be viewed as a prayer, a blessing and a prophecy similar to the blessing Jacob gave to his sons (Genesis 49:1–28).

Just reign (verses 1–7)

The psalm begins with a prayer request—'Give the king ...' (verse 1) and it sets the tone for the rest of the psalm. As we find in Psalm 2, there is a close link between God and 'his anointed' (see also Isaiah 33:17,22). He is God's viceroy: he rules on behalf of God and is one with God. The parallel lines in verse one suggest that 'the king' and 'the king's Son' refer to the same person, the second reference emphasising that he is the authentic successor. King Jesus is great David's greater son as the angel informed Mary: 'He will be great ... and the Lord God will give him the throne of his father David' (Luke 1:31–33). Like the tribal leaders and judges in Israel who were to decide cases impartially on behalf of God ('for the judgment is God's', Deuteronomy 1:17; see 2 Chronicles 19:6), so God's anointed must conform to divine standards in governing the people. Unlike the tyrants of this world who govern to satisfy their own pleasures and bolster their own egos the true king is to exhibit to perfection God's righteous rule in which sound moral principles ('righteousness') are coupled to sound moral practice ('judgments'). Solomon asked God for the wisdom to rule well (1 Kings 3:7–9) and there were kings like Jehoshaphat, Hezekiah and Josiah who endeavoured to lead God's people in a God-honouring way but all fell short of the ideal. Wisdom proclaims that it is by her 'kings reign and rulers decree justice' (Proverbs 8:15). It is for this reason we are urged to pray for rulers that law and order might be maintained and provide conditions beneficial to the spread of the gospel (Jeremiah 29:7; Romans 13:1–4; 1 Timothy 2:1–6).

Those to whom he is to administer justice ('He will judge', verse 2; see Psalm 9:8) are not in the first place the king's people but God's people ('your people') who are described as God's humble 'poor' or 'afflicted' ones (see Psalms 9:18; 10:2,9; etc.). These are the ones who belong to God's heavenly kingdom (Matthew 5:3; Luke 6:20). This righteous rule results from the prayer of verse 1 and it brings about a righteous 'peace' (verse 3), a wholesome state of well-being and prosperity. The mountain slopes and little hills of Canaan (see Psalm 65:12) where the crops grow and the vines and olive trees thrive are illustrative of the blessings associated with Messiah's reign. He will undo the effects of the initial curse on the ground (see Genesis 3:17–19; Amos 9:13). Isaiah's description of the reign of King Jesus contains the same interest in righteousness and justice for the poor and the experience of harmony and security (Isaiah 9:6–7; 11:1–9; 32:1–2,16–19; 55:12–13).

A charity formed in 1919 called 'The Save the Children Fund' was set up to provide relief to children suffering the effects of war and continues to give support and protection to vulnerable children. These noble efforts and those of other similar organizations to alleviate poverty in the world are to be applauded and witness to God's general gracious activity through the lives of individuals whether Christian or not. But in this sinful world under the curse of God poverty and oppression will never be eradicated. It is emphasised again, however, that under Messiah's reign there will be no more miscarriages of justice and all that disfigures human society will be completely eliminated. For that to happen, decisive action has to be taken to crush 'the oppressor' (verse 4). If such people are not humbled by becoming 'crushed' or broken in spirit (Isaiah 57:15) they will be 'crushed' or 'broken in pieces' in judgment as was the Servant of the Lord when he was 'crushed' or 'bruised' in the place of sinners (Isaiah 53:5,10). The kind of treatment the poor had received ('break in pieces'; see Psalm 94:5), the oppressor will experience. As the oppressor of God's people was defeated at the Red Sea so Satan has been crushed and bruised through Messiah's work on the cross and as a result, the God of peace will 'crush Satan' under our feet shortly (Romans 16:20; see Revelation 20:10).

Another result of this righteous reign will be that from one generation to another in perpetuity (literally 'with the sun and before the moon') people will reverence God (verse 5, 'fear you'). This was not the case under Solomon for he encouraged the worship of other gods (1 Kings 11:1–10). Messiah's reign will be refreshing and as revitalising as heavy rain showers that pour down on the dry land to restore 'mown grass' that has become lifeless and brown (verse 6; see 2 Samuel 23:4; Proverbs 16:15; Hosea 6:3). Picking up the thought of verse 3, the moon image of verse 5 and continuing the agricultural figure of verse 6, the section closes by indicating that the opening prayer of verse 1 is answered. The 'righteous' person will 'flourish' as will an 'abundance' of well-being which will also be long lasting (verse 7; see Isaiah 60:21).

The picture presented in this opening section, using language and images appropriate to the time, is of the new creation in the eternal state (2 Peter 3:13).

Universal reign (verses 8–11)

Messiah's rule will not only be long lasting it will be worldwide. What is said of humanity at the beginning of creation is the role of this future king—'He shall have dominion' (verse 8; see Genesis 1:26; Psalm 8:6; Hebrews 2:6–9). The phrase 'from sea to sea' (verse 8) recalls the area promised to Israel (Exodus 23:31) from the Red Sea to the Mediterranean. But 'from the River (Euphrates) to the ends of the earth' extends the boundaries beyond anything that Israel acquired even during the David-Solomon era (see Psalm 2:8; Zechariah 9:10). The land of promise was itself not only symbolic of a lost garden in Eden but a picture of the new earth.

'Those who dwell in the wilderness' (verse 9; see Psalm 74:14) probably refers to those desert creatures often associated with demonic elements (see Isaiah 13:21; 34:14; Jeremiah 50:39). These will 'crouch' (a stronger term than the one usually translated 'bow') before him and 'his enemies' will be brought into abject submission—'lick the dust' (see Isaiah 49:23; Micah 7:17). Jesus must reign till all his enemies are under his feet (1 Corinthians 15:25). Tribute, in the form of presents and gifts from foreign nations will be brought to this king. The whole of the then known world is depicted, represented on the far western side of Israel by 'Tarshish' kings (Spain perhaps; verse 10) along with the Mediterranean coastal regions and on the far southern side by the Arabian ('Sheba') kings and those of 'Seba' (south of Egypt) from where perhaps the Queen of Sheba came (1 Kings 10:1–10).

A summary statement in verse 11 rounds off this section of the psalm. What is said of Solomon's reign in 1 Kings 4:34 becomes symbolic of Messiah's literal universal rule. While the wording is used of homage to an earthly ruler, 'fall down' and 'serve' are often found in the worship of God (Psalm 29:2; Exodus 20:5). The visit made by those important men from the east at Jesus' birth (Matthew 2:11) was a foretaste of what was to come with people of all nations acknowledging King Jesus as Saviour and Lord while the apostle John draws on these Old Testament allusions to picture the elect from every nation bringing glory to God in the new Jerusalem (Revelation 21:26; see Isaiah 60).

Benevolent reign (verses 12–14)

The psalm returns to the concerns of verses 2–4, emphasising that this eternal universal reign, unlike the despotic, corrupt rule of the tyrants of this world, is a regime that is the result of compassion ('spare' verse 13) and care as the opening 'For' (verse 12) suggests. This king represents God's regard for 'the poor and needy' (Psalms 9:8–10,12; 140:12). Like God's activity at the exodus, he 'delivers' when they cry to him (verse 12; Exodus 2:23), he 'saves' (verse 13; Exodus 15:2) and 'redeems' (verse 14; Exodus 15:13). The king is like a family member who makes the needs of his people his own. He is the protector not the oppressor of his people. When sinful humans get into positions of power too often they succumb to the temptation to act corruptly and the lives of those under them begin to count for very little. This king values the lives ('precious shall be their blood', verse 14) of all entrusted to his care just as God does (Psalm 116:15). David showed a similar attitude toward Saul his enemy (1 Samuel 26:21,24).

The Gospels, especially Luke, emphasise Jesus' compassion for the poor and needy who are like sheep without a shepherd. While Solomon eventually made the people's yoke heavy (1 Kings 12:4) Jesus' yoke is easy. His call was to all who labour and are heavy laden to find rest in him who is 'gentle and lowly in heart' (Matthew 11:28–30). He came to seek and to save the lost and to give his life a ransom for many.

Perpetual reign (verses 15–17)

As it draws to a close the thoughts of the whole psalm are brought together. First, this king will 'live' (verse 15).[144] What was a respectful wish at Solomon's accession to the throne ('May the king live', 1 Kings 1:34,39), is literally true in the case of Messiah. Other kings lose their lives and their kingdoms but this king, of whom Solomon is a type, will live on. Jesus said, 'I am he who lives, and was dead, and behold, I am alive for evermore' (Revelation 1:18). Because he lives his people will live also (John 14:19).

The very best is offered to him ('the gold of Sheba', verse 15), as was literally presented to Solomon by the Queen of Sheba (1 Kings 10:10) and to Jesus at his birth (Matthew 2:11). 'Prayer' is made for him always in the way that Jesus taught people to pray for God's name, kingdom and will (Matthew 6:9–10) and daily he will be 'praised' (or more literally 'blessed', see Psalm 41:13). The people's well-being is bound up with the king's well-being. With the background of the old covenant blessings for obedience in mind, we have this picture of fruitfulness and plenty so that Zion's 'city' prospers.[145] The unsheltered 'top of the mountains' where the soil is normally thin produces grain in abundance with the crops like the proverbial cedars of Lebanon. A similar picture of the future prosperity of God's people is depicted by the prophets (see Isaiah 4:2; Hosea 14:5-7). That prosperity is linked to the ingathering of people from all nations into the heavenly city (Isaiah 2:3), something that began with the representatives of all the nations receiving God's word on the day of Pentecost (Acts 2:5-11) but will be consummated in the new creation (Revelation 7:9; 14:1-5; 21:1-4).

The king's 'name' (verse 17) sums up everything he is seen to be by his presence and activity. It is almost equivalent to his reputation. Though Solomon's fame was legendary Jesus could say of himself that 'a greater than Solomon is here' (Matthew 12:42). His reputation will always be maintained. The final words of verse 17 echo the promises to Abraham, Isaac and Jacob (Genesis 12:2-3; 18:18; 22:18; 26:4; 28:4,14). Interestingly, those promises concerning people being blessed like them (see Jeremiah 4:2) are now attached to this amazing ruler. God's covenant with Abraham and his family is directly linked to his covenant with David and the references to the royal 'seed' of the chosen line throughout the Genesis narrative point in this direction. The peoples of the world find blessing in him and are blessed just as this king has been blessed. It is as a consequence of King Jesus redeeming us by becoming a curse for us that results in the blessing of Abraham coming upon the Gentiles in Christ Jesus (Galatians 3:12-14).

In their turn, the elect from every nation will congratulate this king by calling him 'blessed'. This is not the usual term for blessed like the one found in the previous phrase. It is interesting that the Psalms began with the exclamation 'Blessed!', 'Happy!' or 'How fortunate!' concerning the righteous person (Psalm 1:1) and this psalm, the last in Book Two, closes its promises concerning the righteous king using a verbal form from the same word family—'call him blessed', 'count him happy' or 'pronounce him fortunate'. Leah, Jacob's wife employed the same language when she bore him a second son. The text reads, 'for the daughters will call me blessed. So she called him Asher' (Genesis 30:13; see Proverbs 31:28; Malachi 3:12). The nations will be excited and amazed like the Queen of Sheba when she exclaimed to Solomon, 'Happy are your men and happy are these your servants!' (1 Kings 10:8).

The positive elements of Solomon's reign are used by him in this psalm to preview the glory of Messiah and his kingdom.

Doxology (verses 18–19)

Please read the comments on verse 13 of Psalm 41 concerning the doxologies that close off each of the five collections that make up the entire Psalter, and also for an explanation of 'Blessed be the LORD, the God of Israel' and 'Amen and Amen!'

Appropriately at the close of such an amazing psalm the doxology is much fuller than the previous one.[146] It speaks of Israel's covenant-keeping God as the one who 'alone does wondrous things' (verse 18; see Psalms 9:1; 40:5) echoing the song of Moses at the Red Sea: 'Who is like you O Lord, among the gods ... doing wonders?' (Exodus 15:11) The wonders seen at the exodus of Israel from Egypt will be more than matched by the wonders associated with the Lord's anointed. The exodus background is again in mind as God's 'glorious name' (verse 19; see 1 Chronicles 29:13; Nehemiah 9:5; Isaiah 63:14) is extolled. God triumphed 'gloriously' and is 'awesome in glorious deeds' (Exodus 15:1,11) and through such actions he displays to people the stunning splendour of his being. The phrase 'for ever' is attached to God's 'name' just as it was attached to the king's name in verse 17. Pharaoh and Israel were both informed that the whole earth belongs to the Lord (Exodus 9:29; 19:5) and God's purpose is that 'all the earth shall be filled with the glory of the Lord' (Numbers 14:21; Habakkuk 2:14; see Isaiah 11:9). Thus the doxology closes with the prayer that 'the whole earth be filled with his glory' (verse 19), a fitting end not only to this psalm's universal emphasis but to God's worldwide dominion that has been the theme of Psalms 64–68. God rules through his king and, as the New Testament indicates, the psalm's expectations become a reality when the new Jerusalem descends from heaven to fill the new earth (Revelation 21:1–2,10–11).

Postscript (verse 20)

The final verse draws our attention to the fact that most of the psalms up to this point have been from the pen of David (see 2 Samuel 23:1; and for a similar editorial note see Job 31:40) and it reminds us that these psalms are comprised of urgent petitions, many of them in life-threatening circumstances, but all in one way or another having a bearing on God's rule over-against the rule of the dark forces of evil.

So many of the previous psalms have taught us that the king of David's line who is destined to rule on behalf of God over the entire world will do so after enduring much suffering on behalf of his people. Using the book of Psalms as well as the other sections of the Hebrew Bible, the risen Messiah informed his disciples that it was in God's plan that he should suffer and 'enter his glory' (Luke 24:26,44–46). Peter then later wrote to remind Christians of the prophecies concerning Christ's sufferings and the glories that would follow as he encouraged them in their sufferings for Christ. He urged them to 'rejoice to the extent that you partake of Christ's sufferings, that when his glory is revealed, you may also be glad with exceeding joy' (1 Peter 1:11; 4:12–13).

Bibliography

I have profited from the following commentaries, some of them not by evangelicals. They are referred to in the commentary by their surname:

Alexander, Joseph A., *The Psalms Translated and Explained*, (reprinted from the 1864 Edinburgh edition), Grand Rapids: Zondervan.

Calvin, John, *Commentary on the Psalms of David* 2 Vols. Translated by James Anderson (The Ages Digital Library Commentary).

Goldingay, John, *Psalms* 3 vols., Baker Academic, vol. 1, 2006; vol. 2, 2007; vol. 3, 2008.

Henry, Matthew, *Bible Commentary* (Many editions and on line).

Hossfeld, Frank-Lothar & Zenger, Eric, *Psalms 2: A Commentary on Psalms 51-100*; *Psalms 3: A Commentary on Psalms 101-150*, English translated by Linda M. Maloney, (Hermeneia series), Minneapolis: Fortress Press, 2005/2011.

Kidner, Derek, *Psalms* 2 vols. (Tyndale Old Testament Commentaries), Leicester: IVP, 1973/75.

McCann, J. Clinton, 'The Book of Psalms: Introduction, Commentary and Reflections' in *The New Interpreter's Bible* Vol. IV, Abingdon Press, 1996.

Motyer, J. Alec, 'The Psalms' in *New Bible Commentary* 21st Century Edition, (editors D. A. Carson, R. T. France, J. A. Motyer, G. J. Wenham), Leicester: IVP, 1994.

Spurgeon, Charles H. *Treasury of David* (Many editions and on line).

Wilson, Gerald H., *Psalms* Vol. 1 (The NIV Application Commentary), Zondervan, 2002.

Endnotes

1. I am indebted to McCann for this reference.

2. The most frequently used are Psalms 2, 22, 33–35, 39, 50, 69, 78, 89, 102, 105–106, 116, 118, 119, 135, 145 and 147.

3. Martin J. Selman, *2 Chronicles* (Tyndale OT Commentaries), IVP, 1994, p. 491.

4. At the end of Book One the Lord is said to 'delight' or to be 'well pleased with' the psalmist, as the blessed man at the beginning is said to 'delight' in the law of the Lord (Psalms 1:2; 41:11).

5. I am indebted to J. Clinton McCann for some of these insights. See 'The Shape of Book 1 of the Psalter and the Shape of Human Happiness' pp. 340–348 in *The Book of Psalms: Composition and Reception*, eds. Peter W. Flint & Patrick D. Miller, Brill, 2005 [Supplements to Vetus Testamentum Vol. XCIX].

6. In the Hebrew Bible the Writings include twelve books in the following order: Psalms, Job, Proverbs, Ruth, Song of Songs, Ecclesiastes, Lamentations, Esther, Daniel, Ezra, Nehemiah, and 1–2 Chronicles.

7. Interestingly, the psalm's first word ('blessed') begins with the first letter of the Hebrew alphabet (*Aleph*) while the final word of the psalm ('perish')

begins with the last letter of the alphabet (*Taw*). Like the acrostic psalms (see Psalm 119), this feature draws attention to the psalm's message.

8. D. Martyn Lloyd-Jones, *True Happiness: An Exposition of Psalm One*, Bryntirion Press, 1997.

9. The five books of the Psalter resemble the five books of Moses so that Psalm 1 could be said to introduce the law of David.

10. *Luther's Works First Lectures on the Psalms I Psalms 1-75*, Concordia Publishing House, 1974, p. 11.

11. For example, Tertullian and Justin and there are some early Greek manuscripts of Acts that make reference to Psalm 2:7 as belonging to Psalm 1.

12. The Aramaic word for son is used here not the Hebrew as in verse 7. Scholars have made heavy weather of it when, in fact, this address to foreign rulers, using *bar* rather than *ben,* is most appropriate and also assists the poetic line.

13. *O Sacred head! sore wounded.*

14. Dale Ralph Davis, *The Way of the Righteous in the Muck of Life Psalms 1-12*, Fearn, Ross-shire: Christian Focus, 2010, p. 67.

15. One commentator suggests that it is related to an Akkadian word for a lamentation song.

16. Some take God as the subject of 'turn back' or 'repent' in the sense of 'relent'; see *New International Version.*

17. See NASA News Release No. 69-83F (13 July 1969).

18. The *Authorised Version* and *New King James* emend the text to read 'You have set your glory'. The text can remain as it stands by reading 'your majesty is repeated' (see Kidner).

19. The ancient Greek translation (the Septuagint or LXX for short), translated

between the third and second centuries before Christ, provided an interpreted paraphrase of this psalm with the words 'perfected praise' for the original 'ordained a bulwark'.

20. 'Son' is used in Hebrew to denote a member of a class or group; e.g. 'son of perdition'.

21. Hebrews 2:7,9 has 'angels' as it follows the ancient Greek version (LXX).

22. The unity of the two psalms is based on the following factors: 1) some Hebrew manuscripts and the original Greek translation, the Septuagint (LXX), treat them as one; 2) the first ends in a 'Selah' and because this marker does not occur elsewhere at the close of a psalm apart from Psalm 3, it suggests this is not the end of the psalm; 3) unusually in this first Book, there is no title to Psalm 10 (the only other case is Psalm 33); 4) there is an acrostic arrangement with Psalm 9 using the first half of the Hebrew alphabet and Psalm 10 using the last letters of the alphabet; 5) both psalms exhibit similarities of style and phraseology such as 'in times of trouble' (9:9; 10:1); 6) it is not unknown for one psalm to express both thanksgiving and lamentation, although it is surprising to find lamentation following a hymn of praise.

23. There is no certainty concerning the phrase 'upon the death of the son'. The Targum connects it with the death of Goliath. The ancient Greek version (LXX) translates it differently: 'concerning the secrets of the son'.

24. Like 'Selah' the Hebrew term 'Higgaion' could be another musical sign.

25. The same Hebrew word can be translated temple or palace. Habakkuk 2:20 quotes the opening words of verse 4 with the warning 'let all the earth keep silence before him'.

26. This is the position of the 'Open Theology' movement. John Goldingay in his recent commentary on the Psalms would seem to favour this opinion (see his comments on Psalms 7:9 (p. 148); 11:4 (p. 192).

27. There is some ambiguity over the last line of verse 5. It could either mean that it is the oppressors who 'puff' or 'pant' after the needy or that it is the needy who 'puff' or 'yearn' for safety from the oppressors.

28. P. C. Craigie, *Psalms 1–50*, Word Biblical Commentary 19, Word, 1983.

29. M. Wilcock, *The Message of Psalms 1–72: Songs for the People of God*. Bible Speaks Today, Leicester: IVP, 2001.

30. Carson, April 9, *For the Love of God*, Leicester: IVP, 1998.

31. See Goldingay, vol. 1, p. 239.

32. Literally it reads: 'Show the wonders of your faithful love, O you who save those who flee from those who rise up by your right hand'. The phrase 'by your right hand' more naturally goes with 'those who rise up' and this is how the Prayer Book version translates: 'From such as resist thy right hand'. The AV and many modern versions associate it with the verb 'save'. This latter interpretation is more in keeping with the exodus parallel.

33. Some interpret the whole verse as continuing the prayer of verse 13. It is thus taken as an imprecatory prayer for the destruction of the enemy. Others take the second half of the verse to refer to God's people, so that the contrast is between David's enemies who will be destroyed and God's 'treasured ones' whom he will so bless that their offspring will be great and will have abundant provisions.

34. The translation 'shrewd' does tone down the force of the original which has the idea of being difficult to handle.

35. Some scholars adjust the Hebrew vowel points to give 'your answer' matching the opposite thought in verse 41 where the Lord does not answer the cry of the enemy.

36. The Hebrew pointing suggests a pause after 'Save, LORD!' but, with the Septuagint (LXX), it seems better to place the pause after 'king' to give 'LORD, save the king!' The LXX also indicates that the final verb 'may he answer' is a reference to God not the king by changing the third person 'may he answer' to second person 'answer' thus translating 'Lord, save the king and answer us ...'

37. W. Graham Scroggie, *Psalms* vol.1, Marshall, Morgan & Scott, p. 69.

38. The *New International* follows the ancient Greek (LXX) in placing 'sit' in the first line to read, 'You are enthroned as the Holy One, you are the praise of Israel.'

39. The *Authorised Version* follows the Septuagint (LXX) and Vulgate with 'unicorns'.

40. Two different words are used for 'fear' in verse 23, both similar in meaning in this context.

41. See P. H. Eveson, *The Beauty of Holiness*, pp. 48–55,96–98.

42. One of the 14th century BC clay tablets known as the *Amarna Letters* describe the Pharaoh giving gifts to his vassal rulers of Canaan 'while our enemies look on'.

43. Although many comment that the background to this psalm has to do with pilgrims coming up to Jerusalem at festival times, the absence of any specific rituals associated with worship at the tabernacle suggests the psalm was used in a more general way for approaching God.

44. There is a slight variation in the Hebrew text of verse 4, with 'lift up his soul' being replaced by 'lift up my soul' (that is, 'to lift up God's person'). 'Lift my soul in vain' would then be similar to the Third Commandment where it literally reads 'lift up the name of the Lord your God in vain' (Exodus 20:7). It would be saying that we must not associate the Lord with what is useless.

45. The variation in the Hebrew is slight and cannot be shown in translation—'Who is he, this one who is king of glory?'

46. See the superscription in the ancient Greek Septuagint (LXX) which finds support in the Jewish Aramaic paraphrases, the Targums. Allan Harman in his *Commentary on the Psalms* (Fearn, Ross-shire: Mentor/Christian Focus, 2011) p. 229 mistakenly associates it with the Jewish Sabbath and misquotes the LXX which actually reads 'first day of the week' not 'seventh'.

47. The verse division in the traditional text begins verse 2 with another Aleph

but by moving the initial 'O my God' to the end of verse 1, verse 2 can begin with Beth, 'In you I trust ...' Verse divisions are not original to the text.

48. The word for 'earth' is also translated 'land' when applied to Canaan.

49. In Hebrew the vowel points under the verb 'enlarge' can be changed to give better sense and provide a closer parallel with the second line. Instead of 'The troubles of my heart are enlarged' the original would give 'Relieve the troubles of my heart'. See Psalm 4:1 for the same thought.

50. Geoffrey Grogan, *Psalms*, Eerdmans, 2008, p. 78.

51. There is no word for 'psalm' in the original of Psalm 27.

52. *The Psalms in Human Life*, R. E. Prothero, 1904, p.352.

53. The alternative Hebrew reading is 'his lair' where a lion might conceal its prey from other predators.

54. John Stott *The Canticles and Selected Psalms*, London, 1966.

55. It is similar to the Hebrew oath formula where the first half is assumed. The Massorites responsible for the pointing of the Hebrew text considered the 'unless' suspect and there are a few Hebrew manuscripts that omit the 'unless' to become with the English Standard Version 'I believe that I shall look upon the goodness of the Lord ...'

56. Verse 6 of 'Through all the changing scenes of life' by Nahum Tate & Nicholas Brady.

57. The word for 'supplications' is associated with the term 'grace'.

58. In the original the same words ('deed' and 'work') are used both for the wicked and the Lord.

59. The NIV and ESV with the support of the ancient Greek version (the Septuagint) render 'the strength of *his people*' whereas the traditional Hebrew (Massoretic) Text has 'the strength *of them*'.

60. T. D. Alexander, *From Eden to the New Jerusalem*, IVP, 2008, p. 42. See also G. K. Beale *Temple and the Church's Mission: A Biblical Theology of the Dwelling Place of God*, New Studies in Biblical Theology 17, Apollos, 2004.

61. It could also mean that God is the one who has rescued him from past troubles.

62. Many modern commentators follow the Septuagint (LXX) and Syriac, which reads, 'You have hated' with reference to God. But the contrast in the traditional (Massoretic) Hebrew text helps to underline the psalmist's total commitment to Yahweh.

63. From Wesley's hymn, 'Jesu, Lover of my soul'.

64. The argument over the use of either hymns ancient or modern can find little support from these verses. Reference to singing the song of Moses and the Lamb (Revelation 15:3) might suggest we sing old and new songs! Keeping old songs fresh involves prayerful meditation on their contents while new compositions cannot be assumed to be better. Fervent singing with freshness and accomplished instrumentalists suggest that nothing but our best efforts are good enough for God. In the light of the new covenant and the new creation, Christians have more incentive to sing. See Spurgeon on Psalm 33.

65. The LXX and other ancient versions have 'wineskin' or 'skin bottle' in place of 'heap'.

66. Literally the Hebrew has 'together', which the LXX understands as 'alone' meaning that the Lord alone fashions their hearts.

67. In the psalm heading and 1 Samuel 21:13 the literal reading is, 'when he changed his discernment/reason'.

68. Like Psalm 25 the 'W' (*Waw*) is missing and it ends in verse 22 with an extra 'P' (*Pe*).

69. The words for 'praise' and 'boast' have a common Hebrew root.

70. H. L. Ellison, *The Psalms*, Bible Study Books, Scripture Union, p. 31.

71. In translating verse 12 the *New International* has chosen to ignore the question form of the original.

72. It is unfortunate that our English word 'buckler' is generally used for a small round shield.

73. In place of 'stop' many like the *New International* repoint the Hebrew to give 'javelin' or 'pike'.

74. See Ellison, p. 32.

75. The phrase 'at feasts' translates the Hebrew for 'cake' (see 1 Kings 17:13). The *New International* emends the difficult Hebrew text to a superlative expression 'mockers of the mockers' to give 'maliciouly mocked'.

76. Different Hebrew words are used but with similar meaning.

77. As with many of the alphabetical psalms it is not quite complete. In this case the sixteenth letter does not begin the stanza.

78. D. Martyn Lloyd-Jones, *Romans: An Exposition of Chapter 1, The Gospel of God*, Edinburgh: Banner of Truth Trust, 1985, p. 97.

79. Literally 'peace' *shalom*.

80. See Philip H Eveson, *The Beauty of Holiness*, pp. 170–193.

81. See D. A. Carson, *For the Love of God*, Vol. 1, April 28, IVP, 1998.

82. See P. H. Eveson *Foundation* Spring 2005, pp. 12–19 and D. C Fredericks in Fredericks and Estes *Ecclesiastes & The Song of Songs,* Apollos, 2010).

83. The same word is used of Enoch (Genesis 5:24) with the third person ('he is/was not') instead of the first person ('I am not') as here.

84. This is Donald Coggan's heading to the psalm in *Psalms 1–72 The People's Bible Commentary* (The Bible Reading Fellowship), 1998, p. 100.

85. The term used, 'Rahab', is associated with a mythical sea monster and became a nickname for proud Egypt (see Psalm 87:4).

86. See P. H. Eveson's *The Beauty of Holiness* on Leviticus 1–7 for details.

87. In Psalm 40 instead of 'Psalm of David' the original reads 'Of David. A Psalm'.

88. It is translated 'Contemplation' in some of the psalm headings (see Psalm 32).

89. Some Hebrew manuscripts do join the two psalms.

90. D. M. Lloyd-Jones, *Spiritual Depression, Its Cause & Cure*, Pickering & Inglis, 1965, p. 20.

91. Some Hebrew MSS and the LXX place 'my God' of verse 6 at the end of verse 5 to make it accord with verse 11.

92. It could mean 'my living God' making his reference to the 'living God' (verse 2) more personal.

93. More than thirty Hebrew manuscripts indicate that the two psalms are to be regarded as one while the LXX indicates they are separate by giving Psalm 43 the heading 'A Psalm of David', one that has no support in the original Hebrew.

94. See 'God (*El*) of my life' and 'God (El) of my rock' in Psalm 42:8,9. Here *Elohim* is used.

95. In the original the word has a plural form to emphasise its special status.

96. The links include: 'help' or 'victories' (literally 'salvations'; Psalms 44:4; 42:5,11; 43:5); the desire to 'praise' God (Psalms 44:8; 42:5,11; 43:5); being a 'reproach' (Psalms 44:13; 42:10); being 'rejected' or 'cast off' by God (Psalms 44:9,23; 43:2); the enemy's 'oppression' (Psalms 44:24; 42:9; 43:2).

97. Goldingay seems to suggest this in Vol.2, pp. 46–47.

98. We cannot, as some have tried to do, make too much of the fact that the traditional Hebrew text lacks the definite article. It could be translated either 'a king' or 'the king'.

99. It is not the same Hebrew word that is translated 'righteousness' in verse 7.

100. New King James and Authorised versions consider the Hebrew word minni a poetic form of the preposition min ('from') and translate 'whereby' or *'by which'* but it is better to see the original as a contraction of minnim ('stringed instruments'; see Psalm 150:4).

101. The word translated *'many colours'* refers to needlework that brings together a mixture of colour.

102. Some manuscripts and versions give alternative readings such as 'mysteries' or 'death'.

103. Some follow the Greek translation (LXX) and an Aramaic Jewish interpretation (Targum) and read 'shields' instead of 'waggons'. The Hebrew consonants could be taken either way.

104. Besides the obvious reference to the north (verse 2) and east (verse 7), the 'right hand' (verse 10) is also used for the 'south' and 'following' (verse 13) for the 'west'. The Hebrews worked out their directions by first looking east where the sun rose. Thus, facing the rising sun was 'in front' and stood for the 'east' and what was 'behind' was 'west'. Still facing east, that which lay to the 'right hand' was 'south' and what lay to the 'left hand' was sometimes seen as the 'north' though there was a more common word 'zaphon', which is the term used in our psalm. Two of these direction words could also express time in such a way that is very confusing and contrary to the way we think today. The past was thought of as something that could be seen and so it lay 'in front' whereas the future could not be seen and therefore it lay 'behind'. The generation 'following' in verse 13 is literally 'behind', it cannot be seen.

105. Peter C. Craigie, *Psalms 1-50*, Word Biblical Commentary vol. 19, Word, 1983, p. 353.

106. Tarshish was possibly a Phoenician port on the Mediterranean in what

is now Spain. The phrase may well have been used more generally to describe ocean-going cargo ships; see 1 Kings 10:22.

107. It could be translated 'against dying'. A number of Hebrew MSS reads 'for ever' as does the LXX.

108. See Goldingay Vol. 2, pp. 93–4 who finds it 'wondrous' that God is praised on a daily basis by Jews and Christians and possibly Muslims. He writes: 'It is therefore wondrous that God is praised day-to-day, week-to-week, and year-to-year in this city by Jews and Christians (and Muslims?) and that, through the dispersion of Jews and Christians (and Muslims?) all over the world, the name and the praise of this God reach to the end of the earth. Its story is still designed to be an encouragement to us'. Surely, it is committed Christians whether Jewish, Arab or of other nationalities, that seek to show the praises of God.

109. Hebrew has an idiomatic expression which literally reads 'sons of humankind (*adam*) also sons of an individual person/man (*ish*)'.

110. The ancient Greek version (LXX) has 'their grave' which many modern translations accept but it is not necessary.

111. See the ancient Greek version (LXX) and the *Authorised* and *New King James* versions of Joshua 22:22.

112. See P. H. Eveson, *The Beauty of Holiness* for details concerning sacrifices, especially pp. 28–30,31–98.

113. Iain H. Murray, *D. Martyn Lloyd-Jones: The First Forty Years 1899–1939*, Edinburgh: Banner of Truth Trust, p. 64; also *The Life of Martyn Lloyd-Jones 1899–1981*, Edinburgh: Banner of Truth Trust, 2013, p. 49.

114. John R. W. Stott, *The Canticles and Selected Psalms*, Hodder & Stoughton, 1966.

115. NKJV still has '*turned aside*' here and so fails to indicate that a different verb is used.

116. The 'all' of Psalm 14:4 is omitted in this psalm at verse 4.

117. The plural in place of the singular form in Psalm 14:7 is found here to express fulness.

118. The traditional Hebrew text presents two readings: 'Desolations are upon them' or 'Let death beguile /suddenly take them'.

119. A similar sounding word in Hebrew to 'wandering'.

120. From Charles Wesley's hymn, *Jesu, Lover of my soul.*

121. The AV is a guess from the verb 'to bind' in the sense of people banded together. Most modern translations emend the Hebrew vowel points.

122. W. S. Plumer, *Psalms* (Geneva series reprints), Edinburgh: Banner of Truth Trust, 1975.

123. The participle 'judging' is in the plural. When the plural term *elohim* refers to the one true God the participle would normally be found in the singular but in the plural when pagan gods are the subject.

124. See John N Day, *Crying for Justice: What the Psalms Teach Us About Mercy and Vengeance in an Age of Terrorism*, Leicester: IVP, 2005.

125. Although the traditional text has '*his strength*' (verse 9) some Hebrew manuscripts and the ancient Greek translation (the Septuagint) read 'my strength', agreeing with verse 17.

126. The word '*howl*' or 'moan' is a possible translation by a slight change in the vowel points and is supported by the ancient Greek translation (LXX), but the traditional text has 'they stay all night' suggesting that they cannot settle for the night but must continue searching.

127. Taken to be an Aramaic form of the Hebrew for 'bow', which is how the ancient Greek translation (LXX) understands it.

128. The phrase 'cast my shoe' is often associated with ownership (Ruth 4:7).

129. The word can also mean 'enemy' as it certainly does in verse 12.

130. Augustus Toplady, *The Complete Works of Toplady*, 1794, pp. 12,18.

131. A number of translations make verse 6 dependent on verse 5.

132. John Newton *Begone, unbelief.*

133. From J. M. Scriven popular hymn, *What a Friend we have in Jesus.*

134. Some translators understand the verb to mean 'shake the head' in derision as in Jeremiah 48:27 rather than 'to flee'.

135. See Psalm 45:4 where similarly two nouns 'humility righteousness' are placed together. The ancient Greek translation (LXX) has 'Praise is fitting'.

136. Dale R. Davis, *2 Samuel: Out of Every Adversity*, Christian Focus, 2002, p. 269.

137. From the hymn by I. Watts, *Come, we that love the Lord.*

138. John R.W. Stott, *The Canticles and Selected Psalms*, Hodder & Stoughton, 1966.

139. It appears more often than some English texts reveal; e.g. Exodus 15:2; 17:16; Psalm 118:14.

140. Some MSS have LORD (Yahweh).

141. The word for 'song' is literally 'stringed instruments' as in the heading of Psalms 54,55,61. See also Psalm 77:6.

142. There is a word-play in the original: 'a song (shir) is better than an ox (shor)'.

143. In Ancient Near Eastern Texts 'depths of the earth' means the abode of the dead and 'the land of no return'.

144. To take this to mean that the poor of the previous verses will live is, as Calvin states, forced.

145. There is no justification for the New International Version's emendation of the text or for the plural 'cities' in English Standard Version.

146. See *The Lord's Anointed,* editors Satterthwaite, Hess & Wenham, Paternoster Press, 1995, pp. 236ff. for arguments for and against these verses being an integral part of the psalm.